Applied Models in Urban and Regional Analysis

NORBERT OPPENHEIM

Polytechnic Institute of New York

PRENTICE-HALL, INC., *Englewood Cliffs, New Jersey* 07632

Library of Congress Cataloging in Publication Data

OPPENHEIM, NORBERT.
Applied models in urban and regional analysis.

Includes bibliographies and index.
1. City planning—Mathematical models. 2. Regional
planning—Mathematical models. 3. City planning—Statistical methods. 4. Regional planning—Statistical
methods. I. Title.
HT166.O64   309.2'12'0151   79-19730
ISBN 0-13-041467-0

Editorial/production supervision and interior
design by Gary Samartino
Cover design by Saiki/Sprung Design
Manufacturing buyer: Gordon Osbourne

Printed in the United States of America

10 9 8 7 6 5 4 3 2 1

PRENTICE-HALL INTERNATIONAL, INC., *London*
PRENTICE-HALL OF AUSTRALIA PTY. LIMITED, *Sydney*
PRENTICE-HALL OF CANADA, LTD., *Toronto*
PRENTICE-HALL OF INDIA PRIVATE LIMITED, *New Delhi*
PRENTICE-HALL OF JAPAN, INC., *Tokyo*
PRENTICE-HALL OF SOUTHEAST ASIA PTE. LTD., *Singapore*
WHITEHALL BOOKS LIMITED, *Wellington, New Zealand*

To my parents, with gratitude

Contents

3
Economic Activity
and Employment Analysis   72

4
Models of Land Use
and Travel Demand   III

5
Programming Models   I 70

6
Model Fitting   227

7
Linear Regression Modeling

Appendix A
Statistical Tables

Appendix B
Solutions to Selected Exercises

Appendix C
List of Symbols

Appendix D
Glossary

Appendix E
Selected Bibliography

Index

Preface

The basic purpose of this book is to provide the analysts, managers, and planners of urban and regional systems with rational tools for the study of the operation of these systems, the forecasting of their future conditions, and the choice of the best alternative for changes in their characteristics. As such, the quantitative methods and analytical models presented here should also be of relevance to a variety of other professional and academic fields, including geography, sociology, public administration and management, systems engineering, and the policy sciences in general.

The text is organized in three parts, each covering a substantive area. First, an introduction, (Chapter 1), reviews the basic mathematical tools that are later used to develop the models for those readers who may have forgotten or never had a chance to learn about matrix algebra and probability theory.

The first part begins with Chapter 2, which presents several models of population growth projection, including the standard linear, exponential, logistic, and double exponential models, as well as the cohort-survival models. The comparative methods, as well as the multiregional models, are also presented. Chapter 3 presents some elementary models of economic analysis, beginning with the income and employment multiplier models and their multiregional version. The input/output model and its multiregional extension are then derived. Finally, the "shift and share" model is presented as a simple example of a dynamic model of economic analysis. The last chapter in the first part, Chapter 4, describes models of land use and travel demand forecasting, beginning with the "gravity" and "intervening opportunities" models of spatial activity distribution. Next, models of travel generation, modal split (including the "probit" and "logit" models), and travel assignment (including shortest path models), represent the transportation planning applications.

The second part (Chapter 5) concerns models of decision making. First, the techniques of linear programming are applied to a variety of problems related to the optimal operation of urban and regional systems. Next, the approach of dynamic programming is illustrated in the context of capital budgeting. Finally, the methods of Critical Path and PERT are used for the optimal scheduling of projects.

The third part is concerned with some operational aspects of the analytical models just presented. The problems of the adaptation of the models to specific data sets and the evaluation of their efficiency are considered. Thus, Chapter 6 describes methods of estimation of the quality of input data, of calibration of a given model to a specific empirical situation, and of the evaluation of the resulting precision of the model. The last chapter, 7, is devoted to the examination of the linear regression models and the special features of their development and evaluation.

The text focuses on a few models, selected on the basis of their importance in professional practice, as well as their theoretical generality, thus maximizing their applicability to a large variety of situations. The formal structure and the theoretical rigor of the models are emphasized. This comes from a belief that an understanding of the models' development and properties is a prerequisite to a realistic appraisal of their limitations and of the problems attendent to their use. Proficiency in subsequent practical applications of these models can ultimately best come from direct personal experience in their use under field conditions.

The level of scientific and mathematical background assumed is that of a first course in algebra. An effort was made to make the text selfcontained and to provide all necessary special knowledge in the introductory chapter. The formal exposition is, in most cases, immediately followed by an illustration, using a practical example of application. Because all quantitative methods presented in this text need to be tried and practiced to be fully understood, each chapter ends with a set of exercises. These exercises are direct applications of the models and methods and, in numerous cases, relate to the illustrative examples used in the exposition. The solution for a majority of the exercises (those designated by a bold exercise number) have been grouped in Appendix B.

The text can serve as a primer or as a reference, both to professionals and researchers. It can also be used to cover a two-semester or three-quarter sequence of courses in quantitative methods in urban and regional planning, public administration and management, systems engineering, operations research, and other related disciplines in the policy sciences, either at the upper undergraduate levels or at the graduate level.

I would like to acknowledge my indebtedness to a number of people who have, in various direct or indirect ways, contributed to the writing of this book. In chronological order: My parents, whose sacrifices made possible my education; Professors N. Kennedy and G. Newell for respectively believing in me and making me a believer during my student days at the University of California at Berkeley; Robert Lee, Wayne Stenis, and Laurie Kerr for undertaking most of the mundane aspects of the production while they were students at Texas A&M University; Professors Dimitrios Dendrinos of the University of Kansas and Michael Romanos of the University of Illinois at Urbana for constructive and supportive comments on an earlier draft; and Professor Louis J. Pignataro, Head of the Department of Transportation Planning and Engineering at the Polytechnic Institute of New York for his active encouragement and support. I would also like to thank Hank Kennedy, my editor at Prentice Hall, for his faith and decisiveness and Maryon Fischetti and her typing crew at the Polytechnic—Lucille Babikian, Elaine Cummings, Carol Devlin, Ruth Drucker, Kay Kamara, and Elinor McDonald—for turning a near illegible manuscript into a final copy.

A special paragraph is due to my wife Leslee. Not only did she act as my editor in the initial stages, painstakingly going over every word of several early drafts, but she also managed to compensate for the time I could not devote to our infant while she held a teaching job, advanced her doctoral research, and still managed to cook dinner. All along, she put up with and took joy in the various moods that the progress of my writing induced. May she share in the rewards.

New York City   NORBERT OPPENHEIM

I

Introduction

1.1 The Rational Approach to the Policy Analysis and Planning Process

This text purports to present scientific methods of analysis and decision making for the analysis and planning of urban and regional systems. The view taken of this process in this book is that of a purely rational sequence of steps, each of which relying upon the use of scientific methods. If this view is undoubtedly highly idealized, and perhaps unrealistic, it is, nevertheless, convenient to provide a framework for the conduct of this process, even though it might be inapplicable in certain instances, or diverted from or adapted in others.

Furthermore, this approach relies upon the concept of the subject of this process as a *system*. Thus, the societal organization is viewed as a set of components, i.e., the population, its various activities (residential, economic, etc.), and the spaces they require, which are interrelated and interdependent. This system is susceptible of rational comprehension and possibly explanation. In any event, it can be mathematically described, even if simplistically or incompletely. The description and operation of such mathematical models for the purpose of analysis and planning is the subject of this book.

The process of rational planning for guided change, be it physical, economic, political, etc., can be considered to consist of the sequence of steps, illustrated in Figure 1.1. Before we describe the connections between this process and the articulation of the various quantitative methods presented in this book, let us define more precisely what each of the steps entail.

1. *System examination and problem formulation:* This first phase identifies the problem and specifies its nature. The examination of the system and the subsequent determination of inadequacies is performed through surveys. These surveys will ideally be part of a continuing monitoring activity. In general, they will be provoked by the awareness of a potential problem. A housing survey, for instance, will result in the finding that there may be a housing problem because of a shortage of low-cost housing.

2. *Definition of the value system:* The priorities of the community must be specified before the next phase, definition of the goals and objectives, can take place. For instance, it might be decided that a housing shortage is not as important and critical as a traffic congestion problem, and therefore should not be immediately attended to. This phase will also be achieved through field research, this time not with respect to the physical condition of the community, but with respect to the attitudes of its residents.

3. *Definition of the nature and level of objectives of change:* Once the problem and the attitudes of those it affects have been defined, the desired objectives of change in the existing state of the system will be specified. It might be decided, for instance, that in order to alleviate the shortage of low-cost housing, the number of units of such housing will have to be increased by 20%.

4. *Representation of the system:* This phase is designed to result in a formal tool the analyst/planner can use to study the solutions to the problem more effectively than could be achieved through a subjective approach. There can be various types of representations, and at various levels of sophistication and complexity. In particular, the representation can be purely *descriptive*, i.e., not providing an explanation of the mechanisms of the system. Or it can be *causal*, i.e., identifing the cause–effects relationships. The latter form is naturally more useful to the analyst, since the theory represented by these causal models will be needed to perform the next three phases of the process. For instance, the situation of a shortage of low-cost housing could be represented by a housing inventory map, mathematical models of housing stock, etc. In any case, this replication of reality is used in the next three phases of the process, instead of analyzing and experimenting in the "real world," which can be unrealistically costly or simply infeasible.

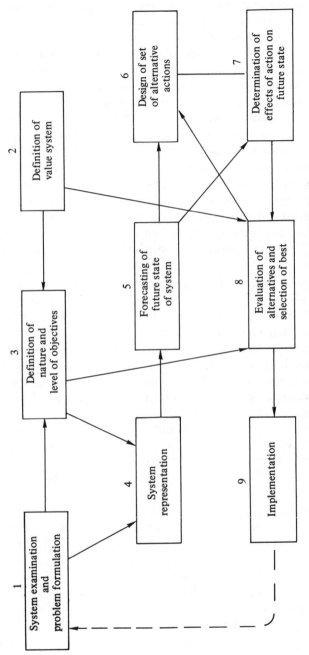

Figure 1.1 The analytical process of policy analysis and planning.

1 System examination and problem formulation

2 Definition of value system

3 Definition of nature and level of objectives

4 System representation

5 Forecasting of future state of system

6 Design of set of alternative actions

7 Determination of effects of action on future state

8 Evaluation of alternatives and selection of best

9 Implementation

5. *Forecasting of the future conditions of the system:* Since any plan for change in urban and regional systems by definition takes place at a future date and is implemented over long periods of time, there will be a need to project the state of the system at future times, in particular its major components of population, economy, and land use. For instance, if it is projected that the population levels are to decrease substantially, there might not be a low-cost housing shortage by the time the housing program could be implemented.

6. *The design of means for the achievement of the objectives:* In this phase, alternative plans of action will be considered. The generation of these alternatives will be constrained by the forecasts of the preceding phase. In general, there will be several solutions to multidimensional development problems, each with a different overall pattern of meeting the stated objectives. For instance, the low-cost housing shortage could be alleviated by a public housing construction program, a financial program of interest-free loans to developers, a renovation program, etc.

7. *The determination of the future effects of the alternative plans:* Using the representation and/or understanding of the mechanisms of the problem obtained during phase 4, the effects on the course of the system of each of the alternatives considered in the preceding phase need to be projected. This is a prerequisite to the next phase. This is gennerally done by assuming that the existing mechanisms which govern the operation of the system remain effective at the future date of implementation and is based on the projected state of the system in the absence of intervention, obtained in phase 5.

   The effects of the various alternatives on the existing resources and their respective costs (time, money, physical requirements, etc.) need to be evaluated as well. For instance, a public housing program may spur a revival of a given area but may require, e.g., the re-zoning of formerly commercial land to residential.

8. *The choice of best alternative:* In a rational approach, the best alternative will be the one that brings the system closest to the levels set in phase 3. Thus, a rational choice of alternative will require systematic consideration of the previous step for each of the alternatives designed in phase 6. However, several (possibly conflicting) objectives may require a formal evaluation procedure. This will be based on the community values identified in phase 2 and might, for example, consist of city council meetings, voting on propositions, etc.

9. *Change implementation and monitoring of the effects:* Although the implementation phase is not, strictly speaking, the responsibility of the analyst/planner, the monitoring of its effects is the analyst's

responsibility. This is important for a comparison with the projected effects of the plan. In other words, the implementation of the change is an opportunity for experimentation in the communal realm which scientists and planners should fully utilize to try out and test the assumptions they have made or the theory they have used in forecasting the evolution of the system.

Let us now describe the place of the models and methods presented in this text in relation to the sequence of steps above. First, the determination of the specific form of the model that describes the system (step 4), as well as the specific values of their parameters, requires the use of the methods described in Chapter 6. (Knowledge of the battery of models described in Chapters 2 to 4 is a prerequisite, however.) Next, the forecasting of the future state of the system (step 5) is usually performed by assuming that the conditions which validate the applicability of the model will remain at the future date. The description of future conditions is thus obtained simply through the operation of the respective models after changing the values of the variables intervening in them to their projected future levels. This approach can also be used in a determination of the effects of future actions on the state of the system, by using not the projected levels, but the planned levels. The evaluation of the alternatives, and also the selection of the "best," step 8, can be aided by use of the optimizing methods of Chapter 5.

To continue our effort to put the subject matter of this book into perspective, let us list the methods and techniques that are not covered herein and suggest where to look for them.

First, the system examination, problem formulation, and definition of the value system (steps 1 and 2, respectively) may involve the performance of surveys and the analysis of the data collected. Thus, standard statistical techniques such as *hypothesis testing* (e.g., to determine if a majority of people in a given community favors a certain planning or political issue) may be used. Other techniques, such as the use of *descriptive statistics* (e.g., to investigate the distribution of housing standards) or *correlation* or *variance analysis* (to determine the effect of geographic location on migration levels), may also be used. Such techniques, although quantitative methods very similar to those presented here, belong more to the area of field research than to analysis. Also, they are mostly nonsubstantive, and consist of the same traditional statistical techniques as are used in a variety of fields, including those close to the policy sciences, such as sociology and political science.

Other analysis and decision-making techniques that could be applied to policy analysis and planning will not be represented herein either because they are too technical or advanced (e.g., *nonlinear, stochastic,* or *multicriteria* optimization), do not fit into the general organization of the book (e.g., *Delphi technique, gaming techniques*), require computer hardware and programming knowledge for exposition (e.g., *simulation*), because their applications to the substantive area of planning have remained minimal to date (e.g., *game theory*), or simply for reasons of space.

In any case, the set of models presented here is only introductory, both at the conceptual and methodological levels. Those readers who want further knowledge about population projections, for instance, will learn about the *life table* approach in more advanced mathematical demography texts, and those who need other economic analysis methods will consult standard *econometrics* texts. In the same fashion, further developments of *spatial models* and *location theory* can be obtained in regional science texts. Also, more powerful or more sophisticated techniques can be obtained from recent developments in *operations research* and *systems analysis*.

This eclectic list reflects the fact that the new field of policy science borrows both substantively and technically from a number of established disciplines. However, the common language is that of rationality, science, and, at least as far as this book is concerned, mathematics.

1.2   Review of Elementary Mathematical Concepts

Having surveyed the organization of the text, let us next review briefly the mathematical tools that will be needed for the development of the analytical models. Readers who have a working proficiency with high school algebra, matrix (linear) algebra, and the elements of probability theory may skip Sections 1.2, 1.3, and 1.4, respectively, and go directly to Chapter 2.

It should be emphasized at the outset that none of the methods and approaches in this text rely on inherent mathematical mysteries. On the contrary, they should be understandable by readers who, although perhaps not very proficient or comfortable with the language of mathematics, are nevertheless willing to accept the premise that these methods are nothing more than the formal translation into mathematical terms of what are always, in the end, common sense notions.

The formal apparatus needed to understand this translation is limited both in scope and in level of complexity. It consists essentially of three components: elementary algebra, matrix algebra, and probability concepts. Elementary algebra will be needed throughout the text, as the "lingua franca." Matrix algebra is the branch of algebra that addresses operations on the class of linear equations and thus will be most useful in Chapters 2 and 3, where a majority of the models are linear. Finally, probability theory is the branch of mathematics that deals with entities whose value is uncertain.

We shall review these three areas successively in the remainder of this introductory chapter. Thus, the overall exposition of the book will be totally self-contained. Let us then begin with a review of algebraic definitions and basic operations.

A *variable* is a quantity whose value can change. For instance, the population of a given city each year is a variable. Variables will be represented and referred to by letters, such as P for the variable "population." The various values of a variable can be indexed to distinguish between them. For instance, 20 values of the population level of a given city (e.g., for a period of time of 20 years) can be in the general case represented by $P_1, P_2, P_3, \ldots, P_{20}$ or more compactly by P_i ($i = 1, 2, \ldots, 20$). Here i is a subscript *index*, not a variable. Several indices may be required to further distinguish values. For example, if it is desired to represent the population levels of several cities simultaneously, we can use the notation P_{ij}. This will refer to the ith observation of the population level of the jth city. Another, equivalent notation is $P_i^{\,j}$, and the set of corresponding values can be arranged along the rows and columns of a *two-way table*, as shown in Figure 1.2. More generally, values can be indexed

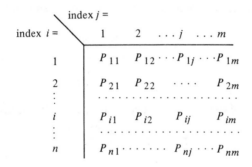

Figure 1.2 Matrix representation of a set of values.

by any number of indices or subscripts. A three-index notation could be P_{ijk} or P_{ij}^k or P_i^{jk}.

There are several operations that one can perform with algebraic quantities, such as, say, the n values X_i of a variable X. The *sum* of the values will be represented by the symbol

$$\sum_{i=1}^{n} X_i \qquad \text{or} \qquad \sum_{i} X_i$$

and will simply mean

$$X_1 + X_2 + \ldots + X_i + \ldots + X_n$$

If, before summing up a series of values X_i, we multiply each one of them by a constant, k, for instance, and we then sum up the resulting values, we can obtain the same result by multiplying the original sum by the constant k.

That is,

$$kX_1 + kX_2 + \ldots + kX_i + \ldots + kX_n = \sum_i kX_i = k(\sum_i X_i) = k \sum_i X_i$$

For instance, $3 \times 5 + 3 \times 10 + 3 \times 8$ is equal to $3 \times (5 + 10 + 8)$. This operation is called *factoring out* the term 3.

The *square* of a given value X is the value obtained by multiplying it by itself. Thus, the square of $X = 5$ is noted X^2 and is equal to $5 \times 5 = 25$. Conversely, the *square root* of a value is the value which when raised to the square is equal to the given value. Thus, the square root of $X = 16$ is denoted $\sqrt{X}$ and is equal to 4, since $4^2 = X = 16$. It is important to remember that the square of a sum of terms is not equal to the sum of the squares of the respective terms. In other words,

$$(\sum_i X_i)^2 \neq \sum_i X_i^2$$

For instance,

$$(5 + 3)^2 = (8)^2 = 64 \neq 5^2 + 3^2 = 25 + 9 = 34$$

Similarly, the square root of a sum is not equal to the sum of the square roots. That is,

$$\sqrt{\sum_i X_i} \neq \sum_i \sqrt{X_i}$$

For instance,

$$\sqrt{16 + 4} = \sqrt{20} \neq \sqrt{16} + \sqrt{4} = 4 + 2 = 6$$

Also, the product of two sums is not equal to the sum of the products. That is,

$$(\sum_i X_i)(\sum_i Y_i) \neq \sum_i X_i Y_i$$

For instance,

$$(2 + 3)(1 + 2) = (5)(3) = 15 \neq (2 \times 1) + (3 \times 2) = 2 + 6 = 8$$

In each of these cases, it is best to follow the basic definition of a sum and a product to compute the various expressions.

A *double sum*,

$$\sum_i \sum_j X_{ij}$$

can be computed by first keeping one of the indices constant, and by summing the terms with respect to the other index. For instance, the sum of the X_{ij}'s given in Table 1.1 can be computed as either

$$\sum_i \sum_j X_{ij} = \sum_i (\sum_j X_{ij}) = (2 + 3) + (4 + 1) = 5 + 5 = 10$$

i.e., summing along successive rows, or as

$$\sum_j (\sum_i X_{ij}) = (2 + 4) + (3 + 1) = 6 + 4 = 10$$

i.e., summing along successive columns.

TABLE 1.1

X_{ij} $\backslash$ $j =$		
$i =$	1	2
1	2	3
2	4	1

The nth *power* X^n of a value X is defined as the product of n times that value. For instance, the fourth power of 5 is noted by 5^4 and is equal to $5 \times 5 \times 5 \times 5 = 625$. In general, the nth power of the mth power of X is equal to the (n times m) power of X. That is, $(X^m)^n = X^{mn}$. Also, the *zero power* of any value is always equal to 1, i.e., $X^0 = 1$, no matter what is the specific value of X. Finally, a *negative power* is defined as the *inverse* of the positive power. That is, $X^{-n} = 1/X^n$. For instance, $5^{-4} = 1/5^4 = 1/625$.

Let us now review the elementary algebraic operations. An *equality* is a statement that two algebraic quantities are equal, i.e., have the same value. For instance, the following statement is an equality: $5 + 2 = 4 + 3$. When some of the terms in an equality are unknown, the equality is called an *equation*. An unknown value can be determined by isolating it on either side of the equality. To achieve that, the only permissible manipulations of the original equality are:

- Both sides of the equality can be multiplied or divided by the *same* positive or negative value (but *not* by zero).

- Both sides of the equality can be added or subtracted by the same positive or negative value.

For instance, the equation $5 + 2X = 4$ can be solved for the unknown X by first subtracting 5 from both sides of the equality:

$$-5 + 5 + 2X = 4 - 5 \qquad \text{or} \qquad 2X = -1$$

Next, both sides of the equality can be divided by 2:

$$\frac{2X}{2} = \frac{-1}{2} \qquad \text{or} \qquad X = -0.5$$

In general, m unknown values can only be evaluated from a simultaneous set of at least m equations. The procedure in this case is to try to isolate one unknown in each equation to get back to the single unknown case.

An *inequality* is a statement that an algebraic quantity is larger or smaller than another. For instance, the statement $5 - 2X < 4$ means that the quantity $(5 - 2X)$ is strictly smaller than 4. The sign $\leq$ would mean "smaller than or equal to," the sign $>$ would mean "strictly larger than," and the sign $\geq$

would mean "larger than or equal to." The solution of an inequality containing an unknown X is not in general a single value as in the case of an equality, but a range of possible values, which are then said to represent an *interval*. The solution of inequalities is also obtained by isolating the unknown on one side. The permissible operations in doing so are the same as in the case of equations, except that when multiplying or dividing both sides by the same *negative* value, the direction of the inequality must be changed, e.g., from "larger than" to "smaller than," and so on. For instance, the inequality at the beginning of this paragraph would be solved by first subtracting 5 from both sides to get $-2X < -1$, and then dividing both sides by -2 to get

$$\frac{-2X}{-2} > \frac{-1}{-2} \quad \text{or} \quad X > 0.5$$

Thus, the solution of the inequality consists of the range of values that are strictly greater than 0.5.

The last concept we will need in standard algebra is that of a *function*. When we represent the variations of a given variable Y against those of another variable X, we say that Y is a function of X. This statement will be represented by $Y = F(X)$ or $Y = Y(X)$. Thus, the notion of function is merely that of a correspondence or *relationship* between the respective values of two variables. For instance, if there is a relationship between the population level P of a given city and its size S, we will say that the variable P is a function of the variable S. This relationship may be represented graphically as shown in the *graph* or *plot* in Figure 1.3.

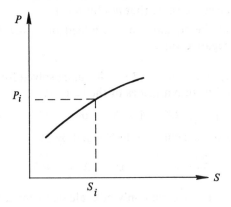

Figure 1.3   Graph of the function $P = F(S)$.

If the exact form of a relationship is specified by a formula that gives the value of the function, or *dependent* variable, as being equal to a specific algebraic expression that contains the value of the *independent* variable, the function can then be used to compute the value of one variable knowing the value of the other. There are various forms of specific functions of a single variable which we will encounter in the course of the text. The first is a *linear function* of the form

$$Y = a_0 + a_1 X \tag{1.1}$$

The graph of this function is a straight line, as represented in Figure 1.4. This basic feature has given the name to the function.

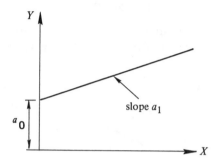

Figure 1.4   Graph of a linear function.

The *parameter* or *constant* a_1, which is the coefficient factor of X, is called the *slope* of the straight line, and the other parameter, a_0, is called the *intercept*. Physically, the slope represents the (constant) rate or speed of variation of Y measured against that of X. In other words, when X varies by 1 unit, Y varies by a_1 units—in the same direction if a_1 is positive, in the other direction if a_1 is negative. a_0 represents the starting level of Y, i.e., its value when the other variable, X, is equal to zero.

Another standard function that we shall use is the *exponential function*, e.g.,

$$Y = a^X \tag{1.2}$$

where a is a given positive parameter. The graph of this function is represented in Figure 1.5. The main property of this function is that to *additive* increments of the variable X correspond *multiplicative* increments of the function Y.

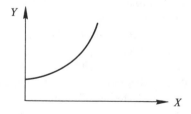

Figure 1.5   Graph of an exponential function.

That is,

$$Y_{(X_0 + X_1)} = a^{(X_0 + X_1)} = a^{X_0} a^{X_1} = (Y_{X_0})(Y_{X_1})$$

by definition of the powers of the value a. In other words, when the variable grows additively (or *arithmetically*), the function growths multiplicatively (or *geometrically*).

Another standard function is the *logarithmic function*, e.g.,

$$Y = \log_a X$$

where a is a parameter indicating the *basis* of the logarithm. The graph of that function is as represented in Figure 1.6. (When the parameter a in the

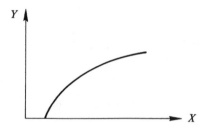

Figure 1.6 Graph of a logarithmic function.

exponential function above is equal to the particular constant $e = 2.7183. \ldots$, the logarithmic function is the *natural* or *Neperian logarithm*.) The main property of this function is that it is the *inverse* of the exponential function. That is, if a variable X is an exponential function of the variable Y, the variable Y will be a logarithmic function of the variable X. This gives the logarithmic function its main feature, which is that to multiplicative increments of the variable X correspond additive increments of the function Y.

That is,

$$Y_{(X_0 X_1)} = \log_a (X_0 X_1) = \log_a X_0 + \log_a X_1 = Y_{(X_0)} + Y_{(X_1)}$$

This property is the basis for the use of the logarithmic function to "scale down" the variations of variables with a high "acceleration."

All the foregoing functions are *univariate functions*; i.e., the variable Y will be a function of only one other variable X. In the general case, a variable Y is a function of the n variables $X_1, X_2, X_3, \ldots, X_n$ if there is a relationship between the value of Y and the *set* of values of the X_i's. (In this formulation, the X_i's are all different variables, each with their own respective set of values. This is not to be confused with the set of values X_i of a single variable X, as described above.) This would be indicated by the statement

$$Y = F_{(X_1, X_2 \ldots, X_i, \ldots X_n)}$$

The variable Y will then be said to be a *multivariate* function of the n variables X_i. When the form of the mathematical relationship between the values of the variables X_i and the values of the variable Y is specified by an algebraic equality, the value of the dependent variable Y can be computed, knowing the n values of the independent variables.

One of the most useful multivariate functions for our purposes will be the *multilinear function*

$$Y = a_0 + a_1 X_1 + a_2 X_2 + \ldots + a_i X_i + \ldots + a_n X_n$$

This function is the multivariate extension of the univariate linear function given above. Its main property is that the variations of the function Y are proportional to the variations of the variables X_i, respectively, weighted by the values of the coefficients a_i. It should be noted that the graph of a multivariate function is impossible to draw for more than three variables at a time, since that is the maximum number of dimensions in the physical space that one can use.

More generally, a (mathematical) *model* is a set of simultaneous equations (of any form) representing the interrelationships among a set of variables. In that sense, a single equation such as the various functions given above can be deemed to represent a model, although in a rather simple sense. The next section, a review of matrix algebra, will present some notations and special procedures for a very important and useful class of models, those in which all equations are multilinear.

1.3 Review of Matrix Algebra

Linear models such as those we have seen in Section 1.2 constitute the simplest type of mathematical models. They are, for that reason, widely used for analytical purposes, and we shall encounter numerous applications of linear models throughout the text. Because of their practical and theoretical importance, a special algebra has been developed to deal with the class of linear models. The core element of that algebra is called a *matrix*. Let us thus begin by defining this term.

A matrix is a rectangular array of numbers. (It may also be a square array of numbers, in which case the matrix is called a *square matrix*.) For example, the set of values represented below is a matrix, which we can call **A**, for instance[1]:

$$\mathbf{A} = \begin{bmatrix} 2 & 0 & 3 \\ 1 & 1 & 2 \end{bmatrix}$$

---

[1] Boldface roman capitals will be reserved to matrices throughout the text.

In general, a matrix $\mathbf{A}$ of size n vertically and m horizontally will be represented as

$$\mathbf{A} = \begin{bmatrix} a_{11} & a_{12} & \cdots\cdots\cdots\cdots & a_{1m} \\ a_{21} & a_{22} & \cdots\cdots\cdots\cdots & a_{2m} \\ \multicolumn{4}{c}{\cdots\cdots\cdots\cdots\cdots\cdots\cdots\cdots} \\ a_{i1} & a_{i2} & \cdots \quad a_{ij} \quad \cdots & a_{im} \\ \multicolumn{4}{c}{\cdots\cdots\cdots\cdots\cdots\cdots\cdots\cdots} \\ a_{n1} & a_{n2} & \cdots \quad a_{nj} \quad \cdots & a_{nm} \end{bmatrix}$$

The order of the subscripts of the entries a_{ij} of the matrix is important. The first index, i, always refers to the vertical dimension, i.e., the *row* number, and the second index, j, to the horizontal dimension, or *column* number. Thus, the entry a_{ij} is found at the intersection of row i and column j. The matrix $\mathbf{A}$ can be written symbolically as $\mathbf{A} = (a_{ij})$.

In the special case where the matrix only has one row, such as

$$[2 \quad 1 \quad 3 \quad 1]$$

it is called a *row vector*. Conversely, when it only has one column, such as

$$\begin{bmatrix} 1 \\ 0 \end{bmatrix}$$

it is called a *column vector*.

The usual algebraic operations of addition, subtraction, multiplication, and division can be effected on matrices. First, the *sum* of two matrices $\mathbf{A}$ and $\mathbf{B}$ can be computed, provided that the two matrices are of the same size, both horizontally and vertically. If that is the case, the sum of $\mathbf{A}$ and $\mathbf{B}$ will be a matrix $\mathbf{C}$, in which the general entry c_{ij} is simply the sum of the respective entries a_{ij} and b_{ij}. For instance, the sum of $\mathbf{A}$ and $\mathbf{B}$,

$$\mathbf{A} = \begin{bmatrix} 0 & 1 \\ 2 & 3 \end{bmatrix} \qquad \mathbf{B} = \begin{bmatrix} 3 & 2 \\ 1 & 0 \end{bmatrix}$$

will be $\mathbf{C}$:

$$\mathbf{C} = \mathbf{A} + \mathbf{B} = \begin{bmatrix} 3 & 3 \\ 3 & 3 \end{bmatrix}$$

In general, using the symbolic notation, if $\mathbf{A} = (a_{ij})$ and $\mathbf{B} = (b_{ij})$, then

$$\mathbf{C} = \mathbf{A} + \mathbf{B} = (a_{ij}) + (b_{ij}) = (a_{ij} + b_{ij})$$

Similarly, the *difference* between matrices of the same size will be a matrix where entries will be the difference between the respective corresponding entries of $\mathbf{A}$ and $\mathbf{B}$. [This, of course, results from the fact that the difference between $\mathbf{A}$ and $\mathbf{B}$ is also the sum of $\mathbf{A}$ and $(-\mathbf{B})$.] Thus, the difference between $\mathbf{A}$ and $\mathbf{B}$ would be

$$\mathbf{D} = \mathbf{A} - \mathbf{B} = \begin{bmatrix} -3 & -1 \\ 1 & 3 \end{bmatrix}$$

In general, symbolically

$$\mathbf{D} = \mathbf{A} - \mathbf{B} = (a_{ij}) - (b_{ij}) = (a_{ij} - b_{ij})$$

One can *multiply* a matrix by a *number*. The result is a matrix in which the entries are the original entries multiplied by the number. For instance, the product of matrix **A** above and 3 would be

$$\mathbf{E} = 3\mathbf{A} = \begin{bmatrix} 0 & 3 \\ 6 & 9 \end{bmatrix}$$

In general, using the symbolic notation

$$\mathbf{E} = k\mathbf{A} = k(a_{ij}) = (ka_{ij}) \qquad \text{where } k \text{ is any rational number}$$

Conversely, *dividing* a matrix by a number results in a matrix in which the entries are the original entries divided by the number. For instance, the division of matrix **A** by 2 is equal to

$$\mathbf{F} = \frac{\mathbf{A}}{2} = \begin{bmatrix} 0 & \frac{1}{2} \\ 1 & \frac{3}{2} \end{bmatrix}$$

In general, symbolically

$$\frac{\mathbf{A}}{k} = \frac{1}{k}(a_{ij}) = \frac{a_{ij}}{k}$$

The next operation we now define for matrices is the multiplication of a row vector by a column vector, *in that order*. If we have a row vector of size n,

$$\mathbf{P} = [p_1 \quad p_2 \quad \cdots \quad p_i \quad \cdots \quad p_n]$$

and a column vector **Q** of the same size,

$$\mathbf{Q} = \begin{bmatrix} q_1 \\ q_2 \\ \cdot \\ \cdot \\ \cdot \\ q_i \\ \cdot \\ \cdot \\ \cdot \\ q_n \end{bmatrix}$$

the result of the product **PQ** is the *number* equal to the sum of the respective double products:

$$p_1q_1 + p_2q_2 + \ldots + p_iq_i + \ldots + p_nq_n = \sum_{i=1}^{n} p_iq_i$$

It is extremely important to note that the result is not another matrix, but a single value. For instance, if

$$\mathbf{P} = [1 \quad 0] \qquad \text{and} \qquad \mathbf{Q} = \begin{bmatrix} 2 \\ 1 \end{bmatrix}$$

then

$$PQ = \begin{bmatrix} 1 & 0 \end{bmatrix} \begin{bmatrix} 2 \\ 1 \end{bmatrix} = (1 \times 2) + (0 \times 1) = 2 + 0 = 2$$

It is equally important to note that the multiplication of **P** and **Q**, in the reverse order, i.e., **QP**, does not have any meaning. In other words, the row vector always comes first in the multiplication.

We shall now extend the definition of the multiplication of two matrices to the case of the multiplication of a matrix by a column vector of the same vertical size, *in that order*. The product of matrix **A** by a column vector **Q** is equal to a column vector **V**, in which the entry in row i is equal to the product of the column vector by row vector i of the matrix **A**, as defined above. For instance, the product of matrix **A** above by column vector **Q** will be a column vector **V** equal to

$$V = \begin{bmatrix} 0 & 1 \\ 2 & 3 \end{bmatrix} \begin{bmatrix} 2 \\ 1 \end{bmatrix} = \begin{bmatrix} 0 \times 2 + 1 \times 1 \\ 2 \times 2 + 3 \times 1 \end{bmatrix} = \begin{bmatrix} 1 \\ 7 \end{bmatrix}$$

In general, the product of **A** and **Q** will then be

$$AQ = \begin{bmatrix} a_{11} & \cdots & a_{1j} & \cdots & a_{1m} \\ & \cdots & & & \\ a_{i1} & \cdots & a_{ij} & \cdots & a_{im} \\ & \cdots & & & \\ a_{n1} & \cdots & a_{nj} & \cdots & a_{nm} \end{bmatrix} \begin{bmatrix} q_1 \\ \vdots \\ q_i \\ \vdots \\ q_m \end{bmatrix}$$

$$= \begin{bmatrix} a_{11}q_1 + a_{12}q_2 + \ldots + a_{1m}q_m \\ \cdots \\ a_{i1}q_1 + a_{i2}q_2 + \ldots + a_{im}q_m \\ \cdots \\ a_{n1}q_1 + a_{n2}q_2 + \ldots + a_{nm}q_m \end{bmatrix} \qquad (1.3)$$

Here again, it is important to note first that in order for the multiplication of a matrix by a column vector to be possible, the number of columns (width) of the matrix must be equal to the number of rows (height) of the vector. Also, the result is another column vector of the same size. Finally, the operation in the reverse order, i.e., the vector first, does not have a meaning.

We are now in a position to define the *product* of two matrices **A** and **B**, *in that order*, i.e., **AB**. This will be possible if the number of columns of the first matrix, **A**, i.e., its horizontal size, is equal to the number of rows of the second matrix, **B**, i.e., its vertical size. The result will be a matrix **C**, in which the entry in position i and j, i.e., at the intersection of row i and column j, will be a number equal to the product of row i of the first matrix, **A**, by column j of the second matrix, **B**. The height (number of rows) of **C** will be equal to the number of rows of **A**, and its number of columns will be equal to the number of columns of **B**.

In general, the product of $\mathbf{A} = (a_{ij})$ and $\mathbf{B} = (b_{ij})$ will be, symbolically

$$\mathbf{G} = \mathbf{AB} = (a_{ij})(b_{ij}) = \left(\sum_{k=1}^{m} a_{ik}b_{kj} \right)$$

This can be visually represented by

$$\mathbf{A} \qquad\qquad \mathbf{B} \qquad\qquad \mathbf{G}$$

where

$$g_{ij} = a_{i1}b_{1j} + \ldots + a_{ik}b_{kj} + \ldots + a_{im}b_{mj} = \sum_{k=1}^{m} a_{ik}b_{kj} \qquad (1.4)$$

For instance, the product of matrices **A** and **B**, in that order, will be another matrix,

$$\mathbf{C} = \mathbf{AB} = \begin{bmatrix} 0 & 1 \\ 2 & 3 \end{bmatrix} \begin{bmatrix} 3 & 2 \\ 1 & 0 \end{bmatrix} = \begin{bmatrix} g_{11} & g_{12} \\ g_{21} & g_{22} \end{bmatrix}$$

where

$$g_{11} = \begin{bmatrix} 0 & 1 \end{bmatrix} \begin{bmatrix} 3 \\ 1 \end{bmatrix} = 1$$

$$g_{12} = \begin{bmatrix} 0 & 1 \end{bmatrix} \begin{bmatrix} 2 \\ 0 \end{bmatrix} = 0$$

$$g_{21} = \begin{bmatrix} 2 & 3 \end{bmatrix} \begin{bmatrix} 3 \\ 1 \end{bmatrix} = 9$$

$$g_{22} = \begin{bmatrix} 2 & 3 \end{bmatrix} \begin{bmatrix} 2 \\ 0 \end{bmatrix} = 4$$

Thus,

$$\mathbf{C} = \mathbf{AB} = \begin{bmatrix} 1 & 0 \\ 9 & 4 \end{bmatrix}$$

It is important to note that the product **AB** is not in general equal to **BA**. For instance, the product **BA** of the two matrices above is equal to

$$\begin{bmatrix} 3 & 2 \\ 1 & 0 \end{bmatrix} \begin{bmatrix} 0 & 1 \\ 2 & 3 \end{bmatrix} = \begin{bmatrix} 3 \times 0 + 2 \times 2 & 1 \times 3 + 2 \times 3 \\ 1 \times 0 + 0 \times 2 & 1 \times 1 + 0 \times 3 \end{bmatrix} = \begin{bmatrix} 4 & 9 \\ 0 & 1 \end{bmatrix}$$

which is not equal to

$$\mathbf{AB} = \begin{bmatrix} 1 & 0 \\ 9 & 4 \end{bmatrix}$$

Finally, we shall define the *division* of a matrix **B** by a matrix **A**, or equivalently the multiplication of a matrix **B** by the inverse of the matrix **A**, for two square matrices of the same size only.

The *inverse* of a square matrix **A**, which will be noted by $\mathbf{A}^{-1}$, is the square matrix which, when multiplied by the original matrix **A**, results in the *unit matrix* of size equal to the size of **A**:

$$\mathbf{I} = \begin{bmatrix} 1 & 0 & \dots & 0 & \dots & 1 \\ 0 & 1 & \dots\dots\dots & 0 \\ 0 & \dots\dots & 1 & \dots & 0 \\ 0 & 0 & \dots & 0 & \dots & 1 \end{bmatrix}$$

[Note that this definition replicates the definition of the inverse $a^{-1} = 1/a$ of a rational number a, as being such that $(a)(a^{-1}) = 1$.]

Thus, for any square matrix $\mathbf{A} = (a_{ij})$, the identification of its inverse is equivalent to finding the values of the entries (α_{ij}) of $\mathbf{A}^{-1}$ such that $\mathbf{A}\mathbf{A}^{-1} = \mathbf{A}^{-1}\mathbf{A} = (a_{ij})(\alpha_{ij}) = \mathbf{I}$. (The order of the multiplication is irrelevant in this case, since if $\mathbf{A}^{-1}$ is the inverse of **A**, then conversely **A** is the inverse of $\mathbf{A}^{-1}$ and $\mathbf{A}^{-1}\mathbf{A} = \mathbf{I}$.)

There are several methods for computing the inverse of a square matrix. The most common uses the *determinant* and *cofactors* of the entries of the matrix. The determinant of a matrix is the value equal to the sum of the products of the entries on any single row or column and their cofactors. Also, the cofactor of any entry a_{ij} is computed as the determinant of the submatrix that remains when row i and column j corresponding to the position of the entry a_{ij} are removed from the original matrix **A**, taking the negative if $(i + j)$ is odd. For instance, in the matrix

$$\mathbf{A} = \begin{bmatrix} 1 & 2 & 0 \\ 0 & 1 & 2 \\ 0 & 2 & 0 \end{bmatrix}$$

the cofactor of a_{11} is the determinant of the submatrix

$$\begin{bmatrix} 1 & 2 & 0 \\ 0 & 1 & 2 \\ 0 & 2 & 0 \end{bmatrix} \longrightarrow \begin{bmatrix} 1 & 2 \\ 2 & 0 \end{bmatrix}$$

[We do not change the sign of the determinant, since $(i + j) = 1 + 1 = 2$ is even.] Since the computation of the determinant of a square matrix involves the computation of cofactors which are themselves determinants but of matrices of size smaller by 1, the process will ultimately cascade down to the computation of determinants of matrices of the smallest possible size, i.e., 2. Thus, we ultimately only need to know how to compute such determinants.

The determinant of a square 2 by 2 matrix is defined as the product of the two terms on the northwest–southeast diagonal minus the product of the two terms on the other diagonal. In other words, the determinant of the matrix

$$\mathbf{A} = \begin{bmatrix} a_{11} & a_{12} \\ a_{21} & a_{22} \end{bmatrix}$$

is equal to $(a_{11}a_{22} - a_{12}a_{21})$.

As an illustration, let us compute the determinant of the 3 by 3 matrix $\mathbf{A}$ above. We first have to compute the cofactors of the entries on the first row. The cofactor of the first entry was determined above as being the determinant of the 2 by 2 matrix $\begin{bmatrix} 1 & 2 \\ 2 & 0 \end{bmatrix}$ and is equal to $(1 \times 0) - (2 \times 2) = -4$. The cofactor of the second entry is equal to the determinant of the matrix

$$\begin{bmatrix} 1 & 2 & 0 \\ 0 & 1 & 2 \\ 0 & 2 & 0 \end{bmatrix} \longrightarrow \begin{bmatrix} 0 & 2 \\ 0 & 0 \end{bmatrix}$$

with a negative sign since $(i + j) = 1 + 2 = 3$ is odd, and thus it is equal to 0. Finally, the cofactor of the third entry is equal to the determinant of

$$\begin{bmatrix} 1 & 2 & 0 \\ 0 & 1 & 2 \\ 0 & 2 & 0 \end{bmatrix} \longrightarrow \begin{bmatrix} 0 & 1 \\ 0 & 2 \end{bmatrix}$$

with a positive sign and is also equal to 0. Thus, the cofactors of the three entries are, respectively, -4, 0, and 0. Therefore, the value of the determinant of the matrix will be equal to the sum of the products of the entries on the first row by their respective cofactors:

$$1 \times (-4) + 2 \times (0) + 0 \times (0) = -4$$

In general, the value of the determinant of a square matrix of any size will be obtained in the same fashion, by first computing the value of the cofactors on any row or any column. These cofactors are themselves defined as determinants, so that the process is iterated. The size of the determinants of the matrices is decreased by one at every iteration until they are reduced to two, when they are easily computed as above. Finally, the value of the determinant is computed as the sum of the double products of the entries in the row or column by their respective cofactors.

This may sound somewhat mystifying, but the social analyst or planner rarely has to compute manually the value of determinants of matrices in real-world applications, because of their usually large size. The computation of the determinants of matrices of a size larger than 4 by 4 is rather cumbersome and time-consuming. This is usually performed by *computer program*, using the same procedure as outlined above.

In any case, the computation of the determinant of a square matrix is principally intended for the determination of the inverse of the matrix. Indeed, the inverse of the square matrix of any size can be obtained in the following fashion by the *method of cofactors*:

- *First*, compute the cofactors of each entry in the matrix.
- *Second*, evaluate the determinant of the matrix using the cofactors. (If the value of the determinant is zero, the matrix does not have an inverse.)
- *Third*, transform the original matrix by replacing each entry by its cofactor, and then flip it along its main diagonal.
- *Fourth*, and finally, divide each entry of the previous matrix by the value of the determinant. The resulting matrix is the inverse matrix.

As an illustration, let us compute the inverse of the matrix $\mathbf{A}$:

$$\mathbf{A} = \begin{bmatrix} 1 & 2 & 0 \\ 0 & 1 & 2 \\ 0 & 2 & 0 \end{bmatrix}$$

First, the cofactors of the entries on the first row were computed above. They are $-4, 0$, and 0. Similarly, the cofactors of the entries on the second row are, respectively, $0, 0$, and -2. (Check as an exercise.) Finally, the cofactors of the entries on the last row are, respectively, $4, -2$, and 1. Therefore, the matrix of cofactors is

$$\mathbf{A}^c = \begin{bmatrix} -4 & 0 & 0 \\ 0 & 0 & -2 \\ 4 & -2 & 1 \end{bmatrix}$$

Second, we compute the value of the determinant of matrix $\mathbf{A}$. This was performed above and is equal to -4.

Third, the transposed (flipped) matrix of cofactors is

$$\mathbf{A}^t = \begin{bmatrix} -4 & 0 & 4 \\ 0 & 0 & -2 \\ 0 & -2 & 1 \end{bmatrix}$$

Finally, the inverse $\mathbf{A}^{-1}$ of the matrix $\mathbf{A}$ is equal to $\mathbf{A}^t$ divided by the determinant:

$$\mathbf{A}^{-1} = \frac{1}{-4} \begin{bmatrix} -4 & 0 & 4 \\ 0 & 0 & -2 \\ 0 & -2 & 1 \end{bmatrix} = \begin{bmatrix} 1 & 0 & -1 \\ 0 & 0 & \frac{1}{2} \\ 0 & \frac{1}{2} & -\frac{1}{4} \end{bmatrix}$$

As a check, we compute the product

$$\mathbf{A}^{-1}\mathbf{A} = \begin{bmatrix} 1 & 0 & -1 \\ 0 & 0 & \frac{1}{2} \\ 0 & \frac{1}{2} & -\frac{1}{4} \end{bmatrix} \begin{bmatrix} 1 & 2 & 0 \\ 0 & 1 & 2 \\ 0 & 2 & 0 \end{bmatrix} = \begin{bmatrix} 1 & 0 & 0 \\ 0 & 1 & 0 \\ 0 & 0 & 1 \end{bmatrix}$$

Thus, $\mathbf{A}^{-1}$ is indeed the inverse of $\mathbf{A}$.

1.4 Review of Probability Theory

The last part of this review of mathematical prerequisites will deal with the branch of mathematics that concerns quantities of a *probabilistic* nature. The algebra exposed in the previous sections concerned quantities that were *deterministic*, i.e., for which there was no uncertainty as to their value. On the other hand, there are some entities that are (or can be considered to be) not known for certain before their actual recording, but can potentially take on a number of possible values, each with a given probability. For instance, the daily level of use of a public facility such as a county hospital is never known for certain before the end of the day of observation, in contrast to, for instance, the number of nurses on the staff. Such quantities are called *random variables*.

Probability theory is concerned with the theoretical derivation of probabilities associated with random variables and of their other properties. The practical application of these concepts to the natural and social sciences comes from interpreting the empirical frequency of observation of natural random phenomena as an approximation of the theoretical probability.

The function that associates the potential values of the variable with their respective probabilities is called the *probability distribution function*. In some cases, it is possible to derive the mathematical expression of that function on the basis of theoretical considerations. In some other cases, this function might be evaluated empirically, on the basis of observations of the values of the random variable.

For example, if we have collected data about car ownership of households in a given urban area, it would be interesting to examine how many people (or what proportion) in the sample have no car, how many have one car, etc. Suppose, for instance, that in a *sample* of 200 we have observed 30 households with no car, 110 with 1 car, 40 with 2 cars, and 20 with 3 cars. The corresponding four frequencies f_1, f_2, f_3, and f_4 with which we have observed the values 1 through 4, respectively ($X_1 = 0$, $X_2 = 1$, $X_3 = 2$, and $X_4 = 3$), of the random variable $X =$ "car ownership" in our sample would then lead to the empirical probability distribution function represented in Table 1.2.

TABLE 1.2 Empirical Frequency Distribution Function

Level number, i	1	2	3	4
Value, X_i	0	1	2	3
Frequency, f_i	30/200	110/200	40/200	20/200

Practically, these frequencies are an indication of the respective chances that we have of observing the various levels of the characteristic in any individual houshold selected at random in the population. For instance, in the example above, the probability of a household selected at random to have 2 cars should be close to $40/200 = 20\%$, or 0.20. However, the exact or *theoretical* probability could only be determined by a survey of all households in the area of interest. We would then obtain, for all practical purposes, the theoretical (sometimes also called *sampling*) distribution function. Equivalently, we could not say that in the total population of households the actual proportion of households owning two cars is 20%. That proportion was observed in a limited sample, and there is a priori no reason to assume that it would remain the same in the overall population. The only thing we can say is that the larger the number of observations, the smaller the difference should be between the value observed in the sample and the theoretical value corresponding to the total population. Later we will learn some of the techniques of extrapolation of the sample values to their exact or *true* values. These are the methods of *statistical inference*, examples of which we will see in Chapters 6 and 7.

Besides the frequencies corresponding to the various values of the characteristic under investigation, we may also be interested in the frequencies corresponding to values of the variable less than or equal to some given value, e.g., the frequency of houses with at most three bedrooms. It is clear that that frequency is simply the *sum* of the frequencies of observation of zero bedrooms, one bedroom, two bedrooms, and three bedrooms. The function that represents the frequencies with which we have observed a value for the characteristic less than or equal to any specified value is called the *cumulative frequency distribution function*. If the value of the frequency distribution for the value X_i is f_i, the value of the cumulative frequency distribution for the value of the variable X_i will, therefore, be equal to

$$F_i = \sum_{j \leq i} f_j$$

For example, the cumulative frequency distribution function for the example above would be as shown in Table 1.3.

TABLE 1.3   Empirical Cumulative Distribution Function

Level number, i	1	2	3	4
Value, X_i	0	1	2	3
Cumulative frequency, F_i	30/200	140/200	180/200	200/200

It should be clear that, conversely, given the cumulative frequency distribution function, one can easily obtain the frequency distribution function. For instance, the frequency with which households with 1 car were observed is equal to the frequency with which households with at most 1 car were observed, minus the frequency of households with at most 0 cars, i.e., $0.7 - 0.15 = 0.55$. Also, it should be obvious that in general the value of the cumulative frequency distribution function for the lowest value of the random variable will be equal to the corresponding value of the frequency distribution function, and that it will be equal to 1 (or 100%) for the largest possible value of the variable.

There are other descriptors of the characteristics of a given random variable besides its frequency distribution. One of the most commonly used is the *mean value* of the variable (or of the distribution), sometimes also called the *expected value*. The purpose of this indicator is to represent the average of the potential values of the variable. Thus, an empirical *estimate* for it would be obtained by adding up all observed values in the sample and dividing by the number of observations. For instance, in the example above, we observed 30 occurrences of the value 0, 110 of the value 1, 40 of the value 2, and 20 of the value 3. Thus, the total value of the variable in the sample (total number of cars observed) is

$$(30 \times 0) + (110 \times 1) + (40 \times 2) + (20 \times 3) = 250$$

Since the sample size was 200, the *sample mean* is 250/200, which is 1.25 (or 1.25 cars per household). In general, for a variable with m levels or values ($i = 1$ to m), corresponding to respective numbers of observations n_i, with a sample size of $n = \sum_{i=1}^{m} n_i$, the sample mean ($\bar{X}$) will, therefore, be computed as

$$\bar{X} = \frac{X_1 n_1 + X_2 n_2 + \ldots + X_i n_i + \ldots + X_m n_m}{n}$$

$$= \frac{X_1 n_1}{n} + \frac{X_2 n_2}{n} + \ldots + \frac{X_i n_i}{n} + \ldots + \frac{X_m n_m}{n} \qquad (1.5)$$

$$= X_1 \left(\frac{n_1}{n}\right) + X_2 \left(\frac{n_2}{n}\right) + \ldots + X_i \left(\frac{n_i}{n}\right) + \ldots + X_m \left(\frac{n_m}{n}\right)$$

Since the *frequencies* n_i/n of observation of the respective values X_i are approximations of the theoretical *probabilities* p_i, the sample mean $\bar{X}$ as computed above is an approximation to the exact, or *true* value of the mean μ_X, which, if we know the theoretical probability distribution function, would then be computed as

$$\mu_X = X_1 p_1 + X_2 p_2 + X_3 p_3 + \ldots + X_i p_i + \ldots + X_m p_m = \sum_{i=1}^{m} X_i p_i \quad (1.6)$$

The mean thus represents a summary of the information contained in the frequency distribution, and is thus an indicator of the probabilistic properties of the random variable. Another such summary indicator is the *variance*, which measures the average (or mean value) of the square deviations of the values from their mean, and is thus related to the spread of the distribution of frequencies around the mean value of the variable.

It would seem more logical to use the average deviation from the mean and not the average square deviation in order to represent the spread of values. However, the definition of the mean implies that if we were to try to measure the average deviation from the mean, we would always get a value of zero. (See Exercise 1.12.) This is the reason for using, instead,

$$\sigma_X^2 = \sum_{i=1}^{m} p_i (X_i - \mu_X)^2 \quad (1.7)$$

The estimated value of the variance or *sample variance* s_X^2 is obtained by first rescaling all the observed values as deviations from the sample mean. Next, the squares of the values of this new variable and the average of the squares are computed. For instance, in the example above, the deviations, $(X_i - \bar{X})$, of the values of the variable "car ownership" from its mean of 1.25 and their squares $(X_i - \bar{X})^2$ are represented in Table 1.4. Since we have observed 30

TABLE 1.4

i	1	2	3	4
X_i	0	1	2	3
n_i	30	110	40	20
$(X_i - \bar{X})$	−1.25	−0.25	0.75	1.75
$(X_i - \bar{X})^2$	1.56	0.06	0.56	3.06

occurrences of the value 1.56, 110 of the value 0.06, 40 of the value 0.56, and 20 of the value 3.06, the total sample value for the squared deviations from the mean will be

$$(30 \times 1.56) + (110 \times 0.06) + (40 \times 0.56) + (20 \times 3.06) = 137$$

Thus, the observed variance will be 119.8/250 = 0.548.

For a better estimate of the "true" value, probability theory indicates that we should divide not by the sample size n but by the *number of degrees of freedom*, defined as $n - 1 = 249$. This is to ensure that as we use more and more observations, the value obtained for the sample variance converges to the value of the "true" variance, i.e., the exact variance in the total population. [Practically, for large sample sizes ($n \geq 100$) the value of the variance is affected beyond the second decimal point only. In the example above, $137/249 = 0.550$, so that, practically, both values would be rounded off to 0.55.] Thus, in the general case, the value of the sample variance, s_X^2, would be evaluated from n observations X_i as

$$s_X^2 = \frac{1}{n - 1} \sum_{i=1}^{n} (X_i - \bar{X})^2 \tag{1.8}$$

The square root of the variance, i.e., the square root of the average of the squares of the deviations from the mean, is called the *standard deviation* and is equal to

$$\sigma_X = \left[\sum_{i=1}^{m} p_i (X_i - \mu_X)^2 \right]^{1/2} = \sqrt{\sigma_X^2}$$

This value is *not* equal to the average deviation of the observed values from the mean, but it is the simplest proxy for it. (See Exercise 1.13.) Thus, in our example, the value of the sample (observed) standard deviation of the number of cars per household would be $\sqrt{0.55} = 0.74$.

In order to correctly interpret the meaning of the standard deviation and the implications of its observed valued, it is convenient to use another theoretical result from probability theory, which is called the *Tchebyscheff theorem*. This property, which is valid irrespective of the particular frequency distribution of the characteristic, states that the range of values of the random variable going from the mean value minus k standard deviations to the mean value plus k standard deviations (k can be any number greater than 1) will correspond to at least $(1 - 1/k^2)$ percent of the total observed frequencies. In the example above, since the mean is 1.25 and the standard deviation is 0.74, the range of values from 0.14 to 2.36 (which corresponds to 1.5 standard deviations on either side of the mean, i.e., $k = 1.5$) should, therefore, contain approximately at least $1 - [1/(1.5)^2] = 0.56 = 56\%$ of all the frequencies of that distribution. We would, therefore, expect that the proportion of households owning at most two cars should be at least approximately 56% of the population. Thus, in that sense, the information condensed in the sample mean and in the sample standard deviation enables us to partially reconstruct the actual distribution of frequencies. However, the penalty is that the estimate of the percentage of the frequencies enclosed by the resulting range of values is usually much more conservative, i.e., smaller, than the actual percentage observed directly in the frequency distribution.

In any case, the standard deviation thus appears to be a measure of the width of the interval of values (centered around the mean) which will contain a given proportion of the total frequency distribution. For instance, if we want to enclose at least 40% of the total distribution of frequencies in an interval built around the mean, i.e., find an interval such that we have a probability of 0.40 to find a random observation of the variable in that interval, then the half-width of that interval should be such that $0.40 = 1 - 1/k^2$, or $1/k^2 = 0.60$, or $k^2 = 1/0.60 = 1.67$. Thus, $k = \sqrt{1.67} = 1.29$ and the half-width is 1.29 standard deviations.

If a random variable can only take a finite number of values, as in the example above, it will be called a *discrete* random variable. If the random variable is *continuous*, i.e., can take on an infinite number of values (such as all rational values), the probability distribution function will not consist of a set of individual values, but will be a continuous function.

The translation of probabilistic concepts to the case of continuous random variables requires the use of calculus tools such as *differentials* and *integrals*. One main difference in this case is that since there is an infinity of values of the random variable, the probability of any single value is always equal to zero. (However, the probability of an *interval* of values, say from a lower value of a to an upper value of b, is equal to the cumulative probability for the value b minus the cumulative probability for the value a.)

$$P(a \leq X \leq b) = F(b) - F(a) \tag{1.9}$$

Two random variables X and Y will be called *independent* if the probability of the *joint* event consisting of the random variable taking on the value X_i and of the random variable Y taking on the value Y_j is *always* equal to the *product* of the respective probabilities that each variable do so independently. In other words, the probabilities of the values of X do not affect those of Y, and vice versa. Mathematically, if X and Y are independent,

$$P(X = X_i \text{ and } Y = Y_j) = P(X = X_i)P(Y = Y_j) \tag{1.10}$$

for all possible values X_i and Y_j. In general, the function of the two variables X and Y that gives the probability $P(X = X_i \text{ and } Y = Y_j)$ is called the *joint* probability distribution function and its values are denoted by p_{ij}. Thus, except when X and Y are independent, it cannot be derived as the simple product of the individual probability distribution functions of the two variables.

The sum of two random variables X and Y, $Z = X + Y$, is itself a random variable, with its own probability distribution function, which can be computed from the knowledge of the individual distribution functions of the two variables. However, that function is *not* equal to the simple sum of the respective probability distribution functions. Similar statements can be made about the distribution function of the difference, product, and, in general, any algebraic function of two random variables. In some cases, the corresponding distributions can be derived analytically. The mean of the sum (or difference) of two random variables is equal to the sum (or difference) of the respective means of the two variables:

$$\mu_{X+Y} = \mu_X + \mu_Y \tag{1.11}$$

$$\mu_{X-Y} = \mu_X - \mu_Y \tag{1.12}$$

Furthermore, but only if the two variables are *independent*, the variance of the sum, as well as the variance of the difference of two random variables, will both be equal to the sum of the respective variances. (Note that this simple property is not applicable to the standard deviation since the square root of a sum is not equal to the sum of the square roots, as seen in the opening section of this review). Thus,

$$\sigma_{X+Y}^2 = \sigma_X^2 + \sigma_Y^2 \tag{1.13}$$

$$\sigma_{X-Y}^2 = \sigma_X^2 + \sigma_Y^2 \tag{1.14}$$

Adding a constant to a random variable X, the distribution of probabilities of the random variable $Y = X + k$ (where k is not a random, but a deterministic quantity) is the same as that of X. However, the corresponding values of Y are transformed from those of X by a shift of k, as is the mean. The variance and standard deviation of X and Y are respectively equal. That is,

$$\mu_{X+k} = \mu_X + k \tag{1.15}$$

$$\sigma_{X+k}^2 = \sigma_X^2 \tag{1.16}$$

If one multiplies a random variable by a constant k, the distribution of the random variable $Y = kX$ has again the same distribution of probabilities, but the corresponding values are k times the values of X. Also, the mean of Y is equal to k times the mean of X and the standard deviation of Y is equal to k times the standard deviation of X, so that the variance of Y is equal to k^2 times the variance of X. That is,

$$\mu_{kX} = k\mu_X \tag{1.17}$$

$$\sigma_{kX}^2 = k^2\sigma_X^2 \tag{1.18}$$

Extending the result of (1.11), we can compute the mean of the sum of n identically distributed random variables, as the mean of

$$Y = (X_1 + X_2 + X_3 + \ldots + X_n)$$

The mean of Y is equal to the sum of the means of the X_i's, i.e., n times the mean μ of their common distribution, i.e., $n\mu$. Then the mean of the average of the n random variables can be computed as the mean of the variable $Z = Y/n$ using (1.17) and is thus equal to $n\mu/n = \mu$. Therefore, the mean of the average of n identically distributed random variables is equal to their common mean. A similar argument, applying (1.13) and (1.18), would show that the variance of their average is not equal to the common variance of the

X_i's, σ^2, but to σ^2/n. Thus, the standard deviation of their average is equal to $\sqrt{\sigma^2/n} = \sigma/\sqrt{n}$.

A very important result in probability theory states that the distribution function of the sum of a large number n of independent variables X_i, with the same probability distribution,

$$Z = X_1 + X_2 + X_3 + \ldots + X_i + \ldots + X_n$$

tends to a specific distribution function, when n, the number of variables, becomes very large, called the *normal distribution function*. This "limit distribution" is converged to irrespective of the specific nature of the common distribution of the variables X_i, and is all the more approximated as the number n of variables grows infinite.

This property is very useful in practice, since it means that even though the exact form of the probability distribution of a random variable might not be known or is impossible to derive, the exact, i.e., theoretical, distribution of a very large number of independent realizations of that variable or of their average will have a "normal" distribution function. For instance, even though we might not know the probabilistic properties of the daily use of a public facility, we know that the use over a month, i.e., 30 observations (and also the daily average), should be approximately distributed with a "normal" probability function.

EXERCISES

1.1 Let

$$A = \begin{bmatrix} 11 & 22 & 33 & 14 \\ 15 & 61 & 21 & 18 \\ 19 & 10 & 11 & 32 \\ 18 & 44 & 15 & 26 \end{bmatrix} \quad \text{and} \quad B = \begin{bmatrix} 11 & 25 & 19 & 20 \\ 22 & 36 & 10 & 33 \\ 18 & 17 & 11 & 49 \\ 34 & 28 & 13 & 50 \end{bmatrix}$$

Compute:
(a) $A + B$
(b) $A - B$
(c) $3A + 4B$
(d) AB

1.2 Let

$$B = \begin{bmatrix} 0.89 & -0.1 & -0.2 \\ 0.0 & 0.9 & -0.3 \\ 0.0 & 0.0 & 0.75 \end{bmatrix}$$

Compute the inverse B^{-1}, and check the solution.

1.3 Given $X_1 = 1$, $X_2 = 3$, $X_3 = 5$, and $X_4 = 7$. Compute:

(a) $\sum_{i=1}^{4} X_i$

(b) $\sqrt{\sum_i X_i}$

(c) $\sum_i \sqrt{X_i}$

(d) $\sum_i X_i^2$

(e) $(\sum_i X_i)^2$

(f) $\sum_i 2X_i$

1.4 Given the following values X_{ij}:

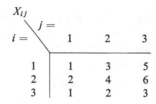

X_{ij} $\diagdown$ $j=$	1	2	3
$i=$			
1	1	3	5
2	2	4	6
3	1	2	3

Compute:

(a) $\sum_{i=1}^{3} \sum_{j=1}^{3} X_{ij}$

(b) $\sum_i \sum_j X_{ij}^{-1}$

1.5 Solve the following equation for X:

$$(3X + 2) = 8X - 6$$

1.6 Plot the graph of the linear function

$$Y = 2X + 3$$

1.7 Solve the following inequation for X:

$$2X + 3 \leq 5$$

1.8 Plot the graph of the exponential function

$$Y = 2^X$$

for all integer values of X between 0 and 6.

1.9 Using a table of decimal logarithms (logarithms of base 10), plot the graph of the function

$$Y = \log_{10} X$$

for all integer values of X between 1 and 10.

1.10 Given the following probability distribution function:

i	1	2	3	4	5
X_i	2	4	6	8	10
p_i	0.2	0.1	0.2	0.3	0.2

Compute:
(a) The mean μ
(b) The variance σ^2
(c) The standard deviation σ

1.11 Following are the data for the number of fire stations observed in 20 different localities:

i	1	2	3	4	5	6	7	8	9	10	11	12	13	14	15	16	17	18	19	20
n_i	3	10	2	1	7	3	6	0	2	8	3	6	5	2	1	3	0	5	1	12

(a) Plot a frequency distribution of the corresponding random variable.
(b) Plot a cumulative frequency distribution function.
(c) Find the average number of fire stations, as observed in the sample.
(d) Find the sample variance.

1.12 Show that the average of the deviations from the sample mean $1/n \sum_i (X_i - \bar{X})$ is always equal to zero. (*Hint:* Factor out the expression.) Justify this on physical grounds.

1.13 Show that the standard deviation is not equal to the average deviation from the mean. (*Hint:* Use the fact that $\sqrt{a^2 + b^2} \neq a + b$.)

REFERENCES

Ang, A. H., and W. Tang. *Probability Concepts in Engineering, Planning and Design*, Vol. 1. New York: John Wiley & Sons, Inc., 1975.

Blalock, H. M. *Theory Construction: From Verbal to Mathematical Formulations*. Englewood Cliffs, N.J.: Prentice-Hall, Inc., 1969.

Chadwick, G. *A Systems View of Planning*. Elmsford, N.Y.: Pergamon Press, Inc., 1971.

Feller, W. *An Introduction to Probability Theory and Its Applications*. New York: John Wiley & Sons, Inc., 1969.

McLoughlin, J. B. *Urban and Regional Planning: A Systems Approach*. New York: Praeger Publishers, Inc., 1969.

Mills, G. *Introduction to Linear Algebra for Social Scientists*. London: George Allen & Unwin Ltd., 1968.

O'Brien, R. J., and G. G. Gareig. *Mathematics for Economists and Social Scientists*. New York: Macmillan Publishing Co., Inc., 1971.

2
Demographic Models

2.1 Introduction

Planning and *analysis* in this book refer to planning for community development and analysis of public policy. Thus, these activities must be based on the knowledge of the makeup of the population to which these plans are directed. The size, age distribution, socioeconomic status, and ethnic distribution of the population are essential factors in the preparation of a plan or the determination of policy alternatives.

Of course, it is always possible to determine the existing values of these characteristics either by census or by survey research methods. However, plans and policy are by nature oriented toward the future. Thus, estimates of the composition of a given population at a future date will be necessary. The purpose of this chapter is to introduce some of the basic methods of *population projection*.

The study of the characteristics of a population and of their evolution through time and space constitutes the field of *demography*. This is a highly technical field, and a thorough exposition would require much more than one chapter. Thus, although one would not expect a planner or policy analyst to be an expert, he or she will need to understand the fundamental demographical methods.

In this chapter, we will begin by introducing *trend* models of population growth. These models treat the population as a whole, i.e., without disaggregation with respect to age, sex, or other characteristics. These models are based on simple physical assumptions about the law that governs the growth of the population. These assumptions are, in turn, translated into simple mathematical formulations.

Next, we shall consider *composite* models. These models treat a given population as an aggregate of various groups, and the evolution of the population results (in part) from the interactions of these groups.

2.2   The Linear Growth Model

The first model we shall describe is the *linear extrapolation model*. The model describes a pattern of population growth where the population level will continue to change at its present rate. Equivalently, the aggregate population level will increase (or decrease) proportionally with time, the proportionality factor being constant. Thus, physically this type of growth is characterized by the fact that the population grows (or decreases) by an equal amount every year (or month, etc.). If that amount is equal to the parameter a, the population levels $P_1, P_2, \ldots, P_n, \ldots$, at years $1, 2, \ldots, n$ are then successively equal to

$$P_1 = P_0 + a$$
$$P_2 = P_1 + a = (P_0 + a) + a = P_0 + 2a$$
$$P_3 = P_2 + a = (P_0 + 2a) + a = P_0 + 3a$$
$$P_n = P_{n-1} + a = P_0 + (n-1)a + a = P_0 + na$$

Therefore, the population level at time n will be

$$\boxed{P_n = P_0 + na} \tag{2.1}$$

where P_0 is the *base population level*, a the *growth per unit time*, and n the time period (measured in months, years, semesters, etc.).

This model is graphically represented by a straight line as in Figure 2.1. Also, it belongs to the general class of linear functions (see Chapter 1). The parameters P_0 and a are, respectively, the intercept and the slope of the straight line.

This model is called the linear extrapolation model because it projects the future population level on the assumption that the linear pattern of growth will remain the same in the future. Its principal characteristic is that the change in population during a given amount of time, equal, for instance,

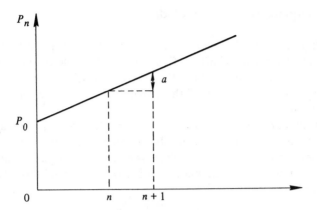

Figure 2.1 Linear growth model.

to k units of time, is constant and equal to ka and is independent of the time of the projection.

In the case of a (constant) decrease in the population level, the parameter a has a negative value, and the plot of the evolution of P_n, although still linear, is now pointed downward.

The practical determination of the values of the parameters a and P_0 of this model will be described in Chapter 6, which is devoted to the empirical methods of model *calibration* and the estimation of empirical parameters, using observational data.

As an illustration of the use of this first model, let us assume that the population level in a given area has been growing by 20,000 every year over the last 20 years. The population level today is 250,000. Assuming that the pattern of growth will remain the same, what will the population levels be 5 and 10 years from now?

Because the increments in population are assumed to be constant and equal to 20,000, the growth of the population level is described by the linear model

$$P_n = P_0 + na$$

Since we know the values of the yearly increments and of the base population level $P_0 = 250,000$, the population level at year n will be

$$P_n = 250,000 + 20,000n$$

Thus, in 5 years it will be

$$P_5 = 250,000 + 20,000(5) = 350,000$$

and in 10 years it will be

$$P_{10} = 250,000 + 20,000(10) = 450,000$$

2.3 The Exponential Growth Model

The simple linear model assumes that the changes in population levels are proportional to the time elapsed. This extremely simple assumption might not be valid in some cases where the rate of growth is not constant, but where there is an acceleration of the growth, i.e., when the rate of growth itself varies with time.

Such a situation might be the case where the population change (per unit time) is not constant, as in the linear model, but proportional to the existing level of population. Physically, this means that the larger the population, the faster it grows. The mathematical translation of this assumption will be

$$P_{n+1} - P_n = rP_n \qquad (2.2)$$

where $(P_{n+1} - P_n)$ represents the increment in population from unit time n to unit time $n + 1$, and r is the proportionality factor.

In physical terms, equation (2.3) also means that the proportionality factor is equal to

$$r = \frac{P_{n+1} - P_n}{P_n} \qquad (2.3)$$

The symbol r therefore represents the *rate of change*, as a percentage (or ratio) of the existing population level. Thus, the basic characteristic of the exponential model is that this rate is constant.

Following the "staircase" procedure used in the linear case, the derivation of the expression of the population level at any time n will be

$$P_1 - P_0 \quad = rP_0 \qquad \text{or} \quad P_1 = (1 + r)P_0$$
$$P_2 - P_1 \quad = rP_1 \qquad \text{or} \quad P_2 = (1 + r)P_1 = (1 + r)(1 + r)P_0 \quad = (1 + r)^2 P_0$$
$$P_3 - P_2 \quad = rP_2 \qquad \text{or} \quad P_3 = (1 + r)P_2 = (1 + r)(1 + r)^2 P_0 = (1 + r)^3 P_0$$
$$\cdots\cdots\cdots\cdots\cdots\cdots\cdots\cdots\cdots\cdots\cdots\cdots\cdots\cdots\cdots$$
$$P_n - P_{n-1} = rP_{n-1} \quad \text{or} \quad P_n = (1 + r)P_{n-1} = (1 + r)(1 + r)^{n-1}P_0$$
$$= (1 + r)^n P_0$$

and the general expression for the population level at time n will be

$$\boxed{P_n = (1 + r)^n P_0} \qquad (2.4)$$

The graphical translation of this type of growth is as represented in Figure 2.2.

Thus, the main characteristic of the *exponential growth model* is that the population level at any time n is proportional to the base population level, with a proportionality factor that is equal to the nth power of (1 plus the growth rate r).

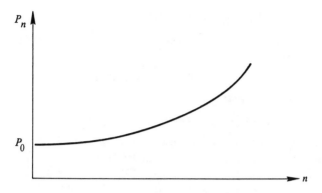

Figure 2.2   Exponential growth model.

In the case of a *decrease* in population, the basic equation (2.3) is now written as

$$r = \frac{P_n - P_{n+1}}{P_n} \tag{2.5}$$

and the equivalent of formula (2.4) is now

$$\boxed{P_n = P_0(1 - r)^n} \tag{2.6}$$

(See Exercise 2.4). The graph of the population level evolution will then have the form represented in Figure 2.3.

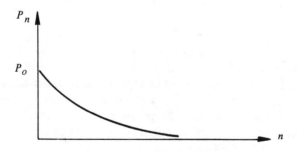

Figure 2.3   Exponential decrease model.

As an illustration of the exponential growth model, let us assume that we know that the population level today is equal to 125,000 and that it is projected to grow at a rate of 5% per year. What will the population level be in 10 years? If the rate of growth is 5%, this means that at the end of every year, the population is equal to what it was at the beginning of the year, plus 5% of that amount. Therefore,

$$P_n = P_{n-1} + 0.05 P_{n-1} = (1 + 0.05) P_{n-1}$$

and we are in the situation described by the exponential growth model, with $r = 0.05$. Therefore,

$$P_n = (1 + 0.05)^n P_0 = (1.05)^n (125{,}000)$$

and at the end of the tenth year,

$$P_{10} = (1.05)^{10} (125{,}000) = 1.63(125{,}000) = 203{,}612$$

It is worth noting that the exponential growth model is similar to the *compounded-interest* formula of financial analysis. Also, the practical computations may be facilitated by the use of *logarithms*. For instance, in the example above, in order to compute the value of $(1.05)^{10}$, we first compute its logarithm[1]:

$$\log (1.05)^{10} = 10 \log (1.05) = 10(0.02118) = 0.2118$$

Also,

$$\log 125{,}000 = \log 125.10^3 = 3 + \log 125 = 5.0969$$

and

$$\log P_{10} = \log 1.05^{10} + \log 125{,}000 = 0.2118 + 5.0969 = 5.3087$$

Thus, $\log P_{10} = 5.3087$ and consequently P_{10}, the "antilog," is equal to 203,564. (The discrepancy with the previous projected figure is due to the rounding of the logarithms.)

In general, if we transform the exponential growth formula of (2.4) by taking the logarithms of both sides, we get

$$\log P_n = \log P_0 + n \log(1 + r)$$

or

$$\log P_n = b + na \qquad\qquad (2.7)$$

where $b = \log P_0$ and $a = \log(1 + r)$, and thus the value of the logarithm of the population level is a linear function of time. The plot of $\log P_n$ will therefore be linear, as represented in Figure 2.4. It might be convenient to use this property to ascertain if the exponential model applies to a given situation, and also to estimate the parameters of the model, P_0 and r, by first graphically evaluating $\log P_0$ and $\log (1 + r)$, or by using the techniques of *linear regression*. (See Chapter 7.)

2.4   The Modified Exponential Growth Model

The respective assumptions behind the linear and the exponential models are reasonable enough in many situations, at least over limited periods of

---

[1]Logarithm values are widely available on pocket calculators, both for logarithms of base 10 (decimal logs), as used in this example, or of base e (natural logs).

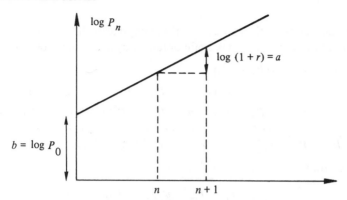

Figure 2.4   Plot of exponential growth model using logarithms.

time. However, a common characteristic of both is that the population level will continue to grow (or decrease) indefinitely. In other words, the population will eventually become *infinite* (or *extinct*). This characteristic might not be appropriate, since it represents a highly undesirable or unrealistic situation.

There are several models which are based on the assumption of a finite, stable limit to the population level. The first we shall consider is a *modified version* of the exponential growth model. The basic assumption behind this model is that the *remaining* growth in population, i.e., the difference between the final population level and the existing population level, is a constant fraction of what it was at the previous time period.

Translated mathematically, this leads to the equation

$$\frac{P_\infty - P_n}{P_\infty - P_{n-1}} = v \qquad (2.8)$$

where P_∞ is the ultimate population level and v a constant smaller than 1. Graphically, this type of growth is represented as in Figure 2.5.

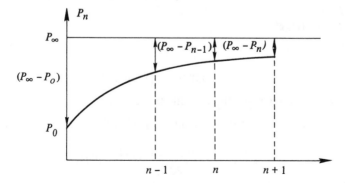

Figure 2.5   Modified exponential growth model.

The derivation of the expression of the population level at any time n as a function of the starting level is again obtained by a cascade procedure:

$$P_\infty - P_1 = v(P_\infty - P_0)$$

$$P_\infty - P_2 = v(P_\infty - P_1) = v \cdot v(P_\infty - P_0) = v^2(P_\infty - P_0)$$

$$P_\infty - P_3 = v(P_\infty - P_2) = v \cdot v^2(P_\infty - P_0) = v^3(P_\infty - P_0)$$

$$\cdots\cdots\cdots\cdots\cdots\cdots\cdots\cdots\cdots\cdots\cdots\cdots\cdots\cdots$$

$$P_\infty - P_n = v(P_\infty - P_{n-1}) = v \cdot v^{n-1}(P_\infty - P_0) = v^n(P_\infty - P_0)$$

and therefore

$$P_n = P_\infty - v^n(P_\infty - P_0) \tag{2.9}$$

Thus, the population level is obtained by subtracting from the ultimate population an expontially decreasing fraction of the overall growth. That fraction is the nth power of the factor v. Consequently, the larger the value of v, the slower the population increase. In the extreme (and unrealistic) case where $v = 1$, the population level remains constant. Conversely, when $v = 0$, the population level would become equal to the final level "immediately," i.e., over a single time period.

As an illustration, let us assume that the enrollment at a university is projected to be stabilized at 30,000, and that it is currently 10,000. The policy of the administration of the university is to have decreasing yearly enrollments in such a fashion that each decade, only a third of the previous decade's growth (measured with respect to the final enrollment) would be allowed. For such a policy, how many years will it take to reach a level of enrollment of 15,000?

The statement of the growth policy indicates that the evolution of the level of enrollment should follow a modified exponential pattern. Thus, at any time (decade) n, the level E_n will be equal to

$$E_n = E_\infty - v^n(E_\infty - E_0)$$

where $E_\infty = 30{,}000$
$\quad\quad E_0 = 10{,}000$
$\quad\quad v = \tfrac{1}{3}$

Thus

$$E_n = 30{,}000 - (\tfrac{1}{3})^n(20{,}000)$$

and $E_n = 15{,}000$ when the time n will be such that

$$15{,}000 = 30{,}000 - (\tfrac{1}{3})^n(20{,}000)$$

or

$$\left(\frac{1}{3}\right)^n = \frac{30{,}000 - 15{,}000}{20{,}000} = 0.75$$

This equation, where n is the unknown, is easily solved by taking the logarithms:

$$n \log \tfrac{1}{3} = \log 0.75$$

or

$$n = \frac{\log 0.75}{\log 0.33} = \frac{-0.125}{-0.478} = 0.261$$

Thus, the level of 15,000 would be reached in only 0.261 decade, or 2.6 years.

2.5   The Double Exponential and Logistic Models

Another model that is based on the assumption of a finite ultimate level of population is the *double exponential model:*

$$\boxed{P_t = P_\infty a^{b^t}} \tag{2.10}$$

The derivation of this model cannot be effected as simply as those described in preceding sections, because it involves the use of calculus. However, it is based on the assumption that the rate of growth of the population is proportional to the population level (as in the exponential model above) but with a proportionality factor which, instead of being constant, increases *exponentially* with time. This provides for a *deceleration* of the rate of growth toward a given limit for the population level. (Note that here t is a continuous variable.)

The main advantage of this model, however, is that after a suitable transformation of the units of measurement of the population level, it becomes a simple *linear* model of growth.

Indeed, if we take the logarithms of both sides of equation (2.10), we get

$$\log P_t = \log P_\infty + b^t \log a$$

or

$$\log \left(\frac{P_\infty}{P_t} \right) = -b^t \log a = b^t \log \frac{1}{a}$$

If we take the logarithms again,

$$\log \log \left(\frac{P_\infty}{P_t} \right) = \log \log \left(\frac{1}{a} \right) + t \log b \tag{2.11}$$

Thus, by using the double logarithms of (P_∞/P_t) and of the inverse of the parameter a, the model becomes a linear model, as illustrated in Figure 2.6. This property can be used to estimate the value of the parameter b, as the slope of the straight line in the plot of the data, after transformation of the population levels into the double logarithms of (P_∞/P_t). This can be done graphically or by using the techniques of Chapters 6 and 7.

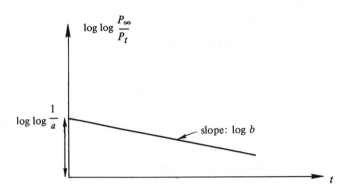

Figure 2.6   Plot of the double exponential model using double logarithms.

The applicability of the model can thus be determined visually by plotting the logarithms of the values of the variable quantity (P_∞/P_t) against time. (This is easily accomplished using commercial *double-log*, or *log-log*, *paper*, i.e., graph paper with a doubly logarithmic scale on the y axis.) The resulting plot should be (approximately) linear.

In any event, this feature of the double exponential model enables us to determine the physical meaning of its parameters a and b. Indeed, at time $t = 0$, we have

$$\log \log \left(\frac{P_\infty}{P_0}\right) = \log \log \left(\frac{1}{a}\right) \qquad \text{or} \qquad \frac{P_\infty}{P_0} = \frac{1}{a}$$

or, finally,

$$a = \frac{P_0}{P_\infty} \tag{2.12}$$

Therefore, a represents the ratio of the base population level to the ultimate level.

Also, the log of b is the slope of the straight line, i.e., the rate of variation of the new unit of measurement of the population level: $\log \log (P_\infty/P_t)$ against time t. The requirement of a finite ultimate level implies that since $a = P_0/P_\infty$ is smaller than 1 (we are assuming growth), b must also be less than 1. Indeed, at time $t = \infty$, $P_t = P_\infty = P_\infty a^{b^\infty}$ or $1 = a^{b^\infty}$. Therefore, $b < 1$; otherwise, b^∞ would be infinitely large, and P_∞ would be infinite. If $b < 1$, b^∞ will be equal to zero and $P_\infty = P_\infty a^0 = P_\infty 1$; the constraint of a finite P_∞ is observed. Since b is smaller than 1, its logarithm is negative and the straight line in Figure 2.6 will be sloping downward. In terms of its original variables, P_t and t, the plot of the double exponential model has the shape represented in Figure 2.7.

As an illustration, let us assume that we would like to fit a double-exponential model to the evolution of a population level starting from a base of 80,000 and stabilizing eventually at a level of 200,000.

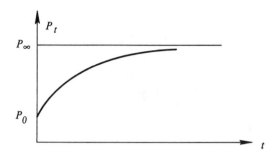

Figure 2.7 Double exponential model.

The model will be of the form $P_t = P_\infty a^{b^t}$. However, we must fit it to our requirements, i.e., estimate the parameters a and b of the model. Equation (2.12) shows that a is equal to (P_0/P_∞). Thus,

$$a = \frac{80,000}{200,000} = 0.4$$

The value of b will be determined from equation (2.11). However, since that equation is time-dependent (i.e., is really the expression of a function), we need the specification of the population level at a given point in time. Thus, suppose that we also know that the level is expected to be 150,000 after 10 years. Plugging these values into equation (2.11), we get

$$\log \log \left(\frac{200,000}{150,000}\right) = \log \log \left(\frac{1}{0.4}\right) + 10 \log b$$

or

$$-0.90 = -0.40 + 10 \log b$$

or

$$\log b = \frac{-0.90 + 0.40}{10} = -0.05 \quad \text{and} \quad b = 0.89$$

Thus, the model that answers our requirements is

$$P_t = (200,000)0.4^{(0.89)^t}$$

[Note that the computations were again performed here using the decimal logarithms, i.e., logs with base 10. The same value for b would have been obtained using the Neperian (or natural) logs, i.e., logarithms of base $e = 2.718\ldots.$]

Let us now conclude our examination of the simple models of extrapolation with a brief description of the *logistic model*. The basic assumption behind the exponential model we have seen in Section 2.3 is that the rate of growth, relative to the population level, is constant. If, however, this is assumed to be a *linearly decreasing* function of the population level, i.e., of the form $(a - bP_t)$, the resulting model is the logistic model:

$$P_t = \frac{1}{\left(\dfrac{1}{P_0} - \dfrac{b}{a}\right)e^{-at} + \dfrac{b}{a}}$$

(2.13)

where $e = 2.718\ldots$ is the base of the Neperian logarithms. The corresponding plot has an "S shape," as represented in Figure 2.8. The resulting

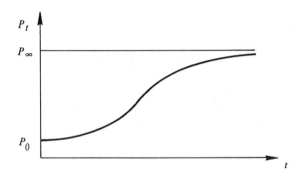

Figure 2.8 Logistic model.

ultimate population level is then equal to a/b. Also, by making b equal to zero in the logistic model, one retrieves the exponential model.

The operation of this model follows essentially the same principles as for the models described previously. (See Exercise 2.7.) Practical determination of the values of the parameters a and b of the model can be effected from the plot of the values of the ratio

$$\frac{P_{n+1} - P_n}{P_n}$$

against those of P_n. If the logistic model applies, the plot will be linear, with an intercept equal to the value of a and a slope equal to the value of b.

2.6 The Comparative Methods

Another group of methods in population projections is based not on the examination of a given area individually but on various assumptions regarding the relative fashion in which two areas or regions are growing. For instance, it might be observed that historically a certain county in a given state has been growing proportionally to the total population of the state. Thus, if the projection for the state P_t^s is available, the projection for the county P_t^c can easily be derived as being

$$P_t^c = kP_t^s$$

(2.14)

where k is the proportionality factor. This simple procedure is sometimes called the *ratio method*.

As an illustration, let us assume that it has been ascertained that the population of a certain metropolitan area C has steadily been 20% of the total population of the state it is in. Also, assume that the population of the state has been projected to grow according to the following linear model:

$$P_t^S = 2 + 0.1t \qquad (P \text{ in millions, } t \text{ in years})$$

In how many years from now will the population of the city double?

If the population of the city, P^C, is assumed to remain 20% of the total population of the state, then, following formula (2.14),

$$P_t^C = 0.2P_t^S$$

Therefore, at any time t, $P_t^C = 0.2(2 + 0.1t)$.

Presently, the level of the population of the city is

$$P_0^C = 0.2[2 + 0.1(0)] = 0.4 \qquad \text{(millions)}$$

For the level to double, i.e., become 0.8, it will take a number of years t such that

$$P_t^C = 0.8 = 0.2(2 + 0.1t)$$

or

$$2 + 0.1t = \frac{0.8}{0.2} = 4$$

and

$$0.1t = 2 \qquad \text{or} \qquad t = 20 \text{ years}$$

In other cases, we might know that the population of a given area S follows the growth of a reference area U, but with a *time lag* T. Then the population level of area S at time t will be equal to the population level of U, T units of time earlier. Translated mathematically,

$$\boxed{P_t^U = P_{t-T}^S} \qquad (2.15)$$

For instance, suppose that the population level P^S of a certain state is known to follow the development of another, P^U, but 15 years later. We know that the population of the reference state, U, is growing exponentially, starting from a base of 2 million and growing by 5% every year. Thus,

$$P_t^U = 2(1 + 0.05)^t$$

How many years will it take the state S to reach a level of 3 million itself?

The model for the population level of the state S is "shifted back" from that of U by 15 years. Thus, following formula (2.15),

$$P_t^S = P_{t-15}^U = 2(1 + 0.05)^{t-15}$$

Therefore, the time at which the level will be 3 million is such that

$$3 = 2(1.05)^{t-15} \qquad \text{or} \qquad \tfrac{3}{2} = 1.5 = 1.05^{t-15}$$

or, taking the logs,

$$\log 1.5 = (t - 15)\log 1.05$$

and

$$t - 15 = \frac{\log 1.5}{\log 1.05} = \frac{0.176}{0.021} = 8.31$$

and

$$t = 8.31 + 15 = 23.31$$

Thus, it would take a little more than 23 years for the state S to reach a level of 3 million people.

Naturally, several of the assumptions about the comparative growth of two areas can be combined. Suppose, for instance, that a given area A has been known to replicate the growth pattern of another area B but with a time lag of 10 years, and with a proportionality factor of 2. In other words, the population level of area A is twice as large as what it was for area B 10 years earlier. The model would thus be

$$P_t^A = 2P_{t-10}^B$$

Finally, in the general case, by plotting the respective graphs of the population levels in two areas A and B, it might be noticed that a horizontal shift, combined with a vertical shift and with a reduction (or enlargement) in a constant ratio will result in the superposition of the two curves. This is illustrated in Figure 2.9. In this case, the population levels are separated by a

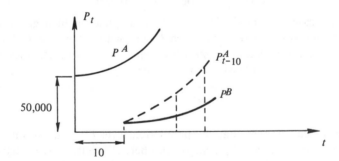

Figure 2.9   Comparative population growths.

time lag of 10 years, a difference in levels of 50,000, and a size factor of 2. The relationship between the levels P^A and P^B of areas A and B would then be

$$P_t^B = \tfrac{1}{2}(P_{t-10}^A - 50,000)$$

and the projection of the population of B can be effected from that of A.

2.7 The Birth Component of the Cohort-Survival Model

The simple projection models presented in the preceding sections treat the population as an aggregate, i.e., without distinguishing among various *age groups* or differentiating with respect to other demographic characteristics, such as sex or ethnic origin. Naturally, it is always possible to apply these models separately to any particular group in the population. However, the evolution of population level is also a function of the interrelationships among the various subgroups that make up the total population. The most obvious example in terms of age groups, for instance, is that some of the people who were in a given age group at a given time will be found (possibly among others) in the next age group at a later time. Also, the groups with females of childbearing age will contribute to the growth of the population in the first age group.

On a methodological level, the analyst/planner needs to know the present and future composition of a given population in terms of the characteristics listed above. This is because various groups in the community have various needs, power, interests, etc. Therefore, the aggregate level of a given population might not be, in some cases, a sufficient basis for planning or policy making.

On a conceptual level, the simple models are *descriptive*, in that they are not based on an explanation of the causes or components of the population growth (or decline), i.e., birth, mortality, and migration. Instead, they are based on some assumption about the relation of the speed (or rate) of growth to time or to the population level itself. Thus, the "explanation" is a mechanistic one but not a "physical" one.

The models that will be presented in this section represent (partially) an attempt to remedy the limitations of the simple models. These belong to the class of *cohort-survival models* and will be described using the matrix notation and algebra. (A succinct exposition of matrix algebra is provided in Section 1.3. It will be beneficial for those readers not proficient with this tool to review it, since it will also be used in several subsequent chapters.)

Let us then first consider the breakdown of a given population in terms of age groups. Let us, for instance, disaggregate the overall population in groups spanning, say, T years. The first group will contain children age 1 to T years, the second group youths from $T + 1$ to $2T$, etc. There will thus be u age groups with respective levels of population $p_1^0, p_2^0, \ldots, p_i^0, \ldots, p_u^0$ at time $t = 0$. The lower index will refer to the age group and the upper index to the time period. This can be represented by a column vector:

$$\mathbf{P}^0 = \begin{bmatrix} p_1^0 \\ p_2^0 \\ \cdot \\ \cdot \\ \cdot \\ p_i^0 \\ \cdot \\ \cdot \\ \cdot \\ p_u^0 \end{bmatrix}$$

Usually, the standard time span for an age group will be $T = 5$ years, and the last group will be the group of age 85 and over. Thus, we would have $u = 18$ groups.

Now that we have defined the structure of the population, let us define the *components of change*. The first factor of change is *birth*. Let us assume that the first age group in which the females are of childbearing age is group k. Similarly, the index of the last such group will be q. The *fertility rates* of the various age groups corresponding to childbearing ages for females will be $b_k, b_{k+1}, \ldots, b_i, \ldots, b_q$. These rates are for a time period of T years equal to the span of the age groups. Thus, b_k will be defined as the ratio of the number of babies (boys and girls) born from females in the kth group in the time period of length T over the total size (male and female) of that group. Equivalently,

$$b_k = \frac{\text{number of births from group } k}{p_k^0} \tag{2.16}$$

or

$$\text{number of births from group } k = (b_k)(p_k^0) \tag{2.17}$$

(The birth rates are the *net* birth rates, i.e., adjusted for mortality of infants at birth.)

Similarly, the number of babies produced by the second childbearing group will be $(b_{k+1})(p_{k+1}^0)$ and that of the last childbearing group will be $(b_q)(p_q^0)$. The total number of babies born in a time period of T years will therefore be

$$b_k p_k^0 + b_{k+1} p_{k+1}^0 + \ldots + b_q p_q^0$$

That number will represent the change Δp_1 in the level of population of the first group over the first time period.[2] Thus, $\Delta p_1 = b_k p_k^0 + b_{k+1} p_{k+1}^0 + \cdots$

---

[2] The symbol ΔX, which will be used in several other instances, represents the difference of two (usually consecutive) values of the variable X. Here

$$\Delta p_1 = p_1^1 - p_1^0$$

$+ b_q p_q^0$. If we consider the birth component of change, in isolation, the population levels of the other age groups do not change in that time interval. In other words, $\Delta p_i = 0$ for all other age groups $i = 1$ to $k - 1$ and $q + 1$ to u.

Using the definition of matrix multiplication, the whole set of population level changes ΔP due to births can, therefore, be represented in matrix notation by the product

$$
\Delta P = \begin{bmatrix} \Delta p_1 \\ \Delta p_2 \\ \cdot \\ \cdot \\ \cdot \\ \cdot \\ \cdot \\ \cdot \\ \Delta p_i \\ \cdot \\ \cdot \\ \cdot \\ \cdot \\ \cdot \\ \cdot \\ \Delta p_u \end{bmatrix} = \begin{bmatrix} 0 & 0 & \cdots & b_k & b_{k+1} & \cdots & b_q & \cdots & 0 \\ 0 & 0 & \cdots\cdots\cdots\cdots & 0 & \cdots\cdots\cdots\cdots\cdots & 0 \\ & & \cdots\cdots\cdots\cdots\cdots\cdots\cdots\cdots\cdots\cdots\cdots \\ & & \cdots\cdots\cdots\cdots\cdots\cdots\cdots\cdots\cdots\cdots\cdots \\ & & \cdots\cdots\cdots\cdots\cdots\cdots\cdots\cdots\cdots\cdots\cdots \\ 0 & 0 & \cdots\cdots\cdots\cdots & 0 & \cdots\cdots\cdots\cdots\cdots & 0 \\ & & \cdots\cdots\cdots\cdots\cdots\cdots\cdots\cdots\cdots\cdots\cdots \\ & & \cdots\cdots\cdots\cdots\cdots\cdots\cdots\cdots\cdots\cdots\cdots \\ & & \cdots\cdots\cdots\cdots\cdots\cdots\cdots\cdots\cdots\cdots\cdots \\ & & \cdots\cdots\cdots\cdots\cdots\cdots\cdots\cdots\cdots\cdots\cdots \\ & & \cdots\cdots\cdots\cdots\cdots\cdots\cdots\cdots\cdots\cdots\cdots \\ & & \cdots\cdots\cdots\cdots\cdots\cdots\cdots\cdots\cdots\cdots\cdots \\ & & \cdots\cdots\cdots\cdots\cdots\cdots\cdots\cdots\cdots\cdots\cdots \\ & & \cdots\cdots\cdots\cdots\cdots\cdots\cdots\cdots\cdots\cdots\cdots \\ & & \cdots\cdots\cdots\cdots\cdots\cdots\cdots\cdots\cdots\cdots\cdots \\ 0 & 0 & \cdots\cdots\cdots\cdots\cdots\cdots\cdots\cdots\cdots & 0 \end{bmatrix} \begin{bmatrix} p_1^0 \\ p_2^0 \\ \cdot \\ \cdot \\ p_k^0 \\ p_{k+1}^0 \\ \cdot \\ \cdot \\ p_i^0 \\ \cdot \\ \cdot \\ p_q^0 \\ \cdot \\ \cdot \\ p_u^0 \end{bmatrix} \qquad (2.18)
$$

or in compact form,

$$\Delta P = BP^0 \qquad (2.19)$$

The column vector ΔP represents the net change due to births only. The matrix B represents the "birth" operator. (Note that only the top row of B has nonzero entries between positions k and q corresponding to the first and last "fertile" age group.) The column vector P^0 represents the population levels at the start of the process.

As an illustration, let us use the data presented in Table 2.1 to model the change in population levels due to births only. Since the age groups have a time span of 10 years, we will adopt the same unit of time for the projection period. There are four age groups that are fertile, groups 2, 3, 4, and 5. Thus, in terms of the notation above, the index of first fertile age group is $k = 2$, and the index of the last is $q = 5$. The total number of age groups is $u = 9$. We now evaluate the fertility rates b_i. These are defined as the ratios

TABLE 2.1

i	Age	Population	Births	Deaths
1	0–9	3,900		42
2	10–19	3,200	35	2
3	20–29	3,300	267	5
4	30–39	2,800	105	6
5	40–49	1,700	12	7
6	50–59	1,800		17
7	60–69	1,100		28
8	70–79	550		35
9	80–89	200		24
Total		18,370	419	166

of the number of births over the total size of the population group. Thus, $b_1 = 0$ and $b_2 = 35/3200 = 0.011$.   Similarly, $b_3 = 267/3300 = 0.081$, $b_4 = 105/2800 = 0.038$, $b_5 = 12/1700 = 0.007$, and $b_6 = b_7 = b_8 = b_9 = 0$. Finally, the increase of the number of babies in the first age group at the beginning of the next time period will be equal to

$$\Delta p_1 = b_2 p_2^0 + b_3 p_3^0 + b_4 p_4^0 + b_5 p_5^0$$
$$= (0.011)(3200) + (0.081)(3300) + (0.038)(2800) + (0.007)(1700)$$
$$= 421$$

(The difference with the given value of $35 + 267 + 105 + 12 = 419$ is due to the rounding of the birth rates.) The increases (changes) for the other population levels are nil, since we are considering the effect of births only.

In matrix notation, the computation above can be represented as

$$\mathbf{\Delta P} = \begin{bmatrix} \Delta p_1 \\ \Delta p_2 \\ \Delta p_3 \\ \Delta p_4 \\ \Delta p_5 \\ \Delta p_6 \\ \Delta p_7 \\ \Delta p_8 \\ \Delta p_9 \end{bmatrix} = \begin{bmatrix} 0 & 0.011 & 0.081 & 0.038 & 0.007 & 0 & 0 & 0 & 0 \\ 0 & 0 & 0 & 0 & 0 & 0 & 0 & 0 & 0 \\ 0 & 0 & 0 & 0 & 0 & 0 & 0 & 0 & 0 \\ 0 & 0 & 0 & 0 & 0 & 0 & 0 & 0 & 0 \\ 0 & 0 & 0 & 0 & 0 & 0 & 0 & 0 & 0 \\ 0 & 0 & 0 & 0 & 0 & 0 & 0 & 0 & 0 \\ 0 & 0 & 0 & 0 & 0 & 0 & 0 & 0 & 0 \\ 0 & 0 & 0 & 0 & 0 & 0 & 0 & 0 & 0 \\ 0 & 0 & 0 & 0 & 0 & 0 & 0 & 0 & 0 \end{bmatrix} \begin{bmatrix} p_1^0 \\ p_2^0 \\ p_3^0 \\ p_4^0 \\ p_5^0 \\ p_6^0 \\ p_7^0 \\ p_8^0 \\ p_9^0 \end{bmatrix}$$

At this point, this approach surely looks like a lot of trouble to formalize something that might look obvious. However, the benefits of putting the relationship between the starting level of population and the changes over the projection period in matrix form using the fertility rates will appear more clearly when the other components of change are included, and when the model is used for calculations over several periods of time.

2.8 The Aging Component

Let us now consider the effect of the other component of change of level of population, i.e., death, or more specifically *survivorship* from one age group to the next. The basic mechanism here is that the fraction of the population in age group i which survives (i.e., does not die) over the period of projection 1 will be found in the next age group $i + 1$, since by the beginning of the next time period they will by then be T years older. (This is the reason for the choice of common length for the projection intervals and the age groups.)

Let us define the *survivorship rate* $s_{i+1,i}$ as the proportion of the population in age group i who survive over one time period, i.e., who make the transition from group i to group $i + 1$ as

$$s_{i+1,i} = 1 - \frac{\text{number of deaths in group } i}{p_i} = \frac{\text{number of survivors in group } i}{p_i}$$

$$s_{i+1,i} = 1 - \frac{d_i}{p_i} = 1 - \text{death rate in group } i \qquad (2.20)$$

The number of survivors in group i is thus equal to $(s_{i+1,i})(p_i)$ from formula (2.20). This is also by definition the new number of people p_{i+1}^1 to be found in group $i + 1$ at the beginning of the next time period, since we are considering only survivorship, not migration or birth.

Thus, the population levels at the beginning of the next time period are, respectively,

$$p_2 = (s_{2,1})(p_1^0)$$
$$p_3 = (s_{3,2})(p_2^0)$$
$$\cdots\cdots\cdots\cdots$$
$$p_i = (s_{i,i-1})(p_{i-1}^0)$$
$$\cdots\cdots\cdots\cdots$$
$$p_u = (s_{u,u-1})(p_{u-1}^0)$$

Finally, the level in group 1 will be zero, since the only change in that group can be caused by either migration or birth, which we are not considering now. Also, the level in the last group u will be the total of the survivors from that group, i.e., $(s_{u,u})(p_u)$, plus the survivors from the penultimate group, $(s_{u,u-1})(p_{u-1})$. In matrix form, this mechanism can be compactly written as

$$
\begin{bmatrix} p_1^1 \\ p_2^1 \\ p_3^1 \\ \cdot \\ \cdot \\ \cdot \\ p_i^1 \\ \cdot \\ \cdot \\ \cdot \\ p_u^1 \end{bmatrix} = \begin{bmatrix} 0 & 0 & 0 & 0 & \cdots & 0 & 0 \\ s_{21} & 0 & 0 & 0 & \cdots & 0 & 0 \\ 0 & s_{32} & 0 & 0 & \cdots & 0 & 0 \\ & & & \cdots\cdots\cdots\cdots\cdots & & & \\ 0 & 0 & 0 & s_{i+1,i} & \cdots & 0 & 0 \\ & & & \cdots\cdots\cdots\cdots\cdots & & & \\ 0 & 0 & 0 & & \cdots & s_{u,u-1} & s_{u,u} \end{bmatrix} \begin{bmatrix} p_1^0 \\ p_2^0 \\ p_3^0 \\ \cdot \\ \cdot \\ \cdot \\ p_i^0 \\ \cdot \\ \cdot \\ \cdot \\ p_u^0 \end{bmatrix}
\tag{2.21}
$$

or in compact form,

$$
\mathbf{P}^1 = \mathbf{S}\mathbf{P}^0
\tag{2.22}
$$

where $\mathbf{P}^1$ is the vector of new population levels and $\mathbf{S}$ the "survivorship" matrix, describing the operation of the individual component "death" on the original population levels $\mathbf{P}^0$. Note that the matrix $\mathbf{S}$, like the previous matrix $\mathbf{B}$, has a distinctive structure. All entries that are not immediately under the main diagonal (except the lower right corner term) are equal to zero. Also, note the *order* of the subscripts in $s_{i+1,i}$: *from* group i (column index) *to* group $i + 1$ (row index).

As an illustration, let us represent the evolution of the population levels given in Table 2.1, considering the effect of death only. The number of deaths in the first age group is 42 for a population of 3900. Thus, the death rate is $42/3900 = 0.011$. Therefore, the survivorship rate from group 1 to group 2 is $s_{21} = 1 - 0.011 = 0.989$. Consequently, the number of people to be found in group 2 at the beginning of the next time period will be $p_2^1 = (s_{21})(p_1^0)$ $= (0.989)(3900) = 3857$. (The difference with $3900 - 42 = 3858$ is again due to rounding of the rates.) Similarly, the death rate of the second group is $2/3200 = 0.0006$ and the survivorship rate from group 2 to group 3 is s_{32} $= 1 - 0.001 = 0.999$. Thus, the number of survivors, i.e., the population level in the third group at the next time period will be $(1 - 0.001)(3200)$ $= 3198$.

Again, it might seem to be perfunctory to write the new population levels as the product of the population base times a survivorship rate, when they could be obtained from a simple subtraction of the number of deaths from the exising levels. The reason is that statistics about the population are usually given in terms of rates of birth and death. Furthermore, the basis of population projections is to assume that these rates remain constant over some period of time. Thus, one then has to convert these rates into absolute population levels at every time period, and then proceed by subtractions and additions. The amount of work involved using matrix multiplication is, however, considerably less than with a "long hand" approach.

In any case, proceeding as above, we obtain the remaining survivorship rates:

$$s_{43} = 1 - \frac{5}{3300} = 0.998$$

$$s_{54} = 1 - \frac{6}{2800} = 0.998$$

$$s_{65} = 1 - \frac{7}{1700} = 0.996$$

$$s_{76} = 1 - \frac{17}{1800} = 0.991$$

$$s_{87} = 1 - \frac{28}{1100} = 0.975$$

$$s_{98} = 1 - \frac{35}{550} = 0.936$$

$$s_{99} = 1 - \frac{24}{200} = 0.880$$

The last survivorship rate, s_{99}, represents the proportion of people who remain in the last age group. Consequently, the size of the last group is now equal to the sum of the survivors from the penultimate group and of the survivors in the last group. Equivalently,

$$p_9^1 = (s_{98})(p_8^0) + (s_{99})(p_9^0) = (0.936)(550) + (0.880)(200) = 691$$

In matrix notation, we can now represent the relationship between the various population sizes at the start and at the end of the first time period as

$$
\begin{bmatrix} p_1^1 \\ p_2^1 \\ p_3^1 \\ p_4^1 \\ p_5^1 \\ p_6^1 \\ p_7^1 \\ p_8^1 \\ p_9^1 \end{bmatrix} =
\begin{bmatrix}
0 & 0 & 0 & 0 & 0 & 0 & 0 & 0 & 0 \\
0.989 & 0 & 0 & 0 & 0 & 0 & 0 & 0 & 0 \\
0 & 0.999 & 0 & 0 & 0 & 0 & 0 & 0 & 0 \\
0 & 0 & 0.998 & 0 & 0 & 0 & 0 & 0 & 0 \\
0 & 0 & 0 & 0.998 & 0 & 0 & 0 & 0 & 0 \\
0 & 0 & 0 & 0 & 0.996 & 0 & 0 & 0 & 0 \\
0 & 0 & 0 & 0 & 0 & 0.991 & 0 & 0 & 0 \\
0 & 0 & 0 & 0 & 0 & 0 & 0.975 & 0 & 0 \\
0 & 0 & 0 & 0 & 0 & 0 & 0 & 0.936 & 0.880
\end{bmatrix}
\begin{bmatrix} p_1^0 \\ p_2^0 \\ p_3^0 \\ p_4^0 \\ p_5^0 \\ p_6^0 \\ p_7^0 \\ p_8^0 \\ p_9^0 \end{bmatrix}
$$

We now have two models which describe, respectively, the effects on the population levels of given age groups of the processes of birth and aging considered separately. It should be obvious that these effects are cumulative, i.e., the total effect of both births and of aging is simply the sum of the effects of these components of change. In formal terms, therefore, the new population levels (considering only birth and death, and not migration, which we shall incorporate into the model next) will be

$$\mathbf{P}^1 = {}^s\mathbf{P}^1 + {}^b\mathbf{P}^1$$

where ${}^s\mathbf{P}^1$ represents the new population levels due to aging (the reshuffling due to the transfer of some people from one age group to the other) and ${}^b\mathbf{P}^1$ represents the addition to the population levels (essentially to the first age group) of the newborn babies. Replacing ${}^s\mathbf{P}^1$ and ${}^b\mathbf{P}^1$ by their expressions from formulas (2.22) and (2.19), respectively, we get

$$\mathbf{P}^1 = \mathbf{S}\mathbf{P}^0 + \mathbf{B}\mathbf{P}^0 = (\mathbf{S} + \mathbf{B})\mathbf{P}^0 = \mathbf{C}\mathbf{P}^0$$

or

$$\mathbf{P}^1 = \mathbf{C}\mathbf{P}^0 \qquad (2.23)$$

where $\mathbf{C}$ is the sum of the matrices $\mathbf{S}$ and $\mathbf{B}$.

In the example above, if we want to represent the relationships between $\mathbf{P}^0$ and $\mathbf{P}^1$ taking into account births and aging at once, we have

$$
\begin{bmatrix} p_1^1 \\ p_2^1 \\ \cdot \\ \cdot \\ p_i^1 \\ \cdot \\ \cdot \\ \cdot \\ p_u^1 \end{bmatrix}
=
\begin{bmatrix}
0 & 0.011 & 0.081 & 0.038 & 0.007 & 0 & 0 & 0 & 0 \\
0.989 & 0 & 0 & 0 & 0 & 0 & 0 & 0 & 0 \\
0 & 0.999 & 0 & 0 & 0 & 0 & 0 & 0 & 0 \\
0 & 0 & 0.998 & 0 & 0 & 0 & 0 & 0 & 0 \\
0 & 0 & 0 & 0.998 & 0 & 0 & 0 & 0 & 0 \\
0 & 0 & 0 & 0 & 0.996 & 0 & 0 & 0 & 0 \\
0 & 0 & 0 & 0 & 0 & 0.991 & 0 & 0 & 0 \\
0 & 0 & 0 & 0 & 0 & 0 & 0.975 & 0 & 0 \\
0 & 0 & 0 & 0 & 0 & 0 & 0 & 0.936 & 0.880
\end{bmatrix}
\begin{bmatrix} p_1^0 \\ p_2^0 \\ \cdot \\ \cdot \\ p_i^0 \\ \cdot \\ \cdot \\ \cdot \\ p_u^0 \end{bmatrix}
$$

In practice, the addition of the two matrices, $\mathbf{S}$ and $\mathbf{B}$, is very simple. It amounts to a superimposition, since matrix $\mathbf{S}$ only has terms along the subdiagonal, where $\mathbf{B}$ only has zeros, and conversely, matrix $\mathbf{B}$ only has nonzero terms along the first row, where all entries in $\mathbf{S}$ are zero.

If there are no migrations into or from the area, or if they are negligible compared to the natural changes internal to the area, the formulation above leads to an extremely convenient process for projecting population levels. Indeed, if we want to evaluate the population levels at time 2, i.e., $\mathbf{P}^2$, we simply replace $\mathbf{P}^0$ by $\mathbf{P}^1$ and $\mathbf{P}^1$ by $\mathbf{P}^2$ in equation (2.23). Thus, we obtain

$$\mathbf{P}^2 = \mathbf{C}\mathbf{P}^1 = \mathbf{C}(\mathbf{C}\mathbf{P}^0)$$

or, directly,

$$\mathbf{P}^2 = (\mathbf{C}\mathbf{C})\mathbf{P}^0 = \mathbf{C}^2\mathbf{P}^0$$

In other words, the projection of the population over two time periods is similar to that over one time period, if we replace the matrix $\mathbf{C}$ by its square. Similarly, the population levels at the beginning of the third time period would be

$$\mathbf{P}^3 = \mathbf{CP}^2 = \mathbf{C}(\mathbf{C}^2\mathbf{P}^0) = (\mathbf{CC}^2)\mathbf{P}^0 = \mathbf{C}^3\mathbf{P}^0$$

In general, it is easy to see that by the same mechanism we encountered in the simple projection models of Sections 2.2 to 2.4:

$$\mathbf{P}^n = \mathbf{CP}^{n-1} = \mathbf{C}(\mathbf{C}^{n-1}\mathbf{P}^0) = \mathbf{C}^n\mathbf{P}^0 \qquad (2.24)$$

Thus, the projection of the population for any time n can be effected directly by first computing the nth power of the matrix $\mathbf{C}$ and then using it in the basic equation (2.24). This is generally easier than repeating the single period projection n times.

As an illustration, assume that we want to infer the population levels $\mathbf{P}^4$, i.e., after four time periods, in the example above. We, therefore, need to compute the fourth power of matrix $\mathbf{C}$, evaluated above. We first compute the second power of $\mathbf{C}$, i.e., $\mathbf{C}^2$. This is equal to

$$
\begin{bmatrix}
0.0 & 0.011 & 0.081 & 0.038 & 0.007 & 0 & 0 & 0 & 0 \\
0.989 & 0 & 0 & 0 & 0 & 0 & 0 & 0 & 0 \\
0.0 & 0.999 & 0 & 0 & 0 & 0 & 0 & 0 & 0 \\
0 & 0 & 0.998 & 0 & 0 & 0 & 0 & 0 & 0 \\
0 & 0 & 0 & 0.998 & 0 & 0 & 0 & 0 & 0 \\
0 & 0 & 0 & 0 & 0.996 & 0 & 0 & 0 & 0 \\
0 & 0 & 0 & 0 & 0 & 0.991 & 0 & 0 & 0 \\
0 & 0 & 0 & 0 & 0 & 0 & 0.975 & 0 & 0 \\
0 & 0 & 0 & 0 & 0 & 0 & 0 & 0.936 & 0.880
\end{bmatrix}
$$

$$\mathbf{C}$$

$$
\times
\begin{bmatrix}
0.0 & 0.011 & 0.081 & 0.038 & 0.007 & 0 & 0 & 0 & 0 \\
0.989 & 0 & 0 & 0 & 0 & 0 & 0 & 0 & 0 \\
0.0 & 0.999 & 0 & 0 & 0 & 0 & 0 & 0 & 0 \\
0 & 0 & 0.998 & 0 & 0 & 0 & 0 & 0 & 0 \\
0 & 0 & 0 & 0.998 & 0 & 0 & 0 & 0 & 0 \\
0 & 0 & 0 & 0 & 0.996 & 0 & 0 & 0 & 0 \\
0 & 0 & 0 & 0 & 0 & 0.991 & 0 & 0 & 0 \\
0 & 0 & 0 & 0 & 0 & 0 & 0.975 & 0 & 0 \\
0 & 0 & 0 & 0 & 0 & 0 & 0 & 0.936 & 0.880
\end{bmatrix}
$$

$$\mathbf{C}$$

$$
= \begin{bmatrix}
0.0109 & 0.0809 & 0.0379 & 0.0070 & 0 & 0 & 0 & 0 & 0 \\
0 & 0.0109 & 0.0802 & 0.0376 & 0.0069 & 0 & 0 & 0 & 0 \\
0.9890 & 0 & 0 & 0 & 0 & 0 & 0 & 0 & 0 \\
0 & 0.9970 & 0 & 0 & 0 & 0 & 0 & 0 & 0 \\
0 & 0 & 0.9960 & 0 & 0 & 0 & 0 & 0 & 0 \\
0 & 0 & 0 & 0.9940 & 0 & 0 & 0 & 0 & 0 \\
0 & 0 & 0 & 0 & 0.9870 & 0 & 0 & 0 & 0 \\
0 & 0 & 0 & 0 & 0 & 0.9662 & 0 & 0 & 0 \\
0 & 0 & 0 & 0 & 0 & 0 & 0.9126 & 0.8237 & 0.7744
\end{bmatrix}
$$

$$\mathbf{C}^2$$

We next compute $\mathbf{C}^4$. This can be computed simply as the square of $\mathbf{C}^2$, since $\mathbf{C}^4 = (\mathbf{C}^2)^2$. Repeating the same procedure, we get

$$\mathbf{C}^4 =$$

$$
\begin{bmatrix}
0.0376 & 0.0088 & 0.0069 & 0.0031 & 0.0006 & 0 & 0 & 0 & 0 \\
0.0793 & 0.0376 & 0.0078 & 0.0004 & 0 & 0 & 0 & 0 & 0 \\
0.0108 & 0.0800 & 0.0375 & 0.0069 & 0 & 0 & 0 & 0 & 0 \\
0 & 0.0109 & 0.0799 & 0.0375 & 0.0070 & 0 & 0 & 0 & 0 \\
0.9851 & 0 & 0 & 0 & 0 & 0 & 0 & 0 & 0 \\
0 & 0.9910 & 0 & 0 & 0 & 0 & 0 & 0 & 0 \\
0 & 0 & 0.9831 & 0 & 0 & 0 & 0 & 0 & 0 \\
0 & 0 & 0 & 0.9604 & 0 & 0 & 0 & 0 & 0 \\
0 & 0 & 0 & 0 & 0.9008 & 0.7924 & 0.7067 & 0.6379 & 0.5997
\end{bmatrix}
$$

Finally, the projected population levels at time 4 would then be

$$\mathbf{P}^4 = \mathbf{C}^4 \mathbf{P}^0$$

$$
= \begin{bmatrix}
0.0376 & 0.0088 & 0.0069 & 0.0031 & 0.0006 & 0 & 0 & 0 & 0 \\
0.0793 & 0.0376 & 0.0078 & 0.0004 & 0 & 0 & 0 & 0 & 0 \\
0.0108 & 0.0800 & 0.0375 & 0.0069 & 0 & 0 & 0 & 0 & 0 \\
0 & 0.0109 & 0.0799 & 0.0375 & 0.0070 & 0 & 0 & 0 & 0 \\
0.9851 & 0 & 0 & 0 & 0 & 0 & 0 & 0 & 0 \\
0 & 0.9910 & 0 & 0 & 0 & 0 & 0 & 0 & 0 \\
0 & 0 & 0.9831 & 0 & 0 & 0 & 0 & 0 & 0 \\
0 & 0 & 0 & 0.9604 & 0 & 0 & 0 & 0 & 0 \\
0 & 0 & 0 & 0 & 0.9008 & 0.7924 & 0.7067 & 0.6379 & 0.5997
\end{bmatrix}
$$

$$
\times
\begin{bmatrix}
3900 \\
3200 \\
3300 \\
2800 \\
1700 \\
1800 \\
1100 \\
550 \\
200
\end{bmatrix}
=
\begin{bmatrix}
207 \\
456 \\
441 \\
415 \\
3841 \\
3171 \\
3244 \\
2689 \\
4206
\end{bmatrix}
$$

(Although the methods are somewhat beyond the scope of this book, the computation of the powers of a square matrix can be effected very efficiently through special techniques of matrix algebra.) In any case, the basic equation (2.24) can be used to study the behavior of a given population as time increases, i.e., when n grows larger and larger by iterating the procedure described above.

2.9 The Migration Component

Finally, let us now incorporate the effects of *migration*, the third and last component of change. Let us assume that we know the level of migration corresponding to age group i, which we will denote M_i (a positive value for M_i means a migration to the population, i.e, an inmigration, and a negative value means a migration from the population, i.e., an outmigration). The total set of net migration levels into (or from) the u age groups can then be represented by the column vector

$$
\mathbf{M} =
\begin{bmatrix}
M_1 \\
M_2 \\
\cdot \\
\cdot \\
\cdot \\
M_i \\
\cdot \\
\cdot \\
\cdot \\
M_u
\end{bmatrix}
$$

To reflect the effect of migration, the model must be modified to the extent that after each time-period projection, the vector of migrations is added to the population vector computed from birth and death effects to get the final population level. If this vector is assumed to be constant, i.e., the migration levels are stable, then the basic model can be written

$$\mathbf{P}^1 = \mathbf{CP}^0 + \mathbf{M} \tag{2.25}$$

Repeating,

$$\mathbf{P}^2 = \mathbf{CP}^1 + \mathbf{M} = \mathbf{C(CP}^0 + \mathbf{M)} + \mathbf{M} = \mathbf{C}^2\mathbf{P}^0 + \mathbf{CM} + \mathbf{M}$$

$$\mathbf{P}^3 = \mathbf{CP}^2 + \mathbf{M} = \mathbf{C(C}^2\mathbf{P}^0 + \mathbf{CM} + \mathbf{M)} + \mathbf{M}$$

$$= \mathbf{C}^3\mathbf{P}^0 + \mathbf{C}^2\mathbf{M} + \mathbf{CM} + \mathbf{M}$$

. . . .

$$\mathbf{P}^n = \mathbf{CP}^{n-1} + \mathbf{M} = \mathbf{C(C}^{n-1}\mathbf{P}^0 + \mathbf{C}^{n-2}\mathbf{M} + \mathbf{C}^{n-3}\mathbf{M} + \ldots + \mathbf{M)}$$

$$= \mathbf{C}^n\mathbf{P}^0 + \mathbf{C}^{n-1}\mathbf{M} + \mathbf{C}^{n-2}\mathbf{M} + \ldots + \mathbf{CM} + \mathbf{M}$$

or

$$\boxed{\mathbf{P}^n = \mathbf{C}^n\mathbf{P}^0 + (\mathbf{C}^{n-1} + \mathbf{C}^{n-2} + \ldots + \mathbf{C} + \mathbf{I})\mathbf{M}} \tag{2.26}$$

where the second term in the sum represents the product of the matrix $(\mathbf{C}^{n-1} + \mathbf{C}^{n-2} + \mathbf{C}^{n-3} + \ldots + \mathbf{C} + \mathbf{I})$ by the column vector $\mathbf{M}$. ($\mathbf{I}$ is the identity, or "unit" matrix, so $\mathbf{IM} = \mathbf{M}$). The computation of the sum $(\mathbf{I} + \mathbf{C} + \mathbf{C}^2 + \ldots + \mathbf{C}^{n-1})$ can be effected using the successive powers of $\mathbf{C}$, which have been computed to evaluate $\mathbf{C}^n$. One can show, however, that the sum $(\mathbf{I} + \mathbf{C} + \mathbf{C}^2 + \ldots + \mathbf{C}^{n-1} + \ldots + \mathbf{C}^\infty)$ is equal to the inverse of the matrix $(\mathbf{I} - \mathbf{C})$, as defined in Section 1.3.

Thus, for sufficiently large values of n, i.e., for projections over a large number of time periods, the sum of powers of the matrix $\mathbf{C}$ above can be approximated by $(\mathbf{I} - \mathbf{C})^{-1}$ and the model above can be written as

$$\boxed{\mathbf{P}^n \approx \mathbf{C}^n\mathbf{P}^0 + (\mathbf{I} - \mathbf{C})^{-1}\mathbf{M}} \tag{2.27}$$

When analyzing the effects of a given set of birth, death and migration rates upon the *ultimate* population levels, we would use the exact expression

$$\mathbf{P} = \mathbf{C}^\infty\mathbf{P}^0 + (\mathbf{I} - \mathbf{C})^{-1}\mathbf{M} \tag{2.28}$$

where $\mathbf{C}^\infty$ is the limit to which the successive powers of $\mathbf{C}$ converge. In computational practice this limit will be reached rather quickly.

As an illustration, let us assume that in the example above, the migration levels are given by the following column vector $\mathbf{M}$:

$$\mathbf{M} = \begin{bmatrix} 5 \\ 0 \\ 50 \\ 35 \\ 10 \\ 0 \\ -20 \\ 0 \\ 0 \end{bmatrix}$$

Suppose that we want to evaluate $\mathbf{P}^2$. Using formula (2.26) for $n = 2$, $\mathbf{P}^2$ will be equal to

$$\mathbf{P}^2 = \mathbf{C}^2\mathbf{P}^0 + (\mathbf{I} + \mathbf{C})\mathbf{M}$$

We have already computed the value of $\mathbf{C}^2$ above. Thus,

$$\mathbf{I} + \mathbf{C} = \begin{bmatrix} 1 & 0 & 0 & 0 & 0 & 0 & 0 & 0 & 0 \\ 0 & 1 & 0 & 0 & 0 & 0 & 0 & 0 & 0 \\ 0 & 0 & 1 & 0 & 0 & 0 & 0 & 0 & 0 \\ 0 & 0 & 0 & 1 & 0 & 0 & 0 & 0 & 0 \\ 0 & 0 & 0 & 0 & 1 & 0 & 0 & 0 & 0 \\ 0 & 0 & 0 & 0 & 0 & 1 & 0 & 0 & 0 \\ 0 & 0 & 0 & 0 & 0 & 0 & 1 & 0 & 0 \\ 0 & 0 & 0 & 0 & 0 & 0 & 0 & 1 & 0 \\ 0 & 0 & 0 & 0 & 0 & 0 & 0 & 0 & 1 \end{bmatrix}$$

$$\mathbf{I}$$

$$+ \begin{bmatrix} 0 & 0.011 & 0.081 & 0.038 & 0.007 & 0 & 0 & 0 & 0 \\ 0.989 & 0 & 0 & 0 & 0 & 0 & 0 & 0 & 0 \\ 0 & 0.999 & 0 & 0 & 0 & 0 & 0 & 0 & 0 \\ 0 & 0 & 0.998 & 0 & 0 & 0 & 0 & 0 & 0 \\ 0 & 0 & 0 & 0.998 & 0 & 0 & 0 & 0 & 0 \\ 0 & 0 & 0 & 0 & 0.996 & 0 & 0 & 0 & 0 \\ 0 & 0 & 0 & 0 & 0 & 0.991 & 0 & 0 & 0 \\ 0 & 0 & 0 & 0 & 0 & 0 & 0.975 & 0 & 0 \\ 0 & 0 & 0 & 0 & 0 & 0 & 0 & 0.936 & 0.880 \end{bmatrix}$$

$$\mathbf{C}$$

$$
= \begin{bmatrix}
1 & 0.011 & 0.081 & 0.038 & 0.007 & 0 & 0 & 0 & 0 \\
0.989 & 1 & 0 & 0 & 0 & 0 & 0 & 0 & 0 \\
0 & 0.999 & 1 & 0 & 0 & 0 & 0 & 0 & 0 \\
0 & 0 & 0.998 & 1 & 0 & 0 & 0 & 0 & 0 \\
0 & 0 & 0 & 0.998 & 1 & 0 & 0 & 0 & 0 \\
0 & 0 & 0 & 0 & 0.996 & 1 & 0 & 0 & 0 \\
0 & 0 & 0 & 0 & 0 & 0.991 & 1 & 0 & 0 \\
0 & 0 & 0 & 0 & 0 & 0 & 0.975 & 1 & 0 \\
0 & 0 & 0 & 0 & 0 & 0 & 0 & 0.936 & 1.880
\end{bmatrix}
$$

Finally,

$$\mathbf{P}^2 = \mathbf{C}^2\mathbf{P}^0 + (\mathbf{I} + \mathbf{C})\mathbf{M} =$$

$$
\begin{bmatrix}
0.01088 & 0.08092 & 0.03792 & 0.00699 & 0 & 0 & 0 & 0 & 0 \\
0 & 0.01089 & 0.08019 & 0.03762 & 0.00693 & 0 & 0 & 0 & 0 \\
0.98901 & 0 & 0 & 0 & 0 & 0 & 0 & 0 & 0 \\
0 & 0.99700 & 0 & 0 & 0 & 0 & 0 & 0 & 0 \\
0 & 0 & 0.99600 & 0 & 0 & 0 & 0 & 0 & 0 \\
0 & 0 & 0 & 0.99401 & 0 & 0 & 0 & 0 & 0 \\
0 & 0 & 0 & 0 & 0.98704 & 0 & 0 & 0 & 0 \\
0 & 0 & 0 & 0 & 0 & 0.96622 & 0 & 0 & 0 \\
0 & 0 & 0 & 0 & 0 & 0 & 0.91260 & 0.82368 & 0.77440
\end{bmatrix}
\begin{bmatrix}
3900 \\ 3200 \\ 3300 \\ 2800 \\ 1700 \\ 1800 \\ 1100 \\ 550 \\ 200
\end{bmatrix}
$$

$$
+ \begin{bmatrix}
1 & 0.011 & 0.081 & 0.038 & 0.007 & 0 & 0 & 0 & 0 \\
0.989 & 1 & 0 & 0 & 0 & 0 & 0 & 0 & 0 \\
0 & 0.999 & 1 & 0 & 0 & 0 & 0 & 0 & 0 \\
0 & 0 & 0.998 & 1 & 0 & 0 & 0 & 0 & 0 \\
0 & 0 & 0 & 0.998 & 1 & 0 & 0 & 0 & 0 \\
0 & 0 & 0 & 0 & 0.996 & 1 & 0 & 0 & 0 \\
0 & 0 & 0 & 0 & 0 & 0.991 & 1 & 0 & 0 \\
0 & 0 & 0 & 0 & 0 & 0 & 0.975 & 1 & 0 \\
0 & 0 & 0 & 0 & 0 & 0 & 0 & 0.936 & 1.880
\end{bmatrix}
\begin{bmatrix}
5 \\ 0 \\ 50 \\ 35 \\ 10 \\ 0 \\ -20 \\ 0 \\ 0
\end{bmatrix}
$$

$$
= \begin{bmatrix}
446 \\ 417 \\ 3857 \\ 3190 \\ 3287 \\ 2783 \\ 1678 \\ 1739 \\ 1612
\end{bmatrix}
+ \begin{bmatrix}
10 \\ 5 \\ 50 \\ 85 \\ 45 \\ 10 \\ -20 \\ -20 \\ 0
\end{bmatrix}
= \begin{bmatrix}
456 \\ 422 \\ 3907 \\ 3275 \\ 3332 \\ 2793 \\ 1658 \\ 1719 \\ 1612
\end{bmatrix}
$$

This procedure can be simplified if one can make the assumption that the migration levels are proportional to the levels of the population migrated to (or from). This simple assumption may be valid in certain cases. If this is the case, we can then write

$$M_1 = m_1 p_1$$
$$M_2 = m_2 p_2$$
$$\cdot$$
$$\cdot$$
$$\cdot$$
$$M_i = m_i p_i$$
$$\cdot$$
$$\cdot$$
$$\cdot$$
$$M_u = m_u p_u$$

where m_i is the *migration rate*, defined as the algebraic ratio of the migration level to (from) age group i to the population level of that group. Formally,

$$m_i = \frac{M_i}{p_i} \tag{2.29}$$

In matrix form the preceding equations can be written

$$\mathbf{M} = \begin{bmatrix} M_1 \\ M_2 \\ \cdot \\ \cdot \\ \cdot \\ M_i \\ \cdot \\ M_u \end{bmatrix} = \begin{bmatrix} m_1 & 0 & 0 & 0 & 0 \\ 0 & m_2 & 0 & 0 & 0 \\ 0 & 0 & m_3 & 0 & 0 \\ \hdotsfor{5} \\ 0 & 0 & 0 & m_i & 0 \\ \hdotsfor{5} \\ 0 & 0 & 0 & 0 & m_u \end{bmatrix} \begin{bmatrix} p_1 \\ p_2 \\ p_3 \\ \cdot \\ p_i \\ \cdot \\ p_u \end{bmatrix} \tag{2.30}$$

or

$$\mathbf{M} = \mathbf{mP}$$

where $\mathbf{m}$ is the diagonal matrix of migration rates. Equation (2.25),

$$\mathbf{P}^1 = \mathbf{CP}^0 + \mathbf{M}$$

can now be written as

$$\mathbf{P}^1 = \mathbf{CP}^0 + \mathbf{mP}^0 = (\mathbf{C} + \mathbf{m})\mathbf{P}^0$$

or

$$\mathbf{P}^1 = \mathbf{DP}^0 \tag{2.31}$$

where the matrix $\mathbf{D}$ is the sum of the respective matrices $\mathbf{S}$, $\mathbf{B}$, and $\mathbf{m}$, representing the aging, birth, and migration components of change, respectively. The matrix $\mathbf{D}$ will thus have the structure

$$
\begin{bmatrix}
m_1 & 0 & 0 & b_k & b_{k+1} & \cdots & b_q & \cdots & 0 \\
s_{21} & m_2 & 0 & 0 & 0 & \cdots & 0 & \cdots & 0 \\
0 & s_{32} & m_3 & 0 & 0 & \cdots & 0 & \cdots & 0 \\
\multicolumn{9}{c}{\dotfill} \\
0 & 0 & s_{i,i-1} & m_i & & \cdots & 0 & \cdots & 0 \\
\multicolumn{9}{c}{\dotfill} \\
0 & 0 & 0 & 0 & 0 & \cdots & & s_{u,u-1} & s_{uu}+m_u
\end{bmatrix}
$$

where b_i, $s_{i,i-1}$, and m_i have the definitions given above.

The compact formula (2.31) is much more convenient, since the matrix $\mathbf{D}$ now plays the role of the matrix $\mathbf{C}$ before the inclusion of migration. Therefore, if the migration rates can be assumed to remain constant throughout the projection period, the population levels at any time n will be given by

$$\mathbf{P}^n = \mathbf{D}^n\mathbf{P}^0 \tag{2.32}$$

As an illustration, let us assume that in the example above the migration levels can be assumed to remain proportional to the population levels. We then compute the migration rates:

$$m_1 = \frac{M_1}{P_1} = \frac{5}{3900} = 0.0013$$

$$m_2 = \frac{M_2}{P_2} = \frac{0}{3200} = 0$$

$$m_3 = \frac{M_3}{P_3} = \frac{50}{3300} = 0.0152$$

$$m_4 = \frac{M_4}{P_4} = \frac{35}{2800} = 0.0125$$

$$m_5 = \frac{M_5}{P_5} = \frac{10}{1700} = 0.0059$$

$$m_6 = \frac{M_6}{P_6} = \frac{0}{1800} = 0$$

$$m_7 = \frac{M_7}{P_7} = \frac{-20}{1100} = -0.0182$$

$$m_8 = \frac{M_8}{P_8} = \frac{0}{550} = 0$$

$$m_9 = \frac{M_9}{P_9} = \frac{0}{200} = 0$$

Matrix **D** can then be written simply as the sum of matrix **C** used above and the matrix of migration rates:

$$
\mathbf{m} = \begin{bmatrix}
0.0013 & 0 & 0 & 0 & 0 & 0 & 0 & 0 & 0 \\
0 & 0 & 0 & 0 & 0 & 0 & 0 & 0 & 0 \\
0 & 0 & 0.0152 & 0 & 0 & 0 & 0 & 0 & 0 \\
0 & 0 & 0 & 0.0125 & 0 & 0 & 0 & 0 & 0 \\
0 & 0 & 0 & 0 & 0.0059 & 0 & 0 & 0 & 0 \\
0 & 0 & 0 & 0 & 0 & 0 & 0 & 0 & 0 \\
0 & 0 & 0 & 0 & 0 & 0 & -0.0182 & 0 & 0 \\
0 & 0 & 0 & 0 & 0 & 0 & 0 & 0 & 0 \\
0 & 0 & 0 & 0 & 0 & 0 & 0 & 0 & 0
\end{bmatrix}
$$

Thus,

$$
\mathbf{D} = \begin{bmatrix}
0 & 0.011 & 0.081 & 0.038 & 0.007 & 0 & 0 & 0 & 0 \\
0.990 & 0 & 0 & 0 & 0 & 0 & 0 & 0 & 0 \\
0 & 0.999 & 0 & 0 & 0 & 0 & 0 & 0 & 0 \\
0 & 0 & 0.998 & 0 & 0 & 0 & 0 & 0 & 0 \\
0 & 0 & 0 & 0.998 & 0 & 0 & 0 & 0 & 0 \\
0 & 0 & 0 & 0 & 0.996 & 0 & 0 & 0 & 0 \\
0 & 0 & 0 & 0 & 0 & 0.991 & 0 & 0 & 0 \\
0 & 0 & 0 & 0 & 0 & 0 & 0.975 & 0 & 0 \\
0 & 0 & 0 & 0 & 0 & 0 & 0 & 0.936 & 0.880
\end{bmatrix}
$$

$$
+ \begin{bmatrix}
0.0013 & 0 & 0 & 0 & 0 & 0 & 0 & 0 & 0 \\
0 & 0 & 0 & 0 & 0 & 0 & 0 & 0 & 0 \\
0 & 0 & 0.0152 & 0 & 0 & 0 & 0 & 0 & 0 \\
0 & 0 & 0 & 0.0125 & 0 & 0 & 0 & 0 & 0 \\
0 & 0 & 0 & 0 & 0.0059 & 0 & 0 & 0 & 0 \\
0 & 0 & 0 & 0 & 0 & 0 & 0 & 0 & 0 \\
0 & 0 & 0 & 0 & 0 & 0 & -0.0182 & 0 & 0 \\
0 & 0 & 0 & 0 & 0 & 0 & 0 & 0 & 0 \\
0 & 0 & 0 & 0 & 0 & 0 & 0 & 0 & 0
\end{bmatrix}
$$

$$= \begin{bmatrix} 0.0013 & 0.011 & 0.081 & 0.038 & 0.007 & 0 & 0 & 0 & 0 \\ 0.990 & 0 & 0 & 0 & 0 & 0 & 0 & 0 & 0 \\ 0 & 0.999 & 0.0152 & 0 & 0 & 0 & 0 & 0 & 0 \\ 0 & 0 & 0.998 & 0.0125 & 0 & 0 & 0 & 0 & 0 \\ 0 & 0 & 0 & 0.998 & 0.0059 & 0 & 0 & 0 & 0 \\ 0 & 0 & 0 & 0 & 0.996 & 0 & 0 & 0 & 0 \\ 0 & 0 & 0 & 0 & 0 & 0.991 & -0.0182 & 0 & 0 \\ 0 & 0 & 0 & 0 & 0 & 0 & 0.975 & 0 & 0 \\ 0 & 0 & 0 & 0 & 0 & 0 & 0 & 0.936 & 0.880 \end{bmatrix}$$

The projection of the population levels at any time n would then involve the computation of the successive powers of the matrix D, up to the nth power, as was done above for the matrix C.

2.10 Multiregional and Further Extensions of the Cohort-Survival Model

The basic cohort-survival population projection model presented above and summarized in equation (2.32) can be extended to incorporate further disaggregation of the population beyond age groups. The population can be further broken down in terms of sex, income group, ethnic background, place of residence, etc. Each of such potential characterizations basically involves augmenting the size of the basic matrix C or D. This simple property constitutes a very powerful feature of the matrix formulation of the model, and makes it immensely more attractive for analytical purposes than the longhand approach, in which the essential structure of the changes is lost in the maze of equations.

Let us first consider the extension of the cohort-survival model to the case of several regions, beginning with two regions for the sake of simplicity. We shall now need two sets of indices, to refer to the age group and to the region of residence, respectively. The set of population levels will be represented by the column vector

$$\begin{bmatrix} p_1^1 \\ p_2^1 \\ \cdot \\ \cdot \\ \cdot \\ p_u^1 \\ p_1^2 \\ p_2^2 \\ \cdot \\ \cdot \\ \cdot \\ p_u^2 \end{bmatrix}$$

where the upper index refers to the region and the lower index refers to the age group. Thus, P_k^i refers to the level of the kth age group in the ith region ($i = 1, 2$ and $k = 1, 2, \ldots, u$). In the same fashion, $s_{i+1,i}^i$ will represent the survival rate from age group i to age group $i + 1$ in the ith region, b_k^i will represent the net birth rate for age group k in the ith region, and $m_{i+1,i}^{12}$ will represent the migration rate corresponding to the proportion of people in age group i in region 2 who have migrated to region 1 during the time period and thus are found in age group $i + 1$ at the beginning of the next one. Note the order of the upper indices, *from* the second index *into* the first. This conforms to the same convention for the lower index, which we have so far observed. Also, note that the $m_{i+1,i}^{12}$'s and the $m_{i+1,i}^{21}$'s are positive, that is, represent inmigrations, since the outmigration from region 1 to region 2 is the inmigration into region 2 from region 1. These migration rates can thus, in a sense, be considered to be *cross-regional* survival rates. Finally, to take into account the migrations from (or to) the outside of the two regions, m_i^{11}, will represent the migration level for age group i between region 1 and the outside, and m_i^{22} the equivalent for region 2. These rates are positive if there is inmigration, or negative otherwise, and play the same role as the m_i's in the single-region model seen in the previous section. This set of notations can perhaps be simply represented as in Figure 2.10.

With these definitions, the changes in population levels in the two regions over the unit time period can then be represented in matrix form:

$$
\begin{bmatrix} p_1^1 \\ p_2^1 \\ p_3^1 \\ \vdots \\ p_i^1 \\ \vdots \\ p_u^1 \\ p_1^2 \\ p_2^2 \\ \vdots \\ p_i^2 \\ \vdots \\ p_u^2 \end{bmatrix}^{1}
=
\left[
\begin{array}{cccccc|cccccc}
m_1^{11} & 0 & \cdots & b_k^1 & \cdots & b_q^1 & \cdots & 0 & 0 & \cdots & & 0 \\
s_{21}^1 & m_2^{11} & & & & & & m_{21}^{12} & 0 & & & 0 \\
0 & s_{32}^1 & m_3^{11} & & & & & 0 & m_{32}^{12} & 0 & & 0 \\
\vdots & & & & & & & \vdots & & & & \vdots \\
0 & 0 & \cdots & s_{i,i-1}^1 & m_i^{11} & \cdots & & 0 & 0 & \cdots & m_{i-1,i}^{12} & 0 \\
\vdots & & & & & & & \vdots & & & & \vdots \\
0 & \cdots & & s_{u,u-1}^1 & s_{uu}^1 + m_u^{11} & \cdots & 0 & m_{u,u-1}^{12} & 0 & \cdots & & m_{u,u-1}^{12} \\
0 & & \cdots & & 0 & & & m_1^{22} & 0 & \cdots & b_k^2 & \cdots & b_q^2 & \cdots & 0 \\
m_{21}^{21} & & \cdots & & 0 & & & s_{21}^2 & m_2^{22} & & & & & 0 \\
\vdots & & & & \vdots & & & \vdots & & & & & & \vdots \\
0 & \cdots & m_{i-1}^{21} & \cdots & 0 & & & 0 & \cdots & s_{i,i-1}^2 & m_i^{22} & \cdots & & 0 \\
\vdots & & & & \vdots & & & \vdots & & & & & & \vdots \\
0 & & \cdots & m_{u,u-1}^{21} & \cdots & 0 & & 0 & \cdots & & s_{u,u-1}^1 & s_{u,u}^1 + m_u^{22}
\end{array}
\right]
\begin{bmatrix} p_1^1 \\ p_2^1 \\ \vdots \\ p_i^1 \\ \vdots \\ p_u^1 \\ p_1^2 \\ \vdots \\ p_u^2 \end{bmatrix}^{0}
\tag{2.33}
$$

64

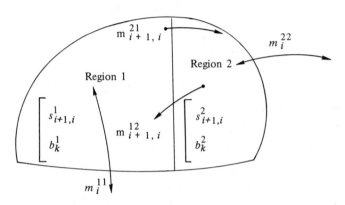

Figure 2.10 Interregional migration rates.

Or, in more compact form,

$$\begin{bmatrix} \mathbf{P}^1 \\ \mathbf{P}^2 \end{bmatrix}^1 = \begin{bmatrix} \mathbf{D}^1 & \mathbf{M}^{12} \\ \mathbf{M}^{21} & \mathbf{D}^2 \end{bmatrix} \begin{bmatrix} \mathbf{P}^1 \\ \mathbf{P}^2 \end{bmatrix}^0 \tag{2.34}$$

where $\mathbf{P}^i$ is the column vector representing the set of population levels in region i, $\mathbf{D}^1$ is the submatrix in the northwest corner of the total matrix in equation (2.33) corresponding to region 1; $\mathbf{D}^2$, in the southeast corner, for region 2; and $\mathbf{M}^{12}$ and $\mathbf{M}^{21}$ in the northeast and southwest corners represent the interregional migrations, from 2 to 1 and from 1 to 2, respectively.

It is worth noting that the submatrices $\mathbf{D}^1$ and $\mathbf{D}^2$ have the same structure as the matrix $\mathbf{D}$ in equation (2.32), corresponding to the single-region model, and play the same role. Matrices $\mathbf{M}^{12}$ and $\mathbf{M}^{21}$ represent the interactions, in terms of migrations, between the two regions. Thus, the structure of the two-regional model is rather simple, since it amounts to little more than a super-position of four matrices which can easily be constructed following the same principles as for the single-region case.

In the general case of v regions, the same approach would lead to the model

$$\begin{bmatrix} \mathbf{P}^1 \\ \mathbf{P}^2 \\ \cdot \\ \mathbf{P}^i \\ \cdot \\ \cdot \\ \mathbf{P}^v \end{bmatrix}^1 = \begin{bmatrix} \mathbf{D}^1 & \mathbf{M}^{12} & \mathbf{M}^{13} & \cdots & & \mathbf{M}^{1v} \\ \mathbf{M}^{21} & \mathbf{D}^2 & \mathbf{M}^{23} & \cdots & \mathbf{M}^{kl} & \cdots \\ & & \cdots & & & \\ \mathbf{M}^{i1} & \cdots & \mathbf{D}^i & & \cdots & \mathbf{M}^{iv} \\ & & \cdots & & & \\ & & \cdots & & & \\ \mathbf{M}^{v1} & & & \cdots & & \mathbf{D}^v \end{bmatrix} \begin{bmatrix} \mathbf{P}^1 \\ \mathbf{P}^2 \\ \cdot \\ \mathbf{P}^i \\ \cdot \\ \cdot \\ \mathbf{P}^v \end{bmatrix}^0 \tag{2.35}$$

where, as above, $\mathbf{P}^i$ is the column vector of population levels in region i, $\mathbf{D}^i$ is the submatrix

$$\mathbf{D}^i = \begin{bmatrix} m_1^i & \cdots & \cdots & b_k^i & \cdots & b_q^i & \cdots & 0 \\ s_{21}^i & m_2^i & & & \cdots & & & 0 \\ 0 & s_{32}^i & & & \cdots & & & 0 \\ 0 & \cdots & & s_{i-1,i}^i & & \cdots & & 0 \\ 0 & & & \cdots & & & s_{uu-1}^i & s_{uu}^i + m_u^i \end{bmatrix} \tag{2.36}$$

and $\mathbf{M}^{kl}$ is the submatrix

$$\mathbf{M}^{kl} = \begin{bmatrix} 0 & & \cdots & & 0 \\ m_{21}^{kl} & 0 & & \cdots & 0 \\ 0 & m_{32}^{kl} & & \cdots & 0 \\ \hdashline 0 & \cdots & m_{i,i-1}^{kl} & \cdots & 0 \\ \hdashline 0 & & \cdots & m_{u,u-1}^{kl} & 0 \end{bmatrix} \tag{2.37}$$

where the positive entry $m_{i,i-1}^{kl}$ represents the migration rate from age group $(i - 1)$ in region l to age group i in region k, i.e., the proportion of the population level p_{i-1}^l that migrates to region k during the time period. The operation of the multiregional model (2.35) is the same as for the single-region model (2.32).

The same framework can conceptually be adapted to represent the changes in population levels in classifications other than geographical, as above. For instance, if the upper indices in the model above are used to represent the type of dwelling unit lived in (one-family detached, two-family, apartment, etc.), the model will provide a dissaggregated description of the evolution of occupancy levels. This, together with a forecast of the aging of the existing housing stock (which can also be effected using a similar type of cohort-survival approach), can then be used to project future housing needs.

Other conceptual extensions of the basic model include dissaggregations with respect to employment (full-time, part-time, retired, unemployed, student, etc.), marital status (not married, married, separated, divorced), with respect to socioeconomic class (professional or income levels), and in general any such typologies. Finally, three-way characterizations of a given population (e.g., in terms of age, place of residence, and employment status) could conceptually be accommodated through the use of two-dimensional, or "cubic" matrices. The method would follow the same basic accounting approach as above, although the handling of three sets of indices would be somewhat trickier.

In closing this chapter, let us briefly mention other approaches, or refinements, to the forecasting of population levels. One potential method, which we shall explore in more detail in Chapter 3, consists of inferring population changes from changes in employment, which are, themselves, projected from forecasts of the level of economic activity of the region(s). This approach can be combined with the cohort survival method, since the migration rates can be used to reflect directly the level of economic opportunities, through changes in the levels of jobs.

Another approach is probabilistic, i.e., is based on treating the appearance or disappearance of a new unit in the population, either from natural causes, or from migration, or both, as a random variable, in the sense we have seen in Section 1.4. The probabilistic law governing this variable is, in turn, based on the passage of time, as in the models examined in this chapter.

Finally, another approach is based on the utilization of the techniques of *statistical regression*, which will be described in Chapter 7. This approach is very general and can be potentially applied to the modelization of a large class of variables besides population levels, and thus loses some of the specificity inherent in the models described above. In turn, it offers the advantage that it is purely descriptive and does not require any causative assumptions. In other words, it can always be tried (provided that empirical data are available to implement the method), in the absence of any insight into the mechanics of the evolution of the population level. This purely *heuristic* approach, however, can be combined with the prior specification of one of the patterns of evolution, seen in Sections 2.2 to 2.5 for the determination of the particular values of its parameters.

EXERCISES

2.1 Assume that the rate of growth of a certain city (as a proportion of its population size) is 5% per year.

    (a) How many years will it take for the city to grow by 30% from its present level?

    (b) Compare this with the growth during the same period of time of a city that grows by a constant 5% of its base population every year.

2.2 Over the last 5 years, the population level of a certain area has gone from 120,000 to 150,000, and seems to follow a double exponential pattern. The physical characteristics of the area limit the total population it can accommodate to 250,000.

    (a) Given this situation, if the same pattern of growth continues, what will be the population level in 10 years?

    (b) How long will it take under the same conditions to reach a population level of 200,000?

2.3 The following (hypothetical) historical data represent the variations in the total population of a certain city.

Year	1970	71	72	73	74	75	76	77	78	79
Population (thousands)	50	52	53.7	55.8	57.6	59.5	61.5	63.7	65.8	67.6

Approximate this pattern of growth with one of the simple extrapolation models seen in Section 2.3.

(a)   If this pattern continues, what would the population level be in 1985? In 1989?

(b)   Define a simple indicator (measure) of the vitality of the area (perhaps connected to the parameters of the model you are using).

(c)   What would be the value characterizing the annual growth of the area?

(d)   The decennial growth?

2.4   A region has been steadily losing population, as reflected in the following data:

Year	1950	55	60	65	70	75
Population (thousands)	500	435	400	370	345	323

(a)   What seems to be the pattern of evolution?

(b)   When (approximately) did the population level go under 350,000?

(c)   If nothing is done to alter this trend, how long will it be before the population goes under 300,000?

(d)   If an economic development program starting in 1980 could induce a fixed number of people to settle in the area every year, what would this amount have to be in order to go back to the 1960 level by year 2000?

2.5   Population estimates can sometimes be effected using base data other than population levels. Let us assume that the number of telephone listings in a certain area, as recorded every 5 years in the past, has been as follows:

Observation number	1	2	3	4	5	present
Number of telephones (millions)	1.24	1.35	1.47	1.54	1.59	1.64

Also, assume that the number of telephones per capita has been 0.26 for the period covered by the first two measurements, 0.28 for the next two, and 0.30 for the last two.

(a)   If both the evolution of telephone listings and per capita ownership continue following their present pattern, when would a population of 6 million be reached?

(b) Does there seem to be an eventual limit to the growth of the area?

(c) If so, what do you estimate it to be? (*Hint:* Try a double-exponential model.)

2.6 Compare the linear extrapolation model, the exponential, and the logistic in terms of what law of change in population increment $(P_{n+1} - P_n)$ they imply. (*Hint:* Show that for the logistic model: $P_{n+1} - P_n = aP_n - bP_n^2$.)

(a) What would be the form of the next model along this progression?

(b) What physical property would such a model translate?

2.7 (a) Fit a logistic model to the following data:

t	0	1	2	3	4	5	6	7
P (tens of thousands)	11.0	11.65	12.30	13.0	13.70	14.45	15.20	15.95

(*Hint:* Plot the values of the quantity $(P_{n+1} - P_n)/P_n$ against those of P_n, and estimate visually the parameters of the logistic model from those of the straight line you expect this plot to be.)

(b) In how many time periods would a population level of 200,000 be reached if the logistic pattern holds up?

(c) Under the same conditions, what would the eventual population level after a very long (infinite) time be?

2.8 The past four decenial censuses for a certain state, its main metropolitan area, and the rest of its counties have resulted in the following figures (in millions):

Census	1940	1950	1960	1970
State	1.365	1.472	1.545	1.688
Metropolitan area	0.480	0.510	0.530	0.602
Rest of state	0.885	0.962	1.015	1.086

(a) Given these past trends, what would you estimate the population of the major metropolitan area A to be when the state reaches a total population of 2 million?

(b) When the rest of the state reaches a total population of 2 million?

(c) What will be the total population of the state when the metropolitan area reaches a population level of 1 million?

2.9 A public housing program is being considered. After considering a variety of factors, including population forecasts and the resulting needs, but also financial and building management considerations, it has been decided to adopt a construction program which, in terms of numbers of units being built, would follow a "diminishing numbers" pattern similar to the modified exponential model of population projections. The program aims at reaching a level of 1000 units after a year. Also, the zoning plan provides for a total capacity of 5000 units.

(a)   Under these constraints, what should be the (constant) fraction of the previous year's level of construction (as characterized by the value of parameter v in the modified exponential model), so that the first-year level is doubled 5 years hence?

(b)   What should that value be so that 90% of the total holding capacity is reached after 10 years?

2.10 Given the data in the accompanying table, broken down by sex, evaluate the population distributions P_{1970} and P_{2000}:

(a)   By sex.

(b)   For the combined population.

[*Advice:* Note that the cohort-survival model has to be adapted for the male population since they do not bear children. Start with the females, using two sets of birth rates, one for the males, and one for the females, but both with respect to the female population levels. (This can easily be handled by adding one supplemental row to the female matrix.) The birth rates row for the male matrix will then in effect be entirely zero. After each independent iteration of the female and male models, add on to the first age group of the males the corresponding number of baby boys, as output by the male birth rates row.]

Age Groups	Pop. 1940	Death	Births	Migration
Males				
0–30	8,000	50	100	100
31–60	10,000	100	80	80
61+	9,000	120	0	50
Females				
0–30	7,500	40	80	80
31–60	6,000	80	110	100
61+	9,000	150	0	50

2.11   Given the following data, and assuming no changes in the birth, death, and migration rates:

Age Group	Pop. 1970	Births 50–65	Deaths 50–65	Migration In	Migration Out
0–14	216	0	36	5	25
15–29	216	162	36	20	30
30–44	216	180	36	10	50
45+	216	54	216	100	0

(a)   What will the population be in 1985 and 2000?
(b)   How would these projections change if the inmigration levels were to go up by 10%?
(c)   What would be the effect of an overall decrease in the birth rates of 0.005%?

2.12   Given the following data, project the population levels in the various age groups over the next 5, 10, 15, 20, and 30 years:

Age Group Number i	Age	p_i	Births/1000 (in last 5 years)	Deaths/1000
1	0–4.9	5985		6.6
2	5–9.9	5306		2.1
3	10–14.9	4184		2.2
4	15–19.9	3203	69	2.3
5	20–24.9	3440	189	2.4
6	25–29.9	3623	155	2.8
7	30–34.9	3903	93	2.9
8	35–39.9	3727	37	3.0
9	40⁺	3109	9	3.1

REFERENCES

KEYFITZ, N. *Introduction to the Mathematics of Population.* Reading, Mass.: Addison-Wesley Publishing Co., Inc., 1968.

KRUECKEBERG, D., et al. *Long Range Population Projections for Minor Civil Divisions: Computer Programs and User's Manual.* New Brunswick, N.J.: Center for Urban Policy Research, Rutgers University, 1973.

MORRISON, P. *Demographic Information for Cities: A Manual for Projecting and Estimating Local Population Characteristics.* Santa Monica, Calif.: The Rand Corporation, 1971.

PITTENGER, D. *Projecting State and Local Population.* Cambridge, Mass.: Ballinger Publishing Company, 1976.

PRESSAT, R. *Demographic Analysis.* London: Edward Arnold Ltd., 1972.

ROGERS, A. *An Introduction to Multiregional Mathematical Demography.* New York: John Wiley & Sons, Inc., 1975.

SHYROCK, H., and J. SIEGEL. *The Methods and Materials of Demography.* Washington, D.C.: Bureau of the Census, 1971.

3
Economic Activity
and Employment Analysis

3.1 Introduction

In Chapter 2, we examined some of the models available to study the evolution of a major component of any urban or regional system, its population. Indeed, no community can be characterized and analyzed without reference to the level of its population and its breakdown with respect to the major socioeconomic characteristics of sex, age, income group, etc.

However, the main factor that sustains the community and enables the individuals in it to live in the area is usually economic activity. In other words, the presence of the population in a given urban or rural area is made possible by the existence of jobs and employment in that area. Thus, there is a rather close association between the levels of employment (or, equivalently, of economic activity) in a given area and the level of population. Specifically, the third major component of change in the population level, migration, is directly connected to the growth or the decline of economic activities in an area. This connection can thus be utilized to estimate migration levels.

In any event, it is clear that the study of the evolution of a given urban or regional system cannot be undertaken in isolation from the study of its economic activity. In this chapter, we shall examine some basic models of economic analysis and their connections with employment projections.

In this sense, the models in this chapter further those in Chapter 2, by providing methods for rational analysis of one of their components. At the same time, however, there is a converse relationship of the population models to the economic activity models. This is because economic activity is, in turn, ultimately determined by demand for goods and services, which is a reflection of the needs and characteristics of a given population(s). Finally, the spatial relationships between residential and economic activities are represented by the models of land use and travel distribution presented in Chapter 4.

Thus, the three blocks of models in Chapters 2, 3, and 4, respectively, are usually used in a feedback fashion, the information generated by one being an input to the other, and vice versa. In large-scale, comprehensive analyses (usually performed with the use of electronic computers), the number and structure of the feedback relationships can be quite large. However, the basic "loops" of the computational algorithms are constituted by the simple models we are examining.

3.2 The Economic Base Model

Let us begin with the simplest model of economic activity, that is, one industrial sector in a single region. Although rather unrealistic, this model will serve to illustrate a basic approach to the building of several economic analysis models, which we shall see later, such as the *economic base model* and the *input–output model*.

Let us assume that we are planning to develop a certain industry in a given region. The corresponding industrial sector will be *basic*, in that the production, which is to be sold outside the region, is its main source of income. The level of basic production has been set at X (in some unit such as dollars, tons, monetary equivalents, etc.). Note that this level of production can be translated in terms of levels of income, through conversion into its market value, or in terms of employment, through conversion into worker-hours required. Thus, the unit of measurement of the quantities we shall be dealing with in this chapter is immaterial, and can be quite flexible, as long as it is used consistently.

Let us assume that part of the income of X will be spent to sustain the ongoing production of the basic sector. This might be because of either the needs of the workers (food, other goods, services, etc.) or those of the production process (materials, capital, etc.). The production sectors that service these respective needs can in this sense be called *nonbasic*, since their production is designed to (indirectly) support that of the basic sector. Some of these nonbasic sectors will be located in the region itself, and some outside. The fraction of the income that is spent in nonbasic sectors will be s, and the fraction of that which is spent locally is l. In other words, the total percentage of the income X which is spent in the region itself is equal to

$$c = s \cdot l \tag{3.1}$$

c is sometimes called the *propensity to consume*.

The percentage $s(1 - l)$ is spent for supporting services outside the area. Thus, the net result is that an additional (nonbasic) income of cX will accrue to the region. This income results from a *second-level* effect of the original production of X units of the basic industry. Consequently, this means that the overall economic activity level of the area has increased by cX from its planned or projected level X.

However, this incremental income will, in turn, be available for spending, and according to our basic assumption, a total of c percent of it will be spent, in the same fashion as above, in the local, nonbasic sector. This results in a *third-level* increment in total economic activity of $c(cX) = c^2 X$. By the same token, c percent of that income will be spent, requiring an additional increment of $c(c^2 X) = c^3 X$.

It is now easy to see that whereas we started with a level for the production of X basic units, if the propensity to consume is c, the total (basic and nonbasic) economic activity will be

$$Y = X + cX + c^2 X + c^3 X + \ldots + c^n X + \ldots + c^\infty X$$

or

$$Y = X(1 + c + c^2 + \ldots + c^n + \ldots + c^\infty) \tag{3.2}$$

For instance, if the basic output is $X = 20,000$ and the propensity to consume is $c = 0.1$ (i.e., 10%), the first-stage increment for X will be $cX = 0.1(20,000) = 2000$. The second will be $c^2 X = (0.1)(0.1)(2000) = 200$. The third will be $c^3 X = 0.001(2000) = 20$. The fourth will be $c^4 X = 0.0001(2000) = 2$. The subsequent increments would be negligible, since they are smaller than the unit of production or income.

Therefore, the total income Y corresponding to the data above would be

$$Y = 20,000 + 2000 + 200 + 20 + 2 = 22,222$$

Formula (3.2) can be simplified, since it can be shown that

$$1 + c + c^2 + \ldots + c^n + \ldots c^\infty = \frac{1}{1 - c} \tag{3.3}$$

(when c is smaller than 1, which is the case here).

Thus, the total amount of activity Y corresponding to the basic activity X, when the area's propensity to consume is c, is equal to

$$\boxed{Y = \left(\frac{1}{1 - c}\right) X} \tag{3.4}$$

The factor $(1/1 - c)$ is called the *economic multiplier*, since c being smaller than 1, $1 - c$ is smaller than 1, and its inverse is larger than 1. Thus, Y will be larger than X. For instance, if the propensity to consume is $c = 0.10$, or 10%, as above, the multiplier will be equal to

$$\frac{1}{1 - 0.1} = \frac{1}{0.9} = 1.1111$$

and

$$Y = \left(\frac{1}{1 - c}\right)X = (1.1111)20,000 = 22,222$$

Thus, either formula (3.2) or (3.4) can be used to compute the total income given the basic production.

Note that in the preceding formulation, all nonbasic activities were lumped together in a single sector. If more differentiation is desired, the value of the propensity to consume can be computed in the following fashion. If there are n nonbasic sectors, and if the fraction of the total income of the region that is spent on sector i is s_i and the fraction of that which is spent locally is l_i, the fraction of the basic income that is spent in nonbasic local sectors will be equal to the sum of the respective fractions for the individual sectors:

$$c = s_1 l_1 + s_2 l_2 + \ldots + s_i l_i + \ldots + s_n l_n = \sum_i s_i l_i \qquad (3.5)$$

Here c, which will then also be a percentage, represents the *overall*, or average propensity to consume, weighed by sector. In the same sense as above, $(1 - c)$ is the propensity to save.

The physical meaning of the propensity to consume can, perhaps, be further illustrated by manipulating formula (3.4). Indeed, we have

$$\frac{Y}{X} = \frac{1}{1 - c} \qquad \text{or} \qquad 1 - c = \frac{X}{Y}$$

and finally

$$c = 1 - \frac{X}{Y} = \frac{Y - X}{Y} \qquad (3.6)$$

Thus, the propensity to consume is equal to the ratio of the absolute increase in total economic activity (i.e., the total level of nonbasic activity) to the total level of activity. Furthermore, since the relation between X and Y as represented in formula (3.4) is linear, it is also valid when the absolute levels are replaced by *changes* in these levels, i.e.,

$$\Delta Y = \left(\frac{1}{1 - c}\right)\Delta X \qquad \text{or} \qquad c = 1 - \frac{\Delta X}{\Delta Y} \qquad (3.7)$$

Equivalently, another interpretation of the propensity to consume is that it is equal to (1 minus the ratio of the increase in the basic activity to the corresponding increase in the total activity). This property might be useful in estimating the propensity to consume from *longitudinal* data.

Equation (3.4) can be used to determine the amount of basic production or employment X, which has to sustain a given total income (or level of employment) Y when the propensity to consume c is known. For instance, if the total level of economic activity in an area Y is 10,000 and if the propensity to consume is 0.15, the activity level in the basic sector X will have to be equal, in the same (unspecified) units, to

$$X = (1 - c)Y$$
$$= (1 - 0.15)10,000 = 8500$$

Finally, equation (3.6) or (3.7) can be used to determine the allowable propensity to consume c when both the total activity Y and the basic activity X are set. For instance, suppose that the propensity c is equated to local taxes. If it is desired that for each dollar of basic production the total, ultimate tax revenue be 10¢, what should be the tax rate? This would mean that to an X of 1 dollar would correspond a Y of $(1 + 0.10) = 1.10$ dollars. Using equation (3.6), we get

$$c = 1 - \frac{1}{1.10} = 1 - 0.91 = 0.09$$

Thus, the tax rate would have to be 9%. (Note that this percentage is not equal to $0.10/1.0 = 10\%$.)

It is worth noting that the same model would be applicable if the supporting goods or services came from the same sector as the basic sector, for instance, if part of the production of the basic sector were acquired by the producers themselves. Consequently, the distinction between basic and nonbasic sectors should be based not on the industrial nature of these sectors, but rather on whether they determine the level of primary activity, or are a consequence of it. This is sometimes reflected in the denomination of the basic sectors as *export* sectors, since their production is to be primarily (but not necessary exclusively) consumed outside the region. The nonbasic sectors, in the same sense, are then called the *domestic*, or *local* sectors.

Also, the effect of the multiplier mechanism is not instantaneous, since the higher-level effects of the original basic production take place after some time lag. Thus, in order to keep the above formulation simple, the activity levels Y and X refer to activities over some interval of time (e.g., a year, or 6 months, etc.), and not to their measurement at a given time.

Before we conclude this section and go on to the case of several basic sectors, let us reformulate this mechanism of multiplication of economic activity in a slightly different fashion, by specifically introducing the nonbasic sector in the previous framework. This approach will be useful later.

We can decompose the total activity into two parts. Thus,

$$Y = X + Z \tag{3.8}$$

where X is the basic production (or income) and Z is the nonbasic production. However, we also know that Z is proportional to the total income Y, the factor of proportionality being the propensity to consume. Thus,

$$Z = cY$$

If we replace Z by its expression in terms of Y in formula (3.8), we get

$$Y = X + cY \tag{3.9}$$

and

$$Y(1 - c) = X \quad \text{or} \quad Y = \frac{X}{1 - c}$$

We thus have the same equation as formula (3.4).

The formulation above assumes that the nonbasic sector acquires the production of the basic sector, as reflected in the propensity to consume. However, it essentially ignores the converse possibility that the basic sector (or any other sector) might need and acquire the production of this nonbasic sector. Thus, although the foregoing (limited) assumption is convenient for the simplicity of illustration of the fundamental multiplier mechanism, it is hardly realistic.

3.3 Multisectorial Extensions of the Economic Base Model

Let us now, therefore, expand the basic model to the case of two mutually interacting economic sectors. (This will later be generalized to the case of any number of such sectors.) In accordance with the notation above, we can write that for each sector, i ($i = 1$ or 2), the total level of production (income) Y_i is equal to the sum of the external (or basic) demand, X_i, and of the internal (or nonbasic) demand, Z_i. However, Z_i is itself made of two parts, the demand from sector 1 itself, and from the other sector 2. Thus, for the first sector,

$$Y_1 = X_1 + Z_{11} + Z_{12} \tag{3.10}$$

where Z_{11} represents the amount of production of the first sector which is required for sustaining the production of the first sector, and Z_{12} represents the amount of the same product required by the second sector. Similarly,

$$Y_2 = X_2 + Z_{21} + Z_{22} \tag{3.11}$$

where Z_{21} represents the demand for the production of the second sector from the first sector, and Z_{22} from the second sector.

Finally, following the approach used in the previous model, we can write

$$Z_{11} = a_{11} Y_1$$

$$Z_{12} = a_{12} Y_2$$

$$Z_{21} = a_{21} Y_1 \qquad (3.12)$$

$$Z_{22} = a_{22} Y_2$$

In other words, we are assuming that the internal demands are proportional, respectively, to the total productions, or incomes, of the acquiring sectors. Equivalently, a_{11} is the propensity of sector 1 to consume its own goods, a_{12} is the propensity of sector 2 to consume the goods of sector 1, a_{21} is propensity of sector 1 to consume the goods of sector 2, and finally a_{22} is the propensity of sector 2 to consume its own goods. Using equations (3.12), equations (3.10) and (3.11) can now be rewritten as

$$Y_1 = X_1 + a_{11} Y_1 + a_{12} Y_2 \qquad (3.13)$$

$$Y_2 = X_2 + a_{21} Y_1 + a_{22} Y_2$$

or in matrix notation:

$$\boxed{\mathbf{Y} = \mathbf{X} + \mathbf{AY}} \qquad (3.14)$$

where $\mathbf{Y}$ is now the column vector or respective total production levels,

$$\begin{bmatrix} Y_1 \\ Y_2 \end{bmatrix}$$

$\mathbf{X}$ is the column vector of external (basic) demand levels,

$$\begin{bmatrix} X_1 \\ X_2 \end{bmatrix}$$

and $\mathbf{A}$ is the matrix of propensity coefficients,

$$\begin{bmatrix} a_{11} & a_{12} \\ a_{21} & a_{22} \end{bmatrix}$$

(Matrix $\mathbf{A}$ is sometimes also called the *production coefficients matrix*, since the coefficients a_{ij} can also be interpreted as the proportion of the total production of sector j that is required by industry sector i.)

It should be noted that the matrix equation (3.14) for the case of two interactive sectors is strikingly similar to classical equation (3.9) for the "unidirectional" activity case above.

As an example of application, let us assume that we are planning to implant two industrial sectors, food producing and clothes manufacturing, in a given area. The levels of required monthly basic (export) production of these respective sectors have been set at 50 and 75, respectively, in thousands of dollars, for instance, from capacity considerations such as availability of land for agriculture, of manpower, etc. The fraction of the total income of the farmers that goes to buy food produced in the region is 35% and the fraction that goes to buy clothes from the seamstresses is 10%. Furthermore, the percentage of the total income of the seamstresses that will be devoted to buying food from the farmers is 0.30 and the fraction of their total income that will be devoted to buying clothes made in the area is 0.15. In terms of formula (3.13), the foregoing situation can be written as

$$Y_1 = 50 + 0.35Y_1 + 0.30Y_2$$
$$Y_2 = 75 + 0.10Y_1 + 0.15Y_2 \tag{3.15}$$

Given these requirements, what are the levels of total production (and thus the numbers of jobs) necessary to satisfy the demands for food and clothing, both internal and external to the area? We can answer this question by solving the above system of two (linear) equations in the two unknowns Y_1 and Y_2. However, applying the iterative method used for the derivation of formula (3.4) might be instructive. If the farmers spend 0.35 of their income of 50 to buy food, and the seamstresses spend 0.30 of their income of 75 for the same purpose, the *first-round* additional requirement on food production will thus be equal to

$$0.35(50) + 0.30(75) = 40$$

Similarly, the first-round increment in clothes production will be

$$0.10(50) + 0.15(75) = 16.25$$

However, these respective increments in production (and thus in total income) will generate additional jobs, and thus income that will, in the same fashion, also be used to buy more food and more clothes. In other words, in the second iteration of the computation of total production requirements, we are in the same position as at the beginning of the first iteration, with the difference that the level of 50 and 75 for the food and the clothes are now replaced by the levels of the increments computed above, i.e., 40 and 16.25, respectively. Thus, the *second-round* increments are now

$$0.35(40) + 0.30(16.25) = 18.9 \quad \text{for the food}$$
$$0.10(40) + 0.15(16.25) = 6.4 \quad \text{for the clothes}$$

We continue this process and compute the *third-round* increment:

$$0.35(18.9) + 0.30(6.4) = 8.5 \quad \text{for the food}$$
$$0.10(18.9) + 0.15(6.4) = 2.8 \quad \text{for the clothes}$$

The *fourth* increment is

$$0.35(8.5) + 0.30(2.8) = 3.8 \quad \text{for the food}$$
$$0.10(8.5) + 0.15(2.8) = 1.3 \quad \text{for the clothes}$$

The *fifth* increment is

$$0.35(3.8) + 0.30(1.3) = 1.7 \quad \text{for the food}$$
$$0.10(3.8) + 0.15(1.3) = 0.6 \quad \text{for the clothes}$$

Since the next increments would be negligible (i.e., under 1, i.e., the unit of measurement), we shall stop the process here. Thus, the total food production should be

$$
\begin{aligned}
Y_1 = {} & X_1 + (X_1 a_{11} + X_2 a_{12}) \\
& + [(X_1 a_{11} + X_2 a_{12})a_{11} + (X_1 a_{21} + X_2 a_{22})a_{12}] \\
& + \{[(X_1 a_{11} + X_2 a_{12})a_{11} + (X_1 a_{21} + X_2 a_{22})a_{12}]a_{11} \qquad (3.16) \\
& + [(X_1 a_{11} + X_2 a_{12})a_{21} + (X_1 a_{21} + X_2 a_{22})a_{22}]a_{12}\} + \cdots \\
= {} & 50 + 40 + 18.9 + 8.5 + 3.8 + 1.7 + \cdots \simeq 123
\end{aligned}
$$

Similarly,

$$
\begin{aligned}
Y_2 = {} & X_2 + (X_1 a_{21} + X_2 a_{22}) + [(X_1 a_{21} + X_2 a_{22})a_{21} \\
& + (X_1 a_{11} + X_2 a_{12})a_{22}] + \cdots \qquad (3.17) \\
= {} & 75 + 16.2 + 6.4 + 2.8 + 1.3 + 0.6 \simeq 102
\end{aligned}
$$

As a check, let us answer the same question by solving equations (3.13):

$$
\begin{array}{ll}
Y_1 = 50 + 0.35\,Y_1 + 0.30\,Y_2 & \quad 0.65\,Y_1 - 0.30\,Y_2 = 50 \\
\qquad\qquad\qquad\qquad\qquad \text{or} & \\
Y_2 = 75 + 0.10\,Y_1 + 0.15\,Y_2 & \quad -0.10\,Y_1 + 0.85\,Y_2 = 75
\end{array}
$$

The solution for Y_2 is obtained immediately by multiplying the second equation by 6.5 and adding it to the first. Thus,

$$0.65\,Y_1 - 0.30\,Y_2 - 0.65\,Y_1 + (0.85)(6.5)\,Y_2 = 50 + 6.5(75)$$

or

$$(5.225)\,Y_2 = 537.5 \quad \text{and} \quad Y_2 = \frac{537.5}{5.225} = 102.9$$

By replacing this value in either of the equations of the original system, the first one, for instance, we get

$$0.65\,Y_1 - 0.30(102.9) = 50 \quad \text{or} \quad 0.65\,Y_1 = 50 + 0.30(102.9) = 80.9$$

and

$$Y_1 = \frac{80.9}{0.65} = 124.5$$

Thus, allowing for the errors due to rounding down the values by stopping the computations after the fifth iteration, we get the same values for the levels of production in the food sector and in the manufacturing sector.

Finally, the same answer would be obtained by using the matrix notation of (3.14) and matrix algebra. Equations (3.15) can be written

$$\begin{bmatrix} Y_1 \\ Y_2 \end{bmatrix} = \begin{bmatrix} 50 \\ 75 \end{bmatrix} + \begin{bmatrix} 0.35 & 0.30 \\ 0.10 & 0.15 \end{bmatrix} \begin{bmatrix} Y_1 \\ Y_2 \end{bmatrix}$$

or

$$\begin{bmatrix} 1 & 0 \\ 0 & 1 \end{bmatrix} \begin{bmatrix} Y_1 \\ Y_2 \end{bmatrix} - \begin{bmatrix} 0.35 & 0.30 \\ 0.10 & 0.15 \end{bmatrix} \begin{bmatrix} Y_1 \\ Y_2 \end{bmatrix} = \begin{bmatrix} 50 \\ 75 \end{bmatrix}$$

and

$$\begin{bmatrix} 1 - 0.35 & -0.30 \\ -0.10 & 1 - 0.15 \end{bmatrix} \begin{bmatrix} Y_1 \\ Y_2 \end{bmatrix} = \begin{bmatrix} 50 \\ 75 \end{bmatrix}$$

Thus,

$$\begin{bmatrix} Y_1 \\ Y_2 \end{bmatrix} = \begin{bmatrix} 1 - 0.35 & -0.30 \\ -0.10 & 1 - 0.15 \end{bmatrix}^{-1} \begin{bmatrix} 50 \\ 75 \end{bmatrix}$$

This method is the application of the general method of resolution of a matrix equation of the form $Y = X + AY$. The solution is given by $Y - AY = X$ or $(I - A)Y = X$, where I is the identity matrix of the same size as the square matrix A. Thus finally, by multiplying both sides to the left by the inverse of the matrix $(I - A)$, we get

$$(I - A)^{-1}(I - A)Y = (I - A)^{-1}X = IY$$

or

$$\boxed{Y = (I - A)^{-1}X} \qquad (3.18)$$

Thus, we have to compute the inverse of the matrix

$$(I - A) = \begin{bmatrix} 1 - 0.35 & -0.30 \\ -0.10 & 1 - 0.15 \end{bmatrix} = \begin{bmatrix} 0.65 & -0.30 \\ -0.10 & 0.85 \end{bmatrix}$$

using the method described in Section 1.3. The reader should check that the inverse is equal to

$$(I - A)^{-1} = \begin{bmatrix} 1.63 & 0.57 \\ 0.19 & 1.24 \end{bmatrix}$$

Thus, the total activity levels Y_1 and Y_2 would be

$$\begin{bmatrix} Y_1 \\ Y_2 \end{bmatrix} = \begin{bmatrix} 1.63 & 0.57 \\ 0.19 & 1.24 \end{bmatrix} \begin{bmatrix} X_1 \\ X_2 \end{bmatrix} = \begin{bmatrix} 1.63 & 0.57 \\ 0.19 & 1.24 \end{bmatrix} \begin{bmatrix} 50 \\ 75 \end{bmatrix} = \begin{bmatrix} 124.25 \\ 102.50 \end{bmatrix}$$

and we again retrieve the same values.

Besides being a more efficient method when the number of sectors is large (the usual case in real-world applications), the computation of the inverse of the matrix $(I - A)$, where A is the matrix of propensities to consume (production coefficients), is very useful to analyze the influence of a marginal change in the level of external demand in a given sector on the total production of all sectors in the economy. This inverse matrix is for this reason sometimes called the *structural matrix*, or matrix of *structural coefficients*.

For instance, suppose that we want to examine the effect of a change in the external food production level X_1 from 50 to 60 in the example above. This means that now Y_1 and Y_2, instead of being equal to

$$\begin{bmatrix} Y_1 \\ Y_2 \end{bmatrix} = \begin{bmatrix} 1.63 & 0.57 \\ 0.19 & 1.24 \end{bmatrix} \begin{bmatrix} 50 \\ 75 \end{bmatrix} \simeq \begin{bmatrix} 124 \\ 102 \end{bmatrix}$$

as computed above are now

$$\begin{bmatrix} Y_1 \\ Y_2 \end{bmatrix} = \begin{bmatrix} 1.63 & 0.57 \\ 0.19 & 1.24 \end{bmatrix} \begin{bmatrix} 60 \\ 75 \end{bmatrix} \simeq \begin{bmatrix} 141 \\ 104 \end{bmatrix}$$

The changes in the respective levels of Y are equal to

$$\Delta Y = \begin{bmatrix} \Delta Y_1 \\ \Delta Y_2 \end{bmatrix} = \begin{bmatrix} 141 \\ 104 \end{bmatrix} - \begin{bmatrix} 124 \\ 102 \end{bmatrix} = \begin{bmatrix} 17 \\ 2 \end{bmatrix}$$

$$= \begin{bmatrix} 1.63 & 0.57 \\ 0.19 & 1.24 \end{bmatrix} \begin{bmatrix} 60 - 50 \\ 75 - 75 \end{bmatrix} = \begin{bmatrix} 1.63 & 0.57 \\ 0.19 & 1.24 \end{bmatrix} \begin{bmatrix} \Delta X_1 \\ \Delta X_2 \end{bmatrix} \qquad (3.19)$$

Thus, in general, to a change ΔX in levels of X will correspond a change $\Delta Y = (I - A)^{-1} \Delta X$ in levels of Y. The coefficient α_{ij} in the matrix $(I - A)^{-1}$ represents the *percent* change in level of total activity Y_i in sector i due to a *unit* change in the basic production X_j in sector j.

This type of analysis is called *sensitivity analysis*, since it determines the sensitivity of the level of effect (here the total production levels) resulting from a change in the level of cause (here the objectives set for the level of basic production). In the example above, we can see that the effect of a change in the exportable production of food, or equivalently on the level of income derived from food, is much more pronounced for the food sector [the required increase in total production being $(141 - 124)/124 = 14\%$, whereas the increase in the total production of the clothing sector is only $(104 - 102)/102 = 2\%$]. In terms of planning, this could mean, for instance, that such an increase might not be possible, because of the amount of agricultural land required to sustain it, the additional requirements on farm roads, etc.

In closing this section, it should be stressed that the two-sector model can conceptually be adapted to represent the interactions between two *regions*, if it is assumed that each sector is located in a different region. The case of several sectors in each of several regions will be addressed at the end of the next section.

3.4　The Input/Output Model

In the example used to illustrate the two-sector interactive model, the final accounting equations for the levels of production (after rounding down),

$$Y_1 = X_1 + a_{11}Y_1 + a_{12}Y_2 = 124 = 50 + 0.35(124) + 0.30(103)$$
$$= 50 + 43 + 31$$
$$Y_2 = X_2 + a_{21}Y_1 + a_{22}Y_2 = 103 = 75 + 0.10(124) + 0.15(103)$$
$$= 75 + 12 + 15$$

can be expanded to reflect more precisely and/or more completely the intersectorial (or interregional) activities. In its present state, this set of equations does balance out in terms of the levels of total *output* (production) of the sectors, as can be seen in the two horizontal levels of Table 3.1.

TABLE 3.1   Economic Transactions Table

Producing Sector	Consuming Sectors			
	Food	Clothes	External	Total Output
Food	43	31	50	124
Clothes	12	15	75	102

However, we might also be interested in obtaining a balance for the levels of *inputs* (i.e., production or activity) going into each of the two sectors. First of all, each of these sectors inputs part of its production into the other, as can be seen in Table 3.1. The level of input from the food sector into itself is 43, and the level of input from the clothes sector into the food sector is 12. Similarly, the level of input of the food sector into itself is 15, and into the food sector, it is 31. Thus, the total internal input, i.e., input which comes from the sectors of the economy themselves into the food sector, is $43 + 12 = 55$, and the total internal input into the clothes sector is $31 + 15 = 46$. Since obviously the total output of each sector must be equal to the total input, the difference between the internal inputs and the corresponding total inputs (or outputs) will come from external supplying (producing) sectors, as represented in Table 3.2.

TABLE 3.2   Input/Output Table

INPUT Producing Sector	OUTPUT Consuming Sector			
	Food	Clothes	External	Total
Food	43	31	50	124
Clothes	12	15	75	102
External	69	56		126
Total	124	102		352

This enlarged multiplier model, which is called the *input/output* model, thus gives us the information that for each unit of total output of the food sector, there must be an input of $69/124 = 0.56$ unit from a producing external sector to the local economy. This might be capital, labor, imported fertilizers, etc. Similarly, the fraction of the total input into the clothing sector that comes from sectors external to the local economy is equal to $56/102 = 0.55$. These coefficients, which play a role similar to the production coefficients, are useful in determining the impacts on the level of outside imports of changes in the levels of basic production.

Table 3.2 can now be translated in matrix form as

$$\begin{bmatrix} 124 \\ 102 \end{bmatrix} = \begin{bmatrix} 0.35 & 0.30 \\ 0.10 & 0.15 \end{bmatrix} \begin{bmatrix} 124 \\ 102 \end{bmatrix} + \begin{bmatrix} 50 \\ 75 \end{bmatrix}$$

$$VA = \begin{bmatrix} 0.56 & 0.55 \end{bmatrix} \begin{bmatrix} 124 \\ 102 \end{bmatrix}$$

(3.20)

where the single figure VA is the *value added* (total external input), which is 56% of 124 plus 55% of $102 = 0.56(124) + 0.55(102) = 126$.

Finally, the grand total input (or output) should be equal to the total internal input, i.e., $(124 + 102)$ plus the value added, i.e., 126. The total level of activity of the economy, including its import and export transactions with the other regions, is thus equal to 352.

If the levels of basic production of the two sectors change, the effects on the required levels of imports can be determined through the use of coefficients in the lower part of the input/output model in (3.20). For instance, pursuing the example above, if the level of sales of food to the outside is now 60 instead of 50, the resultant levels of total production are now $Y_1 = 141$ and $Y_2 = 104$ for food and clothing, respectively, as determined at the end of Section 3.3. The new levels of external inputs required would simply be $0.56(141)$ into the food sector and $0.55(104)$ into the clothes sector, for a total of 136 units.

The input/output model is thus operated in basically the same manner as the multisector multiplier model, but with the addition of the row representing the inports from outside.

In real-world applications, the number of sectors in a local or regional economy is likely to be more than two. We therefore need a general model to accommodate any number of sectors in the economy. We shall now describe the straightforward generalization of the input/output model to the general case of m internal sectors of production, p external sectors of consumption, and q external sectors of importation.

The input/output *tableau* is as represented in Figure 3.1. The definitions of the entries in the tableau are as follows:

OUTPUT / INPUT		Internal Consuming Sectors						External Consuming Sectors			Total
		1	2	3	... j	... m		1	2 ... p		
Internal Producing Sectors	1	Z_{11}	Z_{12}	Z_{13}	$\cdots Z_{1j}$	$\cdots Z_{1m}$		X_{11}	$X_{12} \cdots X_{1p}$		Y_1
	2	Z_{21}	Z_{22}	Z_{23}	$\cdots Z_{2j}$	$\cdots Z_{2m}$		X_{21}	$X_{22} \cdots X_{2p}$		Y_2
	$\vdots$	. . . .						. . . .			. . . .
	i	Z_{i1}	Z_{i2}	Z_{i3}	$\cdots Z_{ij}$	$\cdots Z_{im}$		X_{i1}	$X_{i2} \cdots X_{ip}$		Y_i
	$\vdots$	. . . .						. . . .			. . . .
	m	Z_{m1}		$\cdots$		Z_{mm}		X_{m1}	$X_{m2} \cdots X_{mp}$		Y_m
External Producing Sectors	1	I_{11}	I_{12}		$\cdots I_{1j}$	$\cdots I_{im}$					
	2	. . . .									
	$\cdot$	. . . .	I_{ij}	. . . .							
	q	I_{q1}	I_{q2}	$\cdots$	I_{qj}	$\cdots I_{qm}$					
Total		Y_1	Y_2	$\cdots$	Y_j	$\cdots Y_m$					T

Figure 3.1 Input/output tableau.

- Z_{ij} is the amount of production of sector j that is acquired (consumed) by sector i. It is thus basic production from sector j into sector i.

- X_{ik} is the amount of basic production of sector i that goes to satisfy the demand in external consuming sector number k.

- I_{ij} is the required input into sector j from external producing sector number i.

- Y_j is the total level of input, or output, of sector j.

- T is the grand total level of economic activity, i.e., the sum of the Y_j's for all sectors.

This table corresponds to Table 3.2, where the column of external demand has been disaggregated into p subcolumns and the row of external inputs has been differentiated into q subrows. The external demands X_{ik} and the external supplies I_{ij} do not have to come from the same sectors. For instance, external demand sectors might be demands from certain areas of the country, and supplying sectors might be located in another different set of regions. Also, the external consuming sectors might include such nonbasic local sectors as investments, taxes, private consumption, government consumption, etc. The external supplying sectors might similarly be local nonbasic sectors such as sales taxes, salaries, depreciation, etc.

The matrix of production coefficients **A** corresponding to the table in Figure 3.1 is derived immediately, by dividing each entry by the column total. Therefore,

$$
\mathbf{A} =
\begin{bmatrix}
a_{11} & a_{12} & a_{13} & \cdots & a_{1m} \\
a_{21} & a_{22} & a_{23} & \cdots & a_{2m} \\
\cdots\cdots\cdots\cdots\cdots\cdots \\
a_{i1} & a_{i2} & a_{i3} & \cdots & a_{im} \\
\cdots\cdots\cdots\cdots\cdots\cdots \\
a_{m1} & a_{m2} & a_{m3} & \cdots & a_{mm}
\end{bmatrix}
$$

where

$$
a_{ij} = \frac{Z_{ij}}{Y_j} \tag{3.21}
$$

The row vector of external input coefficients for sector i is

$$
\mathbf{B}_i = [b_{i1} \quad b_{i2} \quad \ldots \quad b_{im}]
$$

where

$$
b_{ij} = \frac{I_{ij}}{Y_j} \tag{3.22}
$$

With these definitions, the balancing equations represented in summary form in Figure 3.1 can be formally written:

$$
\begin{bmatrix} Y_1 \\ Y_2 \\ \cdot \\ \cdot \\ \cdot \\ Y_i \\ \cdot \\ \cdot \\ Y_m \end{bmatrix}
=
\begin{bmatrix}
a_{11} & a_{12} & \cdots & a_{1m} \\
a_{21} & a_{22} & \cdots & a_{2m} \\
\cdots\cdots\cdots\cdots\cdots \\
a_{i1} & a_{i2} & \cdots & a_{im} \\
\cdots\cdots\cdots\cdots\cdots \\
a_{m1} & a_{m2} & \cdots & a_{mm}
\end{bmatrix}
\begin{bmatrix} Y_1 \\ Y_2 \\ \cdot \\ \cdot \\ \cdot \\ Y_i \\ \cdot \\ \cdot \\ Y_m \end{bmatrix}
+
\begin{bmatrix} X_{11} \\ X_{21} \\ \cdot \\ \cdot \\ \cdot \\ X_{i1} \\ \cdot \\ \cdot \\ X_{m1} \end{bmatrix}
+
\begin{bmatrix} X_{12} \\ X_{22} \\ \cdot \\ \cdot \\ \cdot \\ X_{i2} \\ \cdot \\ \cdot \\ X_{m2} \end{bmatrix}
+ \cdots +
\begin{bmatrix} X_{p1} \\ X_{p2} \\ \cdot \\ \cdot \\ \cdot \\ X_{pi} \\ \cdot \\ \cdot \\ X_{pm} \end{bmatrix}
$$

$$\tag{3.23}$$

or $\mathbf{Y} = \mathbf{AY} + \mathbf{X}_1 + \mathbf{X}_2 + \ldots + \mathbf{X}_p$, where **Y** is the column vector of total activity levels for the various sectors, **A** is the matrix of production coefficients defined above, and $\mathbf{X}_1, \mathbf{X}_2, \ldots, \mathbf{X}_p$ are, respectively, the column vectors of the external demands from external sectors $1, 2, 3, \ldots, p$.

The general input/output model is operated in the same fashion as described above. For a desired level of external demands (basic production)

X_j, the corresponding levels of total production Y_i are given by the equation

$$Y = AY + X_1 + X_2 + \ldots + X_p = AY + X \qquad (3.24)$$

where X represents the total external (basic) demand, i.e., the column vector sum of the X individual column vectors X_j. Equation (3.24) is structurally the same as in the two sector case, and thus the solution value of Y is obtained in the same fashion. $Y = (I - A)^{-1}X$.

Thus, we first compute the inverse of the matrix $(I - A)$, using, e.g., the systematic method of the determinants (see Section 1.3). Then we multiply that inverse matrix by the column vector X, and we obtain the vector of total output (input) levels Y. Finally, the total level of external inputs I_i required from supplying sector i is given by

$$I_i = b_{i1}Y_1 + b_{i2}Y_2 + \ldots + b_{im}Y_m = \begin{bmatrix} b_{i1} & b_{i2} & \ldots & b_{im} \end{bmatrix} \begin{bmatrix} Y_1 \\ Y_2 \\ \cdot \\ \cdot \\ \cdot \\ Y_m \end{bmatrix} = B_i Y$$

$$(3.25)$$

The model can also be used to perform analyses of the effects of changes in sales to external sector j. Suppose that the demand from external sector j has changed and is now equal to X'_j. (No other sectors have changed their demand.) In that case, the matrix $(I - A)$ and its inverse stay the same since only the column vector X_j, and thus only the vector X, is changed in equation (3.24). Thus, the new levels of total output (input) are given by

$$Y' = (I - A)^{-1}X' \qquad (3.26)$$

and the new requirements from external supplying sector i are given by

$$I'_i = B_i Y' = B_i(I - A)^{-1}X' \qquad (3.27)$$

The same approach is applicable to changes in the level of demand in any number of external sectors, since they also only result in the change of the vector X. If, however, only the difference in levels of outputs Y is desired (and not the new level), caused by a change in external demand sector j, then it is simply given by

$$\Delta Y = (I - A)^{-1}\Delta X_j \qquad (3.28)$$

and subsequently, the change in level of required input I_i from supplying sector i is given by

$$\Delta I_i = B_i \Delta Y = B_i(I - A)^{-1}\Delta X_j \qquad (3.29)$$

where ΔY, ΔX_j, and ΔI_i are, respectively, the column vectors representing the changes in the vectors Y, X_j, and I_i. These formulas simply represent the generalization of the case above.

3.5 Multiregional Version of the Input/Output Model

Finally, an extension of the single-region multisectorial model of Figure 3.1 can be made to the case of several regions with several sectors of production each, along the same lines as the generalization of the cohort-survival model of Chapter 2. Let us assume that there are n regions, each with the same m activity sectors. With the same notation as above, the model can now be written

$$
\begin{bmatrix} \mathcal{Y}_1 \\ \mathcal{Y}_2 \\ \cdot \\ \cdot \\ \mathcal{Y}_k \\ \cdot \\ \cdot \\ \mathcal{Y}_n \end{bmatrix}
=
\begin{bmatrix}
\mathcal{Q}_{11} & \mathcal{Q}_{12} & \cdots & \mathcal{Q}_{1l} & \cdots & \mathcal{Q}_{1n} \\
\mathcal{Q}_{21} & \mathcal{Q}_{22} & \cdots & \mathcal{Q}_{2l} & \cdots & \mathcal{Q}_{2n} \\
& & \cdots\cdots & & & \\
\mathcal{Q}_{k1} & & \cdots & \mathcal{Q}_{kl} & \cdots & \mathcal{Q}_{kn} \\
& & \cdots\cdots & & & \\
\mathcal{Q}_{n1} & & \cdots & & & \mathcal{Q}_{nn}
\end{bmatrix}
\begin{bmatrix} \mathcal{Y}_1 \\ \mathcal{Y}_2 \\ \cdot \\ \cdot \\ \mathcal{Y}_k \\ \cdot \\ \cdot \\ \mathcal{Y}_n \end{bmatrix}
+
\begin{bmatrix} \mathcal{X}_1 \\ \mathcal{X}_2 \\ \cdot \\ \cdot \\ \mathcal{X}_k \\ \cdot \\ \cdot \\ \mathcal{X}_n \end{bmatrix}
$$

or

$$ \mathcal{Y} = \mathcal{Q} \quad \mathcal{Y} + \mathcal{X} \qquad (3.30) $$

$$
\begin{bmatrix} I_1 \\ I_2 \\ \cdot \\ \cdot \\ I_k \\ \cdot \\ \cdot \\ I_n \end{bmatrix}
=
\begin{bmatrix}
\mathcal{B}_{11} & \mathcal{B}_{12} & \cdots & \mathcal{B}_{1l} & \cdots & \mathcal{B}_{1n} \\
& & \cdots\cdots & & & \\
& & \cdots\cdots & & & \\
& & \cdots & \mathcal{B}_{kl} & \cdots & \\
& & \cdots\cdots & & & \\
\mathcal{B}_{n1} & & \cdots & & & \mathcal{B}_{nn}
\end{bmatrix}
\begin{bmatrix} \mathcal{Y}_1 \\ \mathcal{Y}_2 \\ \cdot \\ \cdot \\ \mathcal{Y}_k \\ \cdot \\ \cdot \\ \mathcal{Y}_n \end{bmatrix}
$$

or

$$ I = \mathcal{B} \quad \mathcal{Y} \qquad (3.31) $$

$\mathcal{Y}_k$ is the column vector of total outputs Y_{kl} of region k with respect to the m sectors:

$$
\mathcal{Y}_k = \begin{bmatrix} Y_{k1} \\ \cdot \\ \cdot \\ \cdot \\ Y_{kl} \\ \cdot \\ \cdot \\ Y_{km} \end{bmatrix} \qquad (3.32)
$$

$\mathcal{Q}_{kl}$ is the matrix of production coefficients representing the interaction of region k and region l with respect to the m sectors:

$$\mathcal{Q}_{kl} = \begin{bmatrix} a_{11}^{kl} & a_{12}^{kl} & \cdots & a_{1m}^{kl} \\ \cdots & a_{ij}^{kl} & \cdots & \\ a_{m1}^{kl} & \cdots & & a_{mm}^{kl} \end{bmatrix} \tag{3.33}$$

where a_{ij}^{kl} is the percentage of the total output of sector j located in region l which is devoted to buying goods from sector i in region k. $\mathcal{X}_k$ is the column vector of outside demands X_{ik} from region k with respect to the m sectors:

$$\mathcal{X}_k = \begin{bmatrix} X_{k1} \\ \cdot \\ \cdot \\ \cdot \\ X_{kl} \\ \cdot \\ \cdot \\ \cdot \\ X_{km} \end{bmatrix} \tag{3.34}$$

I_k is the total value added onto all m sectors in region k, i.e., not a vector but a single value, and $\mathcal{B}_{kl}$ is the row vector of structural coefficients:

$$\mathcal{B}_{kl} = [b_1^{kl} \quad \cdots \quad b_i^{kl} \quad \cdots \quad b_m^{kl}] \tag{3.35}$$

where b_i^{kl} is the amount of value added into region k as a proportion of the total output Y_{il} of sector i in region l.

Although the formulation above might look rather complex, the basic structure of the multiregional model is exactly the same as that of the single regional model, but with the difference that the structural coefficients are now replaced by matrices, and the levels of total and basic outputs, as well as the levels of nonbasic inputs, are replaced by column vectors to accommodate the added dimension introduced by the number of the region. The model is operated through the same basic procedure of computing first the inverse of $(I - \mathcal{Q})$, $\mathcal{Q}$ being the matrix factor of the column vector of $\mathcal{Y}_i$'s in equation (3.30).

Thus, the inclusion of several regions does not change the basic features of the input/output model in its matrix form. In particular, if the inverse matrix is written as

$$(I - \mathcal{Q})^{-1} = \begin{bmatrix} \alpha_{11} & \cdots & \alpha_{1n} \\ \cdots & \alpha_{kl} & \cdots \\ \alpha_{n1} & \cdots & \alpha_{nn} \end{bmatrix} \tag{3.36}$$

where the square submatrix α_{kl} is equal to

$$\boldsymbol{\alpha}_{kl} = \begin{bmatrix} \alpha_{11}^{kl} & \cdots & \alpha_{1m}^{kl} \\ \cdots & \alpha_{ij}^{kl} & \cdots \\ \alpha_{m1}^{kl} & \cdots & \alpha_{mm}^{kl} \end{bmatrix} \qquad (3.37)$$

the physical interpretation of the entry α_{ij}^{kl} is that it represents the part of the total multiplier which transforms the level of external demand on sector i in region k into its total demand, which is related to sector j located in region l.

3.6   The Employment and Population Multiplier Model

In the preceding sections, we have examined how to model the interrelationships between various sectors of a regional or multiregional economy. This then enables us to analyze the effects or changes in given activity sectors on the levels in all other sectors. By translating these levels of economic activity into numbers of jobs (e.g., through the use of *technical coefficients* which define the number of labor-hours required to produce one unit in the respective sectors), these models can thus be used to predict employment levels. In this section, we shall develop models that represent the effect of changes in employment levels in given sectors on the total employment in the area and on the total residential population, respectively. As above, we shall first start with the single-region model, and later expand it to the multiregional case.

We are, therefore, starting from the knowledge of the planned (or projected) levels of jobs in the various sectors of the economy, as determined above. Each of these jobs represents a worker, who will (on the average) have a number of dependents. Furthermore, this family (or household) will require certain services, such as shopping, commercial, transportation, etc. Thus, the changes in the levels of employment in the sectors examined above will affect the total employment level, through the creation (or disappearance) of service-related jobs, and also the total residential population level, through the arrival (or leaving) of the families of workers in both the production sectors and the service sectors.

Let us, therefore, assume that to each worker and his (or her) family corresponds a certain need for services, which in terms of total employment in the service sectors results in α workers. This, therefore, means that each job (in any sector) results in a requirement for α supporting jobs in the service sector. [We are assuming first that the needs for service are the same for all workers in the various employment categories. Also, we are lumping all the service sectors into a single sector. Of course, a dissaggregated approach along the lines followed in the derivation of formula (3.5) in Section 3.2 is possible, if these assumptions are not adequate.] If the projected level of employment in a given production sector is E_p, what will be the total number of jobs E created?

It should be obvious that in this form, this question is essentially the same question as asking what level of total production corresponds to a given level of basic production, knowing the propensity to consume c. Here, the ratio of service jobs E_s to total employment,

$$\alpha = \frac{E_s}{E} \qquad (3.38)$$

plays the role of c. Thus, by the same token as in Section 3.2, we can write that

$$E = E_p + E_s = E_p + \alpha E \qquad \text{or} \qquad E - \alpha E = E_p = E(1 - \alpha)$$

and thus the total employment is

$$\boxed{E = \frac{E_p}{1 - \alpha}} \qquad (3.39)$$

Another way to derive the same result is to start from the level of production employment E_p, compute the corresponding level of service employment αE_p, then compute the level of service employment corresponding to that $\alpha^2 E_p$, etc. The final, total level of employment E created by the employment in the production sector is then

$$E = E_p + \alpha E_p + \alpha^2 E_p + \cdots + \alpha^\infty E_p = \frac{E_p}{1 - \alpha}$$

and we get, of course, the same result.

As an illustration, suppose that we are planning to bring 800 jobs into a certain region through the development of a given industry. On the basis of survey research in areas with the same type of industry, we have found that for each of these production jobs, the various needs of the workers and their families required 0.6 job in the service sector. (This value reflects, in a sense, the propensity of the workers in the production sector to consume services, and thus might depend on the type of production industry and the corresponding wages.) What is the effect of the industrial development on the total employment E in the area?

Using formula (3.39), we get

$$E = \frac{E_p}{1 - \alpha} = \frac{800}{1 - 0.6} = \frac{800}{0.4} = 2000$$

Thus, just as with the economic multiplier, a *job multiplier* $1/(1 - \alpha)$ (here equal to $1/0.4 = 2.5$) has transformed the original 800 production jobs into a total number of 2000 jobs.

In some cases, the service needs of the residents will be more conveniently defined with respect not to the households of workers, but to the overall residential population. Let us then assume that for each person in the total population, β jobs are required in the service sector to answer his or her needs. (α was defined as the ratio of the number of service jobs to the total employment level, whereas β is defined as the ratio of the number of service jobs to the total population level.)

$$\beta = \frac{E_s}{P} \tag{3.40}$$

Let us use the inverse of the proportion of employed people in the population:

$$\gamma = \frac{P}{E} \tag{3.41}$$

We can write that the number of people (originally) brought in by the production jobs is $P = \gamma E_p$. These people require $\beta(\gamma E_p)$ service jobs. In turn, to these service jobs corresponds an additional influx of people: $\gamma(\beta\gamma E_p)$. These people, in turn, require $\beta(\gamma\beta\gamma E_p)$ service jobs, etc. The total number of jobs in the area would be the original production jobs E_p, plus the service jobs they create, $\beta\gamma E_p$, plus the next increment, and the total number of jobs in the area would be

$$E = E_p + \beta\gamma E_p + \beta^2\gamma^2 E_p + \ldots + (\beta\gamma)^\infty E_p$$
$$= E_p[1 + \beta\gamma + (\beta\gamma)^2 + \ldots + (\beta\gamma)^n + \ldots]$$

or

$$\boxed{E = \frac{E_p}{1 - \beta\gamma}} \tag{3.42}$$

Also, the total number of people in the area would be γ times the level of total employment. Thus,

$$\boxed{P = \gamma E = \frac{\gamma E_p}{1 - \beta\gamma}} \tag{3.43}$$

Finally, the total number of service jobs is the difference between the total number of jobs and the total number of production jobs:

$$\boxed{E_s = E - E_p = \frac{E_p}{1 - \beta\gamma} - E_p = \frac{\beta\gamma E_p}{1 - \beta\gamma}} \tag{3.44}$$

This process is, perhaps, best illustrated by Figure 3.2.

As an illustration, assume that we are planning to bring in 10,000 jobs in an area, because of the implantation of an automobile factory. The ratio of total population to active population (i.e., the inverse of the "work-force ratio") is $\gamma = 1.6$. In other words, to each worker corresponds on the average a family of 1.6 people. Also, the ratio of service jobs to total population is

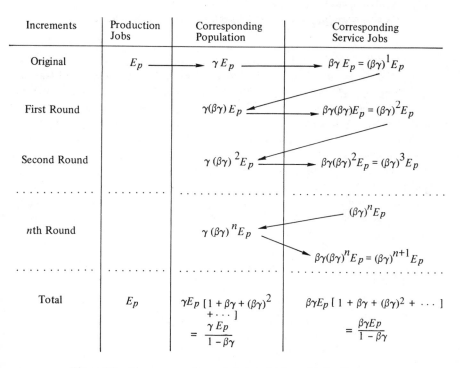

Increments	Production Jobs	Corresponding Population	Corresponding Service Jobs
Original	E_p ⟶	γE_p ⟶	$\beta\gamma\,E_p = (\beta\gamma)^1 E_p$
First Round	$\gamma(\beta\gamma)\,E_p$		$\beta\gamma(\beta\gamma)E_p = (\beta\gamma)^2 E_p$
Second Round	$\gamma\,(\beta\gamma)^2 E_p$		$\beta\gamma(\beta\gamma)^2 E_p = (\beta\gamma)^3 E_p$
nth Round	$\gamma\,(\beta\gamma)^n E_p$	$(\beta\gamma)^n E_p$	$\beta\gamma(\beta\gamma)^n E_p = (\beta\gamma)^{n+1} E_p$
Total	E_p	$\gamma E_p\,[\,1 + \beta\gamma + (\beta\gamma)^2 + \cdots\,]$ $= \dfrac{\gamma E_p}{1 - \beta\gamma}$	$\beta\gamma E_p\,[\,1 + \beta\gamma + (\beta\gamma)^2 + \cdots\,]$ $= \dfrac{\beta\gamma E_p}{1 - \beta\gamma}$

Figure 3.2   The process of population and job multiplication.

assumed to be $\beta = 0.3$. Equivalently, each person in the total population requires on the average a total of 0.3 "service person." Given these data, what is the resultant level of total population that can be expected to migrate to the area, and how many additional service jobs will be created?

Using formula (3.42), we get the level of total employment as:

$$E = \frac{E_p}{1 - \beta\gamma} = \frac{10,000}{1 - (1.6)(0.3)} = 19,231$$

Using formula (3.44), we get the level of service jobs:

$$E_s = \frac{\beta\gamma E_p}{1 - \beta\gamma} = \frac{(1.6)(0.3)10,000}{1 - (1.6)(0.3)} = \beta\gamma E = (1.6)(0.3)19,231$$
$$= 9231$$

This is also

$$E_s = E - E_p = 19,231 - 10,000 = 9231$$

Finally, using formula (3.43), we get

$$P = \frac{\gamma E_p}{1 - \beta\gamma} = 1.6(19,231) = \gamma E = 30,770$$

3.7 Multiregional Version
   of the Employment and Population Multiplier Model

Let us now generalize this single-region multiplier model to the case of several regions. Let us now assume that we are given the numbers of production jobs: $E_1^p, E_2^p, \ldots, E_j^p, \ldots, E_n^p$ in the n regions, respectively. As before, each of the production jobs will result in an increase in the total residential population, corresponding to the workers and their families. In the general case, the workers will not necessarily live in the same region in which they work. Let us assume that the percentage of workers in area j who live in the first area is a_{1j}. In other words, the number of workers who work in area j and live in area 1 will be equal to $a_{1j}E_j^p$. Consequently, the total number of workers W_1 who live in region 1 will be equal to the sum of the numbers who come from all such regions j, i.e.,

$$W_1 = a_{11}E_1^p + a_{12}E_2^p + \ldots + a_{11}E_j^p + \ldots + a_{1n}E_n^p$$

The respective levels of workers W_i living in areas 1 through n can thus be written as

$$W_1 = a_{11}E_1^p + a_{12}E_2^p + \ldots + a_{1j}E_j^p + \ldots + a_{1n}E_n^p$$
$$W_2 = a_{21}E_1^p + a_{22}E_2^p + \ldots + a_{2j}E_j^p + \ldots + a_{2n}E_n^p$$
$$\vdots$$
$$W_i = a_{i1}E_1^p + a_{i2}E_2^p + \ldots + a_{ij}E_j^p + \ldots + a_{in}E_n^p$$
$$\vdots$$
$$W_n = a_{n1}E_1^p + a_{n2}E_2^p + \ldots + a_{nj}E_j^p + \ldots + a_{nn}E_n^p$$

Equivalently, in matrix notation:

$$
\begin{bmatrix} W_1 \\ W_2 \\ \cdot \\ \cdot \\ \cdot \\ W_i \\ \cdot \\ \cdot \\ \cdot \\ W_n \end{bmatrix}
=
\begin{bmatrix}
a_{11} & a_{12} & \cdots & a_{1j} & \cdots & a_{1n} \\
a_{21} & a_{22} & \cdots & a_{2j} & \cdots & a_{2n} \\
& & \cdots & & & \\
a_{i1} & a_{i2} & \cdots & a_{ij} & \cdots & a_{in} \\
& & \cdots & & & \\
a_{n1} & & \cdots & & & a_{nn}
\end{bmatrix}
\begin{bmatrix} E_1^p \\ E_2^p \\ \cdot \\ \cdot \\ \cdot \\ E_i^p \\ \cdot \\ \cdot \\ \cdot \\ E_n^p \end{bmatrix}
$$

or

$$\mathbf{W} = \mathbf{A} \quad \mathbf{E}^p \tag{3.45}$$

where $\mathbf{W}$ is the column vector of resident workers distribution, $\mathbf{E}^p$ is the

94

column vector of production employment (jobs) distribution, and $\mathbf{A}$ is the *work-to-home matrix*.

The entry a_{ij} in matrix $\mathbf{A}$ represents the proportion of workers in area j who live in area i. In that sense, the matrix $\mathbf{A}$ represents (in percentage form) a pattern of commuting from the place of work to the place of residence. In this chapter, we assume that this commuting pattern is known, e.g., from field surveys. In Chapter 4, we shall investigate the implications on the nature of the matrix $\mathbf{A}$, of certain theoretical assumptions concerning the law of interaction between regions i and j.

In any case, the next step is to evaluate the total number of residents in each area corresponding to these workers. Let us assume (in the same fashion as for the single-region case) that the work-force ratio in area i is equal to $1/\gamma_i$. In other words, the ratio of the number of active, employed workers W_i in area i to the total number of residents is $1/\gamma_i$. Therefore, the population level in i will be equal to $P_i = (1/\gamma_i)W_i$. In matrix form, we can write for all areas:

$$
\begin{bmatrix} P_1 \\ P_2 \\ \cdot \\ \cdot \\ P_i \\ \cdot \\ \cdot \\ P_n \end{bmatrix}
=
\begin{bmatrix}
1/\gamma_1 & 0 & \cdots & 0 & \cdots & 0 \\
0 & 1/\gamma_2 & \cdots & 0 & \cdots & 0 \\
& & \cdots & & & \\
0 & 0 & \cdots & 1/\gamma_i & \cdots & 0 \\
& & \cdots & & & \\
0 & 0 & \cdots & 0 & \cdots & 1/\gamma_n
\end{bmatrix}
\begin{bmatrix} W_1 \\ W_2 \\ \cdot \\ \cdot \\ W_i \\ \cdot \\ \cdot \\ W_n \end{bmatrix}
$$

$$\mathbf{P} \quad = \quad\quad\quad\quad \mathbf{\Gamma} \quad\quad\quad\quad\quad\quad \mathbf{W} \qquad (3.46)$$

where $\mathbf{P}$ is the column vector of (total) residential population levels, and $\mathbf{\Gamma}$ is the (diagonal) matrix of inverses of employment ratios.

Finally, by replacing $\mathbf{W}$ in the equality above by its expression as a function of the distribution of employment $\mathbf{E}^p$ in formula (3.45), we get

$$\mathbf{P} = \mathbf{\Gamma W} = \mathbf{\Gamma}(\mathbf{A E}^p) = (\mathbf{\Gamma A})\mathbf{E}^p = \mathbf{H E}^p \qquad (3.47)$$

where $\mathbf{H}$ is the product of $\mathbf{\Gamma}$ by $\mathbf{A}$ and represents the operator matrix that converts the distribution of basic jobs $\mathbf{E}^p$ into the distribution of residential population $\mathbf{P}$.

We now have the distribution of residents in the n areas. The next step is to evaluate the resulting creation of service jobs in the areas. Let us assume that, in the same fashion as in the single-region case, one resident in area i will require the equivalent of β_i service jobs. Thus, the number of service jobs Q_i required by the residents in area i will be equal to

$$Q_i = \beta_i P_i$$

and for all regions

$$
\begin{bmatrix} Q_1 \\ Q_2 \\ \cdot \\ \cdot \\ \cdot \\ Q_i \\ \cdot \\ \cdot \\ \cdot \\ Q_n \end{bmatrix} = \begin{bmatrix} \beta_1 & 0 & \cdots & 0 & \cdots & 0 \\ 0 & \beta_2 & \cdots & 0 & \cdots & 0 \\ & & \cdots & & & \\ 0 & \cdots & & \beta_i & \cdots & 0 \\ & & \cdots & & & \\ 0 & 0 & \cdots & 0 & \cdots & \beta_n \end{bmatrix} \begin{bmatrix} P_1 \\ P_2 \\ \cdot \\ \cdot \\ \cdot \\ P_i \\ \cdot \\ \cdot \\ \cdot \\ P_n \end{bmatrix}
$$

or

$$
\mathbf{Q} \quad = \quad\quad\quad \mathbf{B} \quad\quad\quad\quad \mathbf{P} \tag{3.48}
$$

where $\mathbf{Q}$ is the column vector of service jobs required by each region, and $\mathbf{B}$ is the (diagonal) matrix of inverses of work-force ratios.

However, $\mathbf{Q}$ is not the distribution of actual service jobs, since in the same way that workers from a given area of work are distributed to all areas of residence (through commuting to work), service requirements for residents in a given area are distributed to all areas (through commuting to shop). In other words, residents in area i might go to other areas j to acquire the services they need. Let us assume that the (overall) proportion of residents in area j who go to area i for (all) services is equal to c_{ij}. Equivalently, the number of service jobs created in area i by the residents living in area j will be equal to $c_{ij}Q_j$. Consequently, the total number of service jobs E_i^s created by residents from all areas in area i will be equal to

$$
E_i^s = c_{i1}Q_1 + \ldots + c_{ij}Q_j + \ldots + c_{in}Q_n
$$

and in matrix form we can write

$$
\begin{bmatrix} E_1^s \\ E_2^s \\ \cdot \\ \cdot \\ \cdot \\ E_i^s \\ \cdot \\ \cdot \\ \cdot \\ E_n^s \end{bmatrix} = \begin{bmatrix} c_{11} & c_{12} & \cdots & c_{1i} & \cdots & c_{1n} \\ c_{21} & c_{22} & \cdots & c_{2i} & \cdots & c_{2n} \\ & & \cdots & & & \\ c_{i1} & c_{i2} & \cdots & c_{ij} & \cdots & c_{in} \\ & & \cdots & & & \\ c_{n1} & & \cdots & & & c_{nn} \end{bmatrix} \begin{bmatrix} Q_1 \\ Q_2 \\ \cdot \\ \cdot \\ \cdot \\ Q_i \\ \cdot \\ \cdot \\ \cdot \\ Q_n \end{bmatrix}
$$

or

$$
\mathbf{E}^s \quad = \quad\quad\quad \mathbf{C} \quad\quad\quad\quad \mathbf{Q} \tag{3.49}
$$

where $\mathbf{E}^s$ is the column vector representing the distribution of service jobs in the respective areas, $\mathbf{C}$ is the *home to shop matrix*. Formula (3.49) corresponds to formula (3.45), and matrix $\mathbf{C}$ is the equivalent of matrix $\mathbf{A}$ for the journey to shop. Thus, $\mathbf{C}$ represents the travel patterns corresponding to the demand for services from area j on area i. Finally, by replacing $\mathbf{Q}$ in equality (3.49) by its expression in formula (3.48), we get

$$\mathbf{E}^s = \mathbf{CQ} = \mathbf{C(BP)} = \mathbf{(CB)P} = \mathbf{SP} \qquad (3.50)$$

where $\mathbf{S}$ is the product of $\mathbf{C}$ by $\mathbf{B}$ and represents the operator matrix that converts the distribution of residential population $\mathbf{P}$ into the distribution of service jobs $\mathbf{E}^s$.

We have now obtained the distribution of first-round service jobs, and thus have completed the first iteration of the regionally distributed multiplier process. However, as in the single-region case, these jobs will in turn create an additional residential population, through a distribution of the service workers to areas of residence. We are thus in the same position as at the start of the first cycle, except that we now use the distribution of service jobs $\mathbf{E}^s$ instead of that of the production jobs $\mathbf{E}^p$. The next increment in the total residential population due to the service workers will then be

$$\mathbf{P}^2 = \mathbf{HE}_1^s = \mathbf{H(SHE}^p)$$

These residents in turn will create additional service jobs:

$$\mathbf{E}_2^s = \mathbf{SP}^2 = \mathbf{S[H(SHE}^p)], \qquad \text{etc.}$$

The process is illustrated in Figure 3.3 and the resulting expressions are explicated below. The process is basically similar to that for the single-region case (illustrated in Figure 3.2), with the difference that now all quantities are

Increments Number	Production Jobs Distribution	Resulting Distribution of Population Increments	Resulting Distribution of Service Job Increments
Original	$\mathbf{E}^p$ ⟶	⟶ $\mathbf{HE}^p$ ⟶	⟶ $\mathbf{S(HE}^p) = \mathbf{(SH)E}^p$
First Round		$\mathbf{H(SH)E}^p$ ⟵	⟶ $\mathbf{SH(SHE}^p) = \mathbf{(SH)^2E}^p$
Second Round		$\mathbf{H(SH)^2E}^p$ ⟵	⟶ $\mathbf{SH(SH)^2E}^p = \mathbf{(SH)^3E}^p$
. . . .	. . . .	. . . .	. . . .
			$\mathbf{SH(SH)^{n-1}E}^p = \mathbf{(SH)^nE}^p$
nth Round		$\mathbf{H(SH)^nE}^p$ ⟵	⟶ $\mathbf{SH(SH)^nE}^p = \mathbf{(SH)^{n+1}E}^p$
Total	$\mathbf{E}^p$	$\mathbf{P} = \mathbf{H(I - SH)^{-1}E}^p$	$\mathbf{E}^s = \mathbf{(I - SH)^{-1}SHE}^p$

Figure 3.3   The process of population and job multiplication in multiregional form.

no longer single values, but matrices, i.e., either column vectors or square matrices. The matrix $\mathbf{H}$ plays the role of the parameter α and the matrix $\mathbf{S}$ plays the role of β. (It is important to note that, consequently, the *order* of multiplication is very important.) The total residential population will thus be equal to

$$\mathbf{P} = \mathbf{HIE}^p + \mathbf{H(SH)E}^p + \mathbf{H(SH)}^2\mathbf{E}^p + \ldots + \mathbf{H(SH)}^n\mathbf{E}^p + \ldots$$

or by factoring out $\mathbf{H}$ on the left and $\mathbf{E}^p$ on the right,

$$\mathbf{P} = \mathbf{H}[\mathbf{I} + (\mathbf{SH}) + (\mathbf{SH})^2 + \ldots + (\mathbf{SH})^n + \ldots]\mathbf{E}^p$$

It can be shown that the sum of matrices $\mathbf{I} + \mathbf{X} + \mathbf{X}^2 + \ldots + \mathbf{X}^n + \ldots + \mathbf{X}^\infty$, where $\mathbf{X}$ is a square matrix, is equal to the inverse of the matrix $(\mathbf{I} - \mathbf{X})$. Therefore, the preceding expression for the total residential population distribution vector $\mathbf{P}$ can be written

$$\mathbf{P} = \mathbf{H(I - SH)}^{-1}\mathbf{E}^p \tag{3.51}$$

The distribution of total service jobs $\mathbf{E}^s$ is similarly equal to

$$\mathbf{E}^s = \mathbf{SHE}^p + \mathbf{(SH)SHE}^p + \mathbf{(SH)}^2\mathbf{SHE}^p + \ldots + \mathbf{(SH)}^n\mathbf{SHE}^p + \ldots$$

$$= [\mathbf{I} + (\mathbf{SH})^2 + \ldots + (\mathbf{SH})^n + \ldots]\mathbf{SHE}^p$$

or

$$\mathbf{E}^s = \mathbf{(I - SH)}^{-1}\mathbf{SHE}^p \tag{3.52}$$

Finally, the distribution of total employment (production and service) is

$$\mathbf{E} = \mathbf{E}^p + \mathbf{E}^s = \mathbf{IE}^p + [\mathbf{SHE}^p + \ldots (\mathbf{SH})^n\mathbf{E}^p + \ldots]$$

$$= [\mathbf{I} + \mathbf{SH} + \ldots + (\mathbf{SH})^n + \ldots]\mathbf{E}^p$$

or

$$\mathbf{E} = \mathbf{(I - SH)}^{-1}\mathbf{E}^p \tag{3.53}$$

As an illustration, let us consider a three-region area where we are planning to increase the levels of production jobs by $E_1^p = 200$, $E_2^p = 100$, and $E_3^p = 250$ respectively. We know on the basis of the existing commuting pattern that among people who work in the first region, 20% live in the same region, and the rest are split equally between the other two regions. The workers in the second region reside in equal proportions in all regions. The workers in the third region all live in that region. Furthermore, the work-force ratios are equal to 0.25 for all regions, and all residents require an equivalent of 0.2 service job.

Finally, the residents of the first region have tended in the past to go to service facilities in the first region exclusively. The residents in the second

region go to the other two regions exclusively with equal frequency, and 50%
of the residents in the third region go to the first region, 40% go to the second,
and 10% go to the third.

Given these data, what are the respective projected effects of the additional
production jobs on the three regions, in terms of total resident population
and creation of service jobs, assuming that the past patterns will continue?

The increment in population is given by formula (3.51):

$$P = H(I - SH)^{-1}E^p$$

Let us therefore compute the matrices H and S. H is the product of the matrix
of inverse of work-force ratios Γ by the matrix A of commuting to work.
We have

$$\Gamma = \begin{bmatrix} 1/0.25 & 0 & 0 \\ 0 & 1/0.25 & 0 \\ 0 & 0 & 1/0.25 \end{bmatrix} = \begin{bmatrix} 4 & 0 & 0 \\ 0 & 4 & 0 \\ 0 & 0 & 4 \end{bmatrix}$$

and

$$A = \begin{bmatrix} 0.2 & 0.33 & 0 \\ 0.4 & 0.33 & 0 \\ 0.4 & 0.33 & 1 \end{bmatrix}$$

Thus,

$$H = \Gamma A = \underset{\Gamma}{\begin{bmatrix} 4 & 0 & 0 \\ 0 & 4 & 0 \\ 0 & 0 & 4 \end{bmatrix}} \underset{A}{\begin{bmatrix} 0.2 & 0.33 & 0 \\ 0.4 & 0.33 & 0 \\ 0.4 & 0.33 & 1 \end{bmatrix}} = \begin{bmatrix} 0.8 & 1.32 & 0 \\ 1.6 & 1.32 & 0 \\ 1.6 & 1.32 & 4 \end{bmatrix}$$

Similarly, S is equal to the product of the matrix of service jobs equivalents
B by the "home to shop" matrix C:
Thus,

$$S = \underset{C}{\begin{bmatrix} 1 & 0.5 & 0.5 \\ 0 & 0 & 0.4 \\ 0 & 0.5 & 0.1 \end{bmatrix}} \underset{B}{\begin{bmatrix} 0.2 & 0 & 0 \\ 0 & 0.2 & 0 \\ 0 & 0 & 0.2 \end{bmatrix}} = \begin{bmatrix} 0.2 & 0.1 & 0.1 \\ 0 & 0 & 0.08 \\ 0 & 0.1 & 0.02 \end{bmatrix}$$

We now compute the value of the product SH:

$$\underset{S}{\begin{bmatrix} 0.2 & 0.1 & 0.1 \\ 0 & 0 & 0.08 \\ 0 & 0.1 & 0.02 \end{bmatrix}} \underset{H}{\begin{bmatrix} 0.80 & 1.32 & 0 \\ 1.6 & 1.32 & 0 \\ 1.6 & 1.32 & 4 \end{bmatrix}} = \begin{bmatrix} 0.480 & 0.528 & 0.400 \\ 0.128 & 0.106 & 0.320 \\ 0.192 & 0.158 & 0.080 \end{bmatrix}$$

The matrix $(\mathbf{I} - \mathbf{SH})$ is therefore equal to

$$\underbrace{\begin{bmatrix} 1 & 0 & 0 \\ 0 & 1 & 0 \\ 0 & 0 & 1 \end{bmatrix}}_{\mathbf{I}} - \underbrace{\begin{bmatrix} 0.480 & 0.528 & 0.400 \\ 0.128 & 0.106 & 0.320 \\ 0.192 & 0.158 & 0.080 \end{bmatrix}}_{\mathbf{SH}} = \underbrace{\begin{bmatrix} 0.520 & -0.528 & -0.400 \\ -0.128 & 0.894 & -0.320 \\ -0.192 & -0.158 & 0.920 \end{bmatrix}}_{\mathbf{I} - \mathbf{SH}}$$

We now compute the inverse of $(\mathbf{I} - \mathbf{SH})$. The determinant is equal to 0.246. The matrix of cofactors is

$$\begin{bmatrix} 0.772 & 0.179 & 0.192 \\ 0.549 & 0.402 & 0.184 \\ 0.527 & 0.218 & 0.397 \end{bmatrix}$$

The inverse is now equal to the transposed matrix of cofactors divided by the determinant:

$$(\mathbf{I} - \mathbf{SH})^{-1} = \frac{1}{0.230} \begin{bmatrix} 0.772 & 0.549 & 0.527 \\ 0.179 & 0.402 & 0.218 \\ 0.192 & 0.184 & 0.397 \end{bmatrix} = \begin{bmatrix} 3.356 & 2.387 & 2.291 \\ 0.778 & 1.748 & 0.948 \\ 0.835 & 0.800 & 1.726 \end{bmatrix}$$

The distribution of service jobs is now obtained through formula (3.52) respecting the order of multiplication:

$$\mathbf{E}^s = (\mathbf{I} - \mathbf{SH})^{-1}\mathbf{SHE}^p$$

$$= \underbrace{\begin{bmatrix} 3.356 & 2.387 & 2.291 \\ 0.778 & 1.748 & 0.948 \\ 0.835 & 0.800 & 1.726 \end{bmatrix}}_{(\mathbf{I} - \mathbf{SH})^{-1}} \underbrace{\begin{bmatrix} 0.480 & 0.528 & 0.400 \\ 0.128 & 0.106 & 0.320 \\ 0.192 & 0.158 & 0.080 \end{bmatrix}}_{\mathbf{SH}} \underbrace{\begin{bmatrix} 200 \\ 100 \\ 250 \end{bmatrix}}_{\mathbf{E}^p}$$

$$= \begin{bmatrix} 2.356 & 2.387 & 2.289 \\ 0.779 & 0.746 & 0.946 \\ 0.835 & 0.798 & 0.728 \end{bmatrix} \begin{bmatrix} 200 \\ 100 \\ 250 \end{bmatrix} = \begin{bmatrix} 1282 \\ 467 \\ 429 \end{bmatrix}$$

Next we obtain the distribution of residential population $\mathbf{P}$ through formula (3.51):

$$\mathbf{P} = \mathbf{H}(\mathbf{I} - \mathbf{SH})^{-1}\mathbf{E}^p$$

$$= \underbrace{\begin{bmatrix} 0.800 & 1.320 & 0 \\ 1.600 & 1.320 & 0 \\ 1.600 & 1.320 & 4 \end{bmatrix}}_{\mathbf{H}} \underbrace{\begin{bmatrix} 3.356 & 2.387 & 2.291 \\ 0.778 & 1.748 & 0.948 \\ 0.835 & 0.800 & 1.726 \end{bmatrix}}_{(\mathbf{I} - \mathbf{SH})^{-1}} \underbrace{\begin{bmatrix} 200 \\ 100 \\ 250 \end{bmatrix}}_{\mathbf{E}^p}$$

$$= \begin{bmatrix} 3.711 & 7.929 & 3.084 \\ 6.397 & 6.127 & 4.917 \\ 9.737 & 9.327 & 11.821 \end{bmatrix} \begin{bmatrix} 200 \\ 100 \\ 250 \end{bmatrix} = \begin{bmatrix} 2306 \\ 3121 \\ 5835 \end{bmatrix}$$

Finally, the distribution of total employment can be obtained as

$$\mathbf{E} = \mathbf{E}^s + \mathbf{E}^p$$

$$= \begin{bmatrix} 1282 \\ 467 \\ 429 \end{bmatrix} + \begin{bmatrix} 200 \\ 100 \\ 250 \end{bmatrix} = \begin{bmatrix} 1482 \\ 567 \\ 679 \end{bmatrix}$$

$$\quad\; \mathbf{E}^s \qquad \mathbf{E}^p \qquad \mathbf{E}$$

An equivalent way is to use formula (3.53),

$$\mathbf{E} = (\mathbf{I} - \mathbf{SH})^{-1}\mathbf{E}^p$$

$$= \begin{bmatrix} 3.356 & 2.387 & 2.291 \\ 0.778 & 1.748 & 0.948 \\ 0.835 & 0.800 & 1.726 \end{bmatrix} \begin{bmatrix} 200 \\ 100 \\ 250 \end{bmatrix} = \begin{bmatrix} 1482 \\ 567 \\ 679 \end{bmatrix}$$

$$\qquad\qquad (\mathbf{I} - \mathbf{SH})^{-1} \qquad\;\; \mathbf{E}^p$$

In summary, the effect of bringing 200, 100, and 250 jobs, respectively, to the three regions would be to increase their population levels by 2306, 3121, and 5835, respectively, and to create 1282, 467, and 429 additional jobs, respectively, in the service sector.

The preceding type of analysis can be used to evaluate the impact of alternative regional development plans resulting in changes in the work-force ratios, in the service jobs equivalents, in the commuting-to-work pattern, or in the shopping travel pattern. Suppose, for instance, that one alternative plan involves, in addition to the industrial development represented by the basic jobs above, the development of a commercial center in region 2. It is projected from market analysis studies that the new commercial center would increase the percentage of shoppers from all three regions to region 2 by 10% from the previous levels. This results in a modification of the shopping travel pattern matrix **B**, and thus of matrix **S**. Therefore, the distribution of service jobs and consequently of the residential population will be changed. The new levels can be evaluated in the same fashion as above, after merely changing the value of the entries in the shopping travel pattern matrix **B**. (See Exercise 3.13.)

Similarly, suppose that another, separate alternative involves the development of a residential complex in region 1. In the same fashion, the commuting to work pattern will be changed to reflect the modifications in the choice of place of residence by the workers and their families. This will, in turn, change the levels of shopping and services travel and the requirements for service jobs. These respective changes can be evaluated using the foregoing procedure, after changing the entries in the commuting pattern matrix **A** and thus in **H**. (See Exercise 3.12.)

A very useful feature of the preceding model is its additive property.

Because of the fact that the model is *linear* (i.e., the various levels of population, total employment, and service jobs are all linear f mctions of the levels of production employment), the effects of changes in any number of parameters can be obtained as the sum of the effects of the individual changes. For instance, the effect of yet another alternative plan involving the development of a new commercial center *and* a new residential complex would simply be the sum of the effects of these two changes as considered separately above.

Also, the linear character of the model allows one to evaluate the effect of *marginal* (or incremental) changes by using the same formulas as for changes in the absolute level. For instance, assume that for purposes of analysis, we wanted to evaluate the effect of bringing in 50, 80, and 40 extra basic jobs in the three regions, respectively. Instead of repeating the whole analysis by using levels of basic employment of 200 + 50, 100 + 80, and 250 + 40, respectively, we can evaluate in the same fashion as above the individual effects of 50, 80, and 40 basic sector jobs, and then add those to the effects of the 200, 100, and 250 basic jobs already evaluated.

Finally, the same linear feature of the model allows us to *dissagregate* the effects of changes in any number of regions. For instance, if we wanted to single out the effect of the extra 50 jobs in the first region, we would perform the analysis with a distribution of basic jobs of 50, 0, and 0 respectively, using the same procedure.

Thus, this model of economic base analysis, in spite of its basic simplicity, offers a high degree of flexibility in the analysis of the consequences of various modifications of a given multiregional economic and residential structure.

3.8 Dynamic Models

The preceding models are *static*, in that they describe the levels of economic activity and employment at a given, single point in time. However, these levels are also ultimately dependent on the population levels, and vice versa. On the other hand, the models of population level projection, which we have seen in Chapter 2, were *dynamic*, i.e., contained the element of time. Thus, in order to utilize them in connection with economic analysis and employment projections, we have to make the models in this chapter *time-dependent*. This is the object of this section.

Let us first describe a model of employment level projection. Let us assume that we have a set of regions i, each of which having a set of industrial sectors j. The corresponding employment levels at time 0: E_{ij}^0 are as represented in Figure 3.4. The total employment in sector j in all regions is then

$$\sum_i E^0_{ij} = E^0_{\cdot j}$$

At the beginning of the next time period the employment level in sector j in area i is now E^1_{ij}. This corresponds to an individual growth rate a_{ij} for sector j in region i.

$$a_{ij} = \frac{E^1_{ij} - E^0_{ij}}{E^0_{ij}} \tag{3.54}$$

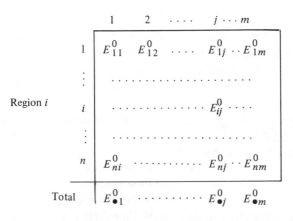

Industrial Sector j

Figure 3.4   Regional distribution of employment at time 0.

In the same fashion, the *overall* rate of growth in all regions for this sector is

$$a_{\cdot j} = \frac{E^1_{\cdot j} - E^0_{\cdot j}}{E^0_{\cdot j}} \tag{3.55}$$

We next compute the rate of growth that would have been observed if sector j had grown in region i at the same rate as the overall regional rate $a_{\cdot j}$ computed in (3.55). The expected employment level, which we can call $\tilde{E}^1_{ij}$ to distinguish it from the actual level E^1_{ij}, would then be

$$\tilde{E}^1_{ij} = \sum_j a_{\cdot j} E^0_{ij} \tag{3.56}$$

which simply represents the sum for all sectors j of the regional base employment E_{ij} multiplied by the global sectorial growth rate $a_{\cdot j}$. The rationale of the model is to attribute the difference between this expected employment level $\tilde{E}^1_{ij}$ and the actual, observable (or predicted) level E^1_{ij}, i.e., $(\tilde{E}^1_{ij} - E^1_{ij})$, to three *components of change*: first, the change in total employment in the region; then the distribution of industrial sectors in the regions; and finally, the relative shares of each region in the production of the sectors. To reflect this approach, we manipulate the expression of this difference by adding the term

$$\left(\sum_j a_{ij} E_{ij}^0 - \sum_j a_{ij} E_{ij}^0 \right)$$

which is of course null, in the following manner:

$$(E_{ij}^1 - \tilde{E}_{ij}^1) = E_{ij}^1 - \sum_j a_{.j} E_{ij}^0$$

$$= E_{ij}^1 - \left(\sum_j a_{ij} E_{ij}^0 - \sum_j a_{ij} E_{ij}^0 \right) - \sum_j a_{.j} E_{ij}^0$$

$$= \left(E_{ij}^1 - \sum_j a_{ij} E_{ij}^0 \right) + \left(\sum_j a_{ij} E_{ij}^0 - \sum_j a_{.j} E_{ij}^0 \right)$$

$$= \left(E_{ij}^1 - \sum_j a_{ij} E_{ij}^0 \right) + \sum_j (a_{ij} - a_{.j}) E_{ij}^0$$

The difference between the actual level of employment and the expected level of employment (in the sense above) is now written as the sum of two terms. The first term represents the difference between the new employment level and the sum $\sum_j a_{ij} E_{ij}^0$, which is the sum of the base employment levels weighed by the rate of growth of the various industrial sectors in region i. This first term can thus be interpreted to reflect the change or *shift* in importance of industrial sector j in region i, over the time period. The second term represents a sum of the base employment levels, weighed by the differences between the sectorial growth rate and the overall growth rate of the sector in all regions. Thus, the second term can be considered to represent the increase (or decrease) in employment due to the relative competitivity of the region with respect to the other regions, that is, the relative mix of industrial sectors across regions. The first term is for that reason sometimes called the "shift" component of employment change, and the second term the "share" component, giving the name "shift and share" to the model.

Both terms can be either positive or negative. If the second term is positive, this means that industrial sector j in area i has grown over the time period at a faster rate than the overall regional rate. If this first term is negative, it means that the sector's relative share of the market in the region has decreased. Of course, if both terms are negative, the employment level will go down, and conversely, if both are positive, it will go up. Their relative influence will determine the direction of change when one is positive and the other negative.

It is important to note that the first term cannot be directly evaluated (as the second term can) from given estimations of projections of the growth rates a_{ij} and $a_{.j}$ since it already contains the new employment levels. In order to break this tautological impasse (the chicken-or-the-egg syndrome, in other words), this first term is in practical applications inferred from projections of the population level in the regions, possibly using the techniques of *statistical regression* (see Chapter 7).

Let us now use this model of employment level changes to transform the models in the preceding sections into dynamic models. We thus assume that we can derive for the production sector an *employment migration matrix G* of the form

$$G = \begin{bmatrix} g_{11} & g_{12} & \cdots & g_{1j} & \cdots & g_{1n} \\ g_{21} & g_{22} & & \cdots & & g_{2n} \\ \cdots\cdots\cdots\cdots\cdots\cdots\cdots\cdots \\ g_{i1} & & \cdots & g_{ij} & \cdots & g_{in} \\ \cdots\cdots\cdots\cdots\cdots\cdots\cdots\cdots \\ g_{n1} & & & \cdots & & g_{nn} \end{bmatrix}$$

where g_{ij} is the proportion of jobs in the production sector that were previously located in region j and have, over the time period of transition, moved or relocated in region i. The terms g_{ii} in the main diagonal are the net rates of change, i.e., taking into account the influx from, or loss of jobs to, the outside. Such a matrix might for instance be inferred from the results of a multiregional population projection, using the methods of Chapter 2. Therefore, the new employment levels in the production sector in the various regions at the beginning of the next time period are given by

$$\begin{bmatrix} E_1^p \\ E_2^p \\ \cdot \\ E_i^p \\ \cdot \\ E_n^p \end{bmatrix}_1 = \begin{bmatrix} g_{11} & \cdots & g_{1n} \\ g_{21} & \cdots & g_{2n} \\ \cdots\cdots\cdots\cdots \\ \cdots & g_{ij} & \cdots \\ \cdots\cdots\cdots\cdots \\ g_{n1} & \cdots & g_{nn} \end{bmatrix} \begin{bmatrix} E_1^p \\ E_2^p \\ \cdot \\ E_i^p \\ \cdot \\ E_n^p \end{bmatrix}_0$$

or

$$\mathbf{E}_1^p = \mathbf{G}\,\mathbf{E}_0^p \tag{3.57}$$

The same concept would apply if the regional activity levels were not represented by the employments E_i^p but by the levels of basic production X_i, for instance:

$$\mathbf{X}_1 = \mathbf{G}\mathbf{X}_0 \tag{3.58}$$

Going back now to the basic input/output equation (3.26): $\mathbf{Y}_1 = (\mathbf{I} - \mathbf{A})^{-1}\mathbf{X}_1$ at time 1 and replacing $\mathbf{X}_1$ by its expression in terms of $\mathbf{X}_0$ as given by formula (3.58), we get for the output at the beginning of the next time period $\mathbf{Y}_1$,

$$\mathbf{Y}_1 = (\mathbf{I} - \mathbf{A})^{-1}\mathbf{X}_1 = (\mathbf{I} - \mathbf{A})^{-1}\mathbf{G}\mathbf{X}_0$$

similarly, at time n, i.e., after n time periods:

$$\mathbf{Y}_n = (\mathbf{I} - \mathbf{A})^{-1}\mathbf{X}_n = (\mathbf{I} - \mathbf{A})^{-1}\mathbf{G}\mathbf{X}_{n-1} = (\mathbf{I} - \mathbf{A})^{-1}\mathbf{G}(\mathbf{G}\mathbf{X}_{n-2})$$
$$= \ldots = (\mathbf{I} - \mathbf{A})^{-1}\mathbf{G}\mathbf{G}\mathbf{G}\ldots\mathbf{G}\mathbf{X}_0$$

or

$$\mathbf{Y}_n = (\mathbf{I} - \mathbf{A})^{-1}\mathbf{G}^n\mathbf{X}_0 \tag{3.59}$$

Equation (3.59) expresses the total levels of regional outputs at time n as functions of the given levels of basic production (or external demand) at time 0: $\mathbf{X}_0$ and of the entries in the nth power $\mathbf{G}^n$ of the transition matrix $\mathbf{G}$.

If this transition matrix $\mathbf{G}$ is not constant, i.e., if the pattern of activity relocation is not stable throughout the n time periods but is equal to $\mathbf{G}_0$ from time 0 to time 1, G_1 from time 1 to time 2, and in general G_{n-1} from time $n - 1$ to n, then formula (3.59) is easily transformed into

$$Y_n = (I - A)^{-1} G_n G_{n-1} \ldots G_1 X_0 \qquad (3.60)$$

Similarly, if the structural matrix $(I - A)^{-1}$ is not stable because the production matrix A changes (e.g., because of technological improvements), and is forecasted to be equal to A_n at time n, formula (3.59) becomes

$$Y_n = (I - A_n)^{-1} G^n X_0 \qquad (3.61)$$

Finally, the combination of changes in both the activity relocation matrix G and the production matrix A would result in

$$Y_n = (I - A_n)^{-1} G_n G_{n-1} \ldots G_1 Y_0 \qquad (3.62)$$

The paragraphs above should not be viewed as mindless exercises in mathematical manipulation. On the contrary, they illustrate the power of the models in their matrix algebra form to incorporate various assumed (or anticipated) conditions. Thus, formulas (3.59) through (3.62), which are barely more complex than their static equivalent (3.26), are operated in the same simple fashion but are much more general and flexible for analytical purposes. In particular, they enable us to study the effects of various patterns of multiregional population changes, as estimated through the multiregional cohort survival model in Chapter 2 and reflected in the matrix G, on the regional activity distributions.

Let us finally briefly expand along the same lines the formulation of the job multiplier model as represented by formulas (3.51) through (3.53). We can write that the distribution of total population levels at time n will be given by the same mechanism as at time 0:

$$P_n = H(I - SH)^{-1} E_n^p \qquad (3.63)$$

However, we also have that the distribution of production jobs is after n time periods equal to

$$E_n^p = G^n E_0^p \qquad (3.64)$$

Combining these last two equations, we get

$$P_n = H(I - SH)^{-1} G^n E_0^p \qquad (3.65)$$

By the same argument, we also have

$$E_n^s = (I - SH)^{-1} SHG^n E_0^p \qquad (3.66)$$

and

$$E_n = (I - SH)^{-1} G^n E_0^p \qquad (3.67)$$

Thus, again, formulas (3.65) through (3.67) are exactly similar to their static counterparts, and are applied in the same fashion, the only difference being that the nth power of the activity relocation matrix **G** is now inserted (at the right place).

The same type of modification as above, allowing for a changing transition matrix **G**, or changing patterns of commuting to work **H**, or commuting to shop **S**, can readily be effected and will not be repeated here.

In any case, we are now in a position to utilize the relationships between the population levels and the economic activity and employment levels. For instance, the entries in matrix **G** can be inferred or deduced from the changing patterns of residential population distribution in the set of regions, as projected using the multiregional methods of Sections 2.7 to 2.10. In turn, the results of economic and employment projections using the various methods in this chapter can be incorporated, through the migration rates, in the population projection models. This feedback relationship between these two components of urban and regional systems will thus lead to consistent estimates of both, and mutually reinforce the accuracy of their individual projections.

EXERCISES

3.1 Given the following input/output data:

OUTPUT INPUT	Sector A	B	C	External Demand	Total Output
Sector A	20	25	80	50	175
B		25	120	105	250
C			100	300	400
External Supply	155	200	100		
Total Input	175	250	400		825

(a) Evaluate the matrix **A** of production coefficients.

(b) If the external demand (basic production) is now

$$\mathbf{X} = \begin{bmatrix} 100 \\ 120 \\ 40 \end{bmatrix}$$

what is the necessary level of total production **Y**? (Use the method of matrix inversion.)

(c) If the level of total output is set to be

$$Y = \begin{bmatrix} 150 \\ 200 \\ 150 \end{bmatrix}$$

what is the available output for export **X**, and what are the respective required external inputs into the three sectors?

3.2 Do Exercise 3.1(b) using the method of successive iterations.

3.3 Do Exercise 3.1(b) using the method of resolution of simultaneous equations.

3.4 Using the following intersectorial table, write the three-sector table for sectors *A*, *B*, and (*C* + *D*), corresponding to a merger of sectors *C* and *D*.

Output / Input		*A*	*B*	*C*	*D*	*External Demand*	*Total Output*
	A	20	25	25	80	50	200
Sector	*B*		25		120	105	250
	C		25	45	40	40	150
	D				100	300	400
Value Added		180	175	80	60		
Total Input		200	250	150	400	495	1000

3.5 Using the table constructed in Exercise 3.4, answer the following questions:

(a) Obtain the structural matrix **A** of intersectorial coefficients.

(b) What is the total output **Y** necessary to sustain an external demand of

$$X = \begin{bmatrix} 100 \\ 120 \\ 40 \end{bmatrix} ?$$

(c) If total output **Y** is $\begin{bmatrix} 150 \\ 200 \\ 150 \end{bmatrix}$, what are the levels of feasible exports from the three sectors?

(d) What would then be the required external inputs into the sectors?

3.6 Given the following interregional flows:

		Purchasing Region			
		A	*B*	*Export*	*Total Output*
Producing	*A*	100	200	100	400
Region	*B*	200	100	100	400
Import		100	100		
Total Input		400	400		

(a) What would be the required level of total production of region A so that it could now export 150 units of production? (Assume no change in the production of B.)

(b) Rework the solution by the method of successive iterations.

(c) What fraction of $1 of total production of region A and region B is exportable?

(d) What is the effect on the total level of production of regions A and B of the export of $1 of commodity from A?

(e) Verbalize the meaning of the entries in the matrices $\mathbf{A}$ and $(\mathbf{I} - \mathbf{A})^{-1}$.

3.7 Using the method of successive iterations, evaluate the total population in an area where $E_b = 10,000$, $\gamma = P/E_s = 1.6$, and $\beta = E_s/P = 0.3$. (Check with the results obtained in Section 3.4.)

3.8 Derive the alternative formula for the final distribution of residential population in the multiregional case:

$$\mathbf{P} = (\mathbf{I} - \mathbf{HS})^{-1}\mathbf{HE}^p$$

3.9 Similarly, derive the alternative formula for the final distribution of total service jobs:

$$\mathbf{E} = \mathbf{S}(\mathbf{I} - \mathbf{HS})^{-1}\mathbf{HE}^p$$

3.10 Derive formulas (3.51) to (3.53) for $\mathbf{E}^s$, $\mathbf{E}^p$, and $\mathbf{P}$ by solving the three equations in three unknowns which describe the relationships between these vectors.

3.11 Using the data in the illustrative multiregional example of Section 3.5, evaluate the effects of a change in the work-force ratio in the second region from 0.25 to 0.35.

3.12 Similarly, evaluate the effects of a change in the pattern of commuting to work resulting from half of the workers of the third region now living in the third region and the rest equally in the other two regions.

3.13 Also, evaluate the effects of a change in the shopping pattern caused by the residents of the first area now shopping among all three areas with equal frequencies.

3.14 Evaluate the effects of all three changes above (Exercises 3.11 to 3.13) taking place simultaneously.

3.15 Derive (from Figure 3.3) the formula

$$\mathbf{E} = \mathbf{H}^{-1}(\mathbf{I} - \mathbf{HS})^{-1}\mathbf{HE}^p$$

obtained in Exercise 3.10.

3.16 Derive the expressions for P, E, and E_s in the single-region case directly from the solution of the equations representing the relationships between them. (*Hint:* Follow the procedure in the solution of Exercise 3.10.)

REFERENCES

BENDAVID, A. *Regional Economic Analysis for Practitioners.* New York: Praeger Publishers, Inc., 1974.

CZAMANSKI, S. *Methods of Regional Science.* Lexington, Mass.: D. C. Heath & Company, 1975.

HOOVER, E. M. *An Introduction to Regional Economics.* New York: Alfred A. Knopf, Inc., 1971.

LEONTIEF, W. *Input–Output Analysis.* New York: Oxford University Press, 1969.

LEVEN, C., et al. *An Analytical Framework for Regional Development Policy.* Cambridge, Mass.: The MIT Press, 1970.

RICHARSON, H. *Input–Output of Regional Economics.* London: George Weidenfeld & Nicolson Ltd., 1972.

4

Models of Land Use
and Travel Demand

4.1 Introduction

In the preceding chapters, we first learned how to project the evolution of the composition and level of populations on the basis of the knowledge of their internal characteristics (birth and death rates), and of the external factors of change (as represented by the migration rates). We next learned how to forecast the effect on the employment (and therefore indirectly on the migration) of changes in the levels of economic activity. These changes may themselves, in turn, be related to changes in the population and its demands for goods and services.

The fact that changes in population level and/or changes in level of economic activity at a given location may be influenced by concurrent changes at other locations was taken into account by the development of the multiregional versions of the population and economic analysis models. Specifically, in the multiregional cohort survival model of population projection, the interregional migration rates in formula (2.37) which measure the proportion of people who have left a given area to go live in another thus represent the relationship between the residential activity levels in two different places or spaces. Thus, in this sense these coefficients represent the level of interaction between the various regions, in a spatial sense, with respect to the activity of migrating, or choice of an area of residence.

Similarly, the interregional input/output coefficients in formula (3.33) reflect the level of spatial interaction in economic activity, since they represent the proportions of goods, or resources, leaving a given physical space to reach another for the purpose of economic production. Finally, in the multiregional employment multiplier model, the coefficients a_{ij} in formula (3.45) measure the level of spatial interaction between areas i and j, with respect to the choice of a place of residence (or of a place of work). The coefficients c_{ij}, in the same model, in formula (3.49) represent the levels of spatial interaction between spaces i and j with respect to the activity of shopping.

Thus far, we have assumed that these measures of spatial interaction were given, or could be determined from observations, i.e., using empirical measurements obtained, for instance, through survey research. However, the application of these models to forecast future conditions requires that we be able to predict the values of these coefficients at a future date. It is logical to assume that they depend not only on the locational characteristics of the activities (e.g., the relative levels of population, or production at various locations), but also on the characteristics of the communication system connecting these locations (principally, the transportation system). Consequently, we cannot in general assume that these coefficients are going to remain at their present values, or even extrapolate them if these characteristics are going to change. This might happen either because of natural evolution (population, for example), or because of planned change (transportation system), or even because of unforeseen changes (demands for production).

In this chapter, we shall see several examples of simple models that translate theories about the mechanics of spatial interaction which will enable us to forecast such spatial interaction, given the levels of their determinants. In a sense, all spatial interaction ultimately is reflected in some *travel*, or movement activity (or more generally *communication* activity), of one sort or another. For instance, matrix **A** in (3.45), which represented the choice of residence, is equivalent to the travel pattern of commuting to work from home (or commuting home from work). Similarly, matrix **C** in (3.49), which represented the choice of a shopping district is equivalent to a shopping travel pattern. Finally, the matrix $\mathcal{C}_{kl}$ in formula (3.33) can be taken to represent the regional pattern of goods movements between regions k and l.

Consequently, the models we are going to see in this chapter can be considered either models of *land use* or of *travel demand* or in some cases both. This is consistent with the physical fact that land use determines travel demand, which determines the characteristics of the transportation system, which in turn influences the evolution of land use, etc. We shall therefore begin with two general models of spatial interaction, the *gravity model* first and then the *intervening opportunities model*, and some of their variants. We shall next survey briefly some of the specific models of travel demand.

4.2 The Theory of the Gravity Model

The first theory of spatial interaction we shall examine is the *gravity theory*. Its name comes from its historical origin as an application of Newton's fundamental law of gravity in physics. This law, which governs the movements of bodies in space, was in the field of social science first applied to the description of the movements of people between areas. It has subsequently been shown to replicate adequately various other kind of spatial phenomena. Concurrently with its empirical validation, theoretical demonstrations from a variety of points of view and assumptions have given it a logical justification which makes it one of the most widely used and important spatial models.

Let us now review briefly the basic concept behind the law of gravity. Newton's law states that the force of attraction, or pull F, between two bodies of respective masses M_1 and M_2, separated by a distance d, will be equal to

$$F = \frac{gM_1M_2}{d^2} = gM_1M_2d^{-2} \qquad (4.1)$$

where g is a constant, or scaling factor which ensures that equation (4.1) is balanced out, i.e., that it indeed represents an equality between the measurements of entities of a completely different nature.

The verbal translation of the law of gravity is thus that the amount of interaction exerted by two physical bodies on each other is proportional to their respective masses, but also inversely proportional to the square of the distance between them. In other words, as the mass of either of the bodies grows, the interaction between them will grow linearly. However, as the distance between them grows, the interaction will decrease parabolically.

In imitation of this gravity law of physics, the gravity concept of spatial interaction states in its simple form that the interaction between two areas, numbered i and j (e.g., the number of people living in area j who work in area i, or the amount of economic output of area j which is consumed in area i, etc.) will be directly proportional to the "masses" of these areas (their size, or population level, or level of expenditures, etc.) but will be inversely proportional to some function of the "distance" between them (travel time, or cost of travel, etc.). Thus, the amount of interaction between the two areas will increase (all other things remaining equal), as the "importance" P_i of the first area increases, and also as that P_j of the second area increases, but will decrease as the "separation" between them, d_{ij}, increases.

In its general mathematical form, therefore, this theory can be stated as: I_{ij}, the amount of interaction between areas, or spaces i and j, is equal to

$$\boxed{I_{ij} = k_i l_j O_j D_i F(d_{ij})} \qquad (4.2)$$

where k_i is a *scaling factor* related to area i, l_j another scaling factor related to area j, so that the product $k_i l_j$ plays the role of the factor g in formula

(4.1). O_j is a measure of the capacity for *interaction producing* of area j, and O_j is a measure of the capacity for *interaction receiving* of area i. Finally, d_{ij} is a measure of the *separation*, or difficulty of interaction between space i and space j, and $F(d_{ij})$ is a mathematical function that can take on various forms, to be specified, which represents the *interaction impedance*.

Several points should be noted in connection with this general model. First, it is important to note that the interaction between areas i and j is *not* a symmetrical concept, i.e., that the action of area j on area i is not in general equal to that of i on j. Thus, the order of the subscripts i and j in formula (4.2) is important, and we shall refer to I_{ij} above as the interaction of area j on area i, or equivalently as the amount of interaction *from j to i* (or by j on i). (This convention for the role of the order of the indices i and j has been adhered to previously in this text, in particular in the multiregional economic base model.)

Also, the measures or scores O_j and D_i can themselves be functions of (i.e., derived from) the values of selected characteristics of the zones i and j. For instance:

$$D_i = a_1 X_{i1} + a_2 X_{i2} + \ldots + a_m X_{im} \tag{4.3}$$

or

$$D_i = X_{i1}^{d_1} X_{i2}^{d_2} \ldots X_{im}^{d_m} \tag{4.4}$$

are two forms of simple functions (*linear* and *power*, respectively) which can be used, where the X_{ij}'s are characteristics of zone i, such as their average income, employment ratios, number of car registrations, etc. The same (or other functions) of the same (or other) characteristics of zone j may (or may not) be applied to the definition of O_j. By replacing D_i and/or O_j by their expressions (4.3) or (4.4), etc., in the model (4.2), the resulting spatial interaction model is of a very general form.

The nature of the factors k_i and l_j should be distinguished from that of the variables O_j and D_i. The latter are given, i.e., are *observable* quantities, which are usually obtained through empirical surveys. In modeling language, they are *exogeneously* determined, and are used as inputs to the model. The latter are endogeneously determined from the internal requirements of the model, usually that the interactions "balance out" according to specified conditions. [In fact, the two versions of the gravity model that we shall examine later in this section represent the outcome of two such sets of conditions applied to the general form (4.2)].

Finally, the functional form of the interaction impedance function $F(d_{ij})$ can be varied as well. Some functions commonly used are

$$F(d_{ij}) = d_{ij}^{-\gamma} \tag{4.5}$$

$$F(d_{ij}) = e^{-\beta d_{ij}} \tag{4.6}$$

$$F(d_{ij}) = d_{ij}^{\alpha} e^{-\beta d_{ij}} \tag{4.7}$$

Each of these forms represents the translation of further hypotheses about the law of interaction between space i and space j. Each of these hypotheses can be given a *behavioristic* basis. For instance, form (4.5), which represents a generalization of the original gravity hypothesis, is the result of the assumption that (all other things being equal) residents in zone j will tend to select a zone i for the location of the activity in geometrically decreasing proportion to the amount of effort involved in reaching i from j, i.e., according to a form of the principle of "least effort." On the other hand, form (4.6) can be derived from the assumption that the distribution of activities is the "most probable," consistent with a given total amount of travel effort between all zones. Finally, form (4.7) can be interpreted to reflect both conflicting desires to choose an activity zone that is away from the zone of residence j (the term $e^{-\beta d_{ij}}$), but at the same time not too far to involve a large travel effort (the term d_{ij}^{α}).

The practical determination of the specific form of the function to use, as well as of the values of the parameters, is effected empirically, using observational data pertaining to a specific situation. This process of *fitting*, or adjusting, the model is conducted through the application of the methods of *model calibration*, which we shall survey in Chapter 6. In any case, this state in the specification of the model should not be confused with the determination of the values of the scaling factors k_i and/or l_j. These factors are not parameters whose values can be changed to make the fit between the output of the model and the observed values as good as is possible, as are the a_i's in (4.3), or α, β, and γ in (4.5), (4.6), or (4.7). On the contrary, they represent structural factors, which can be computed once the logical requirements for the consistency of the model are specified.

4.3 First Application: The Single-Constraint Form

Since the single-constraint form discussed above surely must sound somewhat abstract, we shall proceed with the application of these concepts to the solution of a practical problem which is related to the residential and commercial location models (3.45) and (3.49) that were used in the multiregional employment multiplier model of Section 3.7. This will illustrate the single-constraint," or "one-way," form of the gravity model.

It may be recalled that at that time, we distributed the various numbers of workers E_j working in n zones $j = 1$ to n according to a "work to home" commuting pattern, represented by a matrix $\mathbf{A}$, where the entry a_{ij} measures the proportion of workers living in zone j who live in zone i. These entries were assumed to be given, for the purpose of the model. However, they are clearly related to a spatial interaction between zones j and zone i, in the sense we have discussed above. The gravity model might then be the solution to the problem mentioned above of finding a formal expression for matrix $\mathbf{A}$ that may be used to forecast its values when, and if, the present conditions change.

Indeed, since the gravity model has been shown to adequately describe a large variety of forms of spatial interaction under a wide range of conditions, we might make the assumption that it also governs the commuting pattern between places or work and places of residence in our case.

Let us therefore assume that the spatial interaction represented by the commuting of workers in the area from their places of work to their places of residence follows a gravity-type law. Then, we would expect the number of workers W_{ij} who work in area j and live in area i to be of the form (4.2). That is,

$$W_{ij} = k_i l_j O_j D_i F(d_{ij}) \qquad (4.8)$$

where O_j is some measure, to be specified, of the capacity of area of work j to "produce" such workers, D_i is some measure of the capacity of area i to "receive" them, and d_{ij} is some measure of the difficulty to reach area i from area j. Finally, we will also have to decide on a specific form for the function $F(d_{ij})$.

It seems reasonable, in the absence of prior experiments or of any particular insight, to adopt as a measure O_j, simply the number of workers in the area, i.e, E_j in the notation of Section 3.7. This is about the simplest choice we can make for that measure, and it is logical to at least begin with it. (Of course, later, if it turns out to prevent adequate validation of the reproduced or predicted commuting pattern against the real-world observed pattern, this particular choice can always be modified.) Similarly, since we already utilize the existing residential population levels P_i in the various areas i, we shall choose that characteristic as representing the measure D_i. This means, then, that we are assuming that the residential attractiveness of the zones i is proportional to their population levels, or in other words, that the more people already live in a zone, the more will be attracted to choose it as a place of residence. Although there are undoubtedly other possible hypotheses about the determinants of the capability of area i as a place of residence to attract the workers, this is again one of the simplest we can make at this point, and also one which offers the advantage that we already have the values of the P_i's.

Next, we shall choose a measure of the difficulty d_{ij} of commuting between zones j and i. A simple, logical choice here is to take the physical distance. This measure should itself be closely related to other possible measures such as travel time or cost of travel, and is also fairly simple to evaluate. Finally, let us choose for the function $F(d_{ij})$ the simplest expression we can, i.e., form (4.5) with a parameter $\gamma = 1$. In other words, we are making the assumption that the difficulty of reaching area i from area j is inversely proportional to the distance between them.

The structure of our model for the number of commuters W_{ij} from area of work j to area of residence i is now completely specified as

$$W_{ij} = k_i l_j E_j P_i d_{ij}^{-1} \qquad (4.9)$$

Since we have the values for all the variables E_j, P_i, and d_{ij}, the last step before the model can be operational is the determination of the values of the factors k_i and l_j. These, as was observed above, do not come from empirical data but will be such that they ensure that the formulation (4.9) is consistent with the specific *constraints* we have to observe. In this case, the only such constraint is the fact that the number of workers who commute from a given area of work j and all the areas of residence must be equal to the given number of jobs in that area, i.e., E_j. This set of constraints (one for each area of work j) concerns the areas of work, i.e., production of interaction, and thus the factors l_j only. Since there are no comparable constraints for the attraction of interaction (i.e., conditions relating to the areas of residence i), the factors k_i can be dismissed, and the model (4.9) simplified as

$$W_{ij} = l_j E_j P_i d_{ij}^{-1} \qquad (4.10)$$

This *one-way-distribution model* is sometimes called the *production-constrained version* of the gravity model. Symmetrically, if the constraints concern the receiving areas i, but not the producing areas j (e.g., because of restrictions on the numbers of housing units available in each area i) the corresponding symmetrical model would be called *attraction-constrained*. (See Exercise 4.1.) In any case, for the first area of work, the constraint can be formulated as

$$W_{11} + W_{21} + W_{31} + \ldots + W_{i1} + \ldots + W_{n1} = \sum_{i=1}^{n} W_{i1} = E_1$$

Similarly, for area of work 2,

$$W_{12} + W_{22} + W_{32} + \ldots + W_{i2} + \ldots + W_{n2} = \sum_{i=1}^{n} W_{i2} = E_2$$

and, in general for area of work j,

$$W_{1j} + W_{2j} + W_{3j} + \ldots + W_{ij} + \ldots + W_{nj} = \sum_{i=1}^{n} W_{ij} = E_j \qquad (4.11)$$

Replacing the W_{i1}'s in the first equation by their expression in (4.10), we get

$$l_1 E_1 P_1 d_{11}^{-1} + l_1 E_1 P_2 d_{21}^{-1} + \ldots + l_1 E_1 P_i d_{i1}^{-1} + \ldots + l_1 E_1 P_n d_{n1}^{-1} = E_1$$

and by, factoring the constant terms $l_1 E_1$ in the sum,

$$l_1 E_1 (P_1 d_{11}^{-1} + P_2 d_{21}^{-1} + \ldots + P_i d_{i1}^{-1} + \ldots + P_n d_{n1}^{-1}) = l_1 E_1 \sum_{i=1}^{n} P_i d_{i1}^{-1} = E_1$$

All values are known in this equation but that of l_1. It can thus be used to determine it by solving for the unknown. We thus get

$$l_1 = \frac{1}{\sum\limits_{i=1}^{n} P_i d_{i1}^{-1}}$$

In the same fashion, for the general area of work j, we must have

$$l_j E_j P_1 d_{1j}^{-1} + l_j E_j P_2 d_{2j}^{-1} + \ldots + l_j E_j P_i d_{ij}^{-1} + \ldots + l_j E_j P_n d_{nj}^{-1}$$

$$= l_j E_j \sum_{i=1}^{n} P_i d_{ij}^{-1} = E_j$$

and therefore,

$$l_j = \frac{1}{\sum\limits_{i=1}^{n} P_i d_{ij}^{-1}} \tag{4.12}$$

and of course for the last area,

$$l_n = \frac{1}{\sum\limits_{i=1}^{n} P_i d_{in}^{-1}}$$

We have now evaluated the values for all the unknown factors l_j through the set of equations (4.12). (one for each value of j). The number of workers who work in area j and live in area i can now be computed, since there are no remaining unknowns in the model (4.10). Indeed, by replacing l_j in model (4.10) by its general expression as given by (4.12), we have

$$W_{ij} = \left[\frac{1}{\sum\limits_{i=1}^{n} P_i d_{ij}^{-1}} \right] E_j P_i d_{ij}^{-1} \tag{4.13}$$

or, finally,

$$\boxed{W_{ij} = E_j \left[\frac{P_i d_{ij}^{-1}}{\sum\limits_{i=1}^{n} P_i d_{ij}^{-1}} \right]} \tag{4.14}$$

To summarize the derivation above, if the spatial allocation of workers from places of work to places of residence follows a gravity pattern, represented by the model (4.10), and also if the requirements for consistency represented by equations (4.11) are observed, the values of the scaling factors l_j must be equal to the expressions (4.12). It is worth noting that the foregoing determination of the values of the scaling factors l_j is equivalent to allocating the workers to places of residence. Indeed, the l_j's, and consequently the W_{ij}'s as given by (4.14), are now completely specified in terms of the given values of E_j, P_i. and d_{ij}'s.

The derivation of the expression for W_{ij} would have followed exactly similar lines if the function $F(d_{ij})$ had assumed a form different from that we have chosen above. In fact, the only difference in the final model (4.14) would be that d_{ij}^{-1} would be replaced by $F(d_{ij})$. (See exercise 4.2.) Other possible forms for the definition of the O_j's, for instance $O_j = E_j^{0.5} P_j^{0.5} = \sqrt{E_j P_j}$, might have been used. Similarly, we might have adopted P_i^2 as a measure of the attraction of zone i, etc. The resulting model would again have a form similar to (4.14). (See Exercise 4.2.)

Although its derivation might seem involved, and its appearance forbidding, formula (4.14) can be interpreted in a rather simple physical way. We can look at the product $P_i d_{ij}^{-1}$ as the "residential potential" that area i, with an attraction P_i, and at a distance of d_{ij} from area j, has for the workers in this latter area. In this sense, the factor of E_j between brackets in formula (4.14), which is specific to the couple (i, j), and which we can therefore call a_{ij},

$$a_{ij} = \frac{P_i d_{ij}^{-1}}{\sum_{i=1}^{n} P_i d_{ij}^{-1}} \tag{4.15}$$

is the potential of area i for area j, relative to the sum of the potentials of all areas of residence i for area of work j. This quantity thus represents the *relative share* of area of residence i of the market in area of work j. Another equivalent interpretation of this factor is the (conditional) *probability* that a worker in area of work j will choose area of residence i, *given* the presence (i.e., potentials) of all the other areas. Both interpretations are consistent with the fact that the number of workers which work in j and live in i is equal to the total number of workers in area j, E_j, times the factor a_{ij}. This is easily seen if we rewrite (4.14) using the definition in (4.15):

$$W_{ij} = E_j a_{ij} \tag{4.16}$$

These coefficients a_{ij} are then seen to be precisely the values that characterize the work-to-home commuting pattern in model (3.45), and for which we now have an expression. Indeed, we can now compute the total number of workers W_i who will live in residential area i, coming from all areas of work, as the sum of the numbers of workers who come from area of work 1, plus the number of workers who come from area of work 2, etc.,

$$W_i = W_{i1} + W_{i2} + \ldots + \ldots + W_{ij} + \ldots + \ldots + W_{in} = \sum_{j=1}^{n} W_{ij}$$

or, replacing the W_{ij}'s by their expression in (4.16):

$$W_i = a_{i1} E_1 + a_{i2} E_2 + \ldots + a_{ij} E_j + \ldots + a_{in} E_n = \sum_{j=1}^{n} a_{ij} E_j \tag{4.17}$$

for all areas of residence $i = 1, 2, \ldots n$. (Note that we are now summing with respect to the areas of work j, the "producing" areas.) The system of equalities (4.17) (one for each area of residence i) can also be written in matrix form:

$$
\begin{bmatrix} W_1 \\ W_2 \\ W_3 \\ \cdot \\ \cdot \\ W_i \\ \cdot \\ \cdot \\ W_n \end{bmatrix}
=
\begin{bmatrix}
a_{11} & a_{12} & a_{13} & \cdots & a_{1j} & \cdots & a_{1n} \\
a_{21} & a_{22} & a_{23} & \cdots & a_{2j} & \cdots & a_{2n} \\
a_{31} & a_{32} & a_{33} & \cdots & a_{3j} & \cdots & a_{3n} \\
 & & & \cdots & & & \\
a_{i1} & a_{i2} & a_{i3} & \cdots & a_{ij} & \cdots & a_{in} \\
 & & & \cdots & & & \\
a_{n1} & a_{n2} & a_{n3} & \cdots & a_{nj} & \cdots & a_{nn}
\end{bmatrix}
\begin{bmatrix} E_1 \\ E_2 \\ E_3 \\ \cdot \\ \cdot \\ E_i \\ \cdot \\ \cdot \\ E_n \end{bmatrix}
\tag{4.18}
$$

In this form, (4.18) is exactly similar to (3.45), but with the fundamental difference that we now have a formal expression for the a_{ij}'s. This is
a crucial improvement, since we are now in a position to evaluate the changes
on the distribution of workers from the places of work to the places of
residence that would result from changes in the distribution of residential
population P_i, and from changes in the "distances" d_{ij}, since these factors
are explicitly incorporated in the model, through formula (4.15) for the
a_{ij}'s.

As an illustrative example of this particular form of the gravity model,
let us assume that the development of a three-zone area has been planned. The
existing numbers of residents (in tens of thousands, for instance) are $P_1 = 3$,
$P_2 = 2$, and $P_3 = 2$, respectively. It is also projected that the numbers of
jobs in the three zones will increase by $E_1 = 2$, $E_2 = 3$, and $E_2 = 4$, respectively (in hundreds), over the next 5 years. Finally, the distances in miles
between the three zones are as given below in Table 4.1.

TABLE 4.1

d_{ij}

$i =$ \ $j =$	1	2	3
1	2	8	6
2	8	3	4
3	6	4	3

Previous modeling experiments have shown that the workplace–home
spatial relationship could be adequately described for the area by a general
gravity model of the form (4.10). Given the preceding information, in which
areas, and by how much, will the expected increase in employment result in
residential population increases?

If we assume that the existing gravity pattern, which has so far been stable,
will also prevail at the date of the employment changes, then the forecasting
of the location of the development is the problem we have solved above of
spatially distributing the expected workers to areas of residence according to
the gravity pattern (4.10). The solution of this problem is thus, as we have
seen above, represented by the two sets of formulas (4.15) and (4.16). We
must therefore first compute the values of the a_{ij}'s. To that effect, let us first
compute the values of the terms $P_i d_{ij}^{-1}$ (the potentials, in the language of the
theoretical exposition). Beginning with the first area of residence, the potential
of area of residence 1 for the workers of area 1 is equal to: $P_1 d_{11}^{-1} = P_1/d_{11}$
$= \frac{3}{2}$. Similarly, the potential of area of residence 1 for workers in area of
work 2 is equal to $P_1/d_{12} = \frac{3}{8}$. Proceeding in the same fashion, we obtain the
set of values for the potentials in matrix form, as described in Table 4.2.

TABLE 4.2

$P_i d_{ij}^{-1}$

$i=$ \ $j=$	1	2	3
1	$\frac{3}{2}$	$\frac{3}{8}$	$\frac{3}{6}$
2	$\frac{2}{8}$	$\frac{2}{3}$	$\frac{2}{4}$
3	$\frac{2}{6}$	$\frac{2}{4}$	$\frac{2}{3}$
Total	$\frac{25}{12}$	$\frac{37}{24}$	$\frac{10}{6}$

The next step is to compute the values of the relative potentials or shares a_{ij}. According to formula (4.15), these are easily derived from the absolute potentials computed above by dividing them by their total with respect to all the residential areas i. These totals are represented by the column totals in Table 4.2. Thus, the values of the a_{ij}'s are obtained by dividing each entry in the matrix by the corresponding column total, as given in Table 4.3.

TABLE 4.3

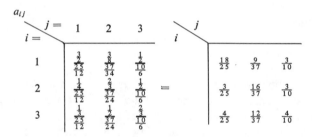

We can now compute the number of workers W_{ij} from area j who will choose area i to reside. According to formula (4.16), this is equal to the product of the coefficient a_{ij} computed above by the number E_j of workers in area j. Thus, the numbers W_{ij} are easily obtained from the entries in the last matrix in Table 4.3 by multiplying each entry by the value E_j corresponding to its column number, as given in Table 4.4.

TABLE 4.4

W_{ij}

$i=$ \ $j=$	1	2	3	Total $= W_i$
1	$2(\frac{18}{25})$	$3(\frac{9}{37})$	$4(\frac{3}{10})$	3.37
2	$2(\frac{3}{25})$	$3(\frac{16}{37})$	$4(\frac{3}{10})$	2.74
3	$2(\frac{4}{25})$	$3(\frac{12}{37})$	$4(\frac{4}{10})$	2.89
				9.00

Finally, the numbers of new residents W_i who should be found in a given area of residence i will be given by summing the numbers of workers W_{ij} coming from all areas j. This is obtained by computing the horizontal row totals in Table 4.4. These are given in the last column of the table.

Thus, area 1 should be chosen by 337 workers, i.e., receive $337/900 = 0.374$, or 37.4%, of the development of the region; area 2 should attract 274 workers, i.e, $274/900$, or 30.4%, of the total development; and area 3 should get 32.2%, the remainder. Indeed, as a (partial) check on the computations, one will note that the total number of resident workers, i.e, 9.00 (9 hundreds) for all three areas, is of course equal to the total number of workers in all areas. That is,

$$\sum_i W_i = \sum_j E_j \qquad (4.19)$$

Thus, the gravity model shuffles the workers from places of work to places of residence, with of course no loss of workers in the process.

The numbers of total new residents (the workers and their dependents) that will result from this distribution can from there on be estimated using the approach of Section 3.4, i.e., converting the figures above into residential population through the use of the work-force ratios $1/\gamma_i$ as in formula (3.46).

The potential uses of the foregoing model for analytical purposes are straightforward. Suppose, for instance, that the characteristics of the transportation system may be changed in the future, perhaps in anticipation of the new commuting pattern. Is this going to change the residential distribution from the projection above, and if so, how? If the characteristics of the transportation system change so that the travel times between zones are affected, for instance because of increased capacity of service, resulting in lower travel time, or perhaps a new pattern of one way streets, etc., we can consider that the distances d_{ij} between zones will also be changed, and consequently the residential potentials of the areas will be changed, through formula (4.15). We can then evaluate these changes by computing the new values of the a_{ij}'s, and from them the new values of the W_{ij}'s and of the W_i's, in the same manner as above. (See Exercise 4.3.)

The gravity model can, of course, be applied to the spatial distribution of activities other than *residential*. In particular, the *shopping activity* of residents of various areas in a given region can be allocated to these areas in the same fashion as above. In this case, the interaction capability of the producing areas (residential) could be represented by the total amount of expenditures coming out of these areas, by the average incomes, by the propensities to consume, etc. The measure of attraction of the receiving areas (commercial) could be represented by their total volumes of sales, or their accessibility, or by their floor space, range of services, etc. The derivation of the "home-to-shop" matrix **C** in the multiregional employment multiplier [formula (3.49)] can then be effected in the same fashion as that of the matrix seen above, thus supplying the other input into the model.

A caveat should be injected in this connection. If the output of a given iteration of the model, i.e., the P_i's and the E_i's or other quantities directly connected, are themselves used as inputs into the gravity model to derive the matrices **A** and **S** as above, these matrices will not remain constant, as was assumed in the model, but change at every iteration of the distributive procedure represented in Figure 3.3. This is because the coefficients in these matrices (the a_{ij}'s and the c_{ij}'s) are assumed to depend, through expressions of the type (4.15) on the existing levels of population, or of service jobs, and that these will then change at every iteration. Therefore, the compact expressions for the final employment and residential distributions (3.51) through (3.53) are not valid anymore. This slight difficulty is, of course, removed if one uses measures of production and attraction that depend on fixed factors, such as the area size or a set value derived from a planning goal. (See Exercise 4.10.)

The gravity model, being a model for the allocation of interactions between areas, can then be used for distributing several urban and regional activities to various spaces. Thus, it can be used also as a model for predicting *land-use patterns*. By combining the preceding analysis for several activities and taking into account the interrelationships, such as conflicts or competition for the same spaces, a general *spatial development model* can be built.

For instance, a new residential distribution might, in turn, provoke changes in the transportation system characteristics, in the commercial distribution, in the availability of housing, and therefore the rent structure, etc. These and similar effects will change the relative desirabilities, or residential potentials of the respective areas. If these changes are reflected in the model, for instance through submodels of rent structure as a function of the housing demand, i.e., of the residential desirability values, then we have an *interactive* model that can represent these feedback effects. This approach, extended to all the principal components of urban and regional systems, such as population, employment, land, housing, services, transportation, etc., is the basis for the *comprehensive* or *general* models of urban and regional systems.

4.4 Second Application: The Double-Constraint Form

In some applications of the general gravity model to modeling situations of the type above, it is necessary to consider constraints on both sets of regions at once. For instance, a standard and very important such case comes from the need to forecast transportation requirements on the basis of separate projections of the amounts of travel generated and received by a set of regions. Another case would be, in terms of the illustrative example above, when both the numbers of workers and the numbers of housing units in each zone are specified. Or, in general, when the amount of activity generated by the producing zones and the amount that can be attracted are both set. The former constraint might come from development plans (economic, residential, etc.), and the latter from land-use considerations (intensity, location, capacity, etc.). This type of double constraint may also be found mixed with single constraints of the type seen in the previous section. In this case the two corresponding versions of the gravity model can be used in conjunction.

In any case let us illustrate the development of this other version of the gravity model in the practical case of a transportation planning study. Let us therefore assume that in a first, preparatory stage, we have forecasted the numbers of trips O_j that will originate in each of the n zones of our region, as well as the number of trips D_i that will terminate in each of the zones. As above, the zones function both as producing and as receiving zones, but are labeled j when they produce, and i when they receive. (We shall describe in some detail in Section 4.8 the methods for travel demand generation.)

In any event, we start now with the knowledge of the number of trips coming out of each area, O_j, and the number of trips coming into each area, D_i. The problem is to find the number of trips between each area and every other area, which we can, for example, call T_{ij}. This can perhaps be described simply as the problem of filling out the entries in the two way table in Figure 4.1, when the horizontal and vertical totals are given and are equal to D_i and

i \ j	1	2	j	n	Total
1	T_{11}	T_{12} $\cdots$ T_{1j}	$\cdots$	T_{1n}	D_1
2	T_{21}	T_{22} $\cdots$ T_{2j}	$\cdots$	T_{2n}	D_2
		$\cdots\cdots\cdots\cdots\cdots\cdots\cdots\cdots\cdots\cdots\cdots$			
i	T_{i1}	T_{i2} $\cdots$ T_{ij}	$\cdots$	T_{in}	D_i
n	T_{n1}	T_{n2} $\cdots$ T_{nj}	$\cdots$	T_{nn}	D_n
Total	O_1	O_2 $\ldots$ O_j	$\cdots$	O_n	I

Figure 4.1   Interzonal travel flows.

O_j, respectively, and also such that the entries have values that conform to the gravity pattern of form (4.2).

If we assume that the travel activity between regions will be distributed according to a gravity law of interaction, we can write that the number of residents T_{ij} traveling from region j to region i should be of the form

$$T_{ij} = k_i l_j O_j D_i F(d_{ij}) \tag{4.20}$$

with the double set of constraints

$$\sum_{i=1}^{n} T_{ij} = O_j \qquad \text{for } j = 1, 2, \dots, n \tag{4.21a}$$

and

$$\sum_{j=1}^{n} T_{ij} = D_i \qquad \text{for } i = 1, 2, \dots, n \tag{4.21b}$$

The first set of constraints expresses the requirement that the total number of travelers leaving region j must be equal to the given level O_j, whereas the second set expresses the symmetrical requirement that the total number of travelers coming into area i must be equal to the given level D_i. Here again, as in the single-constraint case, the solution of this distribution problem, i.e., the assignment of travel demand between zones, will be solved when the unknown values of the factors k_i and l_j (i.e., $2n$ values) will be determined. The $2n$ equations in (4.21a) and (4.21b) can be solved for the k_i's and the l_j's, respectively, since they can be written, using the expression of the T_{ij}'s, in (4.20):

$$\sum_{i=1}^{n} k_i l_j O_j D_i F(d_{ij}) = O_j \qquad \text{for } j = 1, 2, \dots, n \tag{4.22a}$$

and:

$$\sum_{j=1}^{n} k_i l_j O_j D_i F(d_{ij}) = D_i \qquad \text{for } i = 1, 2, \dots, n \tag{4.22b}$$

and by factoring out the constant terms $l_j O_j$ in the sum in (4.22a) and $k_i D_i$ in the sum in (4.22b):

$$l_j O_j \sum_i k_i D_i F(d_{ij}) = O_j \tag{4.23a}$$

and

$$k_i D_i \sum_j l_j O_j F(d_{ij}) = D_i \tag{4.23b}$$

Finally, from (4.23a),

$$l_j = \frac{1}{\displaystyle\sum_{i=1}^{n} k_i D_i F(d_{ij})} \tag{4.24a}$$

and from (4.23b),

$$k_i = \frac{1}{\displaystyle\sum_{j=1}^{n} l_j O_j F(d_{ij})} \tag{4.24b}$$

Thus, the expressions for the values of k_i and l_j that solve the distribution problem resemble those of the previous (single-constrained) case, formula (4.12). There is one fundamental difference, however: the values of the l_j's depend on the values of the k_i's through formula (4.24a), and vice versa through formula (4.24b). In other words, because of this "chicken-or-egg" situation, where one needs the values of one of the sets of unknowns to compute the values of the others, we cannot readily compute them on the basis of the given data, as in the previous case.

The procedure is therefore to give *estimated*, or simply *arbitrary* values to the k_i's, for instance, plug these values into the the formulas for the l_j's, compute the corresponding values, plug back these values into the corresponding expressions for the k_i's, and compare them with the starting values. If they are equal, then the set of values for the k_i's and the l_j's verify equations (4.24a) and (4.24b) and thus they constitute a solution to the allocation problem. If, on the other hand, the first round output values of the k_i's are not equal to the estimated starting values, the process is reiterated. The values of the k_i's are again put into the formulas for the l_j's and the output values for the l_j's are put into the formulas for the k_i's. The output values for the k_i's are compared to the (second-round) starting values. If they are equal, the process stops. If not, it is reiterated until the starting and the ending values for the round for the k_i's are equal. In most cases, this process converges relatively quickly to a stable solution. Also, it is of course possible, if the specific data for the situation make it more convenient, to start with estimated values for the l_j's instead of the k_i's, i.e., to invert the order of the role of the two sets of factors. The process is otherwise the same.

When both sets of values k_i $(i = 1 \ldots n)$ and l_j $(j = 1 \ldots n)$ have thus been evaluated, the values for all T_{ij}'s as given by (4.20) can now be computed and the model is totally specified.

Let us now illustrate what must surely seem to be a convoluted approach with a simple example of application. Let us assume that we have a three-zone region where the respective numbers of commuters $\hat{T}_{ij}$, from area j to area i, observed daily between the zones is as given in Table 4.5.[1]

TABLE 4.5   Observed Values $\hat{T}_{ij}$

$i =$ \ $j =$	1	2	3	Total D_i
1	1,800	3,100	100	5,000
2	3,100	1,500	400	5,000
3	15,100	25,400	4,500	45,000
Total O_j	20,000	30,000	5,000	55,000

The D_i's are the total numbers of commuters coming into the areas, and the O_j's the numbers leaving them. Given this observed pattern of commuting

[1]The notation $\hat{T}_{ij}$ will distinguish the *observed* value from the *predicted* (or theoretical) value T_{ij}.

between the zones, we would like to fit a gravity-type model to the data, so that it can be used to forecast the changes in travel demand between the zones (the T_{ij}'s) that would result from changes in the joint residence–employment spatial distribution (the O_j's and D_i's, respectively). To that effect, we would like to try and empirically test the performance of a model of the form

$$T_{ij} = k_i l_j D_i O_j d_{ij}^2 e^{-0.5d_{ij}} \qquad (4.25)$$

[i.e., a model of the form (4.20) where the function $F(d_{ij})$ is equal to $F(d_{ij}) = d_{ij}^2 e^{-0.5d_{ij}}$], and where the d_{ij}'s are the distances between zones. Although there are numerous other possible choices of variables for the O_j's, the D_i's, and the d_{ij}'s, we will retain this simple formulation if it reproduces the actual levels of travel between the zones to an average error of less than say 8%. The values of the d_{ij}'s have been recorded and are given (in miles) in Table 4.6.

TABLE 4.6   Values of d_{ij}

$i =$ \ $j =$	1	2	3
1	2	4	8
2	5	1	7
3	7	6	3

We therefore need to compute the *theoretical* values of the levels of travel between zones T_{ij} which would be predicted (or reproduced) by model (4.25). To do that, as we have seen above in the model development, we first have to compute the values of the coefficients k_i and l_j, from formulas (4.24a) and (4.24b). [Note that the input into these formulas does not involve the $\hat{T}_{ij}$'s, only the O_j's, D_i's, and the values of the function $F(d_{ij})$.] Let us then first compute these.

We begin by computing the values of d_{ij}^2 for every i and j, by simply raising each entry in Table 4.6 to its square. The results are as presented in Table 4.6(a).

TABLE 4.6(a)   Values of d_{ij}^2

$i =$ \ $j =$	1	2	3
1	4	16	64
2	25	1	49
3	49	36	9

Next, in order to compute the values of the second term in $F(d_{ij})$, i.e., $e^{-0.5d_{ij}}$, we compute the values of $0.5d_{ij}$, which are again simply obtained

from Table 4.6 by multiplying every entry by 0.5. The corresponding values
are given in Table 4.6(b).

TABLE 4.6(b)   Values of $0.5d_{ij}$

$i=$ \ $j=$	1	2	3
1	1	2	4
2	2.5	0.5	3.5
3	3.5	3	1.5

We now compute the values of $e^{-0.5d_{ij}} = 1/e^{0.5d_{ij}}$, for each of the entries in
above. The results are as in Table 4.6(c).

TABLE 4.6(c)   Values of $e^{-0.5d_{ij}}$

i \ j			
	0.3678	0.1353	0.0183
	0.0821	0.6065	0.0302
	0.0302	0.0498	0.2231

We can next compute the values of $F(d_{ij})$ by simply multiplying each
entry in Table 4.6(b) by its corresponding entry in Table 4.6(c). The results
are as given in Table 4.6(d).

TABLE 4.6(d)   Values of $F(d_{ij}) = d_{ij}^2 e^{-0.5d_{ij}}$

i \ j			
	1.472	2.165	1.172
	2.052	0.607	1.480
	1.480	1.792	2.008

We now have the values for all the coefficients O_j, D_i, and $F(d_{ij})$ in equations (4.24a) and (4.24b), which we shall now write out. Since the unit for the
T_{ij}'s and thus for the O_j's and D_i is immaterial, let us use units of ten thousands. (In other words, O_1 will now be equal to 2, etc. This will simplify the
appearance of the formulas.)

Equations (4.24a) for the three values of $j = 1, 2, 3$ are

$$l_1 = \frac{1}{k_1 D_1 F(d_{11}) + k_2 D_2 F(d_{21}) + k_3 D_3 F(d_{31})}$$

$$l_2 = \frac{1}{k_1 D_1 F(d_{12}) + k_2 D_2 F(d_{22}) + k_3 D_3 F(d_{32})}$$

$$l_3 = \frac{1}{k_1 D_1 F(d_{13}) + k_2 D_2 F(d_{23}) + k_3 D_3 F(d_{33})}$$

[Note the systematic position of the k_i's and the D_i's and the fact that the $F(d_{ij})$'s in the first formula are found in the first column of Table 4.6(d) and those in the second formula in the second column, etc. This will facilitate replacing these terms by their given values.] In any case, these formulas are then written

$$l_1 = \frac{1}{k_1(0.5)(1.472) + k_2(0.5)(2.052) + k_3(4.5)(1.480)}$$

$$l_2 = \frac{1}{k_1(0.5)(2.165) + k_2(0.5)(0.607) + k_3(4.5)(1.480)}$$

$$l_3 = \frac{1}{k_1(0.5)(1.172) + k_2(0.5)(1.480) + k_3(4.5)(2.008)}$$

or

$$l_1 = \frac{1}{0.736k_1 + 1.026k_2 + 6.660k_3}$$

$$l_2 = \frac{1}{1.082k_1 + 0.303k_2 + 8.064k_3} \tag{4.26a}$$

$$l_3 = \frac{1}{0.586k_1 + 0.740k_2 + 9.036k_3}$$

Symmetrically, the three equations (4.24b) are written

$$k_1 = \frac{1}{l_1 O_1 F(d_{11}) + l_2 O_2 F(d_{12}) + l_3 O_3 F(d_{13})}$$

$$k_2 = \frac{1}{l_1 O_1 F(d_{21}) + l_2 O_2 F(d_{22}) + l_3 O_3 F(d_{23})}$$

$$k_3 = \frac{1}{l_1 O_1 F(d_{31}) + l_2 O_2 F(d_{32}) + l_3 O_3 F(d_{33})}$$

Here, again, note the systematic positions of the terms l_j and O_j and the fact that the terms $F(d_{ij})$ in the first formula are this time found in the first row of Table 4.6(d), those in the second in the second row, etc. These formulas then become, after replacing these terms by their values and simplifying,

$$k_1 = \frac{1}{2.944 l_1 + 6.495 l_2 + 0.586 l_3}$$

$$k_2 = \frac{1}{4.104 l_1 + 1.821 l_2 + 0.740 l_3} \tag{4.26b}$$

$$k_3 = \frac{1}{2.960 l_1 + 5.376 l_2 + 1.004 l_3}$$

We now have the six equations (4.26a) and (4.26b) in six unknowns $l_1, l_2, l_3, k_1, k_2,$ and k_3, which we need to solve in order to compute the values of the T_{ij}'s. Since, as was noted above, this interlocked system requires the knowledge of one set of values (either the l_j's or the k_i's) to compute the other, we begin by giving arbitrary values of 1 to k_1, k_2, and k_3. By replacing these values in (4.26a), we can now compute the values of the l_j's. These are

$$l_1 = \frac{1}{0.736(1) + 1.026(1) + 6.660(1)} = 0.1187$$

$$l_2 = \frac{1}{1.082(1) + 0.303(1) + 8.064(1)} = 0.1058$$

$$l_3 = \frac{1}{0.586(1) + 0.740(1) + 9.036(1)} = 0.0965$$

We now use these (first-round) values for the l_j's to compute the (second-round) values for the k_i's through formulas (4.26b). The corresponding values are

$$k_1 = \frac{1}{2.944(0.1187) + 6.495(0.1058) + 0.586(0.0965)} = 0.9148$$

$$k_2 = \frac{1}{4.104(0.1187) + 1.821(0.1058) + 0.740(0.0965)} = 1.3312$$

$$k_3 = \frac{1}{2.960(0.1187) + 5.376(0.1058) + 1.004(0.0965)} = 0.9833$$

Since these values for the k_i's are not equal to the last values ($k_1 = k_2 = k_3 = 1$), we continue this process, by computing the next values for the l_i's, through formulas (4.26a), from the latest values for k_1, k_2, and k_3 which have just been obtained. Although we shall not repeat the computations here, it may be noted that they can be very simple, if one uses a systematic (or matrix) framework, such as

$$\begin{bmatrix} 1/k_1 \\ 1/k_2 \\ 1/k_3 \end{bmatrix} = \begin{bmatrix} 2.944 & 6.495 & 0.586 \\ 4.104 & 1.821 & 0.740 \\ 2.960 & 5.376 & 1.004 \end{bmatrix} \begin{bmatrix} l_1 \\ l_2 \\ l_3 \end{bmatrix} \longleftarrow \begin{bmatrix} 1/l_1 \\ 1/l_2 \\ 1/l_3 \end{bmatrix}$$

$$\begin{bmatrix} k_1 \\ k_2 \\ k_3 \end{bmatrix} \longrightarrow \begin{bmatrix} 1/l_1 \\ 1/l_2 \\ 1/l_3 \end{bmatrix} = \begin{bmatrix} 0.736 & 1.026 & 6.660 \\ 1.082 & 0.303 & 8.064 \\ 0.586 & 0.740 & 9.036 \end{bmatrix} \begin{bmatrix} k_1 \\ k_2 \\ k_3 \end{bmatrix}$$

The second set of values of the l_j's, as well as the subsequent values for the k_i's, etc., are given in Table 4.7.

We stop this process when the values for the k's and for the l's do not change from one iteration to the next. This happens in the fourth iteration in our case. These values are the solution to the balancing (equilibrium) problem expressed by equations (4.26a) and (4.26b). The final values are

$$l_1 = 0.1164 \qquad l_2 = 0.1073 \qquad l_3 = 0.0961$$

$$k_1 = 0.9125 \qquad k_2 = 1.3437 \qquad k_3 = 0.9824$$

TABLE 4.7

Iteration Number

	1	2	3	4
k_1	1	0.9148	0.9125	0.9125
k_2	1	1.3312	1.3437	1.3437
k_3	1	0.9833	0.9824	0.9824
l_1	0.1187	0.1164	0.1164	
l_2	0.1058	0.1073	0.1073	
l_3	0.0965	0.0961	0.0961	

We now have the values for all the terms intervening in formula (4.25) for the numbers of commuters between zones. Since this formula involves the respective products $k_i l_j$ and $D_i O_j$, we first compute them systematically. The results are given in Tables 4.8 and 4.9, respectively.

TABLE 4.8   Values of $k_i l_j$

$k_i =$ \ $l_j =$	0.1164	0.1073	0.0961
0.9125	0.1062	0.0979	0.0877
1.3437	0.1564	0.1442	0.1291
0.9824	0.1144	0.1054	0.0944

TABLE 4.9   Values of $D_i O_j$

$D_i =$ \ $O_j =$	2	3	0.5
0.5	1	1.5	0.25
0.5	1	1.5	0.25
4.5	9	13.5	2.25

Next we compute the value of the product $k_i l_j D_i O_j$. This is simply obtained by multiplying each term in Table 4.8 by the corresponding term in Table 4.9. The results are given in Table 4.10. Finally, we obtain the value of the T_{ij}'s by multiplying the entries in Table 4.10 by the factor $F(d_{ij})$, in Table 4.6(d) according to model (4.25). The results are presented in Table 4.11. Translated in terms of the original units, the numbers of commuters between zones are obtained by multiplying these entries by 10,000, and are presented in Table 4.11(a).

A few comments are in order. First, we note that, except for errors due to

TABLE 4.10   Values for $k_i l_j D_i O_j$

j		
0.1062	0.1468	0.0219
0.1564	0.2163	0.0323
1.0296	1.4229	0.2124

TABLE 4.11   Values of T_{ij}

$i =$ \\ $j =$	1	2	3	Total D_i
1	0.1563	0.3178	0.0257	0.4998
2	0.3209	0.1313	0.0478	0.5000
3	1.5238	2.5498	0.4265	4.5001
Total O_j	2.0010	2.9989	0.5000	

TABLE 4.11(a)   Predicted Values T_{ij}

$i =$ \\ $j =$	1	2	3	D_i
1	1,563	3,178	257	4,998
2	3,209	1,313	478	5,000
3	15,238	25,498	4,265	45,001
O_j	20,010	29,989	5,000	

the rounding of all computations to the fourth decimal place, the total for row i, which represents $\sum_j T_{ij}$, i.e., the numbers of travelers whose destination is area i, is in all cases approximately equal to the given levels for the D_i's (i.e., 5000, 5000, and 45,000, respectively) which were used as input into the model. Similarly, the column totals are, within rounding errors, equal to the input levels for the O_j's. In fact, this process of iterative search for the values of the k_i's and of the l_j's is equivalent to the physical distribution of the given levels of travelers between zones, so that we should expect the foregoing equalities to hold if no computational errors have occurred. However, the reproduced levels of the values for the T_{ij}'s, i.e., the predicted values in Table 4.11(a) which represent the output of the model, are not equal to the observed $\hat{T}_{ij}$ values in Table 4.5. These discrepancies are this time not due to the accuracy of the model in a computational sense, but to its validity in a conceptual sense. We can measure the validity of the model or its "fit" to the given situation by evaluating the total, or average error between the actual values $\hat{T}_{ij}$ and the reproduced values T_{ij}. We can then compute the overall precision of the model, as for instance being equal to

$$\sum_i \sum_j \frac{T_{ij} - \hat{T}_{ij}}{T_{ij}} \tag{4.27}$$

i.e., the relative error between the measurement and the prediction. These values, expressed in percentages, are given in Table 4.12.

TABLE 4.12 Relative Errors for T_{ij} (%)

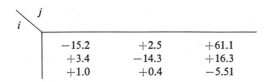

	j	
i		
−15.2	+2.5	+61.1
+3.4	−14.3	+16.3
+1.0	+0.4	−5.51

Thus, we see that the model we are testing tends to allocate less commuters to intrazonal travel, i.e., for the shortest distances, than has been observed. Conversely, zones separated by the largest distances are allocated more travel than exists in reality. Also, the average error is 5.5%, and in absolute value (i.e., when the direction of the error is ignored so that errors of different signs do not compensate for each other) the average error is 13%. (One can choose other measures of the precision of the model, some of which we shall see in Chapter 6.)

Based on these results of the performance of the model, we might at this point decide to try a number of alternatives, to improve on the fit between the model and the data. We may, for instance, change the value of the parameter in the function $F(d_{ij})$ so that the distance effect noted above is attenuated. For instance, we could try an interaction impedance function of the form

$$F(d_{ij}) = d_{ij}^{1.5} e^{-2.0 d_{ij}} \tag{4.28}$$

which, all other factors being equal, will give less weight to large distances. (See Exercise 4.5.) It should be mentioned in this connection that the search for adequate values for the parameters of the model does not have to be random. There are techniques for determining the optimal value for these parameters which result in the best fit, of which we shall see simple examples in Chapter 6.

Another possible alternative would be to change the expression of the function $F(d_{ij})$ altogether, for instance to form (4.5), etc. The computational procedure would follow exactly the same steps as above. Finally, another possibility, as was suggested in the theoretical discussion of the general gravity model, is to change the nature of the variables. We could perhaps try to use the travel time, as an alternative measure of the difficulty of commuting between zones; a combination of cost, time, and distance; etc. Of course, such a heuristic search for a good fit between a descriptive model that is not based on explicit cause-and-effect relationships can be quite time-consuming. However, the simple iterative nature of the procedure makes it well suited for systematic computer-implemented experiments.

4.5 The Theory of the Intervening Opportunities Model

We shall now consider another example of a spatial activity distribution model. This model, called the *intervening opportunities model* for reasons that will become apparent during the course of its derivation, can in principle be used as an alternative to the gravity model in all spatial analyses, including as a module in comprehensive models. However, it has a *microanalytic, behavioral* basis, in that spatial location of the activities is explained by the individual decisions of the residents, based on an explicit mechanism of choice.

Since we did not present the formal derivation of the gravity model, but only indicated that it can be obtained from the optimization of some quantity related to the global or *macroscopic* pattern of travel, we shall show how the intervening opportunity model can be derived, as an example of rational model building. Before going through the mathematics of the derivation, let us state the general principle on which it is based. Individual residents in a given "producing" zone j are assumed to consider opportunities for the location of their conduct of specific activities (residence, shopping, work, etc.) at various places, starting from zone j, and in increasing order of "separation" or difficulty (in the same sense as in the gravity model) from j. Also, each time such an opportunity is considered, there is a given, constant chance (or probability) that it will be selected. Let us now see what these basic assumptions imply for the spatial pattern of activities. [Those readers who wish to skip the derivation of the model can go directly to its final expression, (4.45) on page 139.]

Since the rationale above is based on an explicit consideration of the order with which various "receiving" zones i are considered from zone j, the first thing we need to do is to rank all receiving zones with respect to each zone j. Then, the zone with the easiest access (or in the language of the preceding section, the least difficulty for interaction with j) with respect to zone j will be numbered $i = 1$. It is critical to bear in mind that this index is *relative to* the index j. That is, the index of a given receiving zone i may change, depending on which producing zone it is being considered from. Thus, from producing zone j, zones $i = 1$, $i = 2$, etc., offer opportunities for the location of the activity, in increasing order of difficulty, or "distance" d_{ij}, where

i is the index of the zone with the ith level of difficulty, measured from zone j.

Let us now define a *level of opportunity* found in zone i, as seen from zone j. For instance, this level might be measured by the number of stores, or shopping centers in zone i, which are accessible from zone j if the activity under consideration is travel for shopping, or might be the number of housing units in zone i available to residents of zone j if the activity is residential location, etc.

Let us, furthermore, make the simplyfying assumption that the probability that a given resident in any zone j will select any given zone i is proportional to the level of opportunity in zone i. For instance, we assume that the probability that a resident looking for a place to live will select a given residential location is independent of where he or she works and also of its particular location but is simply proportional to the number of housing units available at that location. Or, in the case of travel for shopping, the foregoing assumption would simply mean that any given shopper residing in any given area has the same probability of selecting a shopping area which is independent of the location of the area, but is proportional to its volume of sales, to its total floor surface, the total size of its parking lot, etc. Although this may be an oversimplification, it may be appropriate in most cases as a first approximation. In any case we shall see examples of the refinement of this assumption at the conclusion of this section. Let us call λ the proportionality factor between the level of opportunity and the probability: Then

$$p(n) = \lambda n \qquad (4.29)$$

where $p(n)$ is the probability of selecting an area where the number, or level of opportunities is equal to n.

Let us now define the variables that will measure the opportunity. First, let us call n_{ij} the level of opportunity, as defined above, found in zone i (for residents in j). Equivalently, let us define N_{ij} as the *cumulative level of opportunity* up to and including the ith area. That is,

$$N_{ij} = n_{1j} + n_{2j} + n_{3j} + \ldots + n_{ij} = \sum_{k=1}^{i} n_{kj} \qquad (4.30)$$

Let us now also define P_{ij} as the probability that a resident in zone j will not choose one of the first i zones (including the ith) as location for the activity. In other words, P_{ij} is also the probability that the resident will continue to look for such a location past zone i.

We are now in a position to establish the relationship between the probability that a resident considers zones beyond zone i before stopping, and the cumulative level of opportunity that he or she encounters in the process. Indeed, we have in (4.29) postulated the existence of such a relationship. Let us start with the first zone, $i = 1$. The basic assumption of the model implies that the probability P_{j1} that the resident will look beyond the first zone, starting from j is the complement (to 1) of the probability that he will choose the first zone. The latter probability, according to formula (4.29), is in turn equal to the number of opportunities n_{1j} in the first zone times the proportionality factor, λ. Therefore,

$$P_{1j} = 1 - \lambda n_{1j} \qquad (4.31)$$

We now evaluate the probability that the resident will look beyond the second zone j, P_{2j}. This event requires two things: that the resident looks beyond zone 1, and that he or she does not choose zone 2. If we assume that these decisions are independent, the probability of going beyond zone 2 is then simply the product of the respective probabilities of the two decisions. [For readers who have forgotten formula (1.10) in Section 1.4, it suffices to think of the probability of getting a "one" and a "six" in a joint toss of two independent dices as being equal to probability of getting a one, i.e., $\frac{1}{6}$, times the probability of getting a six, also $\frac{1}{6}$. The probability of the composite event is thus $(\frac{1}{6})(\frac{1}{6}) = \frac{1}{36}$.]

In any case, the probability of the first decision is P_{1j}, which we have just computed above. Also, the probability of the second decision, i.e., not to choose area 2 (from j), is the complement of the probability to choose it, which is, according again to our basic hypothesis, equal to λn_{2j}, where n_{2j} is the level of opportunity in zone 2 (for residents of i). Thus, combining these two probabilities, we get

$$P_{2j} = P_{1j}(1 - \lambda n_{2j}) \qquad (4.32)$$

In general, we can write that the probability that the resident will choose a location beyond area i is equal to the product of the probability that he or she will choose a location beyond the immediately preceding area in order of consideration, i.e., area number $(i - 1)$, and of the probability that area i itself will not be chosen. Since the probability of choosing area i is proportional to its level of opportunity n_{ij} and equal to λn_{ij}, we have

$$P_{ij} = P_{i-1,j}(1 - \lambda n_{ij}) \qquad (4.33)$$

It is convenient at this point to use the cumulative level of opportunities up to zone i, N_{ij}. According to formula (4.30), the level of opprotunity in zone i, n_{ij}, is simply equal to the difference between the cumulative numbers of opportunities up to and including, zone i, i.e., N_{ij}, and the cumulative number up to the immediately preceding zone $i - 1$, i.e., $N_{i-1,j}$. Thus,

$$n_{ij} = N_{ij} - N_{i-1,j} \qquad (4.34)$$

Replacing n_{ij} in (4.33) by its expression in (4.34), we get

$$P_{ij} = P_{i-j,j}[1 - \lambda(N_{i,j} - N_{i-1,j})]$$

Finally, this can be rewritten as

$$P_{ij} - P_{i-1,j} = \lambda P_{i-1,j}(N_{ij} - N_{i-1,j})$$

or

$$\frac{P_{ij} - P_{i-1,j}}{P_{i-1,j}} = -\lambda(N_{ij} - N_{i-1,j}) \qquad (4.35)$$

At this point, the derivation of the formula that expresses the probability P_{ij} as a function of the cumulative level of opportunities N_{ij} requires the assumption that the cumulative level of opportunity is a *continous* variable (in other words, that the spatial density of such opportunities is high). In this case, we can write the *differential* version of equation (4.35) as

$$\frac{\partial(P_{ij})}{P_{ij}} = -\lambda\partial(N_{ij}) \qquad (4.36)$$

the solution of which is

$$\log P_{ij} = \log k_j - \lambda N_{ij} \qquad (4.37)$$

where k_j is a constant, specific to the solution for area j above.

It is hoped that one will forgive this first and only use of calculus in this text, but it is unavoidable in this case. However, the alert reader will have noticed that there is a similarity between the model in form (4.35) and the exponential model (2.3) of population change in Section 2.3. This suggests that we might resort to the discrete version of that model, since the quantity $(n - 1) - n$, where n was the number of years [which plays the role of $N_{i-1,j} - N_{ij}$ in (4.35)], was constant and equal to 1. Therefore, if we can order the zones in such a manner that the increments in number of opportunities when going from any zone to the next are constant and equal to n, for instance, the simple form

$$P_{ij} = k_j(1 - \lambda n)^i \qquad (4.38)$$

would result.

In any event, an equivalent form for the model can be obtained from (4.37):

$$\log P_{ij} - \log k_j = \log \left(\frac{P_{ij}}{k_j}\right) = \log (e^{-\lambda N_{ij}})$$

and therefore, by taking the "antilogarithms" of both sides,

$$\frac{P_{ij}}{k_j} = e^{-\lambda N_{ij}}$$

or

$$P_{ij} = k_j e^{-\lambda N_{ij}} \qquad (4.39)$$

The constant k_j is a scaling factor, specific to zone j in the same sense as were the constants k_i and l_j in the gravity model.

Now, this derivation of the expression of P_{ij} was originally motivated by the need to evaluate the level of interaction between zone j and zone i. If the level of "interaction-producing" capacity of zone j is measured by the number of residents O_j in it who are engaging in the activity location search described by (4.39), we can write that the proportion of the number of residents in zone j who will go beyond zone i in this search is equal to the product of the total number O_j, by the probability of an individual resident going beyond i, P_{ij}. If we call this number R_{ij}, in keeping with the notational system we have used so far in this section, we then have

$$R_{ij} = O_j P_{ij}$$

or, by replacing P_{ij} by its expression in (4.39),

$$R_{ij} = k_j O_j e^{-\lambda N_{ij}} \tag{4.40}$$

Finally, the number of residents who choose area i as a location, which we can call r_{ij}, is simply equal to the number of residents $R_{i-1,j}$ who go beyond area $(i-1)$ (i.e., who reach area i), minus the number who do not stay in area (i.e., who go beyond area i), $R_{i,j}$. Thus,

$$r_{ij} = R_{i-1,j} - R_{ij} \tag{4.41}$$

where, as for the other quantities, the small letters are reserved for the net values, and the capital letters for the cumulative values. By replacing the R_{ij}'s by their expression in (4.40), we get

$$\boxed{r_{ij} = k_j O_j (e^{-\lambda N_{i-1,j}} - e^{-\lambda N_{ij}})} \tag{4.42}$$

This is the final form of the intervening opportunities model. As for the gravity model, the specific value of the scaling factor k_j will be determined by noting that since we already know that the total number of residents who have to be assigned to the n regions i from region j is O_j, we must therefore have

$$\sum_{i=1}^{n} r_{ij} = O_j$$

or

$$k_j O_j \left(\sum_{i=1}^{n} e^{-\lambda N_{i-1,j}} - \sum_{i=1}^{n} e^{-\lambda N_{ij}} \right) = O_j \tag{4.43}$$

The first sum in equation (4.43) can be written

$$e^{-\lambda N_{0j}} + e^{-\lambda N_{1j}} + \ldots + e^{-\lambda N_{n-1,j}}$$

The first term in the sum is equal to zero, since, in accordance with (4.34), $N_{0j} = 0$ and therefore $e^0 = 1$. Also, the last term when $i = n$ is $e^{-\lambda N_{n-1,j}}$ since the first index for N is $(i-1)$. Similarly, the second sum can be written

$$e^{-\lambda N_{1j}} + e^{-\lambda N_{2j}} + e^{-\lambda N_{3j}} + \ldots + e^{-\lambda N_{nj}}$$

Therefore, the difference between the two sums in (4.43) is equal to

$$(1 + e^{-\lambda N_{1j}} + e^{-\lambda N_{2j}} + \ldots + e^{-\lambda N_{n-1,j}}) - (e^{-\lambda N_{1j}} + e^{-\lambda N_{2j}} + \ldots + e^{-\lambda N_{nj}})$$

which is equal to

$$1 - e^{-\lambda N_{nj}}$$

Finally, going back to (4.43), and replacing the difference between the two sums by its expression above, we obtain

$$k_j O_j (1 - e^{-\lambda N_{nj}}) = O_j$$

or

$$\boxed{k_j = \frac{1}{1 - e^{-\lambda N_{nj}}}} \tag{4.44}$$

Replacing this value for k_j in (4.42), we get the explicit model

$$\boxed{r_{ij} = O_j \left(\frac{e^{-\lambda N_{i-1,j}} - e^{-\lambda N_{ij}}}{1 - e^{-\lambda N_{nj}}} \right)} \tag{4.45}$$

where every quantity is known in terms of the given.[2] The model will be fitted to a specific situation when the value of the parameter λ (which represents, it may be recalled, the probability of choosing a location where the level of opportunity is equal to the unit chosen for the "attracting capacity" of the receiving zones) is determined. A simple, convenient measure for the level of opportunity of a given zone is the number of possible locations, perhaps weighted by importance.

Thus, the value of λ can simply be inferred from equation (4.37) by plotting the logarithms of the cumulative proportion P_{ij} of total activity from a given area j which is found past the various areas $i = 1, 2, \ldots, n$ as a function of the cumulative level of opportunity, or attraction of these areas. Since the proportion P_{ij} is also the ratio of the number of residents who choose areas past area i to the total number of residents O_j, we can plot the logarithm of the observable quantity,

$$P_{ij} = \frac{R_{ij}}{O_j} \tag{4.46}$$

or the alternative, equivalent quantity,

$$P_{ij} = 1 - \frac{\sum_{k=1}^{i} r_{kj}}{O_j} \tag{4.47}$$

that is, the complement to 100% of the observed proportion of the total number of residents choosing areas up to and including area i.

---

[2]It is worth noticing that the factor of O_j in (4.45) plays the role of a_{ij} as defined by (4.15) in the one-way gravity model (4.16); i.e., it can be interpreted as the share of the activities originating in area j which are located in area i.

If the basic assumption of the intervening opportunities model is valid, the resulting plot should be linear and the slope of the line will be equal to the negative of λ, as represented in Figure 4.2. This property provides a graphical way of estimating the value of the parameter.

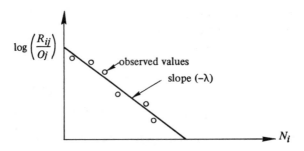

Figure 4.2   Linear property of the intervening opportunities model.

4.6   Application

Let us now illustrate the application of the intervening opportunities model to the following problem. In a given state consisting of four areas, the spatial distribution of the total enrollments of the four state colleges located in each of the zones is as represented in Table 4.13. Also, a total of 15,000 students

TABLE 4.13

| | *Area* | | | | |
	A	*B*	*C*	*D*	*Total*
Enrollment from area C	8,500	275	2,700	3,525	15,000
Total enrollment	30,000	10,000	5,000	65,000	110,000

from area C are attending colleges in the various areas, as described in Table 4.13. The state office of education is concerned for various reasons that students from area C are not represented homogeneously in all four areas. Indeed, the proportions of these students relative to the total enrollments in the four areas, which can be derived from the data in Table 4.13 and which are shown in Table 4.14, show that there is a relative overrepresentation in area C (as could be expected), and a severe underrepresentation in areas B and D.

TABLE 4.14

Area

	A	B	C	D
Proportion of students from area C	$\dfrac{8,500}{30,000} = 0.08$	$\dfrac{275}{10,000} = 0.03$	$\dfrac{2,700}{5,000} = 0.54$	$\dfrac{3,525}{65,000} = 0.05$

The administrators, in the face of a projected decrease in the college-age population in all four areas as predicted using the methods of Chapter 2, are considering various alternative plans for decreasing the capacity of the school system in the various zones. However, they would like at the same time to try to equalize the enrollments of students from area C in the various areas. Therefore, they would like to project, on the basis of the present pattern, how various plans would affect the distribution of enrollment from area C to the four areas. To that effect, a one-way gravity distribution model has already been developed to describe the projected levels of enrollments, whose performance now has to be compared to that of an intervening opportunity model. As we have seen above, the procedure of the model is to distribute activities (here college enrollment) from a given zone j to all other zones i. Since we are more particularly interested in the enrollment from area C, this will be the zone j in the model (4.45) and we shall omit the second index of the producing zone. We next need to assign indices i to the four receiving zones in decreasing order of consideration by students from zone C. To that effect, a small informal survey of applications determines that the first choice ($i = 1$) is zone C itself (as could be expected), the second choice ($i = 2$) is zone A, the third choice ($i = 3$) is zone D, and the last and fourth choice ($i = 4$) is zone B. (Incidentally, it may be seen that this order of preference is at the present time accommodated in the sense that it is also the decreasing order of proportions of students from zone C in the four zones.)

According to (4.45), the intervening opportunities model we are going to try and fit to this situation is of the form

$$r_i = E_c \left(\frac{e^{-\lambda N_i} - e^{-\lambda N_{i-1}}}{1 - e^{-\lambda N_4}} \right) \tag{4.48}$$

where E_c is the total number of students from zone C (i.e., 15,000) to be distributed to the four zones, r_i the number allocated by the model to zone i (as numbered above), N_i the cumulative number of opportunities for location up to and including zone i (as numbered above), and λ a parameter, which value has to be estimated empirically from the data, i.e., the observed values of the variables above.

It seems reasonable to adopt as a measure n_i of opportunity for enrollment, and thus for choice of school location, the total size of the colleges in area i, i.e., the level of total enrollment as given in Table 4.13 and repeated in Table 4.15. Undoubtedly other factors such as number of degrees offered, faculty size, etc., will affect this choice. However, this assumption may well be adequate in a first attempt at modeling the given situation.

TABLE 4.15

Area Name:	C	A	D	B
Area Index, i =	1	2	3	4
Enrollment from C, r_i	2,700	8,500	3,525	275
Total enrollment, n_i	5,000	30,000	65,000	10,000
Cumulative enrollment, $\sum_{k=1}^{i} r_k$	2,700	11,200	14,725	15,000
Cumulative capacity, N_i	5,000	35,000	100,000	110,000

We have now defined all the variables represented in the model, and also have their values, as obtained in a survey of state-wide enrollments. The first step in the development of the model is to ascertain whether the choice of an intervening opportunity model is adequate to represent the existing distribution of enrollments. This can be done using the property that if it is so, the logarithm of the quantity P_i as given in (4.47), where R_i is the proportion of students from area C who go to college in areas with an order index greater than i, will be a linear function of the quantity N_i. Let us therefore compute a table of values for these respective quantities.

The order of the areas, with the corresponding numbers of students from C, as well as the corresponding capacities, are given in Table 4.15 as rearranged from Table 4.14. Table 4.15 also shows the corresponding cumulative quantities. From Table 4.15, we now compute the values of the proportion

$$P_i = 1 - \frac{\sum_{k=1}^{i} r_k}{\sum_{i=1}^{n} r_k} = 1 - \frac{\sum_{k=1}^{i} r_k}{15,000}$$

as well as their logarithms. The corresponding values are given in Table 4.16.

As this point, we can either plot graphically the values of log P_i against those of the N_i's in the last table and verify that the plot is linear, or check that the ratio of the variarions of log P_i to those of N_i when going from a given area i to the next, $(i + 1)$, is constant. The negative of this value will also provide an estimate of the value of the unknown parameter λ, as we have seen in the theoretical exposition.

TABLE 4.16

$i =$	1	2	3	4
$\sum\limits_{k=1}^{i} r_k$	2,700	11,200	14,425	15,000
$\dfrac{\sum r_k}{15,000}$	0.180	0.7467	0.9817	1.000
$P_i = 1 - \dfrac{\sum r_k}{15,000}$	0.820	0.2533	0.0183	0.000
$\log P_i$	-0.1984	-1.3732	-4.009	∞

The logs here are natural logs (base e).

The ratio of these respective variations from $i = 1$ to $i = 2$ is therefore equal to

$$\frac{\log P_2 - \log P_1}{N_2 - N_1} = \frac{-1.3732 + 0.1984}{35,000 - 5,000} = -3.92 \times 10^{-5}$$

Similarly, from $i = 2$ to $i = 3$, the ratio is equal to

$$\frac{\log P_3 - \log P_2}{N_3 - N_2} = \frac{-4.009 + 1.3732}{100,000 + 35,000} = -4.04 \times 10^{-5}$$

(We only can compute two values for this ratio, since the next value for P_i is equal to 0, and its logarithm is therefore infinite.) These two values are very close, and we will thus assume that the intervening opportunity model applies, with a constant λ equal to the negative of the average of the two empirical values above, i.e., 4×10^{-5}.

We are now in a position to evaluate what the enrollments in the four zones would be if we use the following model to predict them:

$$r_i = 15,000 \left(\frac{e^{-4 \times 10^{-5} N_i} - e^{-4 \times 10^{-5} N_{i-1}}}{1 - e^{-4 \times 10^{-5} N_4}} \right) \qquad (4.49)$$

We first compute the values of the quantities $(4 \times 10^{-5} N_i)$ and of $e^{-4 \times 10^{-5} N_i}$ for $i = 1$ to 4. The values are given in Table 4.17.

TABLE 4.17

$i =$	1	2	3	4
N_i	5,000	35,000	100,000	110,000
$4.10^{-5} N_i$	0.2	1.40	4.0	4.4
$e^{-4 \times 10^{-5} N_i}$	0.8187	0.2466	0.0183	0.0123

Finally, we compute the respective shares of the four areas of the total enrollment in area C, according to (4.48):

$$r_1 = 15,000 \left(\frac{1 - e^{-4 \times 10^{-5} N_1}}{1 - e^{-4 \times 10^{-5} N_4}} \right) = 15,000 \left(\frac{0.1813}{0.9877} \right) = 2753$$

$$r_2 = 15,000 \left(\frac{e^{-4 \times 10^{-5} N_1} - e^{-4 \times 10^{-5} N_2}}{1 - e^{-4 \times 10^{-5} N_4}} \right) = 15,000 \left(\frac{0.8187 - 0.2466}{0.9877} \right) = 8688$$

$$r_3 = 15,000 \left(\frac{e^{-4 \times 10^{-5} N_2} - e^{-4 \times 10^{-5} N_3}}{1 - e^{-4 \times 10^{-5} N_4}} \right) = 15,000 \left(\frac{0.2466 - 0.0183}{0.9877} \right) = 3467$$

$$r_4 = 15,000 \left(\frac{e^{-4 \times 10^{-5} N_3} - e^{-4 \times 10^{-5} N_4}}{1 - e^{-4 \times 10^{-5} N_4}} \right) = 15,000 \left(\frac{0.0183 - 0.0123}{0.9877} \right) = 91$$

Thus, the reproduced distribution of enrollments is rather close to the observed distribution, as can be seen from Table 4.18. It is worth noting that the values of the factors in parentheses in the foregoing computations represent the relative shares of the enrollment of $E_c = 15,000$ which go to the four colleges.

TABLE 4.18

Area $i =$	1	2	3	4	Total
Observed enrollment	2,700	8,500	3,525	275	15,000
Reproduced enrollment	2,753	8,689	3,467	91	15,000
Observed share (%)	18.0	56.7	23.5	1.8	100.0
Reproduced share	18.4	57.9	23.1	0.6	100.0

The overall precision of the model we have built thus appears to be rather adequate, and we are now in a position to use it to predict the effect on the distribution of enrollment of various changes in the spatial distribution of college enrollment, e.g., if the capacity of college B were to decrease from 10,000 to 7500. (See Exercise 4.15.) This would require that we assume that the existing pattern of choice of school remains stable, i.e., first, that there is a constant ratio (equal at the present time to 4×10^{-5} or 4/100,000) between the probability of successful application and a given college's capacity. Next, we would have to estimate how the level of this probability might change in the future. We might, in this respect, assume that it will remain the same if the school population in area C and the total state college capacity decrease proportionately, or perhaps that it will increase if a decrease in total capacity is not accompanied by a proportional decrease in the college population of area C; etc.

Next, we would have to forecast what the order of consideration of school areas from area C would be in the future, as it may be affected by such developments as changes in fellowship apportionments, or changes in the relative quality of offerings of the schools, etc. Finally, with the forecast of the future level of school age population in area C, we would then be in a position to repeat the preceding analysis and distribute this level to the four areas, thereby assessing the changes in the corresponding distributions of enrollment from the present distribution.

This example illustrates in a small and simple case the variety of assumptions that need to be made, and the number of operations and computations that have to be performed before a model can be used for planning and policy analysis purposes.

Also, if we need to model the distribution of enrollments from the other areas, A, B, and D, we simply repeat the foregoing analysis independently for each enrollment-producing area. It should be noted in this connection that the intervening opportunities model in this form is a *one-way-distribution* model, in that if, for instance, there were constraints that would limit the total number of students from all areas who can be accepted to colleges in any given area, we would have to adjust the distributed levels so that the totals are equal, respectively, to the given area capacity.

For instance, suppose that we have projected the other three distributions of enrollment, in the same fashion as we have for area C, and that the results are as given in Table 4.19. As can be seen from the table, the total

TABLE 4.19

$j =$ $Ej =$	A $50,000$	B $4,000$	C $15,000$	D $41,000$	Total Enroll- ment, r_i	Enrollment Capacity of the Area
r_{Aj}	18,201	950	8,688	5,230	33,069	30,000
r_{Bj}	2,608	580	91	2,470	5,749	10,000
r_{Cj}	4,651	550	2,753	1,150	9,104	5,000
r_{Dj}	23,541	1,920	3,467	32,150	61,078	65,000

regional enrollments, which are the row totals for each region, are not equal to the given capacities, or permissible enrollments. This can, in general, be expected in the results of a multiregional intervening opportunity model, since there are no formal constraints in the model which assure that the regional allocations will be equal to given values, as for instance in the two-way (doubly constrained) gravity model where the D_j's are given. We must then adjust the entries in the table so that their horizontal totals equal the capacities, and at the same time that their vertical totals equal the given college populations. This requires that these entries be adjusted by a factor (different for each) and related to the corresponding capacity and the corresponding enrollment. If we write the adjustment factor corresponding to r_{ij}

in the above table as $u_i v_j$, for instance, then the values of these factors on the first row should be such that

$$18{,}201u_1v_1 + 950u_1v_2 + 8688u_1v_3 + 5230u_1v_4 = 30{,}000$$

or

$$u_1 = \frac{30{,}000}{18{,}201v_1 + 950v_2 + 8688v_3 + 5230v_4}$$

By writing the other three row conditions, we also obtain four other equations between the u_i's and the v_j's. Similarly, the four column conditions, the first of which is

$$18{,}201u_1v_1 + 2608u_2v_1 + 4651u_3v_1 + 23{,}541u_4v_1 = 50{,}000$$

or

$$v_1 = \frac{50{,}000}{18{,}201u_1 + 2608u_2 + 4651u_3 + 23{,}541u_4}$$

provide the other half of the interlocked system of eight equations in the eight unknowns u_i and v_j. This system, which is of the same nature as that we have seen in (4.26a) and (4.26b) for the doubly constrained gravity model, can be solved using the same *iterative method*. Once the values of the u_i's and the v_j's are found, each entry r_{ij} in Table 4.19 is then adjusted by multiplying it by the corresponding product $u_i v_j$. It should be noted here that there is an equivalent method, sometimes called *row and column factoring*, which consists of first evaluating a set of row adjustment factors, equal to the ratio between the given capacities and the reproduced row totals, respectively, and then multiplying each entry along a given row by that factor, as shown in Table 4.20. The row totals will then equal the given capacities, but the new

TABLE 4.20

	$j = A$	B	C	D	Row Factors
r_{Aj}	16,512	862	7,882	4,745	$\frac{30{,}000}{33{,}069} = 0.9072$
r_{Bj}	4,536	1,009	158	4,296	$\frac{10{,}000}{5{,}749} = 1.7394$
r_{Cj}	2,554	302	1,512	632	$\frac{5{,}000}{9{,}104} = 0.5492$
r_{Dj}	25,052	2,043	3,690	34,214	$\frac{65{,}000}{6{,}078} = 1.0642$
Total Population	48,654	4,216	13,242	43,887	

column totals will in general not equal the given area college population. The process is then repeated, this time using a set of column factors equal to the ratios between the given populations and the latest reproduced column totals. At the end of the interation, the new row totals may not be equal to the given capacities, etc. The process is continued systematically until both row totals and column totals are equal to those given. It is important to note in this connection that this procedure, which is equivalent to the procedure above, will not converge if the grand row total (here 110,000) is not equal to the grand column total. (See Exercise 4.6.)

4.7 Some Variants of the Model

Let us conclude this introduction to the intervening opportunity model by describing some of the variants of its basic form. Just as the general formulation of the gravity model can be adapted to a variety of situations, principally through the changes in the function $F(d_{ij})$ or the definition of O_j and/or D_i, the derivation of the intervening opportunity model can be made to accommodate assumptions that divert from those we have made above. For instance, if the probability that a given resident decides to choose a given location is now assumed to vary in inverse proportion to the number of opportunities *still* to be considered (and not proportional to the number of opportunities being considered, as we have assumed above), the probability of choosing a given single location would be equal to

$$P = \frac{d}{N_\tau - N} \tag{4.50}$$

where N_τ is the total number of opportunities and N the number that have already been considered. [This expression now replaces the probability λn in formula (4.29).] The resulting model, when the mathematical derivations are carried through, is

$$r_{ij} = O_j \left[\left(1 - \frac{N_{i-1,j}}{N_{nj}}\right)^d - \left(1 - \frac{N_{ij}}{N_{nj}}\right)^d \right] \tag{4.51}$$

with the same notation as for model (4.45). The parameter d can be estimated from the formula

$$\log P_{ij} = \log K_j + d \log \left(1 - \frac{N_{ij}}{N_n}\right) \tag{4.52}$$

which is the equivalent of formula (4.37).

Another possible extension of the basic model is to use a probability $\lambda(N_i)$ which, instead of being a constant as in (4.29), is made to be a variable function of the cumulative number of opportunities that have *already* been considered. For instance, the form

$$\lambda(N_i) = \gamma N_i^{-\alpha} e^{\beta N_i} \tag{4.53}$$

can be tried, where the determinination of the values of the parameters can be effected through a linear regression. (See Chapter 7.) A typical form might be, for instance,

$$\lambda(N_i) = 1.5 \cdot 10^{-5} N_i^{-0.5} e^{1.5 N_i} \qquad (4.54)$$

Otherwise, the calibration of the model and its application follow the same principles.

4.8   Travel Generation Models

In the remainder of this chapter, we shall examine models specific to *travel demand analysis*. As we already noted, those are usually the corollary of spatial analysis problems. In fact, although the models we have seen above can be characterized as general *activity distribution models*, as a particular case they can be applied to distribute the travel corresponding to the location of a specific activity. For instance, a model of residential distribution from areas of work is also a model of travel distribution from home to work. Similarly, a model of the distribution of shopping activity from residential zones to commercial zones can be used as a model of travel distribution from home to shopping areas. These models can therefore also be used for transportation planning purposes.

However, these distribution models will require the prior estimation of how much travel there is to distribute, i.e., the estimation of the input values of the O_j's and of the D_i's in the models described above. Furthermore, more information than just the distribution of travel will be needed. The transportation planner might, for instance, be interested in which *modes* are used to travel from zone j to zone i, or in what *itineraries* are followed, etc. Although an adequate coverage of the range of methods specific to transportation systems planning and management would require much more space than we can allocate to them in this chapter, we shall now survey briefly several methods used to answer such questions.

Let us then begin with a description of the overall *transportation planning process*. This is basically composed of four phases, as represented in Figure 4.3. The first phase, *travel generation*, consists of estimating the level of travel demand generated and attracted by various zones. This will in particular provide the input O_j and D_i to the spatial distribution models. This evaluation can be performed either on a *dissagregated* (or micro) basis, i.e., from characteristics of the travelers or of the activity sites, or on an *aggregated* (or macro) basis, from the characteristics of the zones. In the former case, the method, sometimes called *category analysis* or *cross-classification analysis*, essentially consists of identifying in the population homogeneous groups, or "types" of travelers, for whom the travel needs (frequency, purpose, mode,

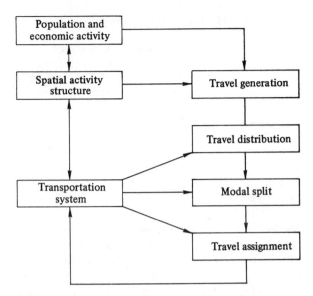

Figure 4.3   Analytical sequence of the transportation planning process.

etc.) are stable (i.e., vary little within groups) and well differentiated (i.e., exhaustively cover the range of travel needs). Characteristics such as car ownership, level of income, number of employed members of the household, etc., may be used, resulting in such groups as "small upper-income households with two cars, living in highly residential areas, or "large low-income families with no cars, living in high-density areas," etc. If the rates of trip making of the various groups in a *typology* of this kind can be accurately measured and easily projected, and if the future composition of the population in terms of the numbers of households belonging to each type can be assessed, this approach will provide a procedure for the estimation of the future levels of travel demand.

The resulting information (in a very simplified case of 20 categories) might then be of the form represented in Table 4.21. The total travel production in a given zone will then be equal to

$$T = \sum_{k=1}^{20} n_k r_k \tag{4.55}$$

where n_k is the number of household in category k and r_k is the corresponding trip rate.

In practical terms, the identification of a "good" classification is an empirical, heuristic problem of finding descriptors that will lead to as few groups as is necessary to account, for instance, for 95% of the travel demand observed. Statistical techniques such as *factor analysis* and *cluster analysis*

TABLE 4.21   Trip Rates Per Household Per Day

		Numbers of Cars Owned			
		0	1	2	3 or more
	1	1.1	2.5	4.2	—
Household Size	2	1.7	4.8	6.6	—
	3	2.5	6.2	8.4	11.1
	4	2.7	7.4	12.1	14.2
	5+	5.2	9.3	14.4	17.6

and other taxonomic procedures may be used to that effect. Also, dissagregate methods such as adaptations of cohort survival projection methods may be used to forecast the future makeup of the population in terms of the chosen groups. Conversely, the levels of travel attraction can also be estimated on a dissagregated basis, this time in relation to a classification of the attracting activities in the recipient zones. For instance, these activities might be grouped in classes of industrial, educational, commercial, governmental, service-oriented, and residential, each corresponding to a certain unit rate of travel production. The method again is to find a typology of such activities which is at once precise (i.e., corresponds to travel attractions rates with little variance within the class) but also exhaustive (i.e., which covers all causes for travel attraction), and which is compatible with the analytical activity forecasting models, such as *input/output*, *shift and share*, and *employment multiplier*, which might be used to estimate the future distribution of activities.

At the aggregate level, travel demand estimation methods usually consist of applying the *multivariate linear regression* techniques to the detection and modeling of a relationship between such zonal characteristics as average car ownership, average income, average family size, distance from central business district (C.B.D), industrial mix, residential character, etc., to either the rate of trip making from a given zone (generation) or to a given zone (attraction). (Regression methods will be described in more detail in Chapter 7.) If the travel generation is measured in terms of absolute levels and not of rates, such variables as population levels, car registrations, etc., may be used for the production of travel, and level of employment, level of retail sales, etc., for the attraction of travel.

It may be important in this case to include descriptors of the transportation system. Indeed, it is reasonable to assume that, just as in the dissagregate approach where the level of car ownership might be a determinant of travel, in the aggregate approach the *level of service* of the transportation system (i.e., density of public transportation stops, capacity of streets, etc.) will affect travel demand.

The typical model for travel generation estimation using this approach would then be

$$Y_i = a_{0j} + \sum_{i=1} a_{ij} X_{ij}$$ (4.56)

where X_{ij} is the ith zonal characteristic for zone j, and the a_{ij}'s are empirically determined coefficients which are produced by the regression analysis. For instance, a typical model might be, in a specific situation,

$$Y = 4.3 + 3.9X_1 - 0.005X_2 - 0.13X_3 - 0.012X_4$$ (4.57)

where Y is the total rate of trip generation per household in the area, X_1 the level of car ownership per household, X_2 the number of residential dwelling units per acre, X_3 the distance from the C.B.D. in miles, X_4 the family income in thousands of dollars.

It is important to note that these models are in general not replicable from geographical area to geographical area. Also, the definition of the spatial zones will affect the value of the resulting coefficients, just as the definition of the categories in the cross-classification analysis would affect the resulting rates of travel generated. The results of this type of analysis are highly *local-specific*.

The foregoing travel generation analysis may be dissaggregated by *trip purpose*, such of travel to work, to shop, etc, to improve the level of precision. Also, further dissaggregations might be necessary, depending on the specific, local situation, such as, for instance, a distinction between *home-based trips* and *work-based trips*, downtown and suburbs, interurban and intraurban, etc. The same general approach is applicable. Finally, account should also be taken of special *travel generators* such as airports, governmental facilities, major shopping centers, manufacturing plants, etc. In each case, typical rates of trip production and attraction can be obtained.

The estimation of *passenger travel demand* may also be supplemented by the estimation of the *freight movements* between zones. In each case appropriate modifications of the approach may be required, such as using an *input/output* model in connection with a regional goods movements estimate, etc.

In summary, the travel generation models require as inputs the outputs of the models of urban and regional activity analysis that we have examined in the preceding chapters. In that sense, they constitute the link between the general urban system models and the subset of transportation systems models we are presently considering.

The next stage in the transportation planning process is the spatial distribution of travel, given the levels generated and attracted as determined above. The spatial distribution models that we have seen in Sections 4.2 to 4.7 can be utilized to that effect, and we shall therefore not elaborate further.

4.9 Models of Mode Choice

The next and third phase in the transportation planning analytical process is the determination of the *modal split*, i.e., the estimation of the fractions of the travel distributed between the zones which will utilize the respective transportation modes available.

Although the theory can be extended to the case of several modes, we shall present it in the context of a choice between two competing modes, mainly the private car and public transportation. This case is in some respects the most important, since one of the critical problems in urban transportation planning is the diversion of travel from the private car to mass transit. The first model of mode choice is the *probit model*. This model equates the probability that a given traveler chooses travel mode 1 instead of mode 2 to the cumulative probability that a standard normal random variable (see Section 1.4) takes on a value less than a given value, called the *utility* of mode 1. This quantity is evaluated as a function of the characteristics of the traveler and of the relative advantages of mode 1 over mode 2. Formally, the probability of the choice of mode 1 is given by

$$P_1 = \Phi(G_k) \tag{4.58}$$

were $\Phi(x)$ is the value of the cumulative standard normal probability distribution function for the value x, and G_k is the value of the "utility" of mode 1 for travelers in population group k. The probability P_2 of the choice of the second mode is, of course, the complement of P_1; that is,

$$P_2 = 1 - P_1 = 1 - \Phi(G_k) \tag{4.59}$$

The rationale for such a formulation derives from the application of principles of mathematical biology to the responses of travelers to the utilities offered by both modes.

In spite of its unusual appearance, the model of mode choice (4.58) is very simple to use, once the expression for the utility G_k has been obtained, since the probability of choice of mode 1 is then computed as the probability that a standard normal random variable takes a value at most equal to G_k. This probability is easily read off Table A.2 in Appendix A, as we shall learn in Section 6.3.

The expression of the utility is usually taken to be a linear function of the relative *attributes* of the two transportation modes (their levels of service, costs, travel times, comfort, etc.) and of the socioeconomic characteristics of the traveler. It is then specified as

$$G_k = a + \sum_s b_s(X_s^1 - X_s^2) + \sum_t c_t Y_t^k \tag{4.60}$$

where the X_s^1's are the values of the characteristics or attributes of mode 1, X_s^2 the corresponding characteristics of mode 2, and the Y_t^k's are personal characteristics of travelers in group k. Other formulations might be based on the ratios X_s^1/X_s^2 instead of the differences $(X_s^1 - X_s^2)$, as measures of the competition between the two modes.

The plot of the values of the probability of choice of mode 1 against the values of the utility can be represented as in Figure 4.4. When the value of the utility is highly negative, mode 2 will be chosen with high probability, and conversely, when it is highly positive, mode 1 will be chosen. The break point, i.e., when mode 1 has the same probability (50%) of being chosen as mode 2 by a traveler in group k, is for a relative utility of zero. Figure 4.4 can be considered to be equivalent to an empirical *diversion curve*, which plots the observed fraction of the total volume of traffic between given areas, using mode 1, as a function of the relative characteristics of the two modes.

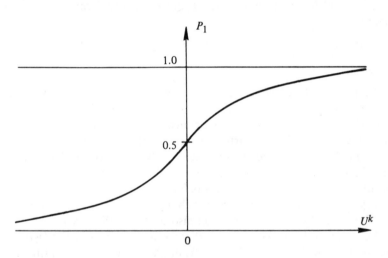

Figure 4.4   Probit model.

In practical terms, probit models of mode choice are calibrated on the basis of empirical observations of the variables above, using the technique of *maximum likelihood* estimation of the coefficients a_0, b_s, and c_t in (4.60). (This technique will be described in detail in Section 6.7 when we consider methods of model calibration.)

As an example of the application of a probit model, let us assume that we have forecasted that the level of travel between areas j and i is 1500 trips per day. At the present time, the only mode available is the private car. It takes 35 minutes (on the average) and costs about \$2.25 (at \$0.15 per mile) to travel by car between the two zones. A public transportation system is planned, which would enable residents to travel between the two zones for

$0.85 and would take 55 minutes. Let us assume further that on the basis of research in areas with similar situations in terms of transportation alternatives and population, it has been determined that the probability P_1 of a traveler choosing the private car can be expressed by the probit model where the utility G is represented by

$$G = 0.8 + 0.11(T_2 - T_1) + 0.1(C_2 - C_1) + 0.01I + 0.005A$$

where T_2 and T_1 are the travel times in hours on the given route with transit and the car, respectively, and C_2 and C_1 the corresponding costs in dollars. I is the income of the traveler, in thousands of dollars and A is his or her age, in years. Given the above, what percentage of the segment of the traveling population of age 35 with an income of $25,000 would be diverted to transit use? Let us compute the value of the probit corresponding to the foregoing comparison of transportation service characteristics (where mode 1 is the car) and to the given traveler. From the above formula, the probit is equal to

$$G = 0.80 + 0.11\left(\frac{55 - 35}{60}\right) + 0.1(0.85 - 2.25) + 0.01(25) + 0.005(35)$$
$$= 1.12$$

The probability of choosing the car is equal to the entry in Table A.2 corresponding to a value of 1.12. This is equal to 0.8686, or about 87%. At this level of service and fare, public transportation would then attract only 13% of the ridership in that particular segment of the population.

The model can be used for the usual analytical purposes by varying the level of the variables. For instance, one could ask how cheap transit would have to become (or faster, or both) before it becomes competitive with the car in the sense of having a higher probability of being used by that particular type of traveler. Similar questions can also be asked. (See Exercise 4.7.)

The other model of mode choice that we shall describe is the *logit* model. This model, which can be derived from the application of principles of mathematical psychology, expresses the probability of the choice of mode 1 as

$$P_1^k = \frac{e^{G_1^k}}{e^{G_1^k} + e^{G_2^k}} = \frac{1}{1 + e^{G_2^k - G_1^k}} \tag{4.61}$$

where as in the probit model above, G_1^k is a function of the characteristics of mode i, as evaluated by a traveler of type k. The expression of this function can take on various forms, linear or otherwise. It is interesting to note that model (4.61) closely resembles the *logistic model* of population projection (2.13). Thus, the plot of the probability P_1 as a function of the values of the variable $(G_2^k - G_1^k)$ has the shape represented in Figure 4.5. Although the general shape of this plot is similar to that of the probit model in Figure 4.4, the specific values of the probabilities are different.

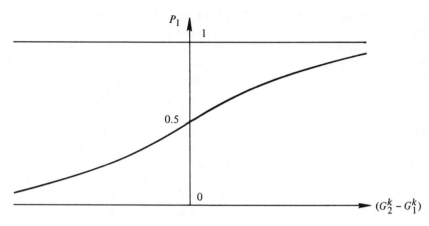

Figure 4.5   Logit model.

Also, the same transformation that enabled us to calibrate the logistic model can be used to evaluate the parameters of the function G_1^k. Indeed, from (4.61) we have

$$1 - P_1^k = 1 - \frac{e^{G_1^k}}{e^{G_1^k} + e^{G_2^k}} = \frac{e^{G_2^k}}{e^{G_1^k} + e^{G_2^k}}$$

and therefore

$$\frac{P_1^k}{1 - P_1^k} = \frac{e^{G_1^k}}{e^{G_2^k}} = e^{G_1^k - G_2^k}$$

so that

$$\log \left(\frac{P_1^k}{1 - P_1^k}\right) = \log \left(\frac{P_1^k}{P_2^k}\right) = \log e^{G_1^k - G_2^k} = (G_1^k - G_2^k) \qquad (4.62)$$

Usually, the function G_i^k, the *utility function* of mode i for traveler k, will be taken to be linear, i.e., of the form

$$G_1^k = a_1 + \sum_s b_{1s} X_s + \sum_t c_{1t} Y_t^k$$

and   (4.63)

$$G_2^k = a_2 + \sum_s b_{2s} X_s + \sum_t c_{2t} Y_t^k$$

where as in (4.60) the X_s's are the attributes, or levels of service common to both the first mode and to the second mode, and the Y_t^k's the characteristics of the traveler in group k. In this (linear) case, (4.62) can be written

$$\log \left(\frac{P_1^k}{P_2^k}\right) = a_1 - a_2 + \sum_s (b_{1s} - b_{2s}) X_s + \sum_t (c_{1t} - c_{2t}) Y_t^k \qquad (4.64)$$

The value of the differences between the coefficients $(a_1 - a_2), (b_{1s} - b_{2s})$, and $(c_{1t} - c_{2t})$, which are the parameters in model (4.61), can then be estimated empirically from the results of a multivariate linear regression of the quantity $\log(P_1^k/P_2^k)$ (as observed from the mode choices of travelers of type k) against the values of the X's and the Y's.

As an illustration, let us assume that the calibration of a logit model of *binary choice* between the private car (mode 1) and commuter train (mode 2) has resulted in a utility difference between the two modes given by

$$G_2 - G_1 = -0.7 + 0.3(c_1 - c_2) + 0.2(t_1 - t_2) \qquad (4.65)$$

where c_i is the cost of travel by mode i in dollars and t_i is the travel time for that mode in hours. [Note that this is a simplified version of (4.64), where the characteristics Y_t of the traveler do not intervene. Consequently, this can be considered to be applicable to all traveler types k, with therefore no index k.]

Given this model and the fact that the difference in travel time on a given route and the car is equal to $t_2 - t_1 = 0.4$ hour, and that the cost of travel by car is equal to \$1.50, what should be the level of the train fare so that it could attract one-third of the commuters? This question can be rephrased by asking what should be the value of c_2 be so that the probability P_2 of choice of mode 2 is equal to $\frac{1}{3}$, or $P_1 = \frac{2}{3}$. From (4.61), we have

$$P_1 = \frac{1}{1 + e^{G_2 - G_1}}$$

and replacing $(G_2 - G_1)$ from (4.65):

$$P_1 = \frac{1}{1 + e^{-[0.7 + 0.3(c_2 - c_1) + 0.2(t_2 - t_1)]}}$$

(Note the importance of the order of the indices.) With the given values,

$$P_1 = \frac{1}{1 + e^{-[0.7 + 0.3(c_2 - 1.5) + 0.2(0.4)]}} = \frac{2}{3}$$

or

$$1 + e^{-(0.33 + 0.3c_2)} = \frac{3}{2} = 1.5$$

Thus,

$$e^{-(0.33 + 0.3c_2)} = 0.5$$

or

$$\log[e^{-(0.33 + 0.3c_2)}] = -(0.33 + 0.3c_2) = \log 0.5 = -0.693$$

so that

$$0.3c_2 = 0.693 - 0.330 = 0.363$$

and $c_2 = 1.21$ or \$1.21 in our units.

Thus, the disadvantage of the train with respect to travel time could in principle be compensated by a lower fare. Similar questions can be answered in the same fashion. (See Exercise 4.8.)

4.10 Travel Assignment Methods

Let us now go on to the fourth and last phase in the transportation planning analytical sequence of Figure 4.3. We now have the levels of the travel flows T_{ij} which are expected between each origin j and each destination i, by mode, possibly by trip purpose, type of traveler, etc. We must now in this final stage assign these travel demands to the various links in the transportation network. Indeed, there may in general be several possible itineraries, or routes to reach area i from area j, each with its own characteristics (capacity, distance or travel time, etc). These individual characteristics of the links between zones j and i may already have intervened in the determination of the *separation*, or *friction* factor $F(d_{ij})$, in the travel distribution phase (possibly through an averaging of their values over all links connecting areas i from area j). However, the problem of *travel assignment* is to determine which fraction of the total demand T_{ij} each of these links will be made to carry.

There are several possible approaches to that problem. However, they all generally rely on the basic principle that the transportation network loading should be such that it minimizes travel effort (i.e,, a composite of time, cost, inconvenience, etc.) between zones, both for an individual traveler choosing between routes for a given trip and for the total effort of the entire population of travelers. Thus, the first step in the methods of travel assignment is the determination of the least-effort route between any given zones, given the efforts associated with each link. This can be accomplished through the application of the *shortest-path* method, as explained below. Let us first, however, define a few basic terms in network theory.

A network will, in general, be a set of *nodes* (or points) in space, connected by *links* (or *arcs*). A network can be *directed*, as in the case of one-way streets, or they can be *undirected*. Similarly, a network can be *capacitated*, meaning that there will be limits on the amounts each link can carry, or it can be *uncapacitated*, or mixed.

There are a number of ways to represent a network. The *graph* of a network will simply be its diagrammatic representation, such as in Figure 4.6, which represents a directed, capacitated network. Arrows along the links

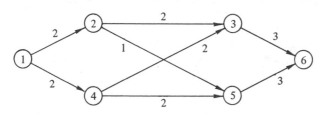

Figure 4.6 The graph of a network.

indicate the directions of travel, and numbers along the links indicate their capacities, or the maximum amounts of travel they can carry. In other instances, such as in the procedure below, the numbers along the links might represent the levels of effort required to travel along them.

The basic principle of the shortest-path method is as follows. From the origin node, we will label all nodes with their shortest distance from the origin in a series of successive steps. At each step, we will determine the node with the shortest possible distance from the origin. This node will be reached directly from the origin, in a *one-step trip*, or will be reached through some previously labeled node in a *multiple-step trip*. In other words, the node with the shortest distance from the origin will be such that it corresponds to the minimum length of either direct links with the origin, or the minimum length of a multilink path first to some already labeled node and then from that node to the origin. When all nodes are labeled, the label of the end node is the length of the shortest path from the origin. We cannot stop the procedure even if the end node is labeled before all the other nodes in the network because of the possibility of a shorter path from the origin through another, yet unlabeled, intermediary node.

As an illustration, let us assume that we want to determine the shortest path between nodes 1 and 7 in the network represented in Figure 4.7. The

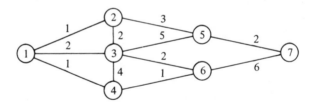

Figure 4.7   Shortest path algorithm.

numbers along the links represent their lengths, either in terms of actual distances or in terms of travel times, generalized effort, cost, etc. (All links are undirected.) We begin by putting the origin, node 1, in the set of labeled nodes (which we will call L) with a label of 0. This is graphically represented in Figure 4.8(a). Next, we determine the shortest trip that can be taken from

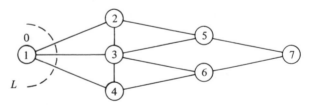

Figure 4.8(a)   Start.

the origin to an unlabeled node. This trip will consist of the shortest of either one-step trips to an unlabeled node, or several-step trips from the origin to some already labeled node and then from that labeled node to an unlabeled node. Since the origin, node 1, is the only labeled node so far, the possible trips are from node 1 to node 2, or node 1 to node 3, or node 1 to node 4, corresponding respectively to a distance of $(0 + 1)$, $(0 + 2)$ and $(0 + 1)$. Therefore, the shortest distance for this first iteration will be

$$d_1 = \text{Min}\left\{0 + \text{Min}\left[0 + \text{Min}\begin{pmatrix}1\\2\\1\end{pmatrix}\right]\right\}$$

The minimum distance between the origin and an unlabeled mode is thus 1, and corresponds to either node 2 or node 4. Let us decide to systematically retain the smallest indexed node in the case of a tie. Thus, we retain node 2, which is now included in the set of labeled nodes $L = (1, 2)$ with a label of 1, its shortest distance from the origin. This is represented in Figure 4.8(b).

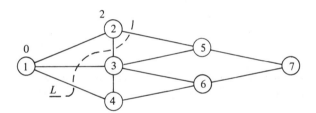

Figure 4.8(b)   First iteration.

Next, we will be trying to reach an unlabeled node with the next shortest possible distance from the origin. This can only be done by either direct one-step trips from the origin or several-step trips, first to some labeled node for which we know the shortest distance from the origin, and then from that labeled node to some unlabeled node. Thus, in our example, the next smallest distance, d_2, to an unlabeled node will be the shortest length, respectively, of a one-step trip from node 1 to the unlabeled node 2 (the only labeled node connected to node 1), or a two-step trip made of first a one-step trip to labeled node 2 and then a one-step trip from node 2 to unlabeled node 3 or 5 (the only nodes connected to node 2). The value for d_2 is then Min [(1); 1 + Min (2 or 3)] = 1, corresponding to node 4. Thus node 4 comes into the set of labeled nodes L with a label of 1. This is represented in Figure 4.8(c). Continuing in this fashion we now look for the next smallest length for trips from the origin to some unlabeled node. The possiblities are a one-step strip to node 3, a two-step trip to node 5 via node 2, a two-step trip to node 3 via

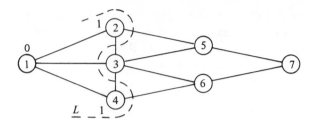

Figure 4.8(c)   Second iteration.

node 4, or a two-step trip to node 6 via node 4. This is summarized as follows:

Third Iteration $L = (1, 2, 4)$

Path

$$d_3 = \text{Min} \begin{cases} 0 + \text{Min (2)} & 1 \longrightarrow 3 \\ 2 + \text{Min (3)} & 1 \longrightarrow 2 \longrightarrow 5 \\ 1 + \text{Min (4, 1)} & 1 \longrightarrow 4 \longrightarrow 3 \end{cases}$$

or $1 \longrightarrow 4 \longrightarrow 6$

Thus, $d_3 = \text{Min} \begin{cases} 2 \\ 5 \\ 2 \end{cases} = 2$, corresponding to either node 3 or node 6. Let us

retain the smallest index, node 3. Thus, node 3 comes into the set of labeled nodes L and its label is 2. This is represented on Figure 4.8(d).

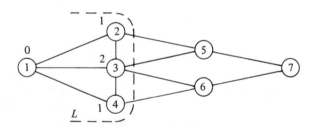

Figure 4.8(d)   Third iteration.

The subsequent iterations are summarized below:

Fourth Iteration $L = (1, 2, 3, 4)$

Path

$$d_4 = \text{Min} \begin{cases} 1 + \text{Min (3)} & 1 \longrightarrow 2 \longrightarrow 5 \\ 2 + \text{Min (5, 2)} & 1 \longrightarrow 3 \longrightarrow 5 \\ & 1 \longrightarrow 3 \longrightarrow 6 \\ 1 + \text{Min (1)} & 1 \longrightarrow 4 \longrightarrow 6 \end{cases}$$
or

Thus,

$$d_4 = \text{Min} \begin{cases} 1 + 3 \\ 2 + 2 \\ 1 + 1 \end{cases} = 2$$

which puts node 6 into the set of labeled nodes with a label of 2 [Figure 4.8(e)].

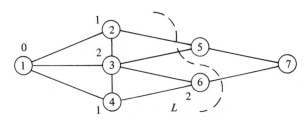

Figure 4.8(e)   Fourth iteration.

Fifth Iteration $L = (1, 2, 3, 4, 6)$

$$\begin{array}{ll} & \text{Path} \\ d_5 = \text{Min} \begin{cases} 1 + \text{Min} (3) & 1 \longrightarrow 2 \longrightarrow 5 \\ 2 + \text{Min} (5) & 1 \longrightarrow 3 \longrightarrow 5 \\ 2 + \text{Min} (6) & 1 \longrightarrow 6 \longrightarrow 7 \end{cases} \end{array}$$

Thus,

$$d_5 = \text{Min} \begin{cases} 1 + 3 \\ 2 + 5 \\ 2 + 6 \end{cases} = 4$$

and node 5 comes into L with a label of 4 [Figure 4.8(f)].

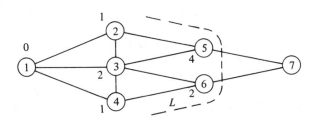

Figure 4.8(f)   Fifth iteration.

Sixth Iteration.   The set of labeled nodes is now $L = (1, 2, 3, 4, 5, 6)$. The only unlabeled node is node 7. Only nodes 5 and 6 are connected to node 7. Therefore, the possibilities are

$$d_6 = \text{Min} \begin{cases} 4 + \text{Min} (2) \\ 2 + \text{Min} (6) \end{cases}$$

The smallest distance from node 1 to node 7 is 6. All nodes in the network have now been labeled [Figure 4.8(g)]. Since all nodes have been labeled, the label of the end node 6 is the length of the shortest path from it to the origin. The shortest path is then determined by retracing how the end point was reached via the intermediary points. In our example, node 7 was reached from node 5, node 5 from node 2, and node 2 from node 1. Thus, the shortest path is 1 → 2 → 5 → 7.

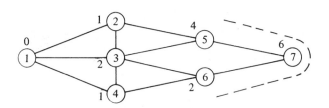

Figure 4.8(g)   Sixth iteration.

There are other possible methods for identifying the shortest path between nodes in a network. In particular it is possible to apply the approach of *dynamic programming*, which will be seen in Chapter 5. Other more sophisticated techniques also provide the *second-shortest* path, the third-, etc. Before leaving this first example, it should be mentioned that there are other applications of network theory to problems of spatial planning. Clearly, the geometry of the transportation network of a region or of an urban area influences its operation in many ways other than just travel. For instance, the individual capacity of the links determines the total level of interaction that can be carried or transmitted through the whole network and therefore constrains the ultimate levels of spatial interaction. Finally, the operational characteristics of the transportation system, e.g., the management of peak hour levels, and other flow control strategies also have a direct bearing on travel assignment. Because of the introductory nature of this text, however, the reader is referred to more specialized texts in the areas of *traffic engineering* and network optimization techniques of *operations research*.

After this diversion, let us now return to the problem of travel assignment. The first and simplest procedure, sometimes called the *all-or-nothing assignment method*, consists of assigning all the travel generated between zones j and i to the minimum path route between the zones. This is a reasonably logical approach in the case when either the minimum path is the only possibility (i.e., there is only one route) or when the second-best route corresponds to a substantially higher effort. However, when the next best route in terms of effort is close to the best route, this approach might lead to serious discrepancies with actual link loadings.

In this case, it may be appropriate to divert some of the travel assigned to the best route to the lower-level routes, in increasing order of effort. Loading splits may be effected on the basis of the relative levels of effort (e_{ij}^2/e_{ij}^1) or of their difference, ($e_{ij}^2 - e_{ij}^1$), possibly through a *route choice model* similar to the modal choice models we have seen in (4.59) and (4.61). (See p. 256.)

Further refinements to these basic approaches may be motivated by the possibility of a relationship between the level of loadings on given links and the corresponding effort they result in. For instance, with increasing volumes on arterials in a street or freeway system, travel times will increase. Consequently, this will change the least-effort routes (in principle, with each new traveler assigned). To take this feedback effect into account, the method of *capacity restraint assignment* consists of adjusting the travel times after each increment of a set number of units of travel volumes (e.g., a hundred cars an hour), identifying the new set of best routes (if any) and assigning the next increment of travel volumes. The procedure is iterated in this fashion until a final stable equilibrium is reached.

Several forms of relationships between travel volume V and travel time T can be used, for instance:

$$T^k = T_0\left(1 + 0.15\frac{V_k}{C}\right)^4 \tag{4.66}$$

or

$$T^k = T_0 \cdot 2\frac{V_k}{C} \tag{4.67}$$

where T_0 is the minimum travel time corresponding to no traffic, V_k the current volume at iteration k, and C the maximum capacity of the link. Needless to say, such procedures are usually implemented on computers, given the large number of computations involved, which grows geometrically with the number of zones considered. At each stage of the assignment, capacity constraints and balance requirements must of course be observed.

Also, *variable link travel efforts* (which might depend, for instance, on the number of turns or passages through interchanges, that is, depend on the actual assignment) may be incorporated into the procedure. Finally, there exist some methods for assigning travel on a *probabilistic* basis, on the assumption that a traveler will not always necessarily choose the least-effort route, especially if the other choices represent close levels of effort.

Mention should also be made, in concluding this section, of models that attempt to treat all four phases of the travel forecasting process simultaneously. The main problems are, as can be suspected, the internal consistency of the relationships between each of the submodels, and the simultaneous estimation of the many parameters. However, at least conceptually, such an integration of individual, travel demand component models is possible.

EXERCISES

4.1   The staff of a State Chamber of Commerce has been analyzing past patterns
of labor migration into the state and would like to develop a formal analytical
model to describe the geographic origin of the new residents. After preliminary discussions and an investigation of the literature on migration models,
it has been decided to try a simple gravity model of the form

$$N_j = P_j d_j^{-1}$$

where N_j is the number of immigrants from state j, P_j the population level
of that state, and d_j the difference between the average income in the state
and in state j, adjusted for cost of living. (Negative differences are put equal
to zero.)

(a)   Verbalize what the formulation above means in practical terms and
what some of its most obvious shortcomings might be.

(b)   Is the model in this form completely specified? Assuming that the
model is to be used to infer the geographic origin of workers when the
total level of work force migration into the state from all other states is
given (or set), how does this affect the form of the model? [*Hint:*
Introduce a scaling factor k, and determine what its value should be
for the predicted migration to the state to be consistent with the given
level. Follow the derivation of the production-constrained version of
the one-way gravity model, (4.10) to (4.14).]

4.2   Derive the final expression of the one-way gravity model (4.14) in the case
when the production measures O_j and the attraction measures D_i, as well
as the friction factors $F(d_{ij})$, are not the simple quantities used in the examples, but can be general functions. (*Advice:* Follow the derivation of the
model, but everywhere replace the quantities above by their final expression.)

4.3   In the illustrative example of the single-constraint gravity model, assume
that proposed changes in the transportation system between the three zones
would result in a decrease of the travel time between zones which, translated
in terms of distance, would be represented by a new distance matrix:

$i =$ $\diagdown$ $j =$	1	2	3
1	2	7	6
2	6	2	4
3	5	4	3

Would these changes have any effect on the commuting pattern from home
to work, assuming that the past gravity mechanism remains stable?

4.4   (a)   Using the original data for the same (single-constraint) example, project what the residential levels would be if the model

$$W_{ij} = l_j E_j P_i^2 d_{ij}^{-2}$$

were used.

(b)   Compare the resulting residential patterns.

4.5 (a) Using the data of the example for the doubly constrained gravity model, project the travel levels T_{ij} that would result from selection of the form

$$F(d_{ij}) = d_{ij}^{1.5} e^{-2d_{ij}}$$

for the "impedance function."

(b) Compare the resulting distribution of travel with the original distribution. Has this choice of function for the friction factor brought the predicted levels closer to the observed levels as given in Table 4.5? Give a measurement of the change.

4.6 Using the data in Table 4.19, adjust the regional distributions of college enrollments so that they conform to the given regional capacities. Use the method of "row and column factoring" as started in Table 4.20. Compare with the resolution of the system of equations in the k_i's and the l_i's as started in the same example.

4.7 Using the probit model (4.60) presented as an illustration, and assuming that a commuter has an income of $40,000 and is 30 years old, give an expression for the combination of values of travel time and transit fare that would result in a probability of at least 30% to obtain his or her patronage.

4.8 (a) Using the logit model (4.65) given in the example, by how much should travel time with transit be lower than that with a private car so that it would attract $\frac{1}{3}$ of the ridership? (Assume that $c_2 = 1$.)

(b) Compare the result with that in the example, and derive an estimate of the "value" of commuting time in monetary terms.

4.9 Assume that we want to investigate, on an indicative basis, the effects on transportation requirements of the growth of three cities H, A, and D, for instance. Assume that the population forecasts for a future year are as follows (in millions):

$$P_H = 3.0$$

$$P_D = 1.5$$

$$P_A = 0.5$$

The present travel times between cities are (in hours):

	H	D	A
H	0.5	6	3
D	6	0.3	3
A	3	3	0.2

The "trips per person per day" rates for the respective populations are as follows:

$$H: \quad 0.70$$

$$D: \quad 0.60$$

$$A: \quad 0.50$$

(a) Given the data above, and assuming that a gravity model of the form $T_{ij} = k_i l_j P_i P_j d_{ij}^{-1}$ applies, what is the expected distribution of travel within and between the three cities?

(b) What would be the effect on intercity travel of a reduction of the travel time between D and H of 20% and between D and A of 10%?

(c) What would be the effect on travel demands of an increase in population (or an error in estimate) of

$$P_H: \quad 30\%$$
$$P_D: \quad 15\%$$
$$P_A: \quad 0\%$$

4.10 Combine the multiregional, economic base mechanism [formulas (3.51) to (3.53)] with the gravity allocation model to evaluate the changes in the regional residential and service employment structure P_i and S_i, respectively, in the data below, resulting from the increase in the number of basic jobs E_i^b, of 5%, minus 3%, and 0% for zones 1, 2, and 3, respectively. Assume a work-force ratio for the new jobs of 1:4 for all population zones, and a service job equivalent of 6:1 for all zones.

Zone i	E_i^b	E_i^s	P_i	T_{ij} (hours)
1	1,000	2,000	30,000	0.1 0.4 0.2
2	1,500	4,000	40,000	0.4 0.1 0.3
3	500	2,000	12,000	0.2 0.3 0.1
Total	3,000	8,000	82,000	

(*Hint:* A simplifying assumption would be that the relative attractions of the zones, both for residential and commercial purposes, are proportional not to the existing populations, or numbers of service jobs at each round of the distribution, but to the original levels.)

4.11 Given the following network, where the numbers along the links represent the distances in miles, determine the itinerary of shortest travel time between points A and G.

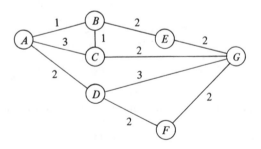

Figure E-4.11

4.12   The Bureau of Economic Analysis of a certain state has been involved in the construction of input/output tables. The staff would now like to test whether the pattern of import/export movements can be modeled according to a gravity formulation. The economic structure of the region has been simplified to three production sectors, *A*, *B*, and *C*, with the respective levels of exports (in millions of dollars per month) as follows:

Sector	A	B	C
Level of exports	3	4	2

These exports go principally to three external regions, 1, 2, and 3. The costs of shipping from each of the production sectors to each of the consumption regions in dollars per hundred pounds are as follows:

		Production Sector		
		A	*B*	*C*
External Sector	1	3	4	2
	2	4	4	5
	3	2	5	3

The model to be tested is based on the rationale that the movements of goods from a given producing sector to a given consuming sector are proportional to the total export level of the producing sector, proportional to the gross economic production of the consuming sector, and inversely proportional to the cost of shipping. The gross economic productions of the three consuming sectors are as given below (in terms of index of base 100):

Sector	1	2	3
Production index	100	50	100

Given the data above, develop a gravity model and use it to predict the movements of goods between regions, so that they can be compared with actual levels,

4.13   (a)   Assuming that the model in Exercise 4.12 is judged adequate, forecast the effects on the freight movements between regions of a change in the economic production index of importing region 2 from 50 to 65.

(b)   What would be the changes in the pattern if the costs of shipping between exporting zone *A* and importing zone 3 were cut by 15%?

(c)   Evaluate the changes in the freight movements that would result from an increase in the export production levels of regions *A* and *C* of 10%.

4.14   The accompanying diagram represents a schematic freeway system, where
the first figure along the links is its (undirected) capacity (in thousands of

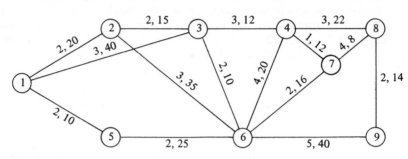

Figure E-4.14

cars per hour), and the second figure is the travel time (in minutes). Also,
the levels of travel demand (in thousands of cars per hour) in 5 years from
now have been projected at the following levels (from j to i):

T_{ij}

$i =$	$j =$ 1	2	3	4	5	6	7	8	9
1		1.1	2.6		0.7				
2	1.3		1.4			2.3			
2	2.2	1		1.8		0.7			
4						2.8	0.4	1.8	
5	0.8					0.9			
6		2.5	0.9	2.7	1.6		0.7		3.2
7			0.8					3.1	
8			2				3.2		0.8
9						3.9		0.7	

Given this information, determine what changes in the individual link capacities would have to be made to accommodate these levels of travel demand.
[*Advice:* Assign the T_{ij}'s on the basis of the least travel time between points,
successively for all couples of zones. Superimpose all such assignments to
obtain the total (directed) loading on each link of the network.]

4.15   (a) Using the intervening opportunities model developed in the illustrative
example (Section 4.6), determine the changes in the choice of college
for students from area C which would result from a decrease of the
capacity of area B from 10,000 to 7,500.

(b) Evaluate the changes resulting from a recruitment campaign that
would be aimed at making colleges in area B the most attractive for
students in area C, i.e., those they would consider first.

REFERENCES

BATTY, M. *Urban Modeling*. New York: Cambridge University Press, 1976.

OLIVER, R. M., AND R. B. POTTS. *Flows in Transportation Networks*. New York: Academic Press, Inc., 1972.

PUTMAN, S. "Urban Residential Location Models," in *Studies in Applied Regional Science*. Leiden, The Netherlands: Martinus Nijhoff's N.V., 1978.

QUANDT, R. E. *The Demand for Travel: Theory and Measurement*. Lexington, Mass.: D. C. Heath & Company, 1978.

STOPHER, P., AND A. MEYBURGH. *Travel Demand Modeling*. Lexington, Mass.: D. C. Heath & Company, 1975.

TRANSPORTATION RESEARCH BOARD. *Urban Travel Demand Forecasting*. Special Report 143, Washington, D.C., 1974.

URBAN MASS TRANSPORTATION ADMINISTRATION. *User Oriented Material for UTPS. An Introduction to Travel Demand Forecasting. A Self-Instructional Text*. Washington, D.C., 1977.

WILSON, A. G. *Urban and Regional Models in Geography and Planning*. New York: John Wiley & Sons, Inc., 1974.

5 ══════════════
Programming Models

5.1 Introduction

In the previous chapters, we have seen a variety of analytical models. These models were designed primarily for *forecasting* purposes, i.e., to analyze the changes in certain predicted variables (the output) resulting from changes in given variables (the input). In that sense these models can be called *descriptive*, since they leave to the analyst the task to decide which of the alternative predicted situations is the most desirable. For instance, the *gravity model* of Chapter 4 only describes the patterns of travel or activity location among zones. The model does not in its own right enable us to evaluate the desirability of each pattern, or equivalently to identify the "best" pattern, but can only generate a variety of such patterns.

Thus, this type of model is not sufficient for *decision-making* purposes. On the other hand, it is usually the case that a descriptive forecast of future conditions under varying assumptions is motivated by the need to select the optimal choice of action which will bring the economic, spatial, or more generally, social system as close as possible to the desired state represented by the development goals. Thus, the decision making being the end product of the overall activity of analysis is at least as important as the forecasting aspect, which usually only represents a preparatory stage.

To return for a moment to Section 1.1, the models of the previous chapters are essentially used in phases 4, 5, and 7, i.e., system representation, forecasting of the future state of the system, and determination of the effects of proposed actions on that future state. The models we are going to see in this chapter are directed toward phase 8, the evaluation of various alternatives and the selection of the optimal one. In that sense, they are models of decision making, as opposed to (or better complementing) the purely analytical models of the previous chapters.

Decision making in our context usually means allocating in the most effective manner scarce (or at least limited) *resources*, to achieve set developmental objectives. These resources are principally physical (such as land, water, housing, etc.), capital (such as budgets, manpower, etc.), and time. The objectives may be financial (cheapest cost of a given project), operational (minimum overall travel to work for a given area), physical (maximum utilization of a given amount of land), social (maximum residential integration), etc., or a combination of these. Although there are still rather few decision-making and evaluative models native to the urban and regional analysis area, several types of optimizing models developed in *management science* and *operations research* have been successfully applied to planning and policy problems. Thus, another characteristic of the models of this chapter (which, incidentally, they share with the statistical models of Chapter 7) is that they are nonsubstantive. That is, they provide a mathematical framework that can be applied to problems involving entities of a quite varied nature, including those which intervened in the substantive models of Chapters 2 to 4, i.e., population levels, economic activity levels, employment levels, etc.

In this chapter, we shall examine three types of methods that are designed to select the "optimal" alternative (in some sense to be defined). They are the *linear programming*, *dynamic programming*, and *CPM–PERT* methods, respectively.

Linear programming is important because it is connected to the class of *linear models* (see the definition in Section 1.2), which we have encountered repeatedly throughout the text. For instance, the *cohort-survival* population projection has a linear form. Also, the *input/output* model belongs to the same class, as well as the multiregional *economic base* model, etc. Furthermore, it can always be attempted to model any situation in a linear form, using the techniques of *linear regression* to be developed in Chapter 7. Thus, because of its inherent simplicity and generality, the linear model is widely used in urban and regional analysis and planning. Consequently, the linear programming model, which, as we shall see expands a linear descriptive model into an optimizing model, has a wide range of applications.

The importance of the dynamic programming model for planning purposes derives from the fact that it optimizes the total outcome of a series of interrelated decisions which are made at several points in time or space, or for various projects. Thus, it has a direct relevance to *long-range program selection* and *incremental planning*. Also, this model does not require that the entity to be optimized be represented by a formal mathematical expression, but only that its values be known. Thus, this second approach to optimization problems is very general in nature, although its central advantage is that it can formally incorporate the dimension of *time* which has intervened repeatedly throughout the models in the text.

The *critical-path* and *PERT* methods essentially concern the optimal scheduling of various activities in a given project, to achieve its completion in the fastest time. Thus, the usefulness of this particular method derives from the fact that the end result of any analysis and decision making will (at least in principle) be an *implementation phase* which will (in general) involve various activities. (In any case, the method can always be applied to the best scheduling of the analytical phase itself!)

Each of these methods, although nonsubstantive, and susceptible as we shall see of variations and of a diversity of applications, is nevertheless, on the whole, directed toward a general class of decision-making problems. For instance, the linear programming approach is better adapted by its nature to the allocation of physical resources, whereas the dynamic programming method is generally superior for budgeting problems, and CPM–PERT is inherently designed for time scheduling problems.

After putting this chapter in perspective, let us now begin with the linear programming method.

5.2 Optimal Development Planning: Several Linear Programming Examples

We recall from Section 1.2 that the variables $X_1, X_2, \ldots, X_i, \ldots, X_n$ are said to have a *linear relationship* if one of them can be expressed as a combination of the others of the form

$$X_i = a_0 + a_1 X_1 + a_2 X_2 + \ldots + a_i X_i + \ldots + a_n X_n$$

where the a_i's are constants. In the same fashion, a model will be called a *linear model*, if all its equations are of the linear form above, i.e., if all the relationships between the variables in the model are linear. Thus, in a compact form a general linear model will be

$$\mathbf{Y} = \mathbf{AX} + \mathbf{B} \tag{5.1}$$

where $\mathbf{Y}$ is a column vector of m (dependent) variables Y_i, $\mathbf{X}$ is a column vector of n (independent) variables X_i, $\mathbf{A}$ is a rectangular n by m matrix, and $\mathbf{B}$ is a column vector of given constants b_i.

As was noted above, we have already seen a number of examples of such linear models in the preceding chapters. For instance, in formula (2.25), **Y** was the vector of new population levels in the *cohort-survival* model, **X** was the vector of starting levels, **A** was the survivorship matrix, and **B** was the vector of migration levels. In formula (3.26), for the *input/output* model, **Y** and **X** were the same vector of total activity, **B** that of basic activity, and **A** was the matrix of production coefficients. In the *economic multiplier* model in its multiregional form, formula (3.14), **Y** was the residential population vector, **X** was the basic employment vector, and **A** was the matrix $\mathbf{H(I - SH)}^{-1}$. (**B** in this case was equal to zero.)

Let us now define formally the general linear programming model. A *linear program* in n variables and m equations is by definition the search for the optimum value (either maximum or minimum) of a linear function of several variables, subject to several constraints which are also of a linear nature, i.e., which are represented by linear relationships between the variables in the sense above. The mathematical formulation of this class of models is, therefore,

---

Find: *Max* or *Min* of:

$Z = (c_1 X_1 + c_2 X_2 + c_3 X_3 + \ldots + c_n X_n)$

   Such That:

$a_{11} X_1 + a_{12} X_2 + a_{13} X_3 + \ldots + a_{1n} X_n = b_1$ (or $\geq b_1$, or $\leq b_1$)

$a_{21} X_1 + a_{22} X_2 + a_{23} X_3 + \ldots + a_{2n} X_n = b_2$ (or $\geq b_2$, or $\leq b_2$)

$\cdots\cdots\cdots\cdots\cdots\cdots\cdots\cdots\cdots\cdots\cdots\cdots\cdots\cdots\cdots\cdots\cdots\cdots\cdots\cdots$

$a_{m1} X_1 + a_{m2} X_2 + a_{m3} X_3 + \ldots + a_{mn} X_n = b_m$ (or $\geq b_m$, or $\leq b_m$)

$$(5.2)$$

This is a program in the n variables $X_1, X_1, X_3, \ldots, X_n$ subject to the m constraints

$$a_{i1} X_1 + a_{i2} X_2 + \ldots + a_{ij} X_j + \ldots + a_{in} X_n = b_i \text{ (or } \leq b_i, \text{ or } \geq b_i)$$

(i going from 1 to m).

Physically, a linear program could be translated as the problem of finding the highest (or lowest) value of a weighed sum of values of n variables x_i, while observing the requirement that m other weighed sums (with different coefficients) remain equal to (or higher, or lower than) prescribed values. Although this might sound somewhat abstract, the following illustrations will clarify the concept.

Let us, for instance, consider the following simple *allocation problem*: assume that we have three residential areas in which 1000, 2000, and 1500 workers live, respectively. Also, assume that there are two areas of work to which 3000 and 1500 workers go to work, respectively. Finally, assume that the distances between the residential areas and the workplaces are as given in Table 5.1.

TABLE 5.1

	Work	
	$j = 1$	2
Residence $i = 1$	15	20
2	10	15
3	10	20

Given this information, what is the travel pattern of workers from workplaces to places of residence which minimizes the total distance traveled to go to work so that pollution, for instance, or total commuting time incurred at the community level, etc. (the "resource" here), is minimized? Although the answer might not be a realistic planning goal (e.g., because of other constraints, such as type of worker needed at the two workplaces or of relocation problems, etc.), it might be useful in determining how far the actual, observed pattern, or a theoretical gravity-type pattern, for instance, deviates from this optimal norm.

In any event, this problem can be put into a linear program form. Let us first define our variables. These will be the respective numbers of workers living in area i who would come from work in area j. Let us call these variables X_{ij} (i going from 1 to 3 and j going from 1 to 2). The problem is then to minimize the sum of all distances traveled by the workers. If X_{ij} workers travel a distance d_{ij} in going from workplace j to residence i, the total mileage traveled from all residential areas to all workplaces is

$$15X_{11} + 20X_{12} + 10X_{21} + 15X_{22} + 10X_{31} + 20X_{32} \qquad (5.3)$$

If there were no other considerations, i.e., constraints on the values of the variables, to be observed, the optimal program (solution) would be trivial; do not have anybody travel to work, i.e., put all X_{ij} at zero. This is obviously unfeasible, because we are ignoring the other given of the problem, the need to go to work.

Therefore, let us write the binding relationships that exist between the variables and their respective values. Since we know that 1000 people live in the first residential area, this number must be equal to the sum of all workers who go from that area to either of the two workplaces. In other words, X_{11} and X_{12} must be such that

$$X_{11} + X_{12} = 1000 \qquad (5.4)$$

Similarly,

$$X_{21} + X_{22} = 2000 \qquad \text{for residential area 2}$$

and

$$X_{31} + X_{32} = 1500 \qquad \text{for residential area 3}$$

By the same token, since we know that workplace 1 is staffed with 3000 workers, that number must be equal to the sum of the number of workers coming from all areas of residence to workplace 1. Therefore, $X_{11} + X_{21} + X_{31} = 3000$. Similarly, $X_{12} + X_{22} + X_{32} = 1500$ for workplace 2. Finally, the total number of workers in all places of work should be equal to the total number of workers in all places of residence:

$$X_{11} + X_{12} + X_{21} + X_{22} + X_{31} + X_{32}$$
$$= X_{11} + X_{21} + X_{31} + X_{12} + X_{22} + X_{32}$$

This last condition is automatically verified (i.e., results in a redundant equation) if the given levels of worker population for all residential areas add up to the same total as the given employment levels for all workplaces. (This is the case with our data, but does not have to be.) Thus, we can dismiss the last equation.

The problem is now completely described. It is clear that with the inclusion of the constraints, the solution is far from trivial. In fact, in the absence of a rational approach to the problem, or of a (miraculous) insight, the only approach would be a systematic examination of all the possible combinations of values for the flows of commuters along the $3 \times 2 = 6$ routes, retaining only those combinations which satisfy all the requirements of balance, such as in equation (5.4). For each combination, the resulting total travel would be computed. The solution would then be the set of six flows corresponding to the lowest total travel. However, it is clear that such an approach, because of the enormous number of combinations of values of six variables, if we consider each of the 4500 travelers, would be unfeasible for all practical purposes.

However, the statement of the problem indicates that this is a linear program, since all constraints of the type (5.4) are linear functions of the variables, and since the quantity to be minimized (called the *objective function*), as represented by formula (5.3), is also a linear function of the variables. The method of resolution of linear programs, which will be described later, provides a systematic approach to the examination of feasible combinations of values, but in such a manner that the value of the objective function is always decreasing (or increasing in the case of a maximization problem) from one examination to the next, thus cutting down very effectively on the number of combinations of variable values to examine.

In any case, to further this introductory illustration of the concept of linear program and of its application to a specific problem, let us now formulate the same problem in its general case.

Assume that there are n residential areas ($i = 1, \ldots, n$). Also assume that there are m workplaces ($j = 1, \ldots, m$). The distance between any residential area i and workplace j is d_{ij}. (If there is no physical link between the areas, then $d_{ij} = \infty$.) Furthermore, assume that the number of trips which originate at residential area i is given, and is O_j, and that the number of trips which terminate at any workplace j is also given, and is D_i. Finally, the total number of workers equals the total number of jobs, i.e., $\sum_i D_i = \sum_j O_j$. Given these constraints, what pattern of travel to workplaces would minimize the total distance traveled (or transportation cost) for the total community? The variables will be the numbers of people that live in area j and go to work in area i, X_{ij}. The relationship between the variables will represent, first, the requirement that we have given numbers of workers at all places of residence. Therefore, $O_j = \sum_i X_{ij}$ at all places of residence j. Similarly, the workplaces have to be staffed at given levels, so that $D_i = \sum_j X_{ij}$ at all workplaces i. Finally, the objective function, which is the total distance traveled is $\sum_i \sum_j X_{ij}d_{ij}$, which we want to minimize. This is, therefore, a linear program of the form (5.2), which may be utilized in connection with the model (3.45).

Another example of application of the linear programming formulation is in the area of *regional development*. Suppose that we are planning for the economic development of a region and that we must determine the levels of operation of two industrial sectors, say, light industry and heavy industry. Each of these two sectors requires three kinds of resources for input: manpower, energy, and capital. Assume that, for instance, the output of 1 unit of the light industry, measured in some unit (i.e., thousands of dollars), requires the input of 0.4 unit of manpower, 0.2 unit of energy, and 0.2 unit of capital. Also, assume that the output of 1 unit of the heavy industry requires the input of 0.2 unit of manpower, 0.5 unit of energy, and 0.2 unit of capital. In the language of Chapter 3, these *production coefficients* are summarized in Table 5.2. Finally, assume that the total amounts of each of the three resources

TABLE 5.2

	Industry	
	$j = 1$	2
Resource $i = 1$	0.4	0.2
2	0.2	0.5
3	0.2	0.2

are in the limited supply of say, 100, 160, and 120 units each year (for manpower, energy, and capital, respectively). Given these constraints, what would be the program of industrial development, i.e., the levels of production at which the two industries should operate, such that the total economic output is maximized?

Note that this problem is directly connected to the input/output model of Chapter 3, since it concerns the optimal allocation of external supplies to the two basic sectors so that the total production is maximized. In other words, given the coefficients a_{ij} of matrix **A** in the model (3.26), what should be the values of Y_1 and Y_2 that make optimal use of given, limited supplies from the external sectors? Thus, this linear programming approach will transform the input/output model from a *projective* model to a *normative* model.

In any case, let us define the variables that we shall use. This should always be the first step in the formulation of a linear program (as, in general, in the formulation of any model). Indeed, the choice of variables will determine the simplicity of the formulation, and even in some cases its feasibility.

Since the unknowns here are the levels of output of the two industries, let us use these as variables. Thus, Y_1 and Y_2 will be the levels of output of the light and heavy industries, respectively. These levels are related to each other by the constraint that they should not jointly use more of the three supply resources than is available. Since 1 unit of output of light industry requires 0.4 unit of manpower and 1 unit of output of heavy industry requites 0.2 unit, a total output of Y_1 units of light industry and Y_2 units of heavy industry will require $(0.4Y_1 + 0.2Y_2)$ units of manpower. This should be less than 100. Similarly, the total requirements for energy, $(0.2Y_1 + 0.5Y_2)$ units, should be less than 160, and for capital, $(0.2Y_1 + 0.2Y_2)$ units, should be less than 120. Given these constraints, we are trying to maximize the total production of the region, $(Y_1 + Y_2)$. Formally, the development problem can be written as

$$Max\ Z = (Y_1 + Y_2)$$
$$Such\ That\ 0.4Y_1 + 0.2Y_2 \leq 100$$
$$0.2Y_1 + 0.5Y_2 \leq 160 \qquad (5.5)$$
$$0.2Y_1 + 0.2Y_2 \leq 120$$

The development problem is, therefore, a linear programming problem of the form (5.2), which can also be written in matrix form

$$Max\ Z = \begin{bmatrix} 1 & 1 \end{bmatrix} \begin{bmatrix} Y_1 \\ Y_2 \end{bmatrix}$$

$$\qquad\qquad \mathbf{C} \qquad \mathbf{Y}$$

$$Such\ That\ \begin{bmatrix} 0.4 & 0.2 \\ 0.2 & 0.5 \\ 0.2 & 0.2 \end{bmatrix} \begin{bmatrix} Y_1 \\ Y_2 \end{bmatrix} \leq \begin{bmatrix} 100 \\ 160 \\ 120 \end{bmatrix} \qquad (5.6)$$

$$\qquad\qquad \mathbf{A} \qquad \mathbf{Y} \leq \mathbf{B}$$

One of the advantages of the linear programming model is that changes in the coefficients of either the matrix $\mathbf{A}$ or the row vector $\mathbf{C}$ can be accommodated with a minimum of new computations, as we shall see later, when we learn about *sensitivity analysis*. Suppose, for instance, that we are now interested in maximizing the total income deriving from the production of the region, each unit of light industry bringing in an income of 0.15 and each unit of heavy industry bringing in an income of 0.25 (in the same units). Thus, the problem is now to maximize $Z = (0.15Y_1 + 0.25Y_2)$. The constraints (matrix **A**) are the same. Only the definition of the objective function (row **C**) is changed. The effects of this type of modification of the objective function on the optimal program (which, in general, will be changed) can be investigated systematically. This feature is, thus, particularly convenient for analytical purposes.

Finally, suppose that we are now interested in maximizing the employment that accrues from the industrial development of the region. The objective function would now be $Z = 0.4Y_1 + 0.2Y_2$, since that expression is the total manpower requirement, as expressed in the first constraint. This time, matrix **A** would change, since it loses its first row, as well as row **C**.

Let us formalize the description of the problem in the general case of m basic industrial sectors and n resource supplying sectors. Let us assume that supplying sector i can only provide the required resource i to a limit of T_i. Also, let us assume that for each unit of output of industry j, a_{ij} units of resource i are needed. Given these constraints, what is the maximum level of total economic output the region can achieve, and what is the corresponding *economic program*, i.e., at what respective levels should the various industrial sectors function?

Again, let us first define our variables, or unknowns. These will most conveniently be the respective total levels of activity Y_i for the industrial sectors, as these levels are directly related to both the goal of maximizing the total output and to the constraints, since the total input of each resource is a linear combination of the levels of output of the industries.

Thus, we will define Y_j to be the level of output of industry j. The objective function is the total output, $\sum_j Y_j$. Next, the relationships between the variables are those derived from the constraints on the resources. This means that the total amount of supply needed from supplying sector i, $\sum_j a_{ij}Y_j$, should be less than T_i. Our problem can, therefore, be written in mathematical terms:

$$Max \quad Z = (Y_1 + \quad Y_2 + \quad Y_3 + \ldots + \quad Y_n)$$
$$Such\ That\ a_{11}Y_1 + a_{12}Y_2 + a_{13}Y_3 + \ldots + a_{1n}Y_n \leq T_1$$
$$a_{21}Y_1 + a_{22}Y_2 + a_{23}Y_3 + \ldots + a_{2n}Y_n \leq T_2 \quad (5.7)$$
$$\cdots\cdots\cdots\cdots\cdots\cdots\cdots\cdots\cdots\cdots\cdots\cdots$$
$$a_{i1}Y_1 + a_{i2}Y_2 + a_{i3}Y_3 + \ldots + a_{in}Y_n \leq T_i$$
$$\cdots\cdots\cdots\cdots\cdots\cdots\cdots\cdots\cdots\cdots\cdots\cdots$$
$$a_{m1}Y_1 + a_{m2}Y_2 + a_{m3}Y_3 + \ldots + a_{mn}Y_n \leq T_n$$

or, in matrix formulation,

$$Max \quad Z = [1 \quad 1 \quad \dots \quad 1 \quad 1] \begin{bmatrix} Y_1 \\ \cdot \\ \cdot \\ \cdot \\ Y_j \\ \cdot \\ \cdot \\ \cdot \\ Y_n \end{bmatrix}$$

$$Such\ That \quad \begin{bmatrix} a_{11} & a_{12} & \cdots & a_{1n} \\ & \cdots\cdots\cdots\cdots & & \\ \cdots & & a_{ij} & \cdots \\ & \cdots\cdots\cdots\cdots & & \\ a_{m1} & & \cdots & a_{mn} \end{bmatrix} \begin{bmatrix} Y_1 \\ \cdot \\ \cdot \\ \cdot \\ Y_j \\ \cdot \\ \cdot \\ \cdot \\ Y_n \end{bmatrix} \leq \begin{bmatrix} T_1 \\ \cdot \\ \cdot \\ \cdot \\ T_i \\ \cdot \\ \cdot \\ \cdot \\ T_n \end{bmatrix} \quad (5.8)$$

and is therefore a linear program of the form (5.3).

Suppose now that we are interested in analyzing the effect of the activity of these industrial sectors on air pollution, for instance, when the manufacture of each unit of the jth sector produces p_j units of air pollutant. We can either require that the total pollution be kept under a certain given level P, and this would merely result in the introduction of an extra constraint:

$$Y_1 p_1 + Y_2 p_2 + \dots + Y_n p_n \leq P$$

or we can be more stringent and require that the total pollution be minimized, while keeping the total regional output above a given level Y. This would then result in changing the objective function to

$$Y_1 p_1 + Y_2 p_2 + \dots + Y_n p_n$$

and introducing the constraint

$$Y_1 + Y_2 + \dots Y_n \geq Y$$

The parameter Y can be set at the optimal level corresponding to the maximization of the income and identified in the original program. If there is a feasible solution to this new program, two goals will have been achieved: maximum income and minimum pollution. If not, the analysis of various combinations of dual objectives of the kind above will provide a basis for a compromise between two, or several (possibly conflicting) objectives. Indeed, other types of objectives might be, for instance, that we would like to maximize the employment in the region, or to keep it above a certain level, etc.

The only new parameters we would need to incorporate the dimension of employment would be the coefficients e_j, which translate a unit of production in each of the sectors into numbers of workers.

Such variations of the basic linear programming theme might appear to be trivial. However, they illustrate the large flexibility of the model in reflecting modifications, or additions to the initial situation. This feature is thus very powerful for analytical purposes such as plan evaluation.

As another example of the application of the linear programming formulation to planning problems, let us consider now the following land-use planning problem. Assume that there is a total amount of land L to be allocated to n land uses. The "cost" of developing a unit of land for use i ($i = 1, 2, \ldots, n$) is c_i. There is the requirement that for each unit of land of type i developed, there must also be at least a_{ij} units of land of type j developed. This reflects the need for supporting activities j to the activity corresponding to land use i. For instance, commercial development will be needed to support residential development; open spaces will be needed to support residential development; residential development will be needed to support industrial development; etc. Given these constraints, what land-use plan minimizes the generalized cost of development?

The unknowns in this problem are, of course, the amounts of land to be allocated to each type of development, or use. Let us set X_i to represent the amount of land allocated to use i. The relationships between the variables are of the type $X_i/X_j \geq a_{ij}$, which simply requires that the ratio between the amounts of land allocated to uses i and j be at least a_{ij} or, equivalently, that X_i be more than $a_{ij}X_j$. Finally, the objective function will be to minimize the total cost of development:

$$C = (c_1 X_1 + c_2 X_2 + \ldots + c_i X_i + \ldots + c_n X_n)$$

We again have a linear problem, which will be written as

$Min \ Z = (c_1 X_1 + c_2 X_2 + \ldots + c_i X_i + \ldots + c_n X_n)$

$Such \ That \ X_i - a_{ij}X_j \geq 0$ for all i and j and $X_1 + X_2 + \ldots + X_n \leq L$

If we have the additional constraints that the amounts of land that can be allocated to any use i are limited (e.g., by zoning or some other constraints) to a maximum of L_i, but have to be at least M_i (e.g., because of population levels), the above formulation would be the same, but we would simply add equations of the type $X_i \leq L_i$ and $X_i \geq M_i$. The land-use planning problem in this form is a linear programming problem.

The same problem can be extended to the case of land-use allocation, or activity distribution, to a set of several regions, thus becoming a *locational* problem. In this case, let us call X_{ij} the amount of land use i allocated to region j, and c_{ij} the corresponding unit cost of development. The overall regional requirements for land may be expressed in the same fashion by

$$\sum_j X_{ij} \leq L_i \qquad \text{(maximum land for use } i)$$

$$\sum_j X_{ij} \geq M_i \qquad \text{(minimum land for use } i)$$

for each use i

Regional constraints on each land use as in the single-region case can be written as:

$$\sum_i X_{ij} \leq L_j \qquad \text{(total land in region } j) \quad \text{for each region } j$$

The objective is to minimize $C = (\sum_i \sum_j c_{ij} X_{ij})$ (total overall cost of development). In this form, the problem is again a linear programming problem of the form (5.2).

Although, as we have stressed above, the linear programming model is essentially a *normative*, or *optimizing* tool, it can also be used for forecasting purposes. One of the earliest such applications is the "Herbert–Stevens" model of land use. The projection of the residential pattern in a given community is made on the basis of the assumption that households in various socioeconomic groups i will choose their individual residential location in such a way that they maximize the communal *utility* derived from their choice. The individual utility is here defined as the difference between the housing budget b_i of the household and the cost c_j of a house in area j.

The constraints on the spatial distribution of residences (i.e., the choice by X_{ij} households in group i to reside in area j) are that each area has a given, limited *holding capacity* of L_j, and that the total number of households in the respective socioeconomic groups are given, and equal to N_i.

Thus, the distribution of households to areas should be the solution to the following linear program in the unknowns X_{ij}:

$$Max \ Z = \sum_j \sum_i X_{ij}(b_i - c_j)$$

$$Such \ That \ \sum_i X_{ij} s_j \leq L_j \qquad \text{for each area } j \qquad (5.9)$$

$$\sum_j X_{ij} = N_i \qquad \text{for each group } i$$

The objective function represents the total utility for the community. The first n constraints (if there are n residential areas) translate the limitation on the total land available in the respective areas j, when the amount of land required per house in area j (which varies across areas since the cost of the house c_j is assumed to vary) is equal to s_j. The next m constraints (if there are m socioeconomic groups) translate the requirements that every household in each group be housed.

The model can be further expanded to differentiate between various types of housing within a given area. This merely results in the addition of another subscript, k, for instance, and of another summation sign $\sum$ in the objective function and the constraints:

$$Min \ Z = \sum_k \sum_i \sum_j X^k_{ij}(b_i - c^k_j)$$

$$Such \ That \ \sum_k \sum_i s^k_j X^k_{ij} \leq L_j \qquad (j = 1, \ldots, n)$$

$$\sum_k \sum_j X^k_{ij} = N_i \qquad (i = 1, \ldots, m)$$

where X^k_{ij} is the number of households in socioeconomic group i which choose to buy a house in category k in area j. This refinement of the model does not change its basic structure, but merely results in an increase in the number of coefficients, i.e., an enlargement of the size of the objective function and of the matrix of coefficients A.

Conversely, the original program can be simplified, if considerations of time or importance of detail so warrant, by omitting the socioeconomic class, i.e., by deleting the subscript i. This would result in the program:

$$Min \ Z = \sum_j X_j(b - c_j)$$

$$Such \ That \ s_j X_j \leq L_j \qquad (j = 1, \ldots, n) \qquad\qquad (5.10)$$

$$\sum_j X_j = N \qquad (i = 1, \ldots, m)$$

This is another illustration of the inherent flexibility of the model.

We have now seen a number of examples of application of a linear program formulation to planning and analysis problems. These only represent a fraction of the variety of possible applications and (as is the case for most chapters in this text) an entire book could easily be devoted to the subject. Other examples are presented in the exercises at chapter's end. The next step, after the formulation, is, of course, the resolution. The standard method for this is called the *simplex method* of linear programming and will be explained below.

5.3 The Graphical Solution for Two-Variable Programs

It is rather seldom that the analyst works out the solution of linear programs with pencil and paper, because the size of real-world problems is usually prohibitive. Fortunately, ready-made computer programs for the implementation of the method are in standard use. However, it is important to understand the workings of the method to effectively communicate one's own needs to whoever (human being or machine) is going to implement it, and also to fully understand its output.

We shall begin with a special case, for which the solution to the linear programming problem can be easily worked out graphically. This is the case of any program in two variables. Let us, for instance, assume that we want to solve the development problem described in model (5.5).

$$Max \quad Z = (Y_1 + Y_2)$$
$$Such \ That \ 0.4Y_1 + 0.2Y_2 \leq 100$$
$$0.2Y_1 + 0.5Y_2 \leq 160$$
$$0.2Y_1 + 0.2Y_2 \leq 120$$
$$Y_1 \geq 0; \quad Y_2 \geq 0$$

Let us translate this problem in terms of a two-dimensional graph in a plane of coordinates Y_1 and Y_2, as represented in Figure 5.1.

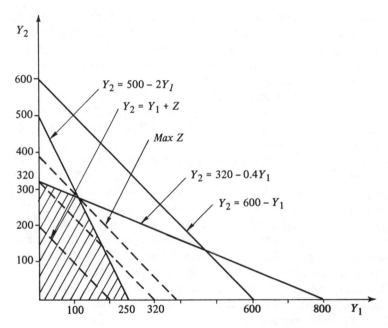

Figure 5.1 Linear program in two variables.

The first constraint, $0.4Y_1 + 0.2Y_2 \leq 100$, requires that we only retain the points of the plane for which the expression $(0.4Y_1 + 0.2Y_2)$ is less than 100. The corresponding region is on one side of the straight line represented by the equation $0.4Y_1 + 0.2Y_2 = 100$, since for the points on the line the equality to zero of this expression is verified by definition of the line. (See Section 1.2.) Therefore, we must determine whether the feasible region is to the left or to the right of the straight line of equation $0.4Y_1 + 0.2Y_2 = 100$, or equivalently, $Y_2 = (100 - 0.4Y_1)/0.2 = 500 - 2Y_1$. This line is represented in Figure 5.1 and has an intercept of 500 and a slope of -2. If we take the origin, i.e., the point in the plane for which $Y_1 = Y_2 = 0$, the expression $(0.4Y_1 + 0.2Y_2)$ is equal to 0, and thus is less than 100. Therefore, the feasible region of the plane is the region that contains the origin, i.e., to the left of the straight line. (Since Y_1 and Y_2 must be positive, we only consider the corresponding quadrant of the plane.)

Similarly, the second constraint $(0.2Y_1 + 0.5Y_2 \le 160)$ requires that we be in the region of the plane determined by the side of the straight line of equation $Y_2 = (160 - 0.2Y_1)/0.5$ for which the quantity $(0.2Y_1 + 0.5Y_2) \le 160$. Since for the origin $(0.2Y_1 + 0.5Y_2) = 0$, we should again be to the left of that line, which has an intercept of $160/0.5 = 320$ and a negative slope of $-0.2/0.5 = -0.4$.

Finally, the last constraint requires that we be to the left of the line of equation $0.2Y_1 + 0.2Y_2 = 120$ or $Y_2 = 600 - Y_1$ (intercept of 600, slope of -1). Thus, the feasible region for our solution to the problem is the part of the (positive) plane common to the three regions identified above, i.e., the shaded region in Figure 5.1.

Next, we want to maximize the value of the quantity $Z = Y_1 + Y_2$. Equivalently, we are looking for the maximum intercept Z for the straight line of equation $Z = Y_1 + Y_2$, or $Y_2 = -Y_1 + Z$. This line has a negative slope of -1. Therefore, we will attempt to give the line (which is represented by a dashed line in Figure 5.1) the highest possible intercept while it remains in the feasible region delineated above. It is clear that the highest possible intercept for that line, while it still has a common point with the shaded area, is when it goes through the northeast corner of the feasible region, i.e., through the point of coordinates $Y_1 = 120$ and $Y_2 = 280$ (approximately). At that point $Z = Y_1 + Y_2 = 120 + 280 = 400$, which represents the value of the maximum intercept of the dashed line in Figure 5.1. Thus, the best program of development is to have the light industry output Y_1 at a level of 120 units and the heavy industry output Y_2 at a level of 280 units. The maximum value for the objective function, i.e., the total regional economic output, will then be $Y_1 + Y_2 = 400$ units.

This graphic method for solving linear programming problems does not depend on the number of constraints, but rather on the number of variables, which can only be two. Conceptually, of course, it would be possible to apply the same approach to problems in three variables, by using a *three-dimensional* representation. However, it is more difficult to visualize the various regions and *surfaces* than in two dimensions. Conversely, if the number of constraints increases, but the number of variables is still two, we simply add more borders to the definition of the feasible region.

5.4 The Simplex Method of Solution for General Programs

For linear programs with any number of variables and constraints, the standard method for obtaining the optimal program is called the *simplex method*. This method is merely an analytical translation of the approach presented above, and consists of the following sequence of steps.

Step 1. Write the problem in *standard form*. The standard form is a minimization problem, with positive variables, with all constraints in equality form, and with positive, right-hand-side constants. Thus, the standard linear programming problem will always be written as

$$Min \quad Z = (c_1 X_1 + c_2 X_2 + \ldots + c_j X_j + \ldots + c_n X_n)$$

$$Such \ That \ a_{11} X_1 + a_{12} X_2 + \ldots + a_{1j} X_j + \ldots + a_{1n} X_n = b_1$$

$$a_{21} X_1 + a_{22} X_2 + \ldots + a_{2j} X_j + \ldots + a_{2n} X_n = b_2$$

$$\ldots \ldots \ldots \ldots \ldots \ldots \ldots \ldots \ldots \ldots \ldots \ldots \ldots \ldots \ldots \ldots \ldots \ldots \ldots \quad (5.11)$$

$$a_{i1} X_1 + a_{i2} X_2 + \ldots + a_{ij} X_j + \ldots + a_{in} X_n = b_i$$

$$\ldots \ldots \ldots \ldots \ldots \ldots \ldots \ldots \ldots \ldots \ldots \ldots \ldots \ldots \ldots \ldots \ldots \ldots \ldots$$

$$a_{m1} X_1 + a_{m2} X_2 + \ldots + a_{mj} X_j + \ldots + a_{mn} X_n = b_m$$

or, in a more compact way:

$$Min \quad Z = \sum_{j=1}^{n} c_j X_j$$

$$Such \ That \ \sum_{j=1}^{n} a_{ij} X_j = b_j \quad for \ i = 1, \ldots, m \quad (5.12)$$

where all b_j's are positive and all X_j's must remain positive-valued. The matrix formulation of a standard linear programming problem is, therefore:

$$Find \ Min \quad Z = \mathbf{CX}$$

$$Such \ That \ \mathbf{AX} = \mathbf{B} \quad (5.13)$$

where $\mathbf{C}$ is a row vector of n cost coefficients c_j, $\mathbf{X}$ is a column vector of n variables, $\mathbf{A}$ is a matrix with m rows and n columns, and $\mathbf{B}$ is a column vector of m given constants (parameters). Z is, therefore, a single value. In this form the standard linear program is clearly related to the general linear model in (5.1), since it is the search for the maximum (or min mum) value of a linear combination of variables interrelated through a relationship of that same general form.

It is very simple to transform a linear problem of any given initial form into a problem in standard form. Indeed, if we have a maximization problem instead of a minimization problem, we simply change the sign of the objective function, since the maximum value of a quantity is also the minimum value of its negative. For instance, suppose that we have to maximize $(3X_1 - 4X_2 + 2X_3 - 6X_4)$. This would be equivalent to minimizing $(-3X_1 + 4X_2 - 2X_3 + 6X_4)$. Also, we can readily transform any constraint written as an inequality into an equality. If we have, for instance, the following constraint:

$$2X_1 + 2X_2 - 1X_3 + 3X_4 \leq 5$$

we can transform this into a constraint in equality form by adding the positive *slack variable* X_5, which will represent the difference between the value of the left-hand side in the foregoing constraint and the value 5. Thus, the constraint can be rewritten as

$$2X_1 + 2X_2 - 1X_3 + 3X_4 + X_5 = 5$$

In general, if we have a "less-than" constraint of the type

$$a_{i1}X_1 + a_{i2}X_2 + \ldots + a_{ij}X_j + \ldots + a_{in}X_n \leq b_i$$

we can always transform it into the equality constraint

$$\sum_{j=1}^{n} a_{ij}X_j + X_{n+1} = b_i$$

by adding an additional positive slack variable X_{n+1} to the left-hand side to reach the upper bound b_i. Conversely, if we have a "greater-than" constraint of the type

$$a_{i1}X_1 + a_{i2}X_2 + \ldots + a_{ij}X_j + \ldots + a_{in}X_n \geq b_i$$

we can transform it into the equality

$$\sum_{j=1}^{n} a_{ij}X_j - X_{n+1} = b_i$$

by subtracting a positive slack variable X_{n+1}.

Next, if we have some variables that are negatively valued, we simply change the signs of all their coefficients, in the constraints, as well as in the objective function. For instance, if the variable X_3 is a variable with negative values and appears in the objective function

$$Max\ (2X_1 - 2X_2 - 4X_3 + 1X_4)$$

and the constraint

$$2X_1 - 2X_2 + 1X_3 - 1X_4 = 4$$

we introduce X'_3, the negative of X_3, which will be positive-valued,

$$X'_3 = -X_3$$

and rewrite the problem as

$$Min\ Z = (2X_1 - 2X_2 + 4X'_3 + 1X_4)$$

$$Such\ That\ \ 2X_1 - 2X_2 - 1X'_3 - 1X_4 = 4$$

Finally, if some of the b_i's are negative, we simply multiply both sides of the corresponding constraints by minus 1. (We thus also have to change the direction of the inequalities, if any; see Section 1.2.) For instance, suppose that in the linear program we have the equality constraint

$$2X_1 - 3X_2 = -3$$

This is equivalent to

$$-2X_1 + 3X_2 = 3$$

or, if we have the inequality

$$2X_1 - 3X_2 \geq -3$$

it becomes

$$-2X_1 + 3X_2 \leq 3$$

for an inequality of the "lower-than" form.

When all these transformations have been effected, the last operation required in step 1 of the method (putting the problem in standard form) is to write the coefficients of the equations in a *tableau*. This simply consists of writing the (possibly transformed) coefficients of the objective function and of the constraints in model (5.11) in tabular form as in Figure 5.2.

X_1	X_2	X_3	$\cdots$	X_j	$\cdots$	X_n	b
a_{11}	a_{12}	a_{13}	$\cdots$	a_{1j}	$\cdots$	a_{1n}	b_1
a_{21}	a_{22}	a_{23}	$\cdots$	a_{2j}	$\cdots$	a_{2n}	b_2
.	.	.		.		.	.
a_{i1}	a_{i2}	a_{i3}	$\cdots$	a_{ij}	$\cdots$	a_{in}	b_i
.	.	.		.		.	.
a_{m1}	a_{m2}	a_{m3}	$\cdots$	a_{mj}	$\cdots$	a_{mn}	b_m
c_1	c_2	c_3	$\cdots$	c_j	$\cdots$	c_n	

Figure 5.2   Linear programming tableau.

The columns corresponding to the respective variables X_j are sometimes called the *activities* and the rows corresponding to the coefficients b_i, the *resources*. The corresponding coefficient a_{ij} can then be interpreted as the amount of resource i required by 1 unit of activity j. The c_j's are the *costs* of operation of a unit of activity j. The linear programming problem can then be interpreted to be the search for the combination of levels of operation of a set of n activities j, given the operational coefficients a_{ij}, given the limits on a set of m resources necessary to that operation, and given the unit cost of operation of each activity, so that the total cost of operation is minimized. (The reader should examine this interpretation in connection with the various examples above.)

Let us now illustrate the process of standardization of a linear problem with the following example of a linear program:

$$\text{Max} \quad (3X_1 + 2X_2 - X_3)$$
$$\text{Such That} \quad 2X_1 + 2X_2 - 5X_3 \leq -3$$
$$3X_1 + X_2 - 3X_3 = 4 \tag{5.14}$$
$$2X_1 + 5X_2 \geq 3$$
$$X_1 \geq 0; \quad X_2 \leq 0; \quad X_3 \geq 0$$

First, we transform the maximization of $(3X_1 + 2X_2 - X_3)$ into the minimization of $(-3X_1 - 2X_2 + X_3)$. Next, we shall transform the inequality constraints into equalities by introducing the positive slack variables X_4 and X_5. The first constraint is equivalent to

$$2X_1 + 2X_2 - 5X_3 + X_4 = -3$$

The second constraint remains unchanged since it is already in equality form. The third constraint becomes

$$2X_1 + 5X_2 - X_5 = 3$$

We shall next transform the negative variable X_2 into the positive variable X_2' by letting $X_2' = -X_2$, and therefore changing the signs of all coefficients of X_2 in the problem, which thus becomes

$$\text{Min} \quad Z = (-3X_1 - 2X_2' + X_3)$$
$$\text{Such That} \quad 2X_1 - 2X_2' - 5X_3 + X_4 = -3$$
$$3X_1 - X_2' - 3X_3 = 4$$
$$2X_1 - 5X_2' - X_5 = 3$$
$$X_1 \geq 0; \quad X_2' \geq 0; \quad X_3 \geq 0; \quad X_4 \geq 0; \quad X_5 \geq 0$$

Finally, since the right-hand side for the first constraint is negative, we have to change its sign by multiplying both sides by minus 1. The new, equivalent first constraint is thus

$$-2X_1 + 2X_2' + 5X_3 - X_4 = 3$$

The other equations in the problem remained unchanged. This problem, which has now been standardized, would then be written in tableau form as in Figure 5.3.

Step 2. When a problem has been written in tableau form, the second step of the simplex method is to find a *feasible solution* to the system of equations. That solution does not have to be *optimal* but should consist of values for the variables which verify the equations of the constraints. This solution is used as a starting point for the search of the optimal solution. Usually, such a feasible solution may easily be found, for instance, by putting all variables on

	X_1	X_2	X_3	X_4	X_5	b_i
	-2	+2	+5	-1	0	3
	3	-1	-3	0	0	4
	2	-5	0	0	-1	3
c_j	-3	-2	+1	0	0	

Figure 5.3 Tableau for standard form.

a given row, but one, at a value of zero and the remaining variable, multiplied by its coefficient, equal to the value of the right-hand side of the corresponding equation. In most cases, in fact, it is always possible to set all original variables equal to zero and the slack variables equal to the right-hand sides b_i. Also, analysts may often know of a heuristic solution to a particular problem. Although this solution is seldom optimal, it is pragmatically feasible and can serve as a start for the application of the systematic simplex method.

In any case, the corresponding set of (nonzero) variables is called the *starting basis*. The method then consists of finding another set of the same number of variables, by dropping one variable from the basis, and introducing another at each iteration of the procedure in such a way that the value of the objective function is increased. Although we shall not explicate completely the subsequent rules for the optimizing *algorithm* below, they basically translate algebraically a progression along the edges of a multidimensional region in the same fashion as in the graphic example for the two-dimensional case seen above.

Step 3. Once the feasible solution (starting basis) to the problem has been determined, the next step of the simplex method is to select the column in the tableau, corresponding to the variable X_j that has the most negative coefficient in the row of objective function coefficients c_j, the last row in the tableau. (If there are no negative coefficients in the objective function, the problem is solved; i.e., the starting solution is optimal.) Let us assume, however, that the column corresponding to the most negative coefficient is column s. (Note that only variables which are not in the basis, i.e., which have a present value of zero, have a nonzero c coefficient.) The position of column s indicates the index of the variable that will be brought into the basis.

To effect this operation, next divide each positive coefficient a_{is} in that column into the value of the corresponding element in the last column of the tableau b_i to obtain a set of values, b_i/a_{is}. Retain level i corresponding to the minimum of these b_i/a_{is}. Let us assume that this is for row r. This indicates that variable r will drop out of the basis to be replaced by variable s. The position in the tableau in row r and column s which has now been identified will be called the *pivot point*. If the value of the tableau entry in that position is a_{rs}, divide each entry in row r of the tableau (the row of the pivot point) by a_{rs}. This means that a_{rs} will be changed into 1 and that all other entries on that row will be modified. Finally, using only linear combinations of the corresponding entries in the other rows of the tableau, transform all entries in column s (the column of the pivot point), including the objective function coefficient, into zeros. (A linear combination of entries a_{kj} in column j will be of the form

$$\alpha_1 a_{1j} + \alpha_2 a_{2j} + \ldots + \alpha_i a_{ij} + \ldots + \alpha_n a_{nj}$$

Therefore, we must find a set of coefficients α_i such that the value of the resulting linear combination of entries in column j is zero. This is often easily found by visual inspection or by trial and error.)

At this stage of the procedure, all coefficients in column s, including the objective function coefficient c_s (but excluding the pivot point), have now become zeros. The variable x_s which corresponded to column s of the pivot point has now entered the basis, and the variable x_r which corresponded to row r of the pivot point has left the basis to replace x_s. Finally, the value of the objective function will have increased, thus improving upon the previous solution.

Step 4.   This procedure is now iterated by again looking for the most negative objective function coefficient in the revised tableau and repeating the subsequent steps. When it is no longer possible to find a negative objective function coefficient, i.e., when all coefficients c_j are either positive or equal to zero, the set of values corresponding to the current basis represents an optimal solution.

Let us now illustrate what surely reads as a rather mystifying description of the simplex method algorithm with an example of its application. Let us assume that we have to solve the following problem, this time in the area of *plan evaluation*. Assume that a municipality has to decide how many building permits to issue. The planning commission has classified the applications into two types, say type 1 and type 2. Type 1 is a three-family unit which requires $\frac{1}{10}$ acre and type 2 is a two-family unit which requires $\frac{1}{4}$ acre. The zoning plan passed by the city council has limited the residential land allocated for these two types of housing units to a total of 10 acres for the coming year. Also, the municipal government estimates that because of limitations on public services capabilities, only 80 new, additional families can be accommodated. Finally, the tax assessor has valued the revenue from type 1 at $3000 per year and from type 2 at $4000.

Given this information, what allocation of building permits to the two types would maximize the tax base, while respecting the constraints on the zoned land and on the capacity of the services?

This program evaluation problem can easily be translated into a linear program. The unknowns here will most conveniently be the numbers of units of each type that will be permitted. Now, each unit of the first type will require 0.1 acre and each unit of the second type 0.4 acres, so that if X_1 units of the first type and X_2 of the second type are built, respectively, the total required land will be $0.1X_1 + 0.4X_2$ acres. This has to be less than the limit of 10 acres. Similarly, since each unit of the first type will house three families and each unit of the second type will house two families, the total number of new families will be $3X_1 + 2X_2$. This has to remain under 80. Finally, the revenue will be $3X_1 + 4X_2$ (in thousands of dollars), which is the objective function to be maximized.

Thus, the problem can be written as follows:

$$Max \ Z = (3X_1 + 4X_2)$$
$$Such \ That \ \ 3X_1 + 2X_2 \leq \ 80$$
$$1X_1 + 4X_2 \leq 100$$
$$X_1; \ \ X_2 \geq 0$$

(5.15)

(Note that since the problem is in two variables only, it could be solved using the graphic procedure above. This will be left to the reader as an exercise.)

The first step is to standardize the problem. This can be done here by adding two slack variables, X_3 and X_4, to transform the inequality constraints and by changing the signs of the coefficients in the objective function to transform the maximization problem into a minimization problem. Thus, the problem can be rewritten as

$$Min \ Z = (-3X_1 - 4X_2)$$
$$Such \ That \ \ \ 3X_1 + 2X_2 + X_3 \ \ \ \ \ \ = \ 80$$
$$1X_1 + 4X_2 \ \ \ \ \ \ + X_4 = 100$$
$$X_1 \geq 0; \ \ X_2 \geq 0; \ \ X_3 \geq 0; \ \ X_4 \geq 0$$

(5.16)

The corresponding tableau is represented in Figure 5.4.

entering basis —

Basis	X_1	X_2	X_3	X_4	b
X_3	3	2	1	0	80
leaving basis → X_4	1	(4)	0	1	100
c_j	-3	-4	0	0	0

Figure 5.4 Starting basis for simplex method.

The feasible starting solution is simply to have $X_1 = X_2 = 0$, $X_3 = 80$, and $X_4 = 100$. This set of values for the variables satisfies the equations, although the corresponding value of the objective function is only zero. Thus, the starting basis will be constituted by X_3 and X_4. Since there are negative coefficients in the objective function, this solution is not optimal. Therefore, the first step is to determine which variable will enter the basis, i.e., become a nonzero variable. This will be X_2, since it corresponds to the most negative coefficient $c_2 = -4$ in the objective function. Both coefficients in the second column are positive. The respective ratios b_i/a_{i2} are $b_1/a_{21} = 80/2$ and $b_2/a_{22} = 100/4$. The smallest value is $100/4$, corresponding to $i = 2$. Therefore, variable X_4 found at the second level of the basis will leave it and take a value of zero. The pivot entry is thus a_{22}, with a corresponding value of 4.

The next step is to divide all elements on row 2 of the initial tableau by the value of the pivot entry, 4. The new row is, therefore, $\frac{1}{4}$, 1, 0, $\frac{1}{4}$, and $\frac{100}{4}$ in the last column. This is represented in Figure 5.4(a).

Basis	X_1	X_2	X_3	X_4	b
X_3	3	2	1	0	80
X_4	1/4	1	0	1/4	100/4
c	-3	-4	0	0	0

Figure 5.4(a)

Finally, we transform all entries of column 2 so that they become zero, except for the entry in the position of the pivot point, which will remain 1. This must be accomplished using linear combinations of the corresponding elements in the other columns only. Thus, a_{12}, which has a present value of 2, can be replaced by a zero simply by multiplying row 2 by 2 and subtracting it from row 1. Therefore, the entries in the new first row will be

$$a_{11} = 3 - \left(\frac{1}{4}\right)2 = \frac{5}{2} \qquad \text{for the first entry}$$

$$a_{12} = 2 - (1)2 = 0 \qquad \text{as we wanted}$$

$$a_{13} = 1 - (0)2 = 1$$

$$a_{14} = 0 - \left(\frac{1}{4}\right)2 = -\frac{1}{2}$$

$$b_1 = 80 - \left(\frac{100}{4}\right)2 = 30$$

Next, we must also transform the last coefficient in column 2 (c_2, the objective coefficient function) into a zero as well. This can be accomplished by multiplying row 2 by 4 and adding it to row 3. Therefore, the entries in the new row 3 of objective function coefficients will now be

$$c_1 = (-3) + \left(\frac{1}{4}\right)4 = -2$$

$$c_2 = (-4) + (1)4 = 0 \qquad \text{as we wanted}$$

$$c_3 = (0) + (0)4 = 0$$

$$c_4 = (0) + \left(\frac{1}{4}\right)4 = 1$$

$$b_3 = 0 + \left(\frac{100}{4}\right)_4 = 100$$

The resulting new tableau at the end of the first iteration is represented in Figure 5.4(b). Notice that X_2 has replaced X_4 in the composition of the basis.

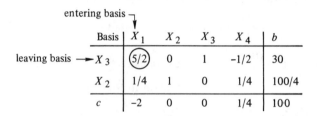

Figure 5.4(b) Second iteration.

There is still one objective function coefficient, c_1, which is negative, indicating that the current solution is not optimal. However, it has improved, since the value of the objective function is now equal to 100. (Note that the negative of the current value of the objective function will, at each step, be found at the intersection of the row of objective function coefficients and the column of right-hand-side values. Thus, in terms of the original maximization objective, the new value of the objective function, that is, b_3 above, is 100.)

Next, we start the second iteration of the procedure on the new tableau. The most (and only) negative objective function coefficient is now $c_1 = -2$. Therefore, X_1 will now enter the basis, i.e., acquire a nonzero value. We again compute the respective values of the ratios b_i/a_{i1}, using the entries in the first column of the new tableau. The values for the ratios are

$$\frac{b_1}{a_{11}} = \frac{30}{5/2}$$

$$\frac{b_2}{a_{21}} = \frac{100/4}{1/4}$$

The minimum corresponds to $i = 1$, i.e., row 1. Thus, X_3 leaves the basis, and the pivot point is $a_{11} = 5/2$. Next, we divide all entries in row 1 by the value of the entry at the pivot point, $5/2$. The resulting tableau is as represented in Figure 5.4(c). Finally, we transform every entry in column 1, except

Basis	X_1	X_2	X_3	X_4	b
X_3	1	0	2/5	–1/5	60/5
X_2	1/4	1	0	1/4	100/4
c	–2	0	0	1	100

Figure 5.4(c)

the pivot point, into zeros, using linear combinations of rows. First, a_{21} can be transformed into a zero by dividing the first row by 4 and subtracting it from row 2. Therefore, the new entries in row 2 will be

$$a_{21} = \frac{1}{4} - \frac{(1)}{4} = 0 \qquad \text{as we wanted}$$

$$a_{22} = 1 - \frac{(0)}{4} = 1 \qquad \text{as we expected, since } X_2 \text{ should}$$
$$\text{remain in the base}$$

$$a_{23} = 0 - \frac{(2/5)}{4} = \frac{-1}{10}$$

$$a_{24} = \frac{1}{4} - \frac{(-1/5)}{4} = \frac{3}{10}$$

$$b_2 = \frac{100}{4} - \frac{(60/5)}{4} = \frac{110}{5}$$

Next, c_1 can be transformed into a zero by multiplying row 1 by 2 and adding it to row 3. Consequently, the new entries in the objective function now will be

$$c_1 = -2 + (1)2 = 0 \qquad \text{as we wanted}$$

$$c_2 = 0 + (0)2 = 0$$

$$c_3 = 0 + \left(\frac{2}{5}\right)2 = \frac{4}{5}$$

$$c_4 = 1 + \left(\frac{-1}{5}\right)2 = \frac{3}{5}$$

$$b_3 = 100 + \left(\frac{60}{5}\right)2 = \frac{620}{5}$$

The resulting new tableau is represented in Figure 5.4(d).

Basis	X_1	X_2	X_3	X_4	b
X_1	1	0	2/5	-1/5	60/5
X_2	0	1	-1/10	3/10	110/5
c	0	0	4/5	3/5	620/5

Figure 5.4(d)   Optimal solution.

All coefficients in the objective function row are now positive. Therefore, the current solution is optimal. This solution consists of the variables X_1 and X_2 (original variables) being in the basis, i.e., having a value different from zero, and the X_3 and X_4 (slack variables) being equal to zero. The optimal value X_1^* for X_1 will be equal to the present value of the corresponding level of the right-hand side, 60/5, and similarly, X_2^* will be equal to 110/5. Also, the values of the slack variables are $X_3^* = X_4^* = 0$.[1]

Translated in physical terms, this means that the optimal program of building permits which maximizes the tax base is to allow $X_1^* = 60/5 = 12$ units of the first type (three-family units) and $X_2^* = 110/5 = 22$ units of the second type (two-family units). The fact that both slack variables X_3^* and X_4^* are equal to zero means that the upper bounds for the constraints are both reached. Thus, this program will result in using all the available land (180 acres) and result in the maximum number of families allowed (80). Indeed,

$$3X_1^* + 2X_2^* = 3\left(\frac{60}{5}\right) + 2\left(\frac{110}{5}\right) = \frac{180}{5} + \frac{220}{5} = 80$$

for the number of families, and

$$1X_1^* + 4X_2^* = 1\left(\frac{60}{5}\right) + 4\left(\frac{110}{5}\right) = \frac{500}{5} = 100$$

for the land used.

Finally, the value of the objective function (tax revenue) can be obtained directly in the optimal tableau at the lower right-hand-side corner, and is equal to 620/5 = 124 (thousands of dollars). Alternatively, it can also be computed directly from its definition:

$$3X_1^* + 4X_2^* = 3(12) + 4(22) = 124$$

Although the procedure is the same for larger problems, which, for instance, would incorporate other types of housing units and other types of planning requirements, the computations become rather cumbersome and time-consuming. It is then beneficial to resort to the use of ready-made computer programs for the implementation of the simplex method. These

---

[1] The notation X^* will represent the optimal value for the variable X.

programs exist in every computer center and are very simple to use since they basically require only specifying the value of the coefficients in the tableau, in the format specific to the particular program used.

5.5   Sensitivity Analysis of a Linear Program

The linear programming approach, besides its generality, offers other analytical advantages. The main one is the possibility to obtain, with very little additional work once the optimal solution has been obtained, further information about the properties of the optimum program, or the effects of changes in the definition of the original problem on it. This type of analysis is called *sensitivity analysis*, and will be briefly described in this section before we leave the area of linear programming.

First, a very convenient feature of the linear programming method is the existence of an alternative procedure for obtaining the optimal solution. This may be useful, in particular, in the case when all the coefficients c_j's are positive in the standard form. (One will recall that if, at the same time, all the coefficients b_i are also positive, then the original tableau is optimal.) If not all the b_i's are positive, whereas the foregoing procedure would not allow to proceed, one can use the "dual method" to arrive at the optimal solution.

The *dual method* uses the same original tableau, but looks first for the most negative right-hand-side coefficient b_i. The corresponding row (r, for instance) determines the row position of the pivot point. The column position is determined by the minimum value of the ratios $(c_j/-a_{rj})$ evaluated along that row r, for the negative-valued a_{rj}'s only. (If all a_{rj}'s along row r are positive, the problem has no solution.) The rest of the procedure is the same as in the primal algorithm and uses the same transformations to go from one basis to the next. The only difference is that one first identifies the variable that leaves the basis, and then the column of the variable that enters it, using the rules given above.

This alternative method may be used to check on the results of the application of the original (or *primal*) method. It can also be applied in connection with the solution of the *dual problem*. The dual problem of the standard form is a maximization problem defined as follows. If the original problem has m constraints in equality form, the dual will have m variables, which will be unrestricted in sign (either positive or negative). If the original problem has n positive variables, the dual problem will have n constraints in less-than inequality form. The matrix of coefficients a_{ij} in the dual is the "transposed" of the original matrix (i.e., the coefficients are interchanged symetrically with respect to the main diagonal to become a_{ji}). Finally, the m coefficients b_i of the right-hand sides of the constraints in the original problem become the m objective function coefficients in the dual problem; and conversely, the n objective function coefficients of the original problem become the n right-hand-side coefficients in the dual. Thus, the dual of the primal standard form,

$$Min \quad Z = (c_1X_1 + c_2X_2 + \ldots + c_jX_j + \ldots + c_nX_n)$$

$$Such \ That \ a_{11}X_1 + a_{12}X_2 + \ldots + a_{1j}X_j + \ldots + a_{1n}X_n = b_1$$

$$a_{21}X_1 + a_{22}X_2 + \ldots + \ldots \ldots + a_{2n}X_n = b_2 \quad (5.17)$$

$$\cdots\cdots\cdots\cdots\cdots\cdots\cdots\cdots\cdots\cdots\cdots\cdots$$

$$a_{m1}X_1 + a_{m2}X_2 + \ldots + \ldots \ldots + a_{mn}X_n = b_n$$

becomes the dual problem:

$$Max \quad Z = (b_1Y_1 + b_2Y_2 + \ldots\ldots\ldots + b_mY_m)$$

$$Such \ That \ a_{11}Y_1 + a_{21}Y_2 + a_{31}Y_3 + \ldots + a_{m1}Y_m \leq c_1$$

$$a_{12}Y_1 + a_{22}Y_2 + a_{32}Y_3 + \ldots + a_{m2}Y_m \leq c_2 \quad (5.18)$$

$$\cdots\cdots\cdots\cdots\cdots\cdots\cdots\cdots\cdots\cdots\cdots\cdots$$

$$a_{1n}Y_1 + a_{2n}Y_2 + \ldots + \ldots + a_{mn}Y_m \leq c_m$$

For example, the dual of the problem (5.23), which we have been using in the illustrative example, and which was

$$Min \quad Z = (-3X_1 - 4X_2 + 0X_3 + 0X_4)$$

$$Such \ That \quad 3X_1 + 2X_2 + \ X_3 + 0X_4 = \ \ 80$$

$$1X_1 + 4X_2 + 0X_3 + 1X_4 = 100$$

would be

$$Max \quad Z = (80Y_1 + \ 100Y_2) \leq -3$$

$$Such \ That \quad 3Y_1 + \quad 1Y_2 \ \leq -3$$

$$2Y_1 + \quad 4Y_2 \ \leq -4 \quad (5.19)$$

$$Y_1 \leq 0; \quad Y_2 \ \leq 0$$

The optimal solution of the dual problem provides further information on the optimal solution of the original (primal) problem. First, it can be shown that the optimal value of the dual objective function is equal to the optimal value of the primal objective function Z^*. That is,

$$Z^* = c_1X_1^* + c_2X_2^* + \ldots + c_iX_i^* + \ldots + c_nX_n^*$$

$$= b_1Y_1^* + b_2Y_2^* + \ldots + b_jY_j^* + \ldots + b_mY_m^* \quad (5.20)$$

This equality can then provide a check on the optimal value of the primal objective function. Formula (5.20) provides an alternative interpretation of the optimal values Y_i^* of the dual variables as the relative importance, or *weights*, which the various resources in the original problem in the respective amounts b_i have on the optimal value of the objective function. Equivalently, by taking the *incremental* version of formula (5.20), we get

$$Y_i^* = \frac{\Delta Z^*}{\Delta b_i} \tag{5.21}$$

Physically, this means that the optimal value of the ith variable in the dual problem measures the *rate of change* of the value of the original objective function for a (small) change in the value of the limit b_i on the ith resource. Thus, it can also be interpreted to represent the "price" of that resource, in that it measures the effect of a unit change on the availability (or supply) of the resource i on the optimal value of the objective.

Another useful relation in which the optimal values Y_i^* intervene is

$$c_j^* = c_j - (a_{1j}Y_1^* + a_{2j}Y_2^* + \ldots + a_{ij}Y_j^* + \ldots + a_{mj}Y_m^*) \tag{5.22}$$

where c_j^* is the updated objective function coefficient in the optimum tableau for the jth variable, the a_{ij}'s are the coefficients along the jth column, i.e., corresponding to the jth activity in the original starting tableau, and c_j is the corresponding objective function coefficient. This alternative formula for the computation of the entries in the objective function row at the optimum can be used to check that, as expected, the values are zero for the basic variables and are positive for the nonbasic variables, by definition of the optimum, as we have seen in the simplex method above.

Finally, it can also be shown that for the optimal solution of the primal, if the ith primal resource is not used up to its available limit (i.e., there is a positive slack variable for the ith constraint), the value of the ith dual variable will be equal to zero.

Although the optimal solution to the dual problem can be obtained by applying the simplex method to the dual, it is not necessary to solve the dual problem in order to compute the optimal values of its variables Y_i^*, since these are respectively equal to the negatives of the objective function coefficients for the ith nonbasic variable in the optimal tableau. Formally,

$$Y_i^* = -c_{j_i}^* \tag{5.23}$$

where j_i is the column index of the ith nonbasic variable, at the optimum.

Since the number of variables in the dual is equal to the number of constraints i in the primal, it may be more advantageous to solve the dual when the primal has a large number of variables but few constraints. In particular, a primal problem in any number of variables, but with only two constraints, can therefore be transformed into a two-variable problem which can then be solved graphically.

As an illustration, let us go back to the example above. At the optimum, as represented by Figure 5.4(d), the variables in the basis were X_1 and X_2, the original variables, and the nonbasic variables were X_3 and X_4, the slack variables. The respective c_j coefficients for these two nonbasic variables were, thus, equal to $\frac{4}{5}$ and $\frac{3}{5}$, respectively. Their negatives represent the optimal values of the dual variables. Therefore, using formula (5.23),

$$Y_1^* = -c_{j_1}^* = \frac{-4}{5} \quad \text{and} \quad Y_2^* = -c_{j_2}^* = \frac{-3}{5}$$

Since both of these values are nonzero, this means (as we already knew) that both resources $i = 1$ (families) and $i = 2$ (land) have been entirely used up to their limits of 80 and 100 units, respectively, to attain the maximum tax value of 124.

We can also use formula (5.20) to check on the previously computed value for the maximum tax revenue:

$$Z^* = b_1 Y_1^* + b_2 Y_2^* = \left[80\left(\frac{-4}{5}\right) + 100\left(\frac{-3}{5}\right) \right] = -\frac{620}{5} = -124$$

Furthermore, we infer from formula (5.21) that if the number of allowable families were to be marginally increased by 1 unit, the resulting effect on the maximum tax revenue Z^* would be equal to

$$\Delta Z^* = Y_1^* \, \Delta b_1 = \left(\frac{-4}{5}\right) 1 = \frac{-4}{5}$$

[We get the negative since the original problem, before transforming into standard (minimization) form, was a maximization of the revenue.]

Similarly, the marginal effect of a unit increase in the availability of land would be 3/5. Thus, increasing the limit on families is more effective, as far as maximizing the tax revenue under the present constraints, than increasing the amount of land zoned for residential purposes. The respective revenues of 4/5 unit (or $800) and 3/5 (or $600), thus provide a means of assessing the *cost-effectiveness ratio* of these two alternatives in increasing the tax revenue above its present maximum value of 124, by comparing them with the respective costs, externalities, positive effects, etc., of either improving the service capacity of the municipality, or zoning and developing more residential land, or both. In fact, the values of 4/5 = $800 and 3/5 = $600 can be considered to represent the "prices" the municipality could put on providing services for one extra family, and on zoning or developing 1 additional acre of residential land, respectively. Indeed, given the foregoing results, if the actual costs of these two actions are more than $800 and $600, respectively, it would not pay for the municipality to do so, since the incremental tax revenues generated by relaxing the constraints on services and land would only be $800 and $600. Conversely, of course, if these actions cost less, they would be profitable. Thus, in general, the optimal values of the dual variables represent break-even points for the feasibility of increasing (or decreasing) the availability of the resources in the primal problem by one unit.

Let us now turn to the interpretation of formulas (5.22). First we confirm that they hold, for a further check on our optimal solution we have for the first two coefficients:

$$c_1^* = -3 - \left[3\left(\frac{-4}{5}\right) + 1\left(\frac{-3}{5}\right)\right] = 0$$

$$c_2^* = -4 - \left[2\left(\frac{-4}{5}\right) + 4\left(\frac{-3}{5}\right)\right] = 0$$

Thus, for the two basic variables (activities) we retrieve the expected value of zero. For the first nonbasic variable X_3 (the slack on the number of families allowed):

$$c_3^* = 0 - \left[1\left(\frac{-4}{5}\right) + 0\left(\frac{-3}{5}\right)\right] = \frac{4}{5}$$

and for the second nonbasic variable (the slack on the amount of residential land):

$$c_4^* = 0 - \left[0\left(\frac{-4}{5}\right) + 1\left(\frac{-3}{5}\right)\right] = \frac{3}{5}$$

Let us now use the same formula (5.22) to answer the following question. The planning commission has also received applications for permits for a third type of housing unit. This type (a single-family unit) requires 0.15 acre, and would be assessed for a tax of 2.5 thousand dollars. Would it increase the tax base to issue permits for this type of unit, given the existing resources?

To answer this, there is no need to go back to the original starting tableau, augment it with a new variable, say X_5 with coefficients $a_{15} = 1$ (family requirement) and $a_{25} = 0.15$ (land requirement), and $c_5 = -2.5$ (objective function coefficient). Rather, we simply observe that since we already know the values of the optimal "prices" 4/5 and 3/5 for the two resources, we can directly compute the updated (optimal) objective function coefficient c_5^* for the new type using formula (5.22) and the coefficients above. Thus,

$$c_5^* = c_5 - (Y_1^* a_{15} + Y_2^* a_{25}) = -2.5 - \left[\left(\frac{-4}{5}\right)1 + \left(\frac{-3}{5}\right)0.15\right]$$

$$= -2.5 + 0.89 = -1.61$$

Therefore, the objective function coefficient for this type of unit would, at the optimum, have been negative. In other words, it would have been a candidate for inclusion in the basis. Consequently, the optimal tableau consisting of X_1 and X_2 (the first two types of housing units) could be improved on by replacing one of them by the new type. In fact, the result above further indicates that this will be true as long as the negative of the tax c_5 on the new unit is such that $\{-c_5 - [(-4/5)1 + (-3/5)0.15]\}$ remains negative, i.e., $(-c_5 + 0.89) \leq 0$ or when the tax is higher than 0.89, or \$890 in our units.

Similarly, for any type of housing with characteristics: number of families housed a_1, land used a_2, and tax $(-c)$, replacing one of the first two types by this type will result in an improvement of the tax base if $[-c - (-4/5a_1) + (-3/5a_2)] \leq 0$, i.e.,

$$-c \leq -\frac{4}{5}a_1 - \frac{3}{5}a_2 \quad \text{or} \quad c \geq \frac{4}{5}a_1 + \frac{3}{5}a_2 \quad (5.24)$$

This inequality allows for various combinations of values of the parameters of the housing unit type.

Physically, inequality (5.24) states that a new type of activity (housing unit) will be competitive if its total cost (sum of its unit requirements weighed by the prices of the respective resources) is smaller than its unit benefit (objective function coefficient). It can thus be used to systematically compare other alternative activities in a given linear program without performing the entire algorithm.

5.6 Capital Budgeting and Dynamic Programming

In this section, we shall now consider another type of programming and evaluation problem, this time of a very different nature, involving a series, or a set of decisions, either at several points in time or concerning several projects. As for the exposition of the linear programming approach, let us first begin with a specific practical example, which we shall then generalize.

Assume that we have the following *budgeting* problem. We are planning for a multimodal urban transportation system, involving mass transit, arterial improvement, and a new dial-a-ride system. The technical *feasibility analyses* have determined the various levels of improvement in the overall transportation system (as measured, for instance, by the increase in some measure of capacity) which would result from various levels of investment in the three alternatives, considered individually. These are represented in Table 5.3,

TABLE 5.3

Mode Number:	1		2		3	
Name:	Dial-a-Ride		Arterial Improvement		Mass Transit	
	X	$g_1(X)$	X	$g_2(X)$	X	$g_3(X)$
	0	0	0	0	0	0
	1	1	1	2	1	3
	2	3	2	4	2	4
	3	6	3	5	3	7
	4	8	4	6	4	8
	5	9	5	7	5	11

where x is the level of capital outlay (in tens of millions of dollars) and $g_i(x)$ is the corresponding resulting improvement in capacity (in hundreds of commuters per day, for instance) which we can call the *return function*, for mode i ($i = 1, 2, 3$).

Given this information and given the total budget of $50 million, what is the program of allocation of funds to the three modes that would result in the optimal improvement in transportation (we assume that the individual effects are cumulative). It is clear that the number of possibilities for the distribution of funds prohibits, even in this simple case, a straight examination approach.

We shall, therefore, serialize this examination in a systematic, efficient manner such that we only have to consider possibilities which improve upon previous decisions, just as in the case of the linear programming algorithm.

Also, it is clear that our problem would be substantially simpler if we were dealing with only two modes. Indeed, in that case we would then only have to look at six possibilities: namely, allocating either 0, 1, 2, 3, 4, or 5 units of capital to one mode, and the remainder to the other, and selecting the allocation that results in the maximum efficiency. (We assume that capital outlays are *discrete*, for instance, in units of tens of millions of dollars. Of course, finer differentiation is possible by merely introducing more values for x in Table 5.3.

In any case, it should also be clear that the optimal allocation of funds between the three modes should be such that it combines the optimal allocation between any two with the optimal allocation between this subset of two and the remaining mode. (The order of consideration of the modes obviously does not matter as far as the overall, total allocation is concerned, since there is only one maximum value for the overall improvement in capacity.) In other words, if there is anything less than optimality in these two suballocations, the overall allocation between the three could not possibly be optimal. This deceptively simple principle (sometimes known as the *principle of optimality* of dynamic programming) gives us the key to the simplification of the problem, since we can now deal with only two modes at a time. Let us, therefore, examine the possible allocations of funds between the first two modes, dial-a-ride and arterial development only. We have to consider all levels of subtotal funding for these two modes under 5 units ($50 million), to reserve for the (yet unknown) remainder allocation to the third and last mode. Thus, if we allocate a subtotal of zero units to the first two, there is only one possibility of doing so, which, obviously, is to allocate nothing to dial-a-ride ($X_1 = 0$) and also nothing to arterial improvement ($X_2 = 0$). The effect of that decision is no improvement on the capacity, that is, $g_1(X_1) + g_2(X_2) = 0$.

Next, we consider the allocation of a total of 1 unit between these two modes. Here, there are two ways of doing so. The first is to allocate 1 unit to the first mode and nothing to the second, i.e., $X_1 = 1$ and $X_2 = 0$. The combined effect of that decision, measured by the sum of the corresponding values of the returns, $g_1(1) + g_2(0)$, can be read off the first two columns of Table 5.3 and is equal to $1 + 0 = 1$. The second, and only other possibility is to allocate nothing to the first mode and 1 unit to the second. In the same fashion, the corresponding effect on system capacity would be measured by an improvement of $g_1(0) + g_2(1) = 0 + 2 = 2$. This combination is, therefore, superior to the first one, for the same suballocation of 1 unit. Regardless of whatever subsequent allocation we shall make to the third mode, it is clear that we should retain the optimal allocation for these first two modes. Thus, we shall retain as the best allocation for a total budget of 2 units for modes 1 and 2 the combination $X_1 = 0$, $X_2 = 1$, and a combined return, which we will note g_{12} of: $g_{12}(1) = 2$.

Continuing in this fashion, we now examine the possibilities corresponding to a suballocation of 2 units to the first two modes. There are three such possibilities, which are as represented in Table 5.4. We shall, therefore, retain

TABLE 5.4

Allocation to First Mode, X_1	Allocation to Second Mode, X_2	Combined Return, $g_{12} = g_1(X_1) + g_2(X_2)$
0	2	$0 + 4 = 4$
1	1	$1 + 2 = 3$
2	0	$3 + 0 = 0$

as the best allocation of 2 units to the first two modes the combination $X_1 = 2$, $X_2 = 0$, which results in a combined improvement of 4 units. We continue in the same fashion to identify the best suballocation, corresponding to subtotals of 3, 4, and 5 units, respectively, between the first two modes. The results are as represented in Table 5.5, as the function $g_{12}(X)$, where X is the subtotal level of allocation, and X_1^* and X_2^* are the optimal levels of allocation for mode 1 and 2, respectively. (In the case where there are several com-

TABLE 5.5

X	$g_{12}(X)$	X_1^*	X_2^*
0	0	0	0
1	2	0	1
2	4	0	2
3	6	3	0
4	8	3	1
5	10	4	1

binations which result in the same optimal value for g_{12}, either all such combinations can be recorded, or only one selected arbitrarily.)

The function $g_{12}(X)$ of the suballocation level X thus represents the maximum value of all possible sums of values for $g_1(X_1)$, the effect of allocating X_1 units of funds to the first mode, and $g_2(X_2)$, the effect of allocating X_2 units to the second mode, when the sum $(X_1 + X_2)$ is kept at the given level of the subtotal X. Thus, the formal expression for the function $g_{12}(X)$ is

$$g_{12}(X) = Max\,[g_1(X_1) + g_2(X_2)]$$
$$Such\ That\ X_1 + X_2 = X$$

(5.25)

We now have to combine this suballocation with the remaining allocation of funds to the third mode, so that the overall, combined effect of the three modes is optimized. We do this by combining optimally, as we have done above for the first two modes, the return for the first two, as represented by the function g_{12} in Table 5.5, with the return $g_3(X)$ for the third and last mode, as given in Table 5.3.

We thus repeat the same procedure, this time using g_{12} and g_3 instead of g_1 and g_2 as in the first step of the procedure. (This is where the procedure of dynamic programming is very efficient, since g_{12} summarizes the best, i.e., only relevant, combinations between g_1 and g_2.)

We begin by considering a total allocation of zero units between the first two modes, and the third. This can only be done in one way, i.e., allocating both 0 to (1 and 2) and 1 to 3. The effect is, of course, a return of zero.

Next, an allocation of a total of 1 unit can be effected in two ways: first, by allocating one unit to (1 and 2) and nothing to 3. This results in a return of $g_{12}(1) + g_3(0)$ (i.e., the sum of the returns corresponding to the best allocation of 1 unit between modes 1 and 2, and the given return corresponding to an allocation of 0 units to mode 3) and is equal to $2 + 0$. Second, it can be effected by allocating 0 to (1 and 2) and 1 to 3. The corresponding effect is equal to $g_{12}(0) + g_3(1) = 0 + 3 = 3$. Thus, the second allocation is superior. Since allocating 0 to (1 and 2) really means allocating 0 to 1 and 0 to 2, we have a complete description of that particular optimal allocation.

Continuing, we now consider a total allocation of 2 units between modes (1 and 2) and 3. There are three ways of doing this, which are represented in Table 5.6. Thus, the optimum allocation is a subtotal of 1 to the first two modes and 1 to the third. Going back to the Table 5.5, we recall that the suboptimal allocation of 1 to (1 and 2) consisted of allocating 0 to the first mode and 1 to the second, thus completely describing the allocation.

Continuing in this fashion, we successively examine the allocation of totals of 3, 4, and 5 units between the three modes. The results are summarized in Table 5.7, which is the equivalent of Table 5.5 for the first two modes only.

The solution to our original problem is then described by the last row in Table 5.6, which indicates that the optimal allocation of a total of 5 units

TABLE 5.6

Allocation to First and Second Mode	Allocation to Third Mode	Total Return, $g_{123} = g_{12} + g_3$
0	2	$0 + 4 = 4$
1	1	$2 + 3 = 5$
2	0	$4 + 0 = 4$

TABLE 5.7

X	g_{123}	X_1^*	X_2^*	X_3^*
0	0	0	0	0
1	3	0	0	1
2	5	0	1	1
3	7	0	0	3
4	9	0	1	3
5	11	0	0	5

of capital ($50 million in funding) results in the maximum improvement of transportation capacity of 1100 commuters per day. The optimal decision is $X_1^* = X_2^* = 0$ (allocate nothing to the first mode, dial-a-ride, and nothing to arterial improvement), and $X_3^* = 5$ ($50 million to the mass transit system, mode number 3).

Further information derives from this solution, which can also be read off the same Table 5.7. For instance, if we only have a level of funding of $40 million (e.g., to anticipate possible cutbacks), then the optimal allocation of funds under the same conditions would be to allocate $10 million to arterial improvement, $30 million to the mass transit system, and nothing to the dial-a-ride system. Similar findings can be inferred for lower levels of total funding.

Another analytical advantage of the dynamic programming approach is that if we wanted to include another mode or several other modes in this budgeting problem, we would not have to start the procedure all over again. Indeed, if, for instance, we would like to consider a fourth mode, for which the individual return function $g_4(X)$ is given, the allocation problem for the four modes is simply obtained from the best allocation between the first three modes combined with the allocation to the fourth mode. In other words, we simply use the two return functions $g_{123}(X)$, as represented in Table 5.7, and $g_4(X)$.

Generalizing, the problem of the optimal allocation of a total number X of units of a given resource to n projects or programs $i = 1, 2, 3, \ldots, n$, for which the individual return functions $g_i(X)$ are given for values of X between

0 and X, can formally be written as

$$
\begin{aligned}
Max \quad & [g_1(X_1) + g_2(X_2) + \ldots + g_i(X_i) + \ldots + g_n(X_n)] \\
Such\ That \quad & X_1 + X_2 + \ldots + X_n \leq X \\
& 0 \leq X_i \leq X \qquad \text{for all } i
\end{aligned}
\tag{5.26}
$$

[Note that when the return functions $g_i(X)$ are all linear functions, the problem becomes a linear programming problem.]

The solution, consisting of the optimal allocation or set of values X_i^*, and of the maximum value of the objective function above can be represented by the model

$$
\begin{aligned}
g_{123\ldots n}(X) = & Max\ [g_{123\ldots n-1}(X - X_n) + g_n(X_n)] \\
Such\ That \quad & 0 \leq X_n \leq X \qquad \text{for each activity } n = 1, 2, 3, \ldots
\end{aligned}
\tag{5.27}
$$

where X_n is the allocation to activity n, $g_{12\ldots n-1}(X)$ is itself the optimal allocation to the set of $(n - 1)$ first activities, and $g_n(X)$ is the individual return function for the nth activity.

The procedure, which computes $g_{123\ldots n}(X)$ knowing the values of $g_{123\ldots n-1}(X)$ through formula (5.27), is iterated with $g_1(X)$, being, of course, the individual return function for the first activity

$$
\begin{aligned}
g_{12}(X) = & Max\ [g_1(X - X_2) + g_2(X_2)] \\
Such\ That \quad & 0 \leq X_2 \leq X
\end{aligned}
\tag{5.28}
$$

Formula (5.28) can be used to implement the dynamic programming procedure on computers.

A great advantage of the dynamic programming approach is the fact that the evaluation of the effectiveness of various levels of investment [the return functions $g_i(X)$] does not have to be specified mathematically, as opposed to, for instance, the linear programming procedure, where the objective function had to be specified. Here, the knowledge of the values of the return functions is sufficient. The only requirement is that these functions be monotonically increasing, i.e., that when the investment grows, the return grows, or at least does not diminish. Thus, the procedure can be applied to a wide generality of situations.

Another advantage is the fact that it can also be transformed easily into a procedure for the allocation of resources, not to several projects at the same time, but to the same project at several points in time. In this case, the indices $1, 2, \ldots, n$ in formulas (5.26) and (5.27) would represent not the projects or activity numbers, but the time periods. Otherwise, the procedure for capital budgeting would be exactly the same. One requirement, however, would be, just as above, that the returns be measured in comparable units. This would imply that for projects taking place at various future dates, the benefits be discounted to the present (or to a common future date), using, for instance, the formula

$$b_0 = \frac{b_n}{(1 + r)^n} \tag{5.29}$$

where b_n is the future value at time n, b_0 the present value, and r the rate of interest, inflation, etc.

A very powerful feature of the method in its application to future capital budgeting is that as we have seen above, the optimal solution for the time frame (year 1 to year n) would also lead to the knowledge of the optimal solution for all smaller time frames: (1 to 2), (1 to 3), (1 to i), . . . , (1 to $n - 1$). Thus, in the case when the objective is not to maximize the total return but to attain a certain (minimum) level Z_0, the allocation procedure can be stopped at year i as soon as the subreturn for time frame (year 1 to year i), i.e., $g_{12\ldots i}(X)$, goes above the value Z_0. Consequently, this approach might result in not spending all of the initially planned budget.

For instance, in the illustrative example above, if we have determined that an increase in capacity of more than 700 commuters is sufficient for the purposes of the project, then we do not have to spend all of the original budget of 5 units, which was allocated before its effects were known. We then have a choice of retaining the three modes as originally planned and spending only 3 units (Table 5.7), or spending 4 units in the first two modes only (Table 5.5), etc. This type of sensitivity analysis is thus very useful for incorporating the value of time in planning and budgeting considerations.

Another useful feature is that the various time periods can be grouped together to form *stages* in the development of the project. For instance, time periods 1 through i might constitute a first stage for which the optimal budget allocation is obtained through the dynamic programming procedure for $n = i$ time periods, resulting in a return function $g_{12\ldots i}(X)$. Next, the second stage, say, time periods $i + 1$ through j, can be optimized independently, resulting in a return function $g_{i+1, i+2\ldots j}(X)$. Then the total time frame corresponding to time periods 1 through j can be optimized by treating it as a two-time period problem, with the return function $g_{12\ldots i}(X)$ to be combined with $g_{i+1, i+2\ldots j}(X)$. The same approach would be used for any number of stages, and is particularly convenient in the case of *developmental planning*, where budgets defined for fiscal years might need to be translated into allocations for projects stages. In particular, the property above allows analysis of the effect of various schemes for the grouping of project activities into stages on the individual stage efficiencies. (The overall return for the total project is not changed, however, as we have seen above.)

5.7 Extensions to Multiresources Allocation

Finally, we will conclude this section with an extension of the dynamic programming procedure to the case of the allocation of two resources, i.e., when the return functions are functions of two variables, X and Y. Let us assume, for instance, that we are planning for the reorganization of a health care delivery system, involving three branch clinics in areas 1, 2, and 3, respectively. Because of differences in the facilities and the needs of the populations at these three locations, their individual efficiency, as measured by the additional number of outpatients that could be treated per day (in tens of people), as a function of the level of additional staffing X (number of doctors and nurses, in tens), and as a function of the level of additional funding Y (equipment, fee subsidy, etc., in millions of dollars), has been projected at the levels represented in Table 5.8. Also, the maximum levels of funding for the

TABLE 5.8

Location 1					Location 2					Location 3				
X_1 Y_1	0	1	2	3	X_2 Y_2	0	1	2	3	X_3 Y_3	0	1	2	3
0	0	1	3	6	0	0	2	4	5	0	0	3	4	7
1	2	3	5	7	1	1	3	5	6	1	2	4	5	8
2	4	5	6	8	2	3	5	7	8	2	4	6	7	9
3	6	6	7	9	3	4	6	8	9	3	5	7	8	10

regional program that can be allocated between the three centers are $3 million and 30 staff, respectively. Given these constraints, what is the distribution of funds and of staff that would maximize the total number of additional people who could be treated per day in the region?

This problem is of the same nature as the one-dimensional allocation problem discussed above, with the difference that we now have to consider all possible joint combinations of allocation of additional funds and staff, with their combined effects (return function values) as represented in the above two-way tables. Let us, therefore, consider in the same fashion as for the one-resource problem, the first two locations only. The very first possibility, which is to allocate no funds and no staff to the first two centers, can only be effected in one way: allocate nothing for both resources and to both centers. The combined return is, of course, 0; and $X_1^* = X_2^* = Y_1^* = Y_2^* = 0$.

The next possibility, keeping the subtotal level of funding Y for the two centers at zero but allocating a subtotal X of 1 unit of staffing can be effected in two ways: $(Y_1 = 0; X_1 = 0)$ for the first center with $(Y_2 = 0; X_2 = 1)$ for the second; or $(Y_1 = 0; X_1 = 1)$ for the first and $(Y_2 = 0; X_2 = 0)$ for the second. The two possibilities are represented diagrammatically in Figure 5.5(a), where positions marked by the same symbol are combined. They lead to respective returns of $(0 + 2) = 2$ and $(1 + 0) = 1$. Thus, the second combination is retained as the best and recorded in the position $X = 1$ and $Y = 0$ of the table of values of the function $g_{12}(X; Y)$, as represented in Table 5.9, where we also record the corresponding optimal values $X_1^*, X_2^*, Y_1^*, Y_2^*$ here: $(Y_1^* = 0; X_1^* = 1)$ and $(Y_2^* = 0; X_2^* = 0)$.

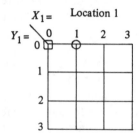

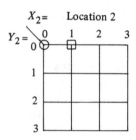

Figure 5.5(a)

TABLE 5.9

$g_{12}(X, Y)$

Y \ X	0	2	3
0	0	2	4	6
1	2	4	6	7
2	4	6	8	9
3	6	8	10	11

Legend:
$$\boxed{\begin{array}{c} X_1^* \,;\, Y_1^* \\ X_2^* \,;\, Y_2^* \end{array}}$$

Y \ X	0	1	2	3
0	0; 0 / 0; 0	1; 0 / 0; 0	0; 0 / 1; 0	3; 0 / 0; 0
1	0; 1 / 0; 0	0; 1 / 1; 0	0; 1 / 2; 0	1; 1 / 2; 0
2	0; 2 / 0; 0	0; 2 / 1; 0	0; 2 / 2; 0	1; 2 / 2; 0
3	0; 3 / 0; 0	0; 3 / 1; 0	0; 3 / 2; 0	0; 3 / 3; 0

We consider next the allocation of a total of $Y = 0$ units of funds and $X = 2$ units of staff to the first two centers. Since again $Y = Y_1 + Y_2 = 0$, we are restricted to consider possibilities such that $Y_1 = 0$ and $Y_2 = 0$, i.e., combining positions along the first row of the first table and the first row of the second. Within this first constraint, however, we can now look for all combinations such that $X = X_1 + X_2 = 2$. There are three such possibilities, corresponding to $X_1 = 0; X_2 = 2$, or $X_1 = X_2 = 1$, or $X_1 = 2; X_2 = 0$. These are in the locations represented in Figure 5.5(b), and lead to the respec-

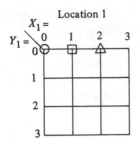

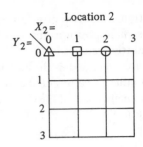

Figure 5.5(b)

tive combined returns of $0 + 4 = 0$, $1 + 2 = 3$, and $3 + 0 = 3$. Thus, the first combination is the best and is recorded in the position $Y = 0$; $X = 2$ in Table 5.9, together with the record of the optimal values: $(X_1^* = 0; Y_1^* = 0)$, and $(X_2^* = 1; Y_2^* = 0)$. Continuing in this fashion, we fill out the last entry in the first row of the table, retaining the best of the combinations on Figure 5.5(c), thus exhausting all allocations such that the total of funds Y is zero, but with varying levels of subtotal staffing X.

Symetrically, we fill out the entries in the first column of Table 5.9, corresponding to a total level of funding between the first two centers of zero and varying levels of staffing X. The corresponding combinations for the case $(X = 0; Y = 2)$, for example, are represented in Figure 5.5(d).

We next consider the case $X = 1$; $Y = 1$, corresponding to a subtotal

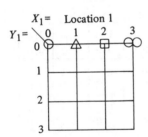

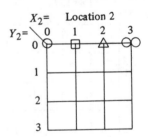

Figure 5.5(c)

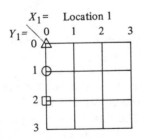

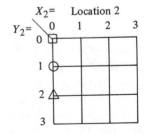

Figure 5.5(d)

allocation of 1 unit of staffing and 1 unit of funding between the first two centers. We have to consider all possibilities such that the sum of X_1 and X_2 is equal to 1, and the sum of Y_1 and Y_2 is equal to 1.

There are only four such possibilities, since we can only combine the first row of either table with the second of the other table, together with the same requirement for the columns. The corresponding possibilities are represented in Figure 5.5(e). The maximum value for the combined return is equal to 4, corresponding to the position marked by the triangle in Figure 5.5(e), i.e., $X_1 = 0$; $Y_1 = 1$ and $X_2 = 1$, $Y_2 = 0$. This is then recorded in Table 5.9.

We continue this process until we fill out all entries in the table of values of $g_{12}(X; Y)$. For instance, the possible combinations corresponding to the position $X = 2$ and $Y = 3$ (i.e., an allocation of a total of 2 units of staffing and 3 units of funding between the first two centers) are represented as Figure 5.5(f). (It should now be clear how these possibilities are generated by keeping the sum of the numbers of the columns combined equal to X *and* that of the row numbers equal to Y.)

The complete table $g_{12}(X; Y)$ then represents the best return possible for the allocation of a total of X units of staffing and Y units of funding to the first two regional centers, for all values of X and Y between 0 and 3. (When several combinations result in the same combined return, it is sufficient to retain only one, chosen arbitrarily. However, recording the other equivalent possibilities might be useful for later flexibility in the allocation for the three centers.)

In the same fashion as for the single-resource case, the best allocation between the three centers is next obtained by combining Table 5.9 with the

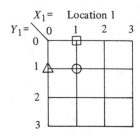

Figure 5.5(e)

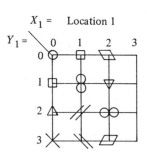

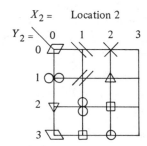

Figure 5.5(f)

table of return for the third center, given in Table 5.8. The computations will not be repeated here, but are conducted in exactly the same fashion. Note, however, that only the information concerning the optimal values X_3^* and Y_3^* needs to be recorded, since the remaining values to be allocated to the first two centers can be obtained by taking the difference from the known totals X and Y. By going back to the corresponding position in Table 5.9, we can then get a complete description of the optimal allocation:

$$(X_1^*; Y_1^*); \quad (X_2^*; Y_2^*) \quad \text{and} \quad (X_3^*; Y_3^*)$$

The resulting optimal allocation between the three centers is represented in Table 5.10.

TABLE 5.10

$g_{123}(X; Y)$					$(X_3^*; Y_3^*)$			
X Y	0	1	2	3	X Y	0	1	2	3
0	0	3	5	7	0	0;0	1;0	1;0	3;0
1	2	5	7	9	1	0;0	1;0	1;0	3;0
2	4	7	9	11	2	2;0	1;0	1;0	1;0
3	6	9	11	13	3	0;1	1;0	1;0	1;0

Thus, for a total budget of \$3 million and a total level of staffing of 30, the optimal total number of additional patients that could be treated is equal to 130 per day. The optimal allocation is to staff the third center at a level X_3^* of 1 unit (10 people) and to allocate a level Y_3^* of 0 units (no additional funds). This means that there remains a subtotal of $3 - 1 = 2$ units of staffing and $3 - 0 = 3$ units of funding for the first two centers. Going back to position $X = 2$ and $Y = 3$ in Table 5.9 for $g_{12}(X; Y)$, we deduce that the corresponding best allocation would be at a level of $(X_1^* = 0; Y_1^* = 3)$ and $(X_2^* = 2; Y_2^* = 0)$. This means that the first center should not be additionally staffed and funded with \$3 million, and the second center should have 20 staff added but receive no additional funding. (Note, as expected, the totals $X_1^* + X_2^* + X_3^* = 3$ and $Y_1^* + Y_2^* + Y_3^* = 3$.)

The problem of the optimal allocation with two resources can formally be written in the general case, using the same notation as in formulas (5.26) through (5.28), as

$$
\begin{aligned}
Max\,[g_1(X_1; Y_1) &+ g_2(X_2; Y_2) + \cdots \\
&+ g_i(X_i; Y_i) + \cdots + g_n(X_n; Y_n)] \\
Such\ That \quad X_1 + X_2 + &\cdots + X_i + \cdots + X_n = X \\
Y_1 + Y_2 + &\cdots + Y_i + \cdots + Y_n = Y
\end{aligned}
\tag{5.30}
$$

for which the solution can be computed as

$$
\begin{aligned}
&g_{123\ldots n}(X;\, Y) = \\
&Max\,[g_{123\ldots n-1}(X - X_n;\, Y - Y_n) + g_n(X_n;\, Y_n)] \\
&Such\ That\quad 0 \le X_n \le X \\
& 0 \le Y_n \le Y
\end{aligned}
\tag{5.31}
$$

and starting the recursive procedure with

$$
\begin{aligned}
&g_{12}(X;\, Y) = Max\,[g_1(X - X_2;\, Y - Y_2) + g_2(X_2;\, Y_2)] \\
&Such\ That\quad 0 \le X_2 \le X \\
& 0 \le Y_2 \le Y
\end{aligned}
\tag{5.32}
$$

Conceptually, the same approach can be applied to an allocation problem in any number m of resources. The computations would in this case be programmed on electronic computers using a generalization of formulas (5.31) and (5.32) to m variables: $x, y, \ldots, z$. Also, just as the case of one resource, application to n time periods, instead of n projects is straightforward.

Before leaving the area of dynamic programming, although we shall not elaborate, it should be mentioned that as a technique of allocation of scarce resources between competing regions or activities, dynamic programming is well suited structurally to accommodate uncertainty concerning the effect of decisions, i.e., for instance, when the values of the return functions are *random variables*, and not deterministic quantities as we have seen above. Such a situation might arise when high, average, or low estimates with corresponding probabilities of occurrence are used to represent the effects of various levels of objectives (or decisions). In that case, the solution approach is essentially similar. (On the contrary, although linear programming is somewhat better suited to represent the mix of effects resulting from a set of concurrent programs, the method becomes substantially different and more complicated when probabilistic coefficients are introduced.) Also, dynamic programming is well suited to represent a general class of problems relevant to *public management* and *planning*, those dealing with the *optimal service delivery* routes along a communication network, such as sanitation, police protection, postal service, etc.

5.8 Scheduling and the Critical-Path Method

To conclude this exposition of allocation methods, we shall now describe a standard model for optimal scheduling, i.e., allocation of time between various activities in a project. Although its applications and variants are much more limited than the other two methods we have seen above, the single problem of scheduling of activities or tasks is sufficiently common that its usefulness is also very great. Furthermore, as we shall see, the method is somewhat simpler.

Let us, therefore, assume that we have to undertake a certain project whose completion involves the performance of a number of tasks. Each of the tasks requires a certain amount of time for its performance, and cannot be initiated before a certain number of preceding tasks have been completed, as represented in Table 5.11. Given these constraints, the problem is to determine the minimum total time required for the completion of the project and the corresponding sequencing of tasks.

TABLE 5.11 Project Activities Data

Activity Number	Preceding Activity	Duration of Activity (days)
1	None	6
2	None	8
3	None	5
4	3	3
5	2	4
6	2	3
7	3	11
8	2, 4, 5	7
9	2, 4, 5	9
10	6, 8	4
11	7, 9	8
12	7, 9	3
13	10	8
14	11, 13	7
15	12	5

The solution to this standard problem can be obtained by translating it into the problem of the optimization of itinerary through a network in the following fashion: We shall represent each of the tasks to be performed by a *link* whose length will be the completion time required for the task. The starting *node* of the link will represent the point in time at which the activity begins, and the end node the point in time at which it ends. Thus, the network nodes will represent dates, i.e., the dates on which a certain number of tasks in the project are initiated or are completed.

For instance, the project described in Table 5.11 is graphically represented as the network in Figure 5.6. The link numbers, which are circled, are simply the activity numbers. The noncircled numbers along the links represent their length, i.e., the time required for the completion of the individual activity. Since no activities precede activities 1, 2, and 3, they can all originate at the

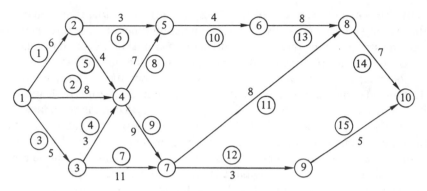

Figure 5.6   CPM chart.

same time (start of the project), which will be represented by node 1. The next activity, number 4, represented by link 4 in the network, cannot start before activity 1 is completed. It will thus be linked to the end node of link 3 and given a length of 3. Similarly, activity 5 originates at the completion of activity 2 and takes 4 days to complete. Activity 8, on the other hand, has to wait until all three activities 2, 4, and 5 are completed before it can be started. Thus, it will originate at the common ending node for the corresponding links. Activity 9, which is subject to the same constraints, will also start at that node, number 4.

We complete the graphical description of the project in this fashion, until all activities are represented. (If need be, it is possible to link simultaneous points in time, i.e., points that are not in fact connected by the performance of an activity, by a fictitious link of length zero, or *dummy link*.)

Once all activities in the project have been represented as a network in this fashion, the first step in CPM is to determine the *earliest starting time* for each activity. That time is defined as the earliest date for the node at which the activities originate. For instance, it is clear that since there are no activities preceding them, activities 1, 2, and 3 can start at time zero. To represent this fact, we will label node 1 (which represents the date at which these activities will be initiated) with a 0. Task 4, however, cannot start before task 3 is completed. Thus, the earliest possible starting time for activity 4 will be the earliest completion time of activity 3 (5 days). Therefore, node 3 will be labeled with a 5. Similarly, node 2 will be labeled with a 6. Generally, in the case of a node at which only one activity terminates, such as node 3, that activity's earliest completion time is also the earliest starting time for all activities that originate at the node.

On the other hand, in the case of a node at which several activities terminate, such as node 4, the activities which originate at that node, such as activity 8, cannot be started before all preceding activities (here the three activities 2, 4, and 5) are completed. Thus, the earliest starting time would be the maximum of the respective earliest completion times of these three activities. In turn, it is clear that the *earliest completion time* of an activity is equal to its earliest starting time plus the activity completion time. Now, activity 2 can be completed in 8 days. Activity 4, which cannot start before day 5 (as determined earlier and as is reflected in the label of node 3), cannot, therefore, be completed before day $5 + 3 = 8$. Finally, activity 5 cannot be completed before day $6 + 4 = 10$. We will therefore have to wait until the longest of these three completion times (which is the maximum of 8, 10, and 8), which is 10. The earliest date for node 4 is therefore 10 days. Generally, in the case of a node at which several activities terminate, the maximum of their respective earliest completion times will also be the earliest date for the node, i.e., the minimum starting time for the activities which are initiated at the node. Proceeding in this fashion, and using the rules given above, we label all nodes of the network with the earliest dates of the activities that are initiated there, as represented in Figure 5.7(a). The label of the end node (which is 36 in our example) represents the earliest total completion time for the overall project.

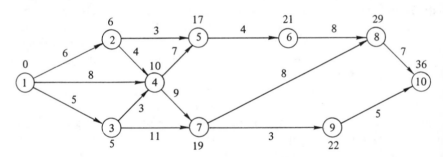

Figure 5.7(a)   Earliest completion times.

As additional information, we might be interested also in evaluating the latest date for these nodes, i.e., the *latest starting time* at which the activities that originate at the node could be started without jeopardy to the project. This will tell us which activities are *critical* (in the sense that they cannot be delayed) and, conversely, which activities can afford a *slack* in their completion time. The second stage in CPM consists of evaluating, systematically, the latest starting times for all activities and labeling all nodes with their latest possible completion times.

Going backwards from the last node, we see that we cannot afford to begin activity 14 later than $36 - 7 = 29$ days if we do not want to increase the total earliest completion time. Thus, the date of the 29th day is critical, because there cannot be any slack between the completion of activities ending that day, i.e., activities 13 and 11, and the start of the next activity, number 15.

Similarly, the latest starting time of activity 13 is day $29 - 8 = 21$ days. In general, then, in the case of a node at which only one activity ends, the latest starting time of that activity is equal to the earliest starting time for the succeeding activities minus the activity duration time. For instance, the latest starting time of activity 11 is $29 - 8 = 21$, corresponding to a starting date early enough to allow for the completion of activity 11 before day 29. Also, the latest starting time for activity 12 is $31 - 3 = 28$. Therefore, the latest date for node 7 at which both these activities can begin will be the minimum of 21 and 28, i.e., 21. Similarly, the latest starting time for the activities which are initiated at node 4 (activities 8 and 9) will be the minimum of $17 - 7$ (latest starting time for node 5 minus duration of activity 8) and $21 - 9$ (latest starting time for node 7 minus duration of activity 9). Therefore, the latest starting time will be the minimum of 10 and $12 = 10$.

Thus, we obtain a second set of labels which indicate the latest starting time of the activities in the project. In general, the latest date for the node, i.e., maximum starting time, will be the minimum of the differences between the latest completion times of all activities which originate at that node and the corresponding duration times. The latest completion time of the end node with which we initiate the labeling is, of course, equal to its earliest completion time. These latest starting times are, thus, as represented in Figure 5.7(b).

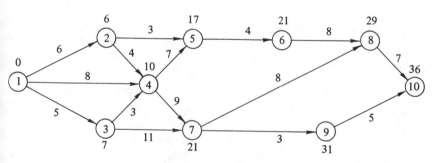

Figure 5.7(b) Latest starting times.

The nodes for which the earliest date equals the latest date, in other words, the set of points at which there is no slack, are on the *critical path*. (There can only be one critical path for a given project.) In our example, the critical path is ①→②→④→⑤→⑥→⑧→⑩, corresponding to activities number $i = 1, 5, 8, 10, 13, 14$, as represented in Figure 5.7(c). This means that activity 1 is critical, in the sense that it takes place between two points in time (nodes 1 and 2) at which the latest starting times are equal to the earliest completion times. Therefore, this activity cannot be delayed without increasing the total completion time of the overall project. Another consequence is that the com-

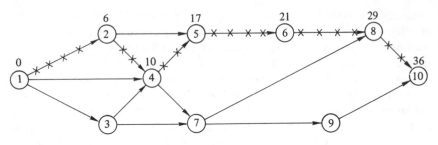

Figure 5.7(c)   Critical path.

pletion time for this activity cannot be increased without delaying the project. On the other hand, activity 2 can suffer any starting delay (or any increase in completion time) of less than $10 - 8 = 2$ days, since its completion does not have to take place before both activities 1 and 5 are completed. Also, activities 3 and 4 can suffer a total delay (between the two activities) of $10 - (5 + 3) = 2$ days.

5.9   Extension to the Case of Uncertainty: The PERT Method

Let us now briefly describe an extension of the CPM method to its *probabilistic* version. The *PERT method* (Program Evaluation and Review Technique) is devised to take into account the uncertainty of the duration times for the various activities.

Suppose that instead of assuming that the completion time of activity 1 in the example above is 6 days (a rather unrealistic assumption given possible delays that can affect any project), we instead forecast that the most likely estimate of the completion time will be 6 days and that at best the activity could be completed in 4 days and at worst in 8 days. Thus, for all practical purposes, we are replacing the single, deterministic estimate of the completion time t by a set of three times. These are, respectively, a *pessimistic estimate t^p*, a *most likely estimate t^l*, and an *optimistic estimate t^o*. Given these estimates, the PERT method essentially resembles the CPM method, but where the activity completion times are now treated as random variables, whose mean (expected value) is

$$\bar{t} = \frac{t^p + 4t^l + t^o}{6} \tag{5.33}$$

(t^p, t^o, and t^l are, respectively, the pessimistic, optimistic, and most likely completion times for the given activity) and whose standard deviation σ_t is

$$\sigma_t = \frac{t^p - t^o}{6} \tag{5.34}$$

Next, the expected earliest completion time for the whole project is determined by applying CPM and using the set of expected (mean) times as if they were deterministic times. The resulting minimum total completion time t^* is then assumed to be a normal random variable whose mean is the sum of the expected completion times for the set of critical activities, and whose variance is equal to the sum of the corresponding variances. (The assumption of a normal distribution for the total completion time derives from the fact that it is the sum of a sufficiently large number of independent activity completion times.) Formally,

$$\bar{t}^* = \sum_i \bar{t}_i \qquad \text{for } i = \text{critical} \qquad (5.35)$$

$$\sigma_{t^*}^2 = \sum_i \sigma_{t_i}^2 \qquad \text{for } i = \text{critical} \qquad (5.36)$$

For instance, let us assume that in our CPM example above, the data for the activity completion times are now probabilistic, as given in Table 5.12.

TABLE 5.12 Project Activities Data

Activity Number, i	Earliest Completion Time, t^o	Most Likely Completion Time, t^1	Latest Completion Time, t^p
1	4	6	8
2	7	8	9
3	4	5	6
4	2	3	4
5	3	4	5
6	1	3	5
7	9	11	13
8	6	7	8
9	8	9	10
10	3	4	5
11	6	8	10
12	2	3	4
13	7	8	9
14	6	7	8
15	3	5	7

We first compute the expected completion times and their standard deviations for each of the activities, using, respectively, formulas (5.33) and (5.34). The corresponding values are given in Table 5.13.

The total expected time for the project will be 36 days. (The reader should verify this result by performing the CPM analysis.) However, this can be ascertained by noting that the activities' expected times are equal to the previous deterministic times, since the pessimistic and optimistic estimates are symmetrical with respect to the most likely times. Also, the critical activities

TABLE 5.13

Activity, $i =$	$\bar{t}_i$	σ_{t_i}
1	6	0.67
2	8	0.33
3	5	0.33
4	3	0.33
5	4	0.33
6	3	0.67
7	11	0.67
8	7	0.33
9	9	0.33
10	4	0.33
11	8	0.67
12	3	0.33
13	8	0.33
14	7	0.33
15	5	0.67

are, for the same reason, still activities $i = 1, 5, 8, 10, 13,$ and 14. However, this optimal completion time t^* is a random variable, with a normal distribution. Its mean, according to formula (5.35), will be equal to

$$\bar{t} = \bar{t}_1 + \bar{t}_5 + \bar{t}_8 + \bar{t}_{10} + \bar{t}_{13} + \bar{t}_{14} = 6 + 4 + 7 + 4 + 8 + 7 = 36$$

and its variance, according to formula (5.36), is equal to

$$\sigma_{t^*}^2 = \sigma_1^2 + \sigma_5^2 + \sigma_8^2 + \sigma_{10}^2 + \sigma_{13}^2 + \sigma_{14}^2$$

$$= (0.67)^2 + (0.33)^2 + (0.33)^2 + (0.33)^2 + (0.33)^2 + (0.33)^2 \simeq 1.0$$

Thus, the standard deviation will be equal to $\sqrt{1} = 1$.

We are now in a position to answer any probabilistic questions concerning the length of the optimal completion time of the project. For instance, the probability that the project will take between 35 and 37 days to complete is the probability that a normal random variable, with mean $\mu = 36$ and standard deviation $\sigma = 1$ will fall between these two values. This probability can then be evaluated from a table of the standard normal probability distribution function after standardizing these values, using the procedure outlined in Section 6.3. The probability is thus the probability that a standard normal variable falls between the values of

$$\frac{35 - \mu}{\sigma} = \frac{35 - 36}{1} = -1 \quad \text{and} \quad \frac{37 - \mu}{\sigma} = \frac{37 - 36}{1} = 1$$

The value of the cumulative standard normal probability distribution for $x = 1$ is $\Phi_{(1)} = 0.84$ (rounding off), as can be read off Table A.2 in Appendix A. Similarly, the value for $x = -1$ is equal to $\Phi_{(-1)} = 0.16$. Therefore, the probability of the variable being between the values -1 and $+1$ is equal to the difference $\Phi_{(1)} - \Phi_{(-1)}$, according to formula (1.9) in Section 1.4. This is equal to 0.68, or 68%. Similar questions, such as the probability that the project will take more than 39 days to complete, or less than 33, etc., can be answered in the same fashion.

EXERCISES

5.1 The following problem is an example of the application of linear programming to dynamic budgeting problems. Assume that a regional development commission is considering promoting industrial development through economic incentives to create jobs in two kinds of industry. Preliminary studies and forecasts have indicated that over a development period of 4 years, the amounts of subsidies (tax rebates, reduced utilities rates, etc.) that would have to be given to the first industry for each hundred jobs created are, respectively (in millions of dollars):

Year	1	2	3	4
Amount	1.3	0.6	0.65	0.3

Similarly, the amounts for the second industry would have to be

Year	1	2	3	4
Amount	0.35	0.7	0.5	0.4

The region has allocated a limited budget for this program, which is:

Year	1	2	3	4
Budget	4.55	4.30	3.25	2.40

Also, it desires to attract both types of industry. Given this situation, what is the optimal mix of induced employment that maximizes the number of jobs within the feasibility of subsidies? Solve this problem graphically. (*Hint:* Use X_1 and X_2, the number of jobs created in the respective sectors as variables.)

5.2 Solve Exercise 5.1, using the analytical simplex method. Check your results against those obtained in Exercise 5.1.

5.3 What would be the minimum revenues that would have to accrue to the region from each additional job in the respective sectors (e.g., from personal income tax, sales tax, etc.) for the economic development program to be financially self-sustaining? (*Hint:* Use the concept of "price," as discussed in Section 5.5, and the optimal tableau in Exercise 5.2.)

5.4   If the available budget was not finalized (due to the passage of a bond issue vote, for instance), and only the yearly amounts given below were definite, how would the optimal allocation of subsidies have to be changed?

Year	1	2	3	4
Budget	3	3	2	2

How would the total number of jobs created be affected?

5.5   What would be the effect on the optimal program of Exercise 5.4 of a change in the incentive requirements of the first industry as follows:

Year	1	2	3	4
Amount	1.7	0.8	0.6	0.25

In view of the answers to Exercise 5.3, would these new requirements be justified; i.e., should industry 1 still receive development assistance? [*Hint:* Use formula (5.22).]

5.6   Finally, because of the possibility of automatization in the production techniques of sector 2, the subsidies of Exercise 5.1 might only correspond to the employment of 90 workers (but mean more machinery) instead of the originally projected 100. Would industry 2 still be a competitive candidate against industry 1 for receiving development funds? What would be the minimum number of jobs created in sector 2 per million dollars in subsidies have to be before this changes? [*Hint:* Use formula (5.22).] What would be the effect of this change on the total number of jobs created? [*Hint:* Use formula (5.20) or (5.21).]

5.7   Assume that the percentage p_i of users of a public transportation system in a given socioeconomic group i (low income, commuters, elderly, etc.) can be estimated as a function of the characteristics of the system X_j (fare, level of service, comfort, etc.) as

$$p_i = \alpha_{i0} + \alpha_{i1}X_1 + \alpha_{i2}X_2 + \ldots + \alpha_{ij}X_j + \ldots + \alpha_{in}X_n$$

where the coefficient α_{ij} represents the weight, or importance, people in group i give to characteristic j. (These coefficients could be estimated for instance using the techniques of multivariate linear regression. See Section 7.4.) Assume that the X_i's are all measured in the same monetary unit (e.g., the cost c_i to the operator of the system of 1 unit of characteristic i).

A certain metropolitan area is interested in increasing the levels of usage of its transit system (as measured by the proportions of users in various groups in the population) above its present values by (at least) given amounts

Δp_i in the respective groups i $(i = 1, 2, \ldots, m)$. Relying on this theory of travel demand and the assumption of costs proportional to the levels of service stated above, it decides to attempt to do that by raising the level of service characteristics. You are called as a consultant to determine on which characteristics of the transit system improvements should be made, and by how much, in order to achieve the given goals at the minimum possible cost.

Formulate this problem as a linear programming problem. [*Hint:* The preceding formula, being linear, implies that to changes ΔX_i in the characteristics correspond changes

$$\Delta p_i = \alpha_{i1} \Delta X_1 + \alpha_{i2} \Delta X_2 + \ldots + \alpha_{ij} \Delta X_j + \ldots + \alpha_{in} \Delta X_n$$

$$= \sum_j \alpha_{ij} \Delta X_j$$

in the (percentage) levels of usage. Also, the cost of these changes would be $\sum_j c_j \Delta X_j$. The problem is now almost written.]

5.8 How would you modify the approach in Exercise 5.7 if a better model for the probability p_i is

$$p_i = X_1^{\alpha_1} X_2^{\alpha_2} X_3^{\alpha_3} \ldots X_j^{\alpha_j} \ldots X_n^{\alpha_n}$$

as is sometimes used in travel demand modeling. (*Hint:* Take the logarithms of both sides of the equation, and use new variables equal to the logarithms of the previous ones.)

5.9 The accompanying diagram represents a communication network, such as, for instance, an arterial system of roads. The numbers along the links represent their capacities, in thousands of cars per hour, for instance. Formulate the problem of determining the maximum number of cars per hour that can go through the network between point 1 and point 7 and what the corresponding assignments (loadings) of traffic volume to the various links

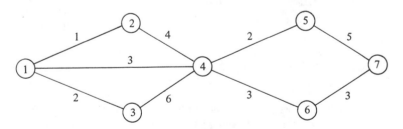

Figure E-5.9

should be. (*Hint:* Use variables F_{ij} equal to the level of flow in link $i - j$. The constraints will be that at each node 2 through 6, the sum of the flows of cars coming into the node must be equal to the sum of the flows coming out of it, since no cars stop at these points. The objective function will simply be equal to either the sum of the flows coming into node 1 or the sum of the flows going out of node 7.)

5.10 Formalize Exercise 5.9 to the general case for any network.

5.11 A state government's civil service is organized in n departments, and its staff is organized in m levels. The minimum levels of staffing of the respective departments, in terms of workloads, are respectively equal to E_i for department i (in numbers of positions). Also, the efficiency, or performance of a worker of level j assigned to department i is A_{ij}. Finally, the salaries for the respective classes are S_i. Given that the payroll budget has been set at a total of B, what should be the levels of staffing in the various departments so that the minimum staffing levels E_i are met, and that the overall efficiency is maximized, within the budget limit? Formulate this as a linear program. (*Hint:* Use variables with two indices X_{ij} representing the number of staffers of level j assigned to department i.)

5.12 A metropolitan area has decided to try to reduce the number of traffic accidents occurring each year. To that effect, it is considering the application of four possible strategies: (1) increase the level of street patroling; (2) improve the streets; (3) change the circulation and signal patterns; and (4) provide incentives (such as free shuttle, free parking, etc.) to use public transportation.

Assume that the effectiveness of each of these schemes, as measured by the projected reduction in hundred of car accidents per year of these respective schemes, has been estimated as follows:

Plan 1		Plan 2		Plan 3		Plan 4	
X	$g_1(X)$	X	$g_2(X)$	X	$g_3(X)$	X	$g_4(X)$
0	0	0	0	0	0	0	0
1	2	1	3	1	1	1	2
2	4	2	3	2	2	2	3
3	5	3	4	3	3	3	6
4	6	4	5	4	4	4	8
5	7	5	8	5	5	5	10

where X is the cost (in millions of dollars) of varying levels of application of plan i ($i = 1$ through 4) and $g_i(X)$ the corresponding estimated accident reduction.

(a)   Given these data, determine the best possible cost/effectiveness ratios for varying levels of funding between $1 and 5 millions from the optimal use of all four alternatives.

(b)   How are the cost/effectiveness ratio values changed if only the first three alternatives can be considered?

(c)   If only alternatives 1, 2, and 4 are considered?

5.13 A given city has decided to renew 3 acres of land each for residential and commercial uses. The plan involves three different locations, which we can call 1, 2, and 3. In order to arrive at the best decision for the location of the renewal effort, the city planning department has prepared individual estimates of the desirability (graded on a scale of 0 to 10) of jointly renewing varying amounts of residential and commercial land, at the three locations, on the simplifying assumption that these benefits could be estimated independently and also that they are additive. These estimates are presented below, where X is the amount of residential land (in acres) and Y is the amount of commercial land (in the same unit); $g_i(X, Y)$ is the corresponding "desirability" at location i.

Location I $g_1(X, Y)$				Location II $g_2(X, Y)$				Location III $g_3(X, Y)$			
$Y \backslash X$	0	1	2	3	$Y \backslash X$	0	1	2	3	$Y \backslash X$	0	1	2	3

Y	0	1	2	3		0	1	2	3		0	1	2	3
0	0	1	3	6		0	2	4	5		0	3	4	7
1	2	3	5	7		1	3	5	6		2	4	5	8
2	4	5	6	8		3	5	7	8		4	6	7	9
3	6	6	7	9		4	6	8	9		5	7	8	9

Given these data, where should renewal take place, and in what amounts, so that the overall desirability of the comprehensive plan is maximum?

5.14 Given the following data concerning the tasks to be performed in a transportation planning study (durations are in months):

Activity	Immediately Preceding Activities	Optimistic t_i^o	Duration Most Likely t_i^l	Pessimistic t_i^p
1. Study design	0	1	2	5
2. Traffic survey	1	2	2	6
3. Network survey	1	2	3	5
4. Land-use survey	0	4	6	9
5. Calibration of travel estimation models	2, 3	3	4	8
6. Travel forecasts	4, 5	1	2	2
7. Transportation plan	6	2	3	9

(a) Determine the minimum completion time for the project (using the most likely estimates of activity duration only).

(b) Indicate the critical activities and events.

5.15   Using the optimistic, most likely, and pessimistic estimates in Exercise 5.14, evaluate the probability for the study to be completed in:
    (a)   Less than 15 months.
    (b)   Between 14 and 16 months.

REFERENCES

GASS, S. *Linear Programming: Methods and Applications*, 3rd ed. New York: McGraw-Hill Book Company, 1969.

HADLEY, G. *Non-Linear and Dynamic Programming*. Reading, Mass.: Addison-Wesley Publishing Company, Inc., 1964.

IBM. *Mathematical Programming System*. White Plains, N.Y.: IBM, 1971.

ISARD, W. *Introduction to Regional Science*. Englewood Cliffs N.J.: Prentice-Hall, Inc., 1975.

LAIDLAW, C. *Linear Programming for Urban Development Plan Evaluation*. New York: Praeger Publishers, Inc., 1972.

WIEST, H. M., AND F. LEVY. *A Management Guide to CPM/PERT*. Englewood Cliffs, N.J.: Prentice-Hall, Inc., 1969.

6
Model Fitting

6.1 Introduction

Chapters 2 through 5 presented models which can be applied to a variety of situations, for the general purpose of forecasting and analyzing urban and regional systems. However, the examination of these models has been consistently conducted at a theoretical level, with only occasional reference to the practical aspects of implementation. It is the purpose of the remaining two chapters of this text to examine some of the *empirical* aspects of the development and use of these analytical models. Whereas we have so far concentrated primarily on the formal properties of the models—their rigor, their generality, and their structure—in Chapters 6 and 7 we will be concerned essentially with the question of their adaptation and application to specific, empirical situations.

This passage from the theoretical to the experimental aspects of the modeling process essentially introduces the use of empirical data and, as a corollary, the notion of the *precision* of a model. We have already illustrated this concept, in particular in the case of the illustration of the gravity model in Section 4.4. In general, a model's applicability or performance can, ultimately, only be judged on the basis of how accurately it reproduces the real world, that is, how much the predicted values it outputs differ from the corresponding observable and measurable values. Thus, the notion of the precision of a model is directly connected to the definition of the error on its predicted or "reproduced" values. Consequently, the practical problems of implementation of these models will ultimately result in problems of definition of the level of precision desired—of methods of attaining, or of improving it. The various methods we shall see in Chapters 6 and 7 are, in different ways, all designed to address one or several of these items.

The precision of a model, or lack thereof, can in general be attributed to several major factors: first, the correctedness of its formulation, which might be called its "structural" precision. For instance, the model may have theoretical flaws, such as wrong assumptions, illogical rationales, or simply erroneous mathematics. The treatment of this type of precision (or rather error) is more related to the first, theoretical part of this text. However, the structural precision of a model may also have an empirical connotation. In some cases, the theory may leave a degree of indeterminacy in the model, which only an empirical approach can resolve. For instance, in the gravity model, it may only be known that the function $F(d_{ij})$ in model (4.2), which measures the effect of the separation between zones on their spatial interaction, is a decreasing function of d_{ij}. Thus, any of the forms in (4.5) through (4.7) is a priori possible, and the determination of which one is appropriate will require experimentation with empirical data. An appropriate method will be presented in Section 6.9.

Another major determinant of the level of precision of a model is the quality or precision of the input data it uses. This is sometimes illustrated by a "proverb": "A model is only as good as its input data," or in a more extreme version: "garbage in–garbage out." The influence of the data on the precision of the model comes from the fact that the input values for the model (as well as subsequently its parameters) will be estimated from observational data. Therefore, measurement errors will be incorporated into the model and transmitted to the output values. Although there are methods for evaluating the level of expected error in the values output by a given model (of any mathematical form), knowing the precision of its input values (or independent variables) and that of its parameters, we shall not describe them here, since they require familiarity with advanced calculus. In any event, even if we are not able to measure the resulting level of error produced by a model, it should be the case that the "best" estimates we can obtain for its parameters and for its input values should result in the best precision for the model. Methods for determining and controlling the quality of input data will be presented in Sections 6.3 to 6.5.

Finally, the precision of a given model depends also on determination of the values of the parameters in it. In general, the theory will not assign a specific value to the parameters but only incorporate their effects. For instance, if we determined that the assumptions on which the intervening opportunities model are validated in a given situation, this does not determine the specific value of the parameter λ in model (4.45). Its value must then be determined on the basis of empirical experiments. Thus, the estimation of the parameters will also involve the use of observational data, whose precision will then be reflected (as a second-level effect), through the precision of the parameter values, in the model output values. The methods of *parameter estimation* will be developed in Sections 6.6 and 6.7.

In summary, the various aspects of model fitting, i.e., the specification of a general model to a given empirical situation, will involve questions of data precision, functional form selection, and parameter estimation. Since all of these ultimately result in the use of observational data, let us begin by briefly outlining the steps of the survey research process.

6.2   The Survey Research Process

As was noted above, the task of *fitting* a model, which precedes model implementation, will generally involve the use of data. In most cases, these data will have to be gathered through research, either bibliographic or field observations. Although to be treated adequately the subject of *survey research* would necessitate a book in itself (and there are, in fact, many excellent sources listed in the references), we shall briefly outline its major stages. These are, respectively: definition of information needed, definition of the population, choice of the type of survey, sample design, design of survey strategy, survey administration, and data processing.

There are various types of surveys, designed to obtain various types of information under different conditions. Thus, the first step in the survey research process is the definition of the type of information to be gathered. This will be directly determined by the nature of the variables that intervene in the model. However, the levels of measurement of these variables must also be defined. For instance, the variable "household income," which might appear in a *category analysis* type of travel demand generation model (Section 4.8), might be defined with respect to levels going from $5000 to $50,000, by increments of $1000, or in another case from $15,000 to $450,000, by increments to $10,000, etc. Such decisions will in general be determined by local considerations, together with given constraints such as space on survey forms or in computer memories, comparability with other variables' measurement levels, etc. Finally, of course, the chosen level of precision of the measurement should reflect the level of specification of the variables in the model. For instance, if socioeconomic classes in the categorization of households are defined with respects of levels varying by $2500, it would be pointless to record incomes within $1000. In these instances, as in fact in most instances in survey research, common sense is the surest guide in such considerations.

The second step in the survey research process is the definition of the object of the survey, which is sometimes called the "population" (even in cases that have nothing to do with demography). This will also in most instances be determined by the nature of the model and of its variables. For instance, a population projection *cohort-survival model* will require the survey of all age groups in a given population, whereas a model of *modal split* between private car and mass transit usage would only require the survey of the users of the two modes, etc.

At this stage of the survey research process, the question should be asked whether there is actually a need to observe and collect the required information, as specified in the previous stages, or whether it has already been gathered and is available somewhere else in the form of *secondary data.* Surveys are indeed rather expensive, lengthy, and technically complex undertakings and should be conducted only when necessary. Thus, prior to starting any survey, a bibliographic search should be conducted to ascertain whether related secondary data already exist, and if so, whether their format and content are adequate for the purpose of the model.

There are various possible sources of secondary data on urban and regional systems. A prime source is research centers in urban affairs and urban studies. Some of these organizations are located on the campuses of major universities (the Joint Center for Urban Studies at Harvard and MIT, the Center for Urban and Regional Development at Berkeley, the Center for Urban Studies at Rutgers University, etc.). Others are private institutes or professional organizations. Among them are the Urban Institute in Washington and Battelle Institute in Columbus. A national source for urban and regional data is the federal government, which issues the U.S. Census and other publications. Possible local sources would include city halls, courthouses, chambers of commerce, economic development agencies, and utility companies. Also, individuals such as real estate professionals, researchers, professional planners or city managers, or consulting firms may be sources of data. Also, professional and research publications often report data or provide leads to its location. Finally, the advent and development of centralized information systems will undoubtedly make the search for secondary data easier and faster in the future.

In cases where it is necessary to conduct a survey, there are three major types to choose from: the self-administered survey, the interview survey, and the observation survey.

The Self-Administered Survey.   The main example of the *self-administered* survey is the mail survey. Other examples are surveys conducted by distributing *questionnaires* at a given site, such as workplaces, public facilities, etc., asking people to fill them out and collecting them at a later time. In general, any survey where the respondents themselves record their answers is a self-survey. This type would be appropriate, for instance, to survey shopping travel patterns, or travel to work, or any other such investigation that is simple or short enough not to require a trained field researcher.

The advantages of self-surveys are primarily that the geographical area covered or the number of respondents surveyed can be very large, since the survey will cost considerably less than an interview survey, in which the salary and travel expenses of the interviewers have to be paid. Also, some respondents who might not be willing to let an interviewer invade their privacy or might not be available when the interviewer calls on them might answer a self-survey more readily.

The disadvantages of self-surveys are, first, that the rate of response is usually smaller than for interview surveys, where the presence of the interviewer makes it harder to dismiss the questionnaire and possibly easier to understand the questions. As a very general rule of thumb, and depending on the characteristics of the survey, a rate of response of more than 60% on the first wave of returns in a self-survey must be considered rather successful. Finally, the number of questions it is possible to administer in a self-survey is smaller than in an interview survey. Depending on the questions asked and the interest they will generate in a given population, it will be difficult to ask for more than 20 to 30 answers, or about 10 minutes of a respondent's time.

However, the chances for success of a self-survey will be better if:

- The appearance of the questionnaire, the envelope in which it comes, the covering letter, etc., stress professionalism, clarity, and brevity.

- The cover letter or introduction (which should always be included) stresses the fact that the respondent has been selected at random, that his anonimity will be preserved, and that the results of the survey will be beneficial to the community at large.

- Some inducement to respond (stamped envelope, token gift, etc.) is enclosed.

- A later follow-up (postcard, telephone call, etc.) is conducted on nonrespondents.

The Interview Survey.   The interview survey is characterized by the presence of an interviewer who asks the questions and records the answers. Examples of this type are the telephone survey and the home interview.

This type of survey may be appropriate, for instance, in *attitudinal surveys* in connection with the preferences for various modes of transportation, as input into *modal split models*. In general, it is recommended when the sophistication or the length or number of the research items prohibit self-administration. The main advantage of an interview survey is indeed that the questionnaire can be much longer and complex than in self-surveys, since the interviewer will be present to urge on and help the respondent. The disadvantages lie primarily in the cost (travel, wages) and time (work hours) needed, which may severely restrict the sample size or the size of the survey area. Also, the mere presence of the interviewer may introduce a *bias* in the answers to the questions. The interviewer may, for instance, unconsciously elicit responses which would be different if the respondent were alone. Also, the interviewer may himself or herself distort the responses. This may happen consciously, for instance, by filling in the answers himself or herself to save effort, or unconsciously, by asking the questions as he or she interprets them, and/or recording his or her own interpretation of the respondent's answers.

Some of the factors on which the success of an interview survey depends are:

- Well-trained, objective interviewers with a pleasing personality and appearance.
- Preinterview announcement of visit (for home interviews) by phone or mail.
- Selection of realistic times for the interviews, etc.

Direct Examination Survey. The last major type of survey is the direct examination survey, which does not involve a respondent. Examples are *window surveys* conducted from a moving car, *traffic counts* (which may involve a mechanical recorder), and housing surveys. This type will thus be generally applicable to surveys that do not involve a human respondent.

The main advantage of this type of survey is that it is the simplest kind to conduct, since it does not involve the asking of questions and recording of answers. The disadvantages are that the survey is not much more than a form of inventory. Also, the very presence of the recorder (whether human or not) may in some cases alter the situation and thus distort or bias the answers. For example, in the case of surveying highway traffic speeds or volumes, the drivers may think that the recorders are police radars and consequently decrease their speeds, and thus possibly the volume of flow.

After the need for the conduct of a survey and the choice of its type have been determined, the size and the composition of the sample have to be set. This stage in the survey research process is called "sample design." With respect to the size of the sample, it is intuitively clear that (all other things being equal) the larger the sample, the better the resulting precision of the measurements will be. (We shall see in Section 6.3 how to evaluate the influence of the sample size on the precision.) In any event, the sample size will, in turn, be constrained by consideration of time, funds, manpower, or all of the above.

With respect to the composition of the sample, there might, for instance, be a need for several *subsamples* with different features. For instance, in the case of the *cohort-survival model*, all ages groups must be surveyed, and with equal importance. Or, if we do not disaggregate the model by sex, we may have to sample more women than men, to reflect their (actual) predominance in the population, etc. The various procedures for determining which individual observations to include in the sample or in each of these subsamples are called *sampling techniques*. All these techniques are designed to ensure that the final sample of individual observations is representative of the overall "population" it comes from. Translated in probability theory language, this implies and requires that each unit in the population has a known (controlled) probability of being selected to be part of the sample. When this is the case, the sampling is called a *probability sampling*. There are four basic schemes of probability sampling: simple random sampling, systematic sampling, stratified sampling, and cluster sampling.

Simple Random Sampling. This is conducted by first assigning a reference number, or code, to all units in the total population being sampled. (In some cases, these units are already represented by such a system, e.g., car registration numbers may be used to represent car owners.) The individual cases to be included in the sample are then selected by drawing lots from the numbers until the total sample size has been attained. If the numbers are replaced in the drawing pool after each draw, the scheme is called simple random sampling *with replacement*, which ensures that each member of the total population has the same probability of being included in the sample at any stage of the drawing. In practice, most simple random samplings are conducted by using a *table of random numbers* (random digits or random deviates). Such tables have the property that any series of one or any number of digits taken in any direction (horizontally, vertically, or diagonally) represents the result of consecutive, random drawings with replacement of numbers from 0 to 9 (for the one-digit series), from 0 to 99 (for the two-digit series), and so on. Therefore, they can be used to perform simple random sampling very conveniently by merely reading numbers off the table and selecting the individual cases they represent. An example of such a table is Table A.1 in Appendix A.

For instance, if we need to select at random 50 cases out of a total population of, say, 1000, we would read off the first 50 three-digit entries in a systematic fashion in any consistent direction. If the same number appears again, it is of course dismissed at each subsequent appearance after the first, and the sample size increased accordingly.

Systematic Random Sampling. This is even simpler to conduct, provided that the individual cases to be sampled can be assumed to be ordered randomly, such as in an alphabetical *name list*. Then if we need a sample of size n out of a total population of size N, we will systematically select every other (N/n)th entry in the list, starting with the first position selected at random between 1 and N/n. For example, if we want 150 cases out of a total of 1000, we would systematically select the entry corresponding to every $(1000/150) =$ 6th position in the list, starting from a random position between 1 and 6. (We can obtain the starting entry for instance by throwing a die.) When N/n is not an integer, this fraction will be rounded down to ensure that at least n cases are selected.

Stratified Sampling. This is conducted by first separating the total population according to some characteristic, or set of characteristics, e.g., separating it into males and females, or into socioeconomic groups, etc. Then subsamples are extracted from each of these *strata* using one of the basic sampling procedures above, e.g., by simple random sampling. The total sample will be formed by the juxtaposition of all these subsamples. This sampling procedure is used to control the composition of the sample in terms of such characteristics as noted above to obtain a desired number of cases in each of the subgroups in the population. For instance, if it is desired to have in the sample a 1:1 ratio of basic industries to service industries and direct sampling were used, it is unlikely that such a ratio would be found in the sample if this ratio were, let us say, 1:4 in the industrial structure. Thus, we would first have to stratify the total population of industries into a basic industry strata and a service industry strata and select $3n/4$ observations at random in the first strata (n being the total sample size) and $n/4$ observations in the second strata. The definition of the stratification, of course, depends in each case on the research objectives, but the basic rationale is to define strata that will be as different from each other as possible (*interheterogeneity*), and as homogeneous within each strata as possible (*intrahomogeneity*), so as to ensure the minimum number of strata and the maximum representativeness of each of the subsamples within the strata.

Cluster Sampling. This sampling first delineates in the total population subgroups (or clusters) of individual cases which are as similar to each other and to the general population as possible (*interhomogeneity*), and as diversified and heterogenous within each cluster as possible (*intraheterogeneity*). The set of clusters is thus deemed to represent the total population, much as in the sense of individuals in a sample. Then simple or systematic random sampling is conducted in each of the clusters. This procedure is used when sampling in the total population is not feasible, e.g., because of size considerations or because a list of the total population is not available. For instance, telephone directories may be available for only certain areas in a region, production statistics for only certain sectors, etc.

Naturally, these basic schemes can be compounded. For instance, a *cluster-stratified* systematic random sampling would first define heterogeneous clusters in a population, then define strata in the clusters, and finally include a systematic sampling in each of the strata in each of the clusters. A *stratified-clustered* simple random sampling would first define strata in the total population, then within each of these would only retain representative parts of each strata, and would conclude with a simple random sampling in each.

When the sample has been identified, the *strategy* of administering the survey must be defined. Procedures as to when and how to gather the data must be established. The first task is the selection of a *schedule* for the administration of the survey. This may depend on the personnel and other available resources, such as transportation, the geographical area covered, and of course also on the population sampled (truck drivers have different schedules than civil servants, for instance). Records should be kept of the identification of respondents, should a follow-up be necessary or a later survey address the same respondents again, as in *longitudinal* surveys. Allowance in terms of schedule and resources should be made for *nonrespondents* in the case of mail surveys (in most cases at least 30% of the original sample) and/or for nonexisting cases in interview surveys or direct observation surveys (moved respondents, inexact locations, etc.). Duplicates should be kept of the returns in case the originals are lost or destroyed.

After the data have been gathered, the next step is to put them in a form suitable for analysis. Comprehensive data analysis, except for very small surveys and simple analyses (such as evaluating averages that can be performed by leafing through the questionnaires and using a desk calculator), cannot be directly performed on the questionnaires themselves. However, the ease and efficiency of using electronic computing facilities and ready-made computer programs for data analysis are well worth the added effort of translating the data into electronic form. In particular, the methods of *statistical regression*, which we shall see in Chapter 7, are almost always implemented using standard, computer programs. The data will then be punched onto computer cards, or magnetic tape or disks. It should be pointed out in this connection that survey data will usually be used for analytical purposes other than just model building, e.g., for descriptions of existing conditions or geographical or historical comparisons, testing assumptions about these conditions, etc. These methods involve the use of some of the methods we shall describe in Sections 6.3 to 6.5 as well as other standard methods of statistical analysis and inference which can be found in any standard introductory text. In any case, these other methods are also implemented in a variety of computer program packages. (See the references at the end of the chapter.)

6.3 The Estimation of Input Data: Average Values

Let us now go back to the first question addressed above, that of the evaluation of quantities used as input in a model, as independent variables. To fix ideas, let us consider the case of the application of a *one-way gravity model*, which is being developed to represent the pattern of mass transit usage from work to home, as discussed in Section 4.3. As input into the model, estimates of the daily levels of traffic from a number of points (the originating zones) must be obtained. To that effect, since it is clear that the daily level O_j varies from day to day (in other words, is a random variable in the sense of Section 1.4), a survey of 90 daily levels over 3 consecutive months has been conducted to describe its variations. The question is now how to derive an estimate of the daily level of usage O_j, from the 90 observations of its value.

Intuitively, it seems logical to adopt as a measure of the daily level of traffic the average of the observations as defined in formula (1.5), on the grounds that it represents a single central value which represents "fairly" the 90 (supposedly different) values. Also, this is consistent with the purpose of the model, which is to describe average, typical patterns of usage. Let us, for instance, assume that the average daily level over these 90 days, which we will denote as $\bar{O}_j$, turned out to be equal to $\bar{O}_j = 1250$ passengers. It is clear that if we had collected the data over another time period (let us say, if we repeated the survey over the next 90 days), we would in general not expect to arrive at the same observed value for $\bar{O}_j$. This is, of course, because the random daily levels for these other 90 days will be in principle different from the first 90 values, and therefore their average will be different from the first average. For instance, it might be equal to 1290 for a second period of 3 months, etc.

Such fluctuations in the daily or in the average daily levels are inherent in the nature of probabilistic quantities and are to be expected. However, we must clearly take them into account in the estimation of the level of potential error, or fluctuation, in our estimation of $\bar{O}_j$. Since we cannot hypothetically gather an infinite number of such samples to compute the value of the mean μ_{O_j} of the sample averages (i.e., the *true value* of the average daily level), we will use the value of 1250 as an estimate for it.

The question, however, is how to evaluate the potential error we thus might make, i.e., the *order of magnitude* of the potential fluctuations from one sample average to the next, or equivalently from one observation to its true value? As we have learned in the survey review of probability theory in Section 1.4, one such estimate is provided by the value of the standard deviation of the sample average $\bar{O}_j$. This, as formula (1.19) shows, is equal to the fraction $1/\sqrt{n}$ of the standard deviation of the daily level of passengers O_j. The latter quantity can easily be evaluated from the survey results using formula (1.8) by computing the variance of the 90 observations.

Let us assume, for instance, that the standard deviation of the daily level turned out to be equal to 270 passengers. The standard deviation of the average daily level (over 90 days) is then equal to $270/\sqrt{90} = 28.46$. Therefore, in the sense that the standard deviation of a random quantity is an indication of the order of magnitude of its "typical" fluctuation, we can estimate that the error on the estimation of the average daily level is (roughly) of the order of 28.5/1250, or approximately 2.3%.

However, this estimate of the level of precision on the estimation of $\bar{O}_j$ does not take into account the fact that whereas a fluctuation of 28 people, i.e., of 1 standard deviation for the average daily level is typical, there may be fluctuations of less, or of more, in a given sample. In other words, to every potential level of fluctuation between an observed value for $\bar{O}_j$ and its true value or mean $\mu_{\bar{O}_j}$ corresponds a certain level of probability. This is illustrated on Figure 6.1, where $\mu_{\bar{O}_j}$ is the mean of the (theoretical) probability distribution function, $\bar{O}_j$ is a single observed value, and the probability corresponding to a given level of fluctuation is equal to the area under the curve of the distribution.

Consequently, to each level of fluctuation, or error, between the (unknown) exact value and the observed value $\bar{O}_j$ corresponds a certain level of probability of occurence on any single measurement of $\bar{O}_j$. That is, we have to replace the notion of a single, deterministic level of potential error as above, by a function, whose values depend on varying levels of probability.

Therefore, although we can say that on the average we incur an error of about 2.3% in the estimation of $\bar{O}_j$, we do not know what percentage of the time we would expect the error to be less than 2.3%, or between 2.3% and 5%, etc., over repeated applications of the estimation procedure described above, such as when estimating a large number of zonal levels $\bar{O}_j$ under the same conditions. This is essentially because we do not have the specification of the probability distribution of the quantity $\bar{O}_j$, and thus have resorted to using one of its summaries, the standard deviation.

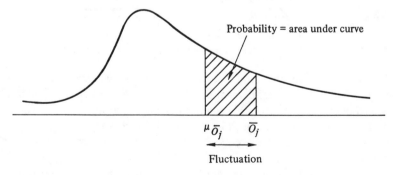

Probability = area under curve

$\mu_{\bar{O}_j}$ $\bar{O}_j$

Fluctuation

Figure 6.1 Fluctuation between an observed value and the true value.

This situation illustrates a very general principle in value estimation. The more the *distributional properties* of a fluctuating quantity are known, the better the corresponding precision can be stated in a more complete, or meaningful sense. In other words, it should be the case that the estimation of the average error is less precise than could be achieved if the complete probabilistic information about the average daily level of usage of the mass transit system $\bar{O}_j$, as represented in the probability distribution, were utilized.

Let us therefore ask the following question: If we choose a level of probability of, say, 90%, given our measurement of 1250 for $\bar{O}_j$, what is the maximum level of error that we may have incurred; that is, how far from 1250 (on both sides) could the true value $\mu_{\bar{o}_j}$ be? This is clearly the same question as: How far can the observed values $\bar{O}_j$ deviate from the mean (or both sides) so that the corresponding fluctuation δ corresponds to a probability of at most 90%? This is illustrated in Figure 6.2.

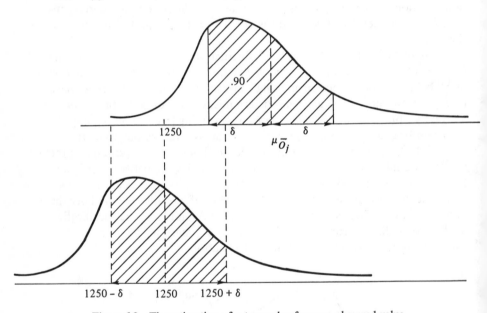

Figure 6.2 The estimation of a true value from an observed value.

It is important to understand that the two questions are strictly equivalent. They both involve the determination of the width of the half-interval δ such that 90% of the probability distribution function of $\bar{O}_j$ is enclosed around either the known mean, to result in a measurement for the maximum level of error, or from the observed value, to result in an interval for the position of the unknown mean.

That is, if an interval of half-width δ centered around the mean encloses with a probability of 0.90 (or in general p) all potential observations of $\bar{O}_j$, then, reciprocally, an interval of the same width centered around a given observation will enclose with probability (or confidence) 90% the unknown value of the mean $\mu_{\bar{O}_j}$, or true value. This is translated graphically in Figure 6.3.

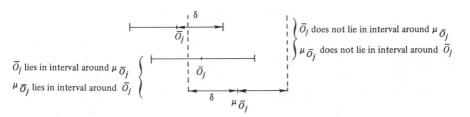

Figure 6.3 Confidence intervals for true values and observed values.

The determination of δ therefore involves the use of the probability distribution function of $\bar{O}_j$ as shown in Figure 6.1. Specifically, we spread out in both directions from the position of the observed value, 1250, until we enclose a total area under the probability curve equal to 0.90. However, as was noted above, we do not know the function's specification. Although we shall see later that under certain conditions we can infer an *approximation* for it, we do not really need to know the exact probability distribution to answer the question posed earlier.

Indeed, let us now recall the *Tchebyscheff theorem*, stated first in Section 1.4 and repeated here: "The interval of values of any random variable going from its mean minus k standard deviations to its mean plus k standard deviations corresponds to a total probability of at least $(1 - 1/k^2)$." This theoretical result, which is valid irrespective of the specific probability distribution function for the random variable, thus applies to $\bar{O}_j$. Therefore, we can evaluate δ as being equal to k standard deviations, where k is such that it corresponds to a level of probability of (at least) p:

$$p = 1 - \frac{1}{k^2} \tag{6.1}$$

so that

$$k = \sqrt{\frac{1}{1-p}} \tag{6.2}$$

and, consequently,

$$\delta = \frac{k\sigma}{\sqrt{n}} = \sigma\sqrt{\frac{1}{n(1-p)}} \tag{6.3}$$

where σ is an estimate of the standard deviation of the observations and $\sigma/\sqrt{n}$ an estimate of the standard deviation of their average. For instance, to a level of probability $p = 0.90$ corresponds a value of $k = \sqrt{1/0.10} = \sqrt{10} = 3.16$. Since, as was estimated above, the standard deviation of the average $\bar{O}_j$ is equal to 28.46, the fluctuation level corresponding to a probability of 0.90 is equal to

$$\delta = 270\sqrt{\frac{1}{90(0.1)}} = 90$$

or 90 passengers per sample, on the average. This result can be interpreted by stating that over a long series of computations of such sample averages under similar conditions, 90% of all observed values for $\bar{O}_j$, would lie within an interval going from $1250 - 90 = 1160$ to $1250 + 90 = 1340$ passengers. Therefore, with probability 90%, the mean of all these observations (which we are trying to estimate) also lies in this interval. Equivalently, given our survey results and the observation for the average daily level $\bar{O}_j$ of 1250, the maximum level of error on its true value, at a level of probability (or certainty) of 0.90, is 90 passengers in either direction.

By choosing another level of probability and repeating the above procedure, we can then construct the function that associates the level of error with its degree of probability. For instance, a level of potential error of 127 passengers would correspond to a level of probability of 0.95, or 95%, etc. Of course, as we expect, the higher the level of probability, the larger the level of error. (See Exercise 6.9.)

Several comments are in order at this point. First, it should be clearly understood that "level of error" means the average error that would be committed over a large number of applications of the estimation procedure, and that therefore, on any single estimation, the error will, of course, not be equal to the given level (90, 127, etc.) but, rather, will be at most equal to that level, with the corresponding given probability. That is, the results above mean that we can assume, with a certainty or *level of confidence* of 90%, that on any single estimation of the average level of daily usage of the mass transit system, using a sample of 90 observations, the true value of the average daily usage will lie within 127 passengers of whatever observed value will be recorded.

Also, it should be kept in mind that this statement is approximate to the extent that, first, the Tchebyscheff theorem provides not an exact value for the probability but a lower bound for it. (The exact value can only come from the probability distribution of $\bar{O}_j$). Second, we have not used the exact value for the standard deviation of $\bar{O}_j$, i.e., $\sigma_{\bar{O}_j}$, which we do not know, but an approximation based on the observed value of the sample standard deviation.

Furthermore, formula (6.3) shows that the level of precision (for a given level of probability) is dependent on the sample size. Let us assume, for instance, that we had used a sample of 30 observations instead of the 90 observations used above. The procedure would be the same except that the standard deviation of the sample average would now be equal to the standard deviation computed from the 30 values, divided by $\sqrt{30}$. Although the sample standard deviation is (just as the sample average) also a random variable, therefore subject to fluctuations from a given sample to another sample, let us assume for the purpose of comparison that we had observed approximately the same value, i.e., 270 passengers. Then the standard deviation of the (30-size) sample average would be equal to $270/\sqrt{30} = 49.29$, i.e., almost twice as large. Consequently, from formula (6.3), the interval δ corresponding to the same level of probability of say 0.90, i.e., to a value of $k = \sqrt{1/0.1} = 3.16$, will now be equal to

$$\delta = 3.16(49.29) = 155.76$$

or about 156 passengers, a smaller level of imprecision. Thus, as could be intuitively expected, the larger the sample size, the better the precision on the estimation of the average daily level of usage. In general, to an increase by a factor of m in the sample size will correspond (for the same level of probability) a decrease by a factor of $\sqrt{m}$ in the potential level of error in the estimation. This relationship, which is reflected in formula (6.3), can be used to determine the necessary sample size for a desired maximum level of error (at a set level of confidence). In this case, δ is given, the probability p is given, the standard deviation is known, and the unknown $\sqrt{n}$ is given by

$$\sqrt{n} = \frac{\sigma}{\delta\sqrt{1 - p}}$$

or

$$n = \frac{\sigma^2}{(1 - p)\delta^2} \tag{6.4}$$

For instance, based on the estimate of the standard deviation of O_j of 270, if we assume that it is a close estimate of the true value of σ_{O_j} and if we wanted to achieve a precision of, say, 35 passengers on the estimation of the true value of the average daily level, again with 90% confidence, we would have to select a sample size according to formula (6.4) such that

$$n = \frac{\sigma^2}{(1 - p)\delta^2} = \frac{(270)^2}{0.10(35)^2} = 595.10$$

Thus, a sample size of 596 would be required to achieve this level of precision at this level of probability.

6.4 Special Cases

Let us briefly describe two special cases, in which the error estimation procedure can be made more precise. Indeed, the price one pays for taking advantage of the generality of the Tchebyscheff approximation is that the estimation of the level of error δ provided by formula (6.3) is in general substantially more conservative than the more exact estimation which would be made on the basis of knowledge of the probability distribution of the quantity being estimated.

However, when the sample size is large, the distribution of the sample average can be approximated by a *normal probability distribution*. This result, which was stated in the probability theory review of Section 1.4, means that for a sufficiently large sample size, the probabilities of given values for the sample average can be read off directly from a table of the normal probability distribution. This is a very useful property of the sample average for our purposes of bettering the estimation of the level of error, since it provides us with knowledge of the probability distribution function that we replaced by the Tchebyscheff approximation.

The definition of "large" sample size depends on the quantity being measured, so that there is no universal minimum number above which the sample size will automatically guarantee that the distribution of repeated sample averages will be normal. This would only be true when, strictly speaking, the sample size is infinite. However, for most quantities related to the models in this text, a sample size of 100 or more will lead for all practical purposes to an adequate approximation. Conversely, a sample size of 25 or less will require great caution in using the normal approximation, as described below.

In any event, let us assume that our sample size of 90 is sufficient for this purpose. Consequently, we can assume that the sample average is a random variable, with a normal probability distribution function, with a mean approximately equal to 1250 (as was estimated above) and a standard deviation of approximately 28.46. Normal random variables have the very useful property that, when their values are rescaled according to formula (6.5),

$$Z = \frac{X - \mu}{\sigma} \longleftrightarrow X = \sigma Z + \mu \qquad (6.5)$$

where X is the original value, μ the mean, and σ the standard deviation of the variable, the rescaled *standardized*, or *normalized*, values Z (which, in fact, represent the fluctuations of the original values from the mean, measured in number of standard deviations) will have a *standard normal distribution*. The practical consequence is that the probability of a normal random variable with any mean and standard deviation can be read off the standard normal table, which is given in Table A.2, Appendix A, after standardizing its values by transforming them according to (6.5).

Let us therefore apply this result to the same estimation that we performed above. Using the same rationale, given a measurement of 1250 for the sample average, we can say that at a level of probability or confidence of 0.90, for instance, the corresponding maximum potential error δ will be such that an interval of half-width δ centered on the mean $\mu_{\bar{O}_j}$ will contain a total probability of 0.90. Rescaling this statement in terms of the corresponding standardized values for $\bar{O}_j$, this means that to a deviation of δ from the mean in the original scale corresponds a deviation of

$$Z = \frac{\delta}{\sigma / \sqrt{n}} \tag{6.6}$$

in the standardized scale. Therefore, the determination of δ is effected simply by looking for the entry $Z_{0.45}$ in Table A.2, which corresponds to a probability of $0.90/2 = 0.45$, since the standard normal distribution function is symmetrical with respect to the value zero. This is illustrated in Figure 6.4.

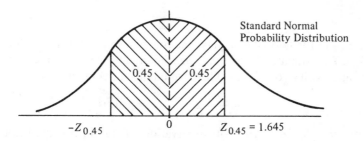

Standard Normal
Probability Distribution

$-Z_{0.45}$ 0 $Z_{0.45} = 1.645$

Figure 6.4 Determination of the cutoff value $Z_{p/2}$ corresponding to a probability p.

The value of $Z_{0.45}$ is 1.645. Therefore, translated back in terms of the original scale of measurement for $\bar{O}_j$, through formula (6.5), this corresponds to a fluctuation, or error, of

$$\delta = Z \frac{\sigma}{\sqrt{n}} \tag{6.7}$$

and

$$\delta = \frac{270}{\sqrt{90}}(1.645) = 48.82$$

or about 49 passengers. Similarly, the level of error δ, at a level of probability of 0.95, would be equal to about $1.96(28.46) = 55.78$ or, about 56 passengers.

In general, the error δ_p corresponding to a level of probability p will be equal to

$$\boxed{\delta = \pm Z_{p/2} \frac{\sigma}{\sqrt{n}}} \tag{6.8}$$

where $Z_{p/2}$ is the entry in the standard normal table that corresponds to a cumulative probability of $p/2$ measured from zero. It is important to notice that for the same level of probability, the resulting estimate of the level of error is smaller than that given by the Tchebyscheff formula. This confirms the intuitive expectation that the bounds on the interval of possible values for the average daily number of passengers (i.e., from $1250 - 49 = 1201$ to $1250 + 49 = 1299$, with a confidence of 90%) should be more precise than before, since we are using more information about $\bar{O}_j$ (the knowledge of the specific nature of its probability distribution). Thus, although the Tchebyscheff approach might constitute a useful shortcut, it provides worse estimates of the error level than the use of the normal distribution function, which, however, requires a "large" number of observations.

In the same fashion, formula (6.4) for the minimum sample size to achieve a given level of maximum error δ_p at a given level of confidence now becomes

$$n = \frac{\sigma^2 Z_{p/2}^2}{\delta^2} \tag{6.9}$$

since $Z_{p/2}$ in the normal case plays the role of k in the Tchebyscheff approximation. The estimate of the sample size required to achieve a precision of ± 35 passengers with a confidence of 0.90 would then be computed as

$$n = \frac{(270)^2 (1.645)^2}{(35)^2} = 161.04$$

i.e., as a sample size of 162 daily observations. Thus, for this application also, the use of the normal approximation (when legitimate) is more beneficial than the use of the Tchebyscheff approximation, since the estimation of the sample size is more economical; i.e., the estimated required sample is smaller.

Finally, one should be aware of the fact that although formulas (6.6) through (6.9) contain the true value σ of the standard deviation of the daily average number of passengers, we used the approximate observed value of 28.46 instead. In cases when the sample size is large, however, the observed value should approximate closely the true value. (There are methods for estimating the level of error on the observed value of a variance, based on principles similar to those we have seen above. Because of space constraints, we shall not present them here. They will be found in any introductory statistics text.)

Therefore, in the case of large samples, the foregoing method remains applicable. In the case of small samples, however, i.e., in most cases below size 30, not only might the sample average no longer be normally distributed, but the observed sample standard deviation might be a very poor estimate of the true standard deviation.

In such cases, provided that the quantity under estimation (here the daily level of usage) is normally distributed, the procedure described above can be used for any sample size by simply replacing the standard normal distribution by the "T distribution." The table of the T distribution is given in Table A.3 of Appendix A. One will notice that it is characterized by a parameter, called the *number of degrees of freedom*. This number is equal to the sample size minus 1. Otherwise, the procedure remains the same, and we shall not illustrate it again. (Although the requirement that the quantity be normally distributed is theoretically strict, in practice, of course, when the sample size is small, the use of the T distribution is the only choice, whether the requirement is observed or not.)

There is, however, one difference with the "normal" case, in the computation of the required sample size for a given precision. When we use the normal approximation, the term $Z_{p/2}$ in formula (6.9) does not depend on the sample size, since it is derived from the standard normal distribution. On the contrary, when we use the T distribution, for which the parameter (number of degrees of freedom) is equal to the sample size minus 1, we do not know which particular T distribution to use (and thus what the value of $T_{p/2}$ is), since it depends on the unknown sample size. In this case, we must then resort to a *trial-and-error* approach, where we first guess the required sample size, derive the value of $T_{p/2}$ from the T distribution with $(n - 1)$ degrees of freedom (as we have done using the normal distribution table), and then use that value to compute the sample size through formula (6.9). If the result is equal (or sufficiently close) to the original guessed value, it is the solution for the required sample size. Otherwise, another value is tried, which reduces the discrepancy, etc., until there is equality of the guessed and the retrieved values.

Let us now conclude this exposition of the estimation procedures for average values in two important special cases. First, the case when the quantity to estimate is the difference between two (sample) averages or, equivalently, the average of a quantity that is the difference between two random variables. This case was encountered, it may be recalled, in the models for *modal split*, (4.60) through (4.64), where the variables $(X_s^1 - X_s^2)$ or $(G_1^k - G_2^k)$ represent the difference between the same quantity in two different samples. In this case, if it can be assumed that the standard deviations of the respective two quantities X_1 and X_2 are equal, probability theory shows that the appropriate estimate of the standard deviation of the difference between the two averages is

$$s_{\bar{X}_1 - \bar{X}_2} = \sqrt{\frac{[(n_1 - 1)s_1^2 + (n_2 - 1)s_2^2](n_1 + n_2)}{(n_1 + n_2 - 2)n_1 n_2}} \qquad (6.10)$$

where s_1^2 and s_2^2 are the observed sample variances (not the variances of the sample averages) of the two variables respectively, and n_1 and n_2 the corresponding sample sizes. (There are methods of "hypothesis testing" to determine whether the two sample variances can be assumed to be equal. However, we shall not present them here, because of lack of space, since they can be found in standard texts on statistical methods.) Furthermore, the standardized value for the difference in the observed sample averages $\bar{X}_1$

and $\bar{X}_2$,

$$t = \frac{\bar{X}_1 - \bar{X}_2}{s_{\bar{X}_1 - \bar{X}_2}} \tag{6.11}$$

will have a T distribution with $(n_1 + n_2 - 2)$ degrees of freedom. Subsequently, the estimation of the maximum level of error, for a given level of confidence, follows the same procedure as above.

6.5   The Estimation of Input Data: Proportions

An important case is that of the estimation of values which are *proportions*, or *percentages*. For instance, to estimate the value of the entry a_{ij} in the multiregional employment multiplier model (3.45), we would need to record the proportion of residents working in a given area who live in another. Or, we might have to measure the proportion of the production of a given economic sector which is consumed in another, as a parameter of an input/output model of the form (3.23). Or, we might need estimates of the migration rates m_i for model (2.31), or the value of the "work-force ratio" γ in (3.46). In all these instances the value of the proportion, or percentage, is computed as the ratio of the number of cases surveyed (residents, units of production, etc.) which exhibit the quality of interest (being born, going to shop in area i, being consumed by sector i, etc.) to the total number of cases surveyed or, equivalently, the number of such cases found in a sample of size 100. For instance, if we wanted to estimate the proportions of commuters who use public transportation to go to work, we would interview a sample of n commuters, record the total number Y of "yes" responses to the question "Do you ride transit to work?", and estimate the proportion by Y/n.

Thus, the random quantity being recorded in connection with the estimation of proportions is of a particular nature. It only has two levels: 0, when the property of interest is not exhibited by the case, and 1, when it is. The proportion is then the *sample average* for that variable, i.e., the total number of 1's observed, divided by the sample size. Therefore, when the sample size is large, we can again use the normal approximation for the estimation of proportions. However, when the sample size is small (typically less than 25), the special nature of the variable (discrete with only two levels) prohibits the use of the T distribution, which assumes that the variable is continuous. Although we could in principle use the Tchebyscheff approximation, it would be even less precise than it already is in typical situations, because of the discrete nature of the variable. Incidentally, although less convenient analytically than the case of large samples, the estimation of averages from small samples is a very important practical case, since one of the main problems in model building is the lack or insufficiency of data. This may be the case, for instance, in a multiregional survey, where the number of cases surveyed which will be found in each of the cells of a two-way table (i, j), even for large surveys, may end up rather small if there are many zones. Also, the small-sample case is important because it is typically the format of the *pilot runs* prior to the administration of the survey. These are used to derive initial estimates of the order of magnitude of the quantities involved (means, standard deviations, etc.) so that a determination of the final sample size (using the methods we have seen above) can be effected. Finally, in some cases, the savings derived from administering a small-sample survey may be worth the resulting lack of precision.

In any event, let us illustrate the approach to this problem using a practical example. Suppose that we are polling several areas about their local attitudes toward a certain proposed transit system, e.g., by querying a few representative citizens. In order to estimate what proportion of municipalities in the region are in favor of the transit system (e.g., to have an initial rough estimate of what the outcome of a vote on a bond might be), we decide to poll a sample of 10 areas by questioning representative citizens. The results of the survey show that of the 10 areas, 6 were opposed to the system and 4 were in favor of it ("don't know"s were not allowed). On the basis of this experimental result, in which interval of values can we estimate the (true) value of the percentage of areas in favor of the transit system in the entire region?

Since none of the probability distribution methods we have used so far is really applicable, the only recourse is to try and infer the (theoretical) probability distribution of the number of areas in favor of the system, in a sample of size n, so that we can derive the percentage. Let us denote by π the probability that an individual area is in favor of the transit system (i.e., the probability that a single value of the variable "Are you in favor of the system" is "yes." Consequently, the probability that the answer is "no" is $(1 - \pi)$. Let us assume that this probability is the same for all areas in the region. Then π also represents the proportion of areas in the entire region which are in favor of the proposition[1]. Under this assumption, probability theory shows that the distribution of the total number of areas in favor of the proposition in a sample is size n is a certain distribution, called the *binomial* distribution with parameters n, the sample size, and π, the probability of a "yes" answer

[1] This is obviously a simplifying assumption which is convenient for our purpose, since we are trying to get an estimate of the true value of π. However, it may well be justified, at least within subsamples of areas, corresponding, for instance, to geographic clusters. These subsamples may then be chosen so that they represent the overall region, e.g., using the techniques of *stratified sampling* as described in Section 6.2. The overall proportion would then be the average of the proportions in the subsamples, weighed by their relative importance in the entire region.

in an individual area. As in the case of the normal distribution, this is an example of a specific distribution whose probabilities can be evaluated theoretically given the conditions noted above. The mean of such a distribution is equal to $n\pi$ and its variance is equal to $n\pi(1 - \pi)$. [For instance, the true value of the average number of areas observed to be in favor of the proposition in samples of size 10 with $\pi = 0.5$ would be $10(0.5) = 5$, and the true value of the variance would be equal to $10(0.5)(1 - 0.5) = 0.25$.] Tables for the binomial distribution function with various values of its two parameters n and π are given in Table A.4 of Appendix A.

Thus, our sample statistic (the number of areas in a sample of size 10 who will be observed to be in favor of the proposition) is distributed with a binomial distribution of parameters $n = 10$ and π equal to the unknown true value but which should be (more or less) approximated by the observed value of $4/10 = 0.4$. Let us assume that we want to estimate the true value of that proportion at a level of confidence of 0.95. Since our random variable surveyed is the number of areas in the sample in favor of the transit system, we shall first build an interval of estimation for that quantity and then translate it into terms of estimation of the percentage. This means building an interval around the observed value of 4, which encloses a 0.90 total probability. However, the binomial distribution is not symmetrical with respect to its mean (except when $\pi = 0.50$). This is easy to conceive of, since when π is equal to 0.30, for instance, the probability of observing 4 "yes" responses should not be equal to the probability of observing $10 - 3 = 7$ "yes" responses. (It is, however, equal to the probability of observing $10 - 3 = 7$ "no" responses, which is also the probability of observing 7 "yes" responses when $\pi = 1 - 0.3 = 0.7$. This property explains why binomial tables are often given only for values of x, the number of "yes" responses up to half the total sample size. The probabilities for the remaining values can be inferred from changing x into $n - x$ and π into $1 - \pi$.) At any rate, the consequence of the asymmetry of the distribution is that we will have to build the estimation interval by spreading out from the observed value alternatively in both directions until we enclose a probability at least equal to the confidence level, here 0.90. (Since the binomial distribution function is a discrete distribution with integer values only, we cannot in general expect to enclose a probability exactly equal to the confidence level.)

The parameters of the binomial table are then $n = 10$ (sample size) and $\pi = 0.4$ (observed value of the proportion). The corresponding binomial table shows that the probability of the value $x = 4$ is equal to 0.2508. Since this is less than our desired level of 0.90, we now add the value $x = 3$ to the interval. This value has a probability of 0.2150. This brings the total probability of the interval constituted by these two values to $0.2508 + 0.2150 = 0.4658$. We now add the value $x = 5$ corresponding to the probability 0.2007. The total interval probability is now $0.4658 + 0.2007 = 0.6665$. Adding the value $x = 2$ we have a total probability of $0.6665 + 0.1207 = 0.7872$. Adding the value $x = 6$, the probability becomes 0.8987. Finally, adding the value $x = 1$, we get a total interval probability of 0.939. Since we have now exceeded our chosen level of confidence, we stop, and the final estimation interval for the true number of areas in favor of the transit system in a sample of size 10 is anywhere between 1 and 6 areas. This estimation is at a level of certainty of 90%.

In terms of the true value of the proportion of areas who favor the system in the entire region, this means that the proportion could be anywhere between $1/10 = 0.1$, or 10%, and $6/10 = 0.6$, or 60% (at 0.90 confidence). Therefore, the level of potential error we might incur in using our estimate of 0.4 may be as high as $0.4 - 0.1 = 0.3$, or 30 percentage points, i.e., 30%. This large degree of imprecision is, of course, due to the very small sample size. This example, although perhaps somewhat extreme, illustrates well the model calibration problems due to limited data. When the sample size becomes larger, the precision is improved significantly. (See Exercise 6.8.)

As a final refinement to all the various procedures for value estimation given above, when the population being sampled is itself small (e.g., in the case of small geographical areas, where the number of residents might only be several hundreds), the estimate of the sample standard deviation (and consequently also of the sample average's standard deviation) must be adjusted (multiplied) by the factor

$$C = \sqrt{\frac{P - n}{P - 1}} \tag{6.12}$$

where P is the population size and n the sample size. (See Exercise 6.1.)

6.6   Model Calibration: Minimum-Sum-of-Squares Method

In the preceding sections, we have seen methods of evaluating the quality (or precision) of data which will be used in connection with the development and/or application of an analytical model. In this section, we turn to the problem of the estimation of the *parameters* of a model.

A parameter is a quantity appearing in the specification of a model [such as the parameter r in the exponential population projection model (2.4), or the parameter λ in the intervening model (4.45)] which in general cannot be observed (and thus estimated) directly. On the other hand, other numerical values, such as the value P_0 in the same population model (2.3) or the values N_j in the intervening opportunity model (4.45), are *exogeneous* variables, i.e., quantities that are external inputs into the model and can be observed independently. The determination of their values is thus simply a matter of empirical observation, and is subject to the procedures outlined in the previous sections.

On the contrary, model parameters are internal (endogenous) quantities whose value will be derived indirectly, as a factor that allows an adjustment of the output of the model with the information given. In some special cases, such as the exponential model (2.4), where the parameter r has a simple physical definition as shown in formula (2.3), it is possible to measure the value of the parameter directly, from observational data. This was done in several cases throughout this text. For instance, the determination of the parameters of the linear population projection model (2.1) can be effected from its definition as the unit time population change, or equivalently graphically, as the slope of the plot of the variations of the population level against time. In the case of the intervening opportunity model, we can empirically derive the value of the parameter λ in model (4.45) from formula (4.37) as the intercept of the corresponding linear plot of log P_{ij}. However, when this type of approach to the determination of the value of a model parameter is possible, it still entails a certain degree of subjectivity. More specifically, we would expect fluctuations in the actual population increments a, or a deviation from a linear pattern in the observed values of log P_{ij}, in the first and in the second instances above, respectively. Thus, unless we choose a value representative of all the yearly population increments, or approximate the variations of log P_{ij} by a straight line, we cannot estimate these respective parameters. The choice of value in the first case (to take the average yearly increment, the median, etc.), and the choice of which specific straight line best approximates the locus of points in Figure 4.2 in the latter case, are thus left unresolved. Therefore, in the absence of a *criterion* for such choices, the parameter estimation remains typically an "eyeball" procedure. Furthermore, in most cases, such an approach is not even possible. For instance, there is no definition or interpretation for the parameters of the gravity model (4.20) which would allow the same type of graphical fitting.

It is the purpose of this section to present examples of more rational and systematic approaches to this problem. We shall begin by an exposition of the basic rationale behind a first type of approach, and then illustrate it in a practical case.

One logical rationale which can guide the determination of the values of model parameters is that they should be such that they minimize the difference between the values predicted by the model (the output, or reproduced values) Y_i, and the actual, observed values $\hat{Y}_i$.[1] For instance, in a gravity model, we would want the parameters α and β in the impedance function (4.7) to be such that the level of error, i.e., the "overall difference" between the values of the

---

[1] The symbol $\wedge$ over a variable (i.e., $\hat{Y}_i$) will refer to the observed value, as opposed to the predicted value, Y_i.

levels of travel T_{ij}, as predicted by the model and given in Table 4.11(a), and the observed values $\hat{T}_{ij}$ given in Table 4.5, be as small as possible. (The parameter values were $\alpha = 2.0$ and $\beta = 0.5$, as may be recalled from the example.) There are several potential choices for the definition of the criterion to use for the measure of this overall difference. One such criterion would be to minimize the average error, i.e.,

$$\frac{1}{n} \sum_{i=1}^{n} (Y_i - \hat{Y}_i)$$

where Y_i is the value predicted by the model and $\hat{Y}_i$ is the actual value. However, this quantity would not be very representative of the overall level of error between the prediction and the observation, since errors of opposite signs could cancel each other out, and thus reduce the average error. Another possiblity to alleviate this problem would be to use the average of the absolute value of the error, i.e.,

$$\frac{1}{n} \sum_i | Y_i - \hat{Y}_i |$$

However, this is not a very convenient mathematical expression to manipulate. A common measure of the overall level of error is the total or average sum-of-squared errors (or deviations) between predicted and actual values:

$$\boxed{S = \sum_i (Y_i - \hat{Y}_i)^2} \tag{6.13}$$

(This particular measure of the level of prediction error of a model offers other advantages, which we shall see in more detail in Chapter 7, when we consider the methods of linear statistical modeling.) Consequently, the unknown parameters of a given model will be chosen such that their values minimize the value of the criterion S above.

Since the predicted values Y_i are a function of the unknown parameters (i.e., depend on the values of the parameters), the problem *Find Min S* (possibly subject to constraints on the values of α, β, etc.) will in general lead to a system of equations in the unknown parameters. In principle, then, it is possible to solve these equations analytically, to determine the "exact" values of the parameters. However, such a rigorous approach, besides requiring the use of advanced calculus, is not always possible, for reasons of the intractability of the mathematics involved. Thus, an alternative approach is an empirical search, in which several values of the parameter(s) are tried, and that value (or set of values) that results in the smallest value for S is retained. Such a *heuristic* approach, however, does not guarantee that the absolute minimum for S is attained (as in linear statistical modeling) and therefore that the "best" model is derived.

Let us now illustrate this procedure in the case of the calibration of a logistic model of population projection of the form (2.13). Let us assume (using the data of Exercise 2.7) that we would like to fit a logistic model to the pattern of population change represented by the observed values $\hat{P}_t$ in Table 6.1. The expression for the logistic model is

$$P_t = \frac{1}{\left(\dfrac{1}{P_0} - \dfrac{b}{a}\right)e^{-at} + \dfrac{b}{a}} \qquad (6.14/2.13)$$

TABLE 6.1

Time, t	0	1	2	3	4	5	6	7
Observed population, $\hat{P}_t$ (thousands)	11	11.65	12.30	13.0	13.70	14.45	15.20	15.95

The value of the exogenous variable P_0, the base population level, is 11, as given in Table 6.1. Thus, the specification of the model requires determination of the values of the two parameters a and b. Although an eyeball approach was indicated in Section 2.5 and suggested for the solution of Exercise 2.7, it will be instructive to compare its outcome to the application of the procedure above.

Let us assume, to save time, that we have identified in a first stage the "ballpark" range of values where the two parameters lie. This can be obtained by trying a few guessed values, or on the basis of knowledge of other calibrations of the model under similar conditions. In any case, let us assume that we know that the parameter a is of the order of 10^{-2} (or 0.01) and that the parameter b is of the order of 10^{-3} (or 0.001). We would then choose a joint set of values in these respective ranges, for instance the nine values represented in Table 6.2. These nine combinations of values for a and b

TABLE 6.2   Model Number

$b =$	$a = 0.04$	0.08	0.12
0.001	1	2	3
0.002	4	5	6
0.003	7	8	9

define nine individual models. For instance, the first combination would lead to the specific expression

$$P_t^1 = \frac{1}{\left(\dfrac{1}{11} - \dfrac{0.001}{0.04}\right)e^{-0.04t} + \dfrac{0.001}{0.04}}$$

or

$$P_t^1 = \frac{1}{0.0659e^{-0.04t} + 0.025}$$

where the superscript refers to the model number. We would then compute the respective sets of predicted values for the population levels from each of the nine models: P_t^j, for $j = 1, 2, 3, \ldots, 9$ and $t = 0, 1, 2, \ldots, 7$. For each series of projections we would then compute the value of the total sum of squared errors S^j,

$$S^j = \sum_{t=0}^{7} (P_t^j - \hat{P}_t^j)^2$$

and retain the model for which this criterion has the smallest value.

Let us describe the corresponding computations in the cases of model 4 and 8 only. Model 4 corresponds to the combination $a = 0.04$ with $b = 0.002$. The model is therefore

$$P_t^4 = \frac{1}{0.041e^{-0.04t} + 0.05} \tag{6.15}$$

Similarly, the combination of parameter values for model 8 is $a = 0.08$ and $b = 0.003$. The model is therefore

$$P_t^8 = \frac{1}{0.053e^{-0.08t} + 0.038} \tag{6.16}$$

First, we compute systematically the values of the predicted population levels for all values of t between 0 and 7. The sequence of computations is presented in Table 6.3.

Next, we compute the respective errors between the prediction from model 4, P_t^4, and the actual corresponding value of the population level $\hat{P}_t$, as given in Table 6.1, and similarly, for model 8. We then compute the value of the squares of these errors and compute their totals, as shown in Table 6.3. Model 8 results in a total sum of squared errors of 4.299, whereas model 4 leads to a sum of 35.169. Thus, model 8 is the better model, i.e., fits the given data more closely and would be retained.

Naturally, it is possible to try and reduce this level of total squared error, e.g., by trying other combinations of values. (see Exercise 6.14.) The definition of a level for the criterion S below which such a search should stop is somewhat arbitrary, since S is not a normalized (or standardized) indicator which could be compared from model to model, such as average percent error, for instance. However, in cases where the errors can be assumed to be normally distributed random variables, another related criterion, the *coefficient of linear correlation*, which will be defined in Chapter 7, can then be used.

Also, it is clear that such (blind) searches can be quite time-consuming, even for a modest number of parameter values. Indeed, a two-parameter

TABLE 6.3

$t =$	0	1	2	3	4	5	6	7	$\sum_t$
$0.04t$	0	0.04	0.08	0.12	0.16	0.20	0.24	0.28	
$0.08t$	0	0.08	0.16	0.24	0.32	0.40	0.48	0.56	
$e^{-0.04t}$	1	0.961	0.923	0.887	0.852	0.819	0.787	0.756	
$e^{-0.08t}$	1	0.923	0.852	0.787	0.726	0.670	0.619	0.571	
$0.041e^{-0.04t}$	0.041	0.039	0.038	0.036	0.035	0.034	0.032	0.031	
$0.053e^{-0.08t}$	0.053	0.049	0.045	0.042	0.038	0.036	0.033	0.030	
$0.041e^{-0.04t} + 0.05$	0.091	0.089	0.088	0.086	0.085	0.084	0.082	0.081	
$\dfrac{1}{0.041e^{-0.04t} + 0.05} = P_t^4$	10.989	11.236	11.364	11.628	11.765	11.905	12.195	12.346	
$0.053e^{-0.08t} + 0.038$	0.091	0.087	0.083	0.080	0.076	0.074	0.071	0.068	
$\dfrac{1}{0.053e^{-0.08t} + 0.038} = P_t^8$	10.989	11.494	12.048	12.500	13.158	13.514	14.085	14.706	
$P_t^4 - \hat{P}_t$	-0.011	-0.414	-0.936	-1.372	-1.935	-2.545	-3.005	-3.604	
$(P_t^4 - \hat{P}_t)^2$	0	0.171	0.876	1.882	3.744	6.477	9.030	12.989	35.169
$P_t^8 - \hat{P}_t$	-0.011	-0.156	-0.252	-0.500	-0.542	-0.936	-1.115	-1.244	
$(P_t^8 - \hat{P}_t)^2$	0.000	0.024	0.064	0.250	0.294	0.876	1.243	1.548	4.299

gravity model with six trial values for each parameter, applied to a 25-zone region, would lead to $6 \times 6 \times 25 \times 25 = 22{,}500$ computations of the predicted values for the T_{ij}'s. However, some methods are available for guiding the search by choosing the next interval of trial values on the basis of the performance of the preceding one. One such method is the *golden section search*, and another uses *Fibonacci numbers*. Interested readers are referred to the specialized literature. Finally, the simple, iterative nature of the procedure makes it ideally suited for implementation on high-speed computers, and even on programmable pocket calculators.

6.7 Model Calibration:
Maximum Likelihood Method

Let us now describe the second main approach to the parameter estimation problem, which is based on the *principle of maximum likelihood*. This principle postulates that the parameters of the model should be such that they result in a maximum probability for the sample of observed values. Consequently, suppose that we can evaluate the (joint) probability of occurrence of the respective observed values for the variable(s) being predicted. In general, this probability will be a function of the unknown parameters, which we can then call the *likelihood function*. Then, since we did, in fact, observe these values, the probability should (a posteriori) be maximum. This rationale thus gives us another criterion for selecting among various specifications of a given model. In the same fashion as above, we shall retain that model which corresponds to the maximum value of the likelihood function. This requirement of a maximum for the function can also, in principle, be translated into a set of equations in the unknown parameters, which can then be solved. In practice, however, and for the same reasons, an empirical search procedure for the maximum is usually used instead.

Let us now illustrate this approach in the case of a doubly constrained gravity model of the form

$$T_{ij} = k_i l_j O_i D_j d_{ij}^{-\alpha} \qquad (6.17/4.2/4.5)$$

where the T_{ij} are the predicted levels of interaction between zone j and zone i, e.g., the number of travelers from j to i. We also, assume that we have the corresponding observed values $\hat{T}_{ij}$.

Let us then evaluate the likelihood function. The model states that the total number of travelers between zones j and i is equal to T_{ij} as given in (6.17). Therefore, the probability that an individual traveler will travel between these two zones can be predicted (a priori) by the model to be equal to

$$P_{ij} = \frac{T_{ij}}{T} \qquad (6.18)$$

where T is the total number of travelers between all zones (i.e., $T = \sum_i \sum_j T_{ij}$). Therefore, the probability that exactly $\hat{T}_{ij}$ travelers (i.e., the observed number) would travel between zone j and zone i is (assuming that the travelers are independent)

$$P(\hat{T}_{ij}) = (P_{ij})^{\hat{T}_{ij}} = \left(\frac{T_{ij}}{T}\right)^{\hat{T}_{ij}} \qquad (6.19)$$

i.e., the product of $\hat{T}_{ij}$ times the individual theoretical probability (remember the probability of getting two 1's in two tosses of a die?). Therefore, if the zonal numbers of travelers are independent of one another, another application of the multiplicative rule for the probability of joint (independent) events gives the probability of the whole set of observed travel levels between zones $\hat{T}_{ij}$ as the product of the individual terms in (6.19):

$$P(\text{sample}) = \prod_{ij} P(\hat{T}_{ij}) = \prod_{ij} \left(\frac{T_{ij}}{T}\right)^{\hat{T}_{ij}} \qquad (6.20)$$

where the symbol $\prod$ means "product of."

Because the T_{ij}'s are functions of the parameter α, through (6.17), this expression for the probability or likelihood is also a function of α. Now, as observed above, it seems logical to require that this theoretical probability be a maximum, since we did, in fact, observe the respective numbers of travelers $\hat{T}_{ij}$ between zones. Thus, the value of α should be chosen so as to maximize the expression in (6.20); equivalently, since when a variable's value increases, so does its logarithm, it should maximize its logarithm, which has a simpler form.

Thus, we would be trying to maximize the "log-likelihood function":

$$L = \log[P(\text{sample})] = \sum_{ij} \hat{T}_{ij}(\log T_{ij} - \log T) \qquad (6.21)$$

The $\hat{T}_{ij}$'s are given (observational data) and the T_{ij}'s and their sum T are the output of the model. This expression is then evaluated for various sets of output values of the model, corresponding to various values of the parameter α. The model corresponding to the value that leads to the maximum value for L is then retained. (See Exercise 6.15.)

Let us illustrate this approach with a practical example, this time concerning the calibration of a probit model of *route choice* of the form (4.58 to 4.60). Let us assume that a traffic department has been surveying the proportion of drivers who change their usual itinerary to go to work as a function of the delay and this "cost" in travel time caused by increases in traffic. The results are presented in Table 6.4.

The agency would like to try to develop a probit model for the probability $P(t)$ that a given driver does not change itinerary as a function of the amount of delay, t, of the form

$$P(t) = \Phi(Y) \qquad (6.22/4.58)$$

TABLE 6.4

Delay level, i	1	2	3	4	5	6	7
Delay, t (minutes)	0	5	10	15	25	35	50
Number of drivers not changing itinerary, $\hat{N}_i$ (per hundred)	97	93	86	72	35	9	4

where $\Phi(Y)$ is the value of the cumulative standard normal probability distribution function for the value Y. Y (the probit value) is assumed to be a linear function of the delay t:

$$Y = a + bt \qquad\qquad (6.23/4.60)$$

The calibration of the model, i.e., determination of the values of the parameters a and b, will be attempted in the range of values for a around 2.0 and for b around -0.05, on the basis of estimates of other such calibrations. (Incidentally, it is always useful to have an idea of the typical values of the various parameters of the models we have seen, since although they do vary from case to case, their order of magnitude remains relatively stable.) Consequently, the grid of trial combinations is as represented in Table 6.5.

TABLE 6.5   Model Number

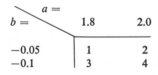

$b =$	$a =$ 1.8	2.0
-0.05	1	2
-0.1	3	4

The four respective models corresponding to the combinations of values of the parameters above are

$$Y^1 = 1.8 - 0.05t \qquad\qquad (6.24)$$

$$Y^2 = 2 \;\; - 0.05t$$

$$Y^3 = 1.8 - 0.1t$$

$$Y^4 = 2.0 - 0.1t \qquad\qquad (6.25)$$

Let us now write the likelihood function corresponding to the foregoing model. This is the joint probability of the observed numbers of drivers not changing their itinerary as a function of the delay t. Thus, we first compute the predicted probability P_i that an individual driver does not change itineraries, for various values t_i of t. This is equal to the value of the cumulative of the standard normal probability distribution for the value given by $Y(t_i)$.

Next, we translate this in terms of the predicted number of drivers in a sample of 100 who would not change itineraries, i.e., the predicted value N_i corresponding to the observed $\hat{N}_i$'s in Table 6.4. This is, of course, simply equal to the foregoing probabilities times 100:

$$N_i = 100P_i \qquad (6.26)$$

Then we compute the total number of such drivers who would not change itineraries, for all possible values of the delay:

$$\sum_i N_i = N \qquad (6.27)$$

Next, we compute the probability that a given driver chosen at random would not change itineraries when the delay is t_i. This is simply equal to

$$p_i = \frac{N_i}{\sum_i N_i} \qquad (6.28)$$

i.e., the normalized values for the N_i's expressed in terms of frequencies. (Note that this is different from P_i.) Next, we compute the probability that $\hat{N}_i$ (the observed number) drivers would not change their itinerary when the delay is t_i. Following the same principle of multiplication of individual probabilities, this is equal to

$$(p_i)^{\hat{N}_i} = \left(\frac{N_i}{\sum_i N_i}\right)^{\hat{N}_i} \qquad (6.29)$$

So the final probability of the observed *set* of numbers of drivers who do not change their itinerary over the seven levels of the delay is

$$p = \prod_{i=1}^{7} (p_i)^{\hat{N}_i} \qquad (6.30)$$

This expression is a function of the two unknown parameters a and b, since the p_i's are computed from the value of Y_{t_i}, which is dependent on a and b. Therefore, the combination of values for a and b that maximizes the expression above will be retained for the final model. It is equivalent, and somewhat easier (although not necessary), to follow common usage and maximize the logarithm of p in (6.30). Thus, we will compute the value of the expression

$$L = \log p = \sum_{i=1}^{7} \hat{N}_i \log p_i \qquad (6.31)$$

which is the log-likelihood function, for various combinations of values for a and b. The corresponding computations (for models 1 and 4 only) are shown in Table 6.6, with the corresponding formula reference.

Since model 4 (i.e., $Y = 2.0 - 0.1t$) corresponds to the maximum value for the likelihood function, we shall retain it as giving the best fit between predicted values and observed values.[2] In practice, of course, we would want

---

[2]The values of the log-likelihood function being negative, the smallest in absolute value is the largest in algebraic value.

TABLE 6.6

Reference Formula	$i =$	1	2	3	4	5	6	7	$\sum_i$
	t_i	0	5	10	15	25	35	50	
	$0.1t_i$	0	0.5	1	1.5	2.5	3.5	5	
	$0.05t_i$	0	0.025	0.5	0.75	1.25	1.75	2.5	
(6.24)	$Y_i^1 = 1.8 - 0.05t_i$	1.800	1.775	1.300	1.050	0.550	0.050	-0.700	
(6.25)	$Y_i^4 = 2 - 0.1t_i$	2	1.5	1	0.5	-0.5	-1.5	-2.5	
(6.22)	$P_i^1 = \Phi(Y_i^1)$	0.9641	0.9599	0.9032	0.8531	0.7088	0.5199	0.2420	
(6.22)	$P_i^4 = \Phi(Y_i^4)$	0.9792	0.9332	0.8413	0.6915	0.3085	0.0680	0.0062	
(6.26)	$N_i^1 = 100P_i^1$	96	96	90	85	71	52	24	514
(6.26)	$N_i^4 = 100P_i^4$	98	93	84	69	31	7	1	386
(6.28)	$p_i^1 = N_i^1/\sum_i N_i^1$	0.187	0.187	0.175	0.165	0.138	0.101	0.047	
(6.28)	$p_i^4 = N_i^4/\sum_i N_i^4$	0.254	0.241	0.218	0.179	0.080	0.018	0.002	
	$\log p_i^1$	-1.6766	-1.6766	-1.7430	-1.8018	-1.9805	-2.2926	-3.0576	
	$\log p_i^4$	-1.3704	-1.4230	-1.5141	-1.7093	-2.5257	-4.0174	-6.2146	
Table 6.4	$\mathcal{N}_i$	97	93	86	72	35	9	4	396
(6.31)	$\mathcal{N}_i \log N_i^1$	-162.63	-155.92	-149.90	-129.73	-69.32	-20.63	-12.23	-700.36
(6.31)	$\mathcal{N}_i \log N_i^4$	-132.93	-132.34	-130.21	-123.07	-88.40	-36.16	-24.86	-667.97

259

to try several other combinations before finally selecting a model. (See Exercise 6.16.) The final expression for the probability of a given driver not changing itineraries when the delay is t is therefore

$$P(t) = \Phi(2.0 - 0.1t) \qquad (6.32)$$

and conversely, the probability of a driver changing his (or her) itinerary is

$$1 - \Phi(2.0 - 0.1t) \qquad (6.33)$$

6.8   Measures of the Precision of a Calibrated Model

Having now learned how to calibrate models, it would be useful to have a measure of the effectiveness of the calibration procedure or, equivalently, of the resulting overall precision of the model. That is, if the level of error in the model is too large, the search procedure should be continued. However, in that case, we would then also need to know how beneficial this would be, i.e., whether the current value for the criterion used (sum of squared errors, or log-likelihood value) is significantly far from the absolute minimum that can theoretically be attained. Conversely, it would be useful to be able to assess the progress of the iterative procedure, i.e., at what point to terminate it.

Let us therefore reexamine the two criteria we have used as yardsticks in the calibration process, and interpret their meaning in relation to the preceding questions, beginning with criterion S, the sum-of-squared errors, defined by (6.13).

$$S = \sum_{i=1}^{n} (Y_i - \hat{Y}_i)^2$$

Let us call s_e^2 the average squared error for the model, after calibration. This is simply the value of the minimum sum-of-squared errors obtained, divided by the number of observed values (sample size). Therefore,

$$s_e^2 = \frac{1}{n} S_{\min} = \frac{1}{n} \sum_{i=1}^{n} (Y_i - \hat{Y}_i)^2 \qquad (6.34)$$

This quantity is sometimes called the *residual variance*, since it represents the amount of (squared) variation between predicted and observed values, which the calibration will leave attached to the model. Its square root,

$$\boxed{ s_e = \sqrt{\frac{1}{n} \sum_{i=1}^{n} (Y_i - \hat{Y}_i)^2} } \qquad (6.35)$$

which is sometimes called the *standard error of estimate*, therefore represents the typical level of error that will be attached (on the average) to the predicted values, using the model.

For the same reason that the standard deviation of a random variable does not equal the average deviation from the mean, as was seen in Section 1.4 and Exercise 1.13, the standard error of estimate s_e is not equal to the average algebraic prediction error but is a proxy for it. For instance, in the calibration of the population projection model in the preceding section, the residual sum of squared errors corresponding to model 8, at the termination of the procedure, was equal to 4.299, as given in Table 6.3. Thus, the average of the squared errors, or residual variance s_e^2 is equal to $4.299/8 = 0.537$, and the standard error of estimate is equal to $\sqrt{0.537} = 0.733$. Therefore, we can expect a typical error of about 0.733 unit (73 people) on the prediction of the population levels. This is, in fact, the order of magnitude of the differences between the P_t^8's predicted by model 8 and which can be found in row 11 of Table 6.3, and the corresponding observed values in Table 6.1.

However, as has been pointed out, the sum of squared errors does not provide a standardized indicator for the model error, since it is an absolute and not a relative quantity. In other words, this represents a criterion that does not allow comparative evaluations of the effectiveness of the calibration in varying situations. Although we can meaningfully compare the performance of models 8 and 2 in the calibration, we could not, for instance, compare their performance with logistic models calibrated on different data sets. This is a serious drawback from a practical point of view, since it implies the impossibility of meaningfully assessing the potential of transferring a model calibrated in a given geographical area to another, when, for instance, limited resources preclude full recalibration.

What is needed, therefore, instead of an absolute measure of the level of model error is a relative measure. It is logical to try and relate the model error to a "base" level of error, for instance, that which would be incurred when using the least effective possible model. Let us, for instance, consider the case of the prediction of the population levels, for which the logistic model was calibrated. Given the set of eight observed values in Table 6.1, it should be (at least intuitively) clear that the least effective representation of their variations is to equate them all to the average of their observed values. In other words, the least effective model should be

$$P_t = 13.41 \quad \text{(for all values of } t) \qquad (6.36)$$

This model is reasonable (since it would be easy to think of arbitrarily worse models, e.g., with negative values for populations, etc.), in that it is *minimally consistent* with the givens. At the same time, this model has to be the worst of such models, since it does not allow for any variability in the values of the population level for varying values of t. In other words, this (extreme) model corresponds to a prediction of the population levels which is the "safest" if one does not use any information about the covariations of time and population. In general, therefore, for any model, $Y_i = F(X_i, Z_i, \ldots)$, and given any set of observed values, the comparative "least-effective" predictive model is

$$Y_i = \bar{\bar{Y}} \quad \text{for } i = 1, 2, 3, \ldots \tag{6.37}$$

where $\bar{\bar{Y}}$ is the average of the sample of observed values.

Let us therefore compare the respective levels of average prediction errors for the given model and for the least-effective model (6.37), respectively. The given model's error is represented, as we have seen above, by the standard error of estimate s_e, as defined by (6.35). In the case of the least-effective model (6.37), since all values predicted are equal to $\bar{\bar{Y}}$, the corresponding standard error of estimate is

$$s_Y = \sqrt{\frac{1}{n} \sum_i (\bar{\bar{Y}} - \hat{Y}_i)^2} \tag{6.38}$$

that is, (6.37) where $\bar{\bar{Y}}$ has replaced all Y_i's. However, this expression is exactly that of the (sample) standard deviation s_Y of the observed values $\hat{Y}_i$, as given by formula (1.8).[3] Therefore, the indicator of the precision of the given model relative to a "worst" case can be taken to be the ratio of s_e to $s_{\hat{Y}}$:

$$\rho = \frac{s_e}{s_{\hat{Y}}} = \frac{\sqrt{\dfrac{1}{n} \sum_i (Y_i - \hat{Y}_i)^2}}{\sqrt{\dfrac{1}{n} \sum_i (\bar{\bar{Y}} - \hat{Y}_i)^2}} \tag{6.39}$$

A complementary indicator of the overall precision of a given model can also be taken to be the square of ρ:

$$\rho^2 = \frac{s_e^2}{s_{\hat{Y}}^2} = \frac{\displaystyle\sum_{i=1}^{n} (Y_i - \hat{Y}_i)^2}{\displaystyle\sum_{i=1}^{n} (\bar{\bar{Y}} - \hat{Y}_i)^2} \tag{6.40}$$

This indicator physically measures the total squared error attached to the model as a fraction (or percentage) of the total variability of the observed values (data) around their mean. Thus, it can be interpreted to represent the fraction of the original variance $s_{\hat{Y}}^2$ of the observed values which remains after calibration, in the form of residual variance, s_e^2. Finally, another corollary measure of the precision of the model can be taken to be the criterion defined by

$$R^2 = 1 - \rho^2 = \frac{s_{\hat{Y}}^2 - s_e^2}{s_{\hat{Y}}^2} \tag{6.41}$$

[3]We shall here divide the sum of squares by n, not $(n-1)$, to get the "arithmetic" average of the errors.

This simply represents the ratio of the difference between the original "before" variance $s_{\hat{Y}}^2$ in the data and the "after" residual variance to the original variance $s_{\hat{Y}}^2$. Since the difference in "before" and "after" variances can be interpreted as representing the variance that has been accounted for, or captured, by the model, the value of R^2 then measures the percentage of the variance in the observed values which the model "reproduces" or, as is sometimes stated by extension of language, "explains."

The physical meaning of these various criteria may become a little clearer by reference to Figure 6.5. The variance s_e^2 is computed from the

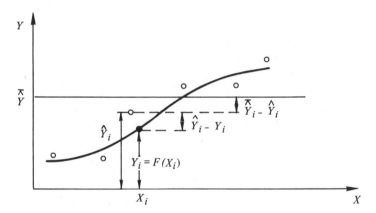

Figure 6.5 Prediction errors.

deviations of the observed values $\hat{Y}_i$ from the predicted values Y_i on the curve corresponding to the plot of the model $Y = F(X)$. The variance $s_{\hat{Y}}^2$ of the $\hat{Y}_i$'s is measured against the fixed value of their mean $\bar{\hat{Y}}$. Thus, a "good" model will be represented by a curve $Y = F(X)$ such that it reduces the "residual variance" to its minimum possible value. The relative degree of reduction is measured by ρ^2. A perfect model would result in a perfect fit between the locus of the observed points in the figure and its plot, resulting in $s_e^2 = 0$, and the corresponding value for ρ^2 (and for ρ) would be zero; equivalently, the value for R^2 would be equal to 1.

Let us now apply these criteria to measure the efficiency of the logistic model fitted in Table 6.3. To compute the values of ρ^2 and of R^2, we first need to evaluate the variance $s_{\hat{Y}}^2$ of the observed values for the population levels This is easily obtained from Table 6.1 and formula (6.39):

$$\bar{\hat{Y}} = \tfrac{1}{8}(11 + 11.65 + \ldots + 15.95) = 13.41$$

$$s_{\hat{Y}}^2 = \frac{1}{n} \sum_i (\hat{Y}_i - \bar{\hat{Y}})^2 = \tfrac{1}{8}[(11 - 13.41)^2 + (11.65 - 13.41)^2 + \ldots$$
$$+ (15.95 - 13.41)^2] = 2.640$$

Therefore, for model 8, for which $s_e^2 = 4.299/8 = 0.537$, as computed in Table 6-3:

$$\rho^2 = \frac{s_e^2}{s_{\hat{Y}}^2} = \frac{0.537}{2.640} = 0.203$$

and

$$\rho = \sqrt{0.203} = 0.451$$

This result means that the typical error in the reproduction of the population levels using model 8 is only 45%, i.e., only about half the typical level of error that would be incurred if variations in population levels for the eight time periods were not taken into account and they were consequently all predicted to be equal to the average observed value of 13.41. Model 8 is in this sense, then, only about half "effective" with respect to a "perfect" model (i.e., 100% effective), for which ρ would equal 1.0.

Since $\rho^2 = 0.203$, the residual variance (or sum of squared errors) relative to the overall variability of the population levels is 20%. This means that the model is adequate, since it results in a typical squared error which is only about one-fifth of the squared fluctuations in the values to be reproduced. Here again, a perfect model would have an infinitely small relative error, i.e., a ρ^2 of 0.

Finally, the value of $R^2 = 1 - 0.203 = 0.797$ indicates that about 80% of the amount of variability contained in the sample of eight observed population levels has been "accounted for" by the model. In other words, if the variability in observed values is taken to represent the amount of information supplied about the population changes, this can be interpreted to mean that the model has incorporated, or "reproduced," 80% of that information. It is, in that sense, 80% successful, if the "model" corresponding to the raw, unreproduced observed data corresponds to an index of 100%.

Thus, these three related indicators ρ, ρ^2, and R^2 describe in various ways the *normalized efficiency*, or performance of the model. They can be applied, for instance, to comparisons of the model above with other models considered in the same calibration (see Exercise 6.19), or to other models (of the same type or not) calibrated on other sets of data.

It may also be interesting to evaluate the precision of the model in relation to the quality of the input data. More specifically, the question would be: What is the order to magnitude of the precision of the reproduced values in relation to the precision of the observed values? This can be measured by the ratio

$$\frac{s_e}{s_{\hat{Y}_t}} \tag{6.42}$$

where s_e is the standard error of estimate and $s_{\hat{Y}_t}$ represents the standard deviations of a single observed value (obtained, e.g., in the case above by making several measurements for the population level during a given time period i. This standard deviation is not to be confused with the standard deviation of the eight observed values $s_{\hat{Y}}$ used above.).

We would expect that for an "efficient" model, this ratio would be less than 1 and as close to zero as is possible. That is, the intrinsic error due to the model should be as small as possible relative to the error in the input data. Although this criterion is not "standardized," as are the others above, it may be useful in assessing the significance of the level of error of the prediction in relation to the reliability of the given information.

Let us now go on to the other criterion used in model calibration, the *log-likelihood function*. In this case, as above, it is logical to compare its value to the value it would take in the "worst" case of a prediction of all observed values equal to their average. The criterion L was defined as

$$L = \sum_{i=1}^{n} \hat{Y}_i \log P(Y_i) \qquad (6.43)$$

If all predicted values Y_i are equal to the constant $\bar{Y}$, the probability of Y_i is $1/m$, where m is the number of levels i of the variable Y (not to be confused with the number of observations). Therefore, the value of L in that (worst) prediction is

$$L_{\min} = \sum_{i=1}^{n} Y_i \log \frac{1}{m} = \log \frac{1}{m} \sum_{i=1}^{n} Y_i \qquad (6.44)$$

The case of "best" or optimal prediction is, of course, when all predicted values are equal to the observed values, i.e., $Y_i = \hat{Y}_i$ for all m values of i. The value of L in this other extreme case is then

$$L_{\max} = \sum_{i=1}^{n} \hat{Y}_i \log P(\hat{Y}_i) \qquad (6.45)$$

By comparing the value of the log-likelihood function at the termination of the calibration to these two extreme values, the efficiency of the model relative to the "best" and "worst" cases of prediction can then be assessed.

For instance, using the example of the calibration of the probit model of mode choice in Section 6.7, as represented in Table 6.6, the value of L for model 4 was equal to -667.97. Since the number of predictions m (i.e., the number of levels of delay) was equal to 7 and the values for the Y_i's from model 4 are given in the tenth row of Table 6.6, we can easily compute the value of $L_{\min}$ through formula (6.44). This is equal to $386 \log(\frac{1}{8}) = -802.66$.

Similarly, to compute the value of $L_{\max}$, we first need to compute the values of $P(\hat{Y}_i)$. This is simply $\hat{N}_i / \sum_i \hat{N}_i$, so that the corresponding values are easily obtained from Table 6.4 or row 15 of Table 6.6.

Combining the logarithms of these values according to formula (6.45) with those of the $\hat{N}_i$'s as given in Table 6.4, we get a value for L_{max} of -662.61. Thus, a scaled indicator of model efficiency between L_{min} and L_{max} could be, for instance,

$$\theta = \frac{L - L_{min}}{L_{max} - L_{min}} \qquad (6.46)$$

Its value would equal, in the case of model 2,

$$\frac{-667.97 + 802.66}{-662.61 + 802.66} = 0.962$$

Thus, although this scale is not linear (i.e., proportional to model efficiency), it could be said (very loosely) that model 2 is about 96 % efficient.

Therefore, if the maximum likelihood criterion is used, it can also be related to a comparative indicator θ of the overall precision of the model. (See Exercise 6.20.) However, this indicator is not as convenient as R^2, which we have seen above. This is principally because, as we shall see in Chapter 7, R^2 offers substantial advantages of simplicity when the model being evaluated has a linear form. Also, under certain conditions, the "distributional properties" of R^2 (in the sense that we have seen in Section 6.3) can be readily ascertained. This is not true of comparative indicators such as θ which are based on the log-likelihood value.

6.9 Functional Form Determination

We now turn to the last topic in this chapter, that of determining which among several possible choices is the most appropriate form for an unspecified function intervening in a model. We shall illustrate the approach to the solution of this problem in the case of the determination of the function $F(d_{ij})$ in the expression of the general gravity model (4.2). The question addressed in this section is thus how, on the basis of the observed values, to make a preliminary determination of the nature of the function $F(d_{ij})$ so that the values of its parameters can be determined, using the methods of Section 6.8.

The procedure consists of first defining levels or intervals of values I_i for the variable in the function $F(\cdot)$, i.e., here d_{ij}. Next, starting with initial guesses for the values of F in the various intervals, $F^1(I_i)$ (the "friction" or "impedance" factors), the model is applied to compute a first round of predicted values T_{ij}. These values will in all probability be different from the observed values $\hat{T}_{ij}$. The next step is then to adjust the factors $F^1(I_i)$ in each of the intervals I_i so that the sum of the predicted values in each interval equals the sum of the observed values. This is achieved when

$$F^2(I_t) = F^1(I_t)\left(\frac{\sum_{I_t} \hat{T}_{ij}}{\sum_{I_t} T_{ij}^1}\right) \tag{6.47}$$

since T_{ij} is proportional to $F(d_{ij})$, as stipulated in (4.2). The procedure is iterated (i.e., the model applied again to compute the next round of predicted values), and the values of $F^2(I_t)$ are adjusted as $F^3(I_t)$ according to (6.47), etc., until there is sufficient stabilization of the values of $F^k(I_t)$ in all intervals from iteration number k to $k+1$. When this has been done, a plot of the final values $F^{k+1}(d_{ij})$ for $F(\cdot)$ against the values of the variable d_{ij} will indicate in which family of standard, common mathematical forms the function $F(\cdot)$ belongs.

Let us apply this procedure in the following case. Assume that the data in Table 6.7 represent the number of workers E_j, the total residential populations P_i in a three-zone region, the distances between zones d_{ij}, and the observed number of commuters between regions $\hat{T}_{ij}$. The units are 1000 people for T_{ij}, E_j, and P_i, and miles for d_{ij}.

TABLE 6.7

	d_{ij}			$\hat{T}_{ij}$						
$j =$	1	2	3	1	2	3	i	P_i	j	E_j
$i = 1$	2	7	4	3.0	0.10	2.85	1	30	1	4
2	8	1	5	0.15	1.45	0.90	2	15	2	2
3	5	4	3	0.85	0.45	3.25	3	25	3	7

On the basis of these data, we want to fit to the pattern of commuting to work a one-way gravity model of the form

$$T_{ij} = l_j E_j P_i F(d_{ij}) \tag{6.48/4.10}$$

or, in its equivalent form, when the balancing factor l_j is explicitly expressed,

$$T_{ij} = E_j\left[\frac{P_i F(d_{ij})}{\sum_i P_i F(d_{ij})}\right] \tag{6.49/4.14}$$

(Note that since only the numbers of workers E_j are given, i.e., the levels of "travel production" of the zones, the one-way or single-constraint form of the gravity model is appropriate.) The unknown in the model is now the expression for $F(d_{ij})$. [It may be recalled that this was assumed to be $F(d_{ij}) = d_{ij}^{-1}$ in the illustrative example of the one-way gravity model in Section 4.3.]

The first step is to define intervals for the variable d_{ij} in the function. Let us choose three levels:

I_1: d_{ij} between 0 and 3.0 inclusive $(0 \leq d_{ij} \leq 3.0)$

I_2: d_{ij} between 3.1 and 6.0 $(3.1 \leq d_{ij} \leq 6.0)$

I_3: d_{ij} between 6.1 and 10.0 $(6.1 \leq d_{ij} \leq 10.0)$

Thus, the couples of interracting zones (i, j) corresponding to these three intervals are, respectively,

$$
\begin{aligned}
I_1&: \quad (11); (22); (33) \\
I_2&: \quad (13); (23); (31); (32) \qquad\qquad (6.50) \\
I_3&: \quad (12); (21)
\end{aligned}
$$

Next, we choose initial values for the values of the function $F(d_{ij})$. Although we do not know the definition of $F(d_{ij})$ (that is precisely the object of the procedure), from (6.48) we know that $F(d_{ij})$, whatever its expression, should have values such that

$$
F(d_{ij}) = \frac{\hat{T}_{ij}}{l_j E_j P_i} \qquad (6.51)
$$

Now, we do not know the values of the l_j's [since at (6.49) or (4.12) show they are equal to $[\sum_i P_i F(d_{ij})]^{-1}$, and thus they are dependent on the expression of $F(d_{ij})$], but we know the values of the E_j's and P_i's as well as those of the $\hat{T}_{ij}$'s. Thus, as starting values for $F(d_{ij})$, and ignoring l_j in (6.48), we may choose the values

$$
F^1(d_{ij}) = \frac{\hat{T}_{ij}}{E_j P_i} \qquad (6.52)
$$

Since we are not estimating the values of $F(d_{ij})$ for every value of d_{ij} but only within the three intervals I_i specified in (6.50), the corresponding starting values are

$$
F^1(d_{ij}) = \text{average in } I_i \text{ of } \left(\frac{\hat{T}_{ij}}{E_j P_i} \right) \qquad (6.53)
$$

where the superscript for F refers to the iteration number and the subscript for I refers to the interval number. The corresponding values for $F^1(I_i)$ are given in Table 6.8. We now have a set of first-approximation values for $F(d_{ij})$, as represented in Table 6.9.

TABLE 6.8   Values for $\hat{T}_{ij}/E_j P_i$

$(i, j) =$	(1, 1)	(1, 2)	(1,3)	(2, 1)	(2, 2)	(2, 3)	(3, 1)	(3, 2)	(3, 3)	Total	$F^1(I_i)$ = Average
Interval I_1	0.025				0.048				0.019	0.092	0.031
I_2			0.014			0.009	0.009	0.009		0.040	0.001
I_3		0.002		0.002						0.004	0.002

TABLE 6.9   Values for $F^1(d_{ij})$

$i =$	$j =$ 1	2	3
1	0.031	0.002	0.001
2	0.002	0.031	0.001
3	0.001	0.001	0.031

Next, we apply the model (6.49) using these values for the $F(d_{ij})$, following the procedure described the illustrative example of Section 4.3 (which will not be presented in detail again here), to obtain the set of first predicted values for the T_{ij}'s. The resulting values are given in Table 6.10. This first set of

TABLE 6.10   Values of T^1_{ij}

$i =$	$j =$ 1	2	3
1	3.08	0.16	1.75
2	0.12	1.26	0.84
3	0.80	0.58	4.41

predicted values for the T_{ij}'s is, of course, different from the corresponding values T_{ij} given in Table 6.7. This is because the unknown exact values for the factors $F(d_{ij})$ have only been approximated, in order to get started. We will now adjust the values for $F(d_{ij})$ according to formula (6.47). Thus, we next compute the sums of the T^1_{ij} in each of the three intervals:

$$\sum_{I_1} T^1_{ij} = T^1_{11} + T^1_{22} + T^1_{33} = 3.08 + 1.26 + 4.41 = 8.75$$

$$\sum_{I_2} T^1_{ij} = T^1_{13} + T^1_{23} + T^1_{31} + T^1_{32} = 1.75 + 0.84 + 0.80 + 0.58$$
$$= 3.97$$

$$\sum_{I_3} T^1_{ij} = T^1_{12} + T^1_{21} = 0.16 + 0.12 = 0.28$$

The corresponding sums for the observed values are, from Table 6.7,

$$\sum_{I_1} \hat{T}_{ij} = 3 + 1.45 + 3.25 = 7.70$$

$$\sum_{I_2} \hat{T}_{ij} = 2.85 + 0.90 + 0.85 + 0.45 = 5.05$$

$$\sum_{I_3} \hat{T}_{ij} = 0.10 + 0.15 = 0.25$$

We now adjust the values of $F^1(I_i)$ according to (6.47), to obtain the second-round approximation values:

$$F^2(I_1) = F^1(I_1)\left(\frac{\sum_{I_1} \hat{T}_{ij}}{\sum_{I_1} T_{ij}^1}\right) = 0.031\left(\frac{7.70}{8.75}\right) = 0.027$$

$$F^2(I_2) = F^1(I_2)\left(\frac{\sum_{I_2} \hat{T}_{ij}}{\sum_{I_2} T_{ij}^1}\right) = 0.010\left(\frac{5.05}{3.97}\right) = 0.013$$

$$F^2(I_3) = F^1(I_3)\left(\frac{\sum_{I_3} \hat{T}_{ij}}{\sum_{I_3} T_{ij}^1}\right) = 0.002\left(\frac{0.25}{0.28}\right) = 0.002$$

Let us decide, based, for instance, on the results of an analysis of the reliability of the measurements for the T_{ij}'s using the techniques of Section 6.3, that we can meaningfully carry up to three decimal points (i.e., a precision of 10^{-3}). Under these conditions, the second-round approximation values for the function $F(d_{ij})$ are not equal to those of the previous iteration. Therefore, we have not obtained the final values and we iterate the procedure. Using the new values $F^2(d_{ij})$, the second round of predicted values T_{ij}'s are then evaluated, as given in Table 6.11. The values for the sums $\sum_{I_i} T_{ij}^2$ are, therefore,

$$\sum_{I_1} T_{ij}^2 = 7.54 \qquad \sum_{I_2} T_{ij}^2 = 5.18 \qquad \sum_{I_3} T_{ij}^2 = 0.28$$

so that

$$F^3(I_1) = F^2(I_1)\left(\frac{\sum_{I_1} \hat{T}_{ij}}{\sum_{I_1} T_{ij}^2}\right) = 0.027\left(\frac{7.70}{7.54}\right) = 0.027$$

$$F^3(I_2) = F^2(I_2)\left(\frac{\sum_{I_2} \hat{T}_{ij}}{\sum_{I_2} T_{ij}^2}\right) = 0.013\left(\frac{5.05}{5.18}\right) = 0.013$$

$$F^3(I_3) = F^2(I_3)\left(\frac{\sum_{I_3} \hat{T}_{ij}}{\sum_{I_3} T_{ij}^2}\right) = 0.002\left(\frac{0.25}{0.28}\right) = 0.002$$

TABLE 6.11   Values for T_{ij}^2

$i =$	$j =$ 1	2	3
1	2.76	0.16	2.17
2	0.12	1.00	1.05
3	1.12	0.84	3.78

These values are (within rounding to the third decimal point) equal to the previous ones. Therefore, we have obtained the final values for $F(d_{ij})$.

In order to determine the expression for $F(d_{ij})$, we may now plot the variations of $F(d_{ij})$ across the various intervals I_t as shown in Figure 6.6. The shape of this plot suggests that the function $F(d_{ij})$ might be of the *negative exponential* form (4.6), which we have already seen in Figure 2.3, i.e., $F(d_{ij}) = e^{-\beta d_{ij}}$, or perhaps of the *hyperbolic* form (4.5), $F(d_{ij}) = d_{ij}^{-\gamma}$.

To determine which of these forms applies, we might compute a few representative values for these two types of functions for various values of their parameters. A comparison of the resulting plots against the graph in Figure 6.6 will then indicate which specific function gives the best approximation.

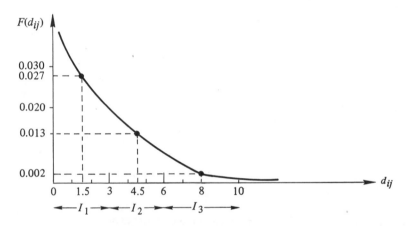

Figure 6.6 Plot of the unknown function $F(d_{ij})$.

Another approach, if we decide, for instance, to try an exponential function, is to make use of its characteristic property that the plot of the logarithms of its values is linear. [This property has already been used in connection with the exponential model of population projection (2.4) and Figure 2.3.] Let us therefore plot the logarithms of the values for $F(d_{ij})$.

The resulting plot, for the three values of d_{ij} corresponding to the middle of the intervals I_1, I_2, and I_3 (i.e., 1.5, 4.5, and 8, respectively), is shown in Figure 6.7. Since this plot is (approximately) linear, the unknown function $F(d_{ij})$ must be of the form

$$F(d_{ij}) = e^{-\gamma d_{ij}}$$

where the value of the parameter γ is equal to the negative slope of the straight line. This is approximately equal to

$$\gamma = \frac{F(8) - F(1.5)}{8.0 - 1.5} = \frac{-6.21 + 3.61}{8.0 - 1.5} = -0.4$$

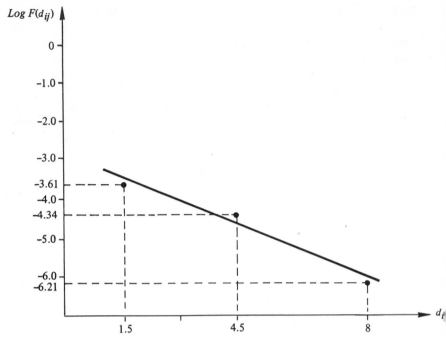

Figure 6.7   Plot of the unknown function using the logarithms.

The function $F(d_{ij})$ is therefore approximated by the expression

$$F(d_{ij}) = e^{-0.4d_{ij}}$$

and the gravity model of the form (6.49) that best describes the commuting pattern given in Table 6.7 can now be completely specified as

$$T_{ij} = E_j \left(\frac{P_i e^{-0.4d_{ij}}}{\sum_i P_i e^{-0.4d_{ij}}} \right) \tag{6.54}$$

It is interesting to note that in this particular instance, the determination of the form of the function $F(d_{ij})$ has also resulted in the identification of the value of the parameter γ. In other words, although this is not always the case for all practical purposes, the calibration of the model has also been achieved. In any event, we can now try to further refine the fitting of the model by using the calibration methods of Sections 6.6 and 6.7 for an unspecified value of the parameter γ, in a range of values around 0.4. (See Exercise 6.17.)

EXERCISES

6.1 In connection with the development of a regional employment multiplier model of the form (3.46), the work-force ratios need to be estimated. Past censuses indicate that in a given area, the percentage of employed people is of the order of 20%, or 0.20.

(a) What would be the level of magnitude of the error that could be expected on the estimation of the true value of the work-force ratio if a sample of 100 people is surveyed?

(b) Now assume that such a survey is conducted, and that the observed value of the percentage of employed people is found to be 23%. Give an estimation interval for the true value (in the overall population) of this percentage, at a level of confidence of 95%.

(c) Finally, although this was ignored in first approximation, the size of the population of the region is only 850. Does this appreciably affect the estimate, and if so, by how much?

6.2 Data concerning the average per capita income in a given area are required for the development of a travel demand generation model of the form (4.56). A previous survey resulted in an estimate of $7500 for this value, together with a standard deviation of $1500. In order to determine whether there is a need for revising this estimate, and therefore to engage in another survey effort, a limited survey of 100 individuals shows that the average per capita income is now $7900. If the desired maximum level of error on the estimation of this quantity is 10%, does the result indicate that the true value has changed since the last survey, and that therefore there should be a new one? (Choose a level of confidence of 98% for your conclusions.)

6.3 As input into a shift-and-share model of economic activity forecast of the form (3.54) to (3.56), the difference between the rate of employment growth in a given area and in the entire region is being estimated as a measure of the "shift" of the area. Suppose that the regional value is a reliable estimate (i.e., a true value). Assume also that the local estimate comes from a sufficiently large number of production measurements that it can be assumed to be normally distributed. Finally, the order of magnitude of the standard deviation of the local rate of growth has historically been about 0.25%. Given this information, what is the level of potential error on an estimate of the differential rate of growth if a level of confidence of 95% is desired?

6.4 For the circumstances described in Exercise 6.3, suppose that both the regional and the local rates of growth were obtained from large samples of measurements of the production of industries and enterprises. How does this affect the resulting precision on the estimation of the differential rate?

6.5 In the situation described in Exercise 6.3, how would the precision be affected if the numbers of industries surveyed could only be equal to 15 and 25, locally and regionally, respectively?

6.6   If you suspect that the proportion of residents in a certain community who work outside it is approximately 75%, how many cases do you need to obtain a 95% confidence estimation interval for the true value of that proportion that will be no wider than 0.03, or 3 percentage points (i.e., a maximum error of $\pm 1.5\%$)?

6.7   A poll of 200 households in a certain area indicates that 54% of them have two or more cars. Can it be assumed, for example for the purpose of devising groups to perform a category analysis of travel demand of the type (4.55), that this is also true in the overall population?

6.8   How would the results of the estimation on the proportion of areas in favor of the mass transit system in the illustrative example of Section 6.5 (which was conducted using the binomial distribution) be affected if the sample size were not 10 but 50?

6.9   (a)   Going back to the example of the application of the Tchebyscheff approximation to the level of error, formula (6.3), compute the values of the error for various levels of confidence between 0.99 and 0.50.

       (b)   Represent the results graphically and elaborate on their practical implications for estimation procedures.

6.10   (a)   Continuing Exercise 6.9, represent graphically the variations of the level of error as a function of the sample size when the level of confidence is fixed at 0.90.

       (b)   On the same figure, represent these variations when the level of confidence is fixed at 0.98.

       (c)   Draw conclusions as to the trade-off between sample size and the level of confidence for a desired level of precision.

6.11   Repeat Exercise 6.9 when (as in the follow-up of the illustrative example in the text) the normal approximation is used instead of the Tchebyscheff approximation. Elaborate on the differences between the results of the two approaches.

6.12   Repeat Exercise 6.10, using the normal approximation. Compare with the results of the use of the Tchebyscheff approximation.

6.13   To develop an input/output model for a region, the proportion of the production of a given sector j that is consumed by another sector i has been on the average approximately 0.20 (20%), with a standard deviation of 0.05 (5%). Since this corresponds to a relative error of $5/20 = 25\%$, it is desired to improve this estimate of the true value of this coefficient by changing the survey size accordingly. Under those conditions, what would be the required sample size to achieve a precision of $\pm 2.5\%$ (i.e., 2.5 percentage points on either side of the observed value)?

6.14   Using the data in Table 6.1 for the illustrative example of the use of the minimum-sum-of-squares criterion for parameter calibration, try the other models corresponding to other values of the two parameters in Table 6.2 to try to improve upon the performance of model 8. Is there a better model fit?

6.15   Verify that (as was assumed in the illustrative example for the doubly constrained gravity model of Section 4.4) the values of the parameters $\alpha = 2$
and $\beta = 0.5$ are optimal in terms of the calibration of the model

$$T_{ij} = k_i l_j D_i O_j d_{ij}^{\alpha} e^{-\beta d_{ij}}$$

to fit the data presented in Tables 4.5 and 4.6. [*Advice:* Try other combinations of values for the parameters, and compute the log-likelihood function,
as given by formula (6.21), with the values output by the model. Then verify
that the value of the function is less than that for the combination $\alpha = 2$
and $\beta = 0.5$.]

6.16   Using the data for the illustration of the use of the maximum likelihood
criterion method of calibration given in Tables 6.4 and 6.6, determine whether
a better model than model 4 can be found.

6.17   Using the result of the example in Section 6.9—that the function $F(d_{ij})$ in
the one-way gravity model (6.48) is an exponential function of the form
$F(d_{ij}) = e^{-\alpha d_{ij}}$ and the data given in Table 6.7—confirm that the exponent
α has a value of approximately 0.4, by calibrating the model using one of
the methods of Sections 6.6 and 6.7.

6.18   Go back to Exercises 6.14 to 6.17, and whenever one of the calibration criteria
was used (sum of squares or log-likelihood function), use the other and
compare both sets of results.

6.19   Compare the relative efficiency of logistic model 2 developed in the illustrative example (Table 6.3) to that of model 8, using the criteria R, R^2,
ρ, and ρ^2.

6.20   Use the criterion defined by (6.46) to compare the performances of the two
modal split models developed in Table 6.6.

REFERENCES

BATTY, M. *Urban Modeling.* New York: Cambridge University Press, 1976.

BATTY, M., AND S. MACKIE. "The Calibration of Gravity, Entropy and Related
Models of Spatial Interaction." *Environment and Planning*, 4 (1972), 131–150.

BLALOCK, H. *Social Statistics*, 2nd ed. New York: McGraw-Hill Book Company,
1972.

HOEL, P. *Introduction to Mathematical Statistics*, 4th ed. New York: John Wiley
& Sons, Inc., 1971.

MENDENHALL, W., R. L. OTT, AND R. L. SCHEAFFER. *Elementary Survey Sampling.*
Belmont, Calif.: Wadsworth Publishing Company, Inc., 1971.

NIE, N. H., C. H. HULL, J. G. JENKINS, K. STEINBRENNER, AND D. H. BENT. *SPSS:
Statistical Package for the Social Sciences* 2nd ed. New York: McGraw-Hill
Book Company, 1975.

OPENSHAW, S. "An Empirical Study of Some Spatial Interaction Models." *Environment and Planning*, 8 (1976), 23–42.

WILLIAMS, I. "A Comparison of Some Calibration Techniques for Doubly Constrained Gravity Models with an Exponential Cost Function." *Transportation Research*, 10 (1976), 91–104.

7

Linear Regression Modeling

7.1 Introduction

The final chapter in this text will be devoted to a special type of model: the *statistical regression model*. Several characteristics distinguish this type of model from the analytical models we have seen in preceding chapters. First, all the previous models were developed deductively; that is, they were derived mathematically from specifically stated assumptions. Thus, they were built theoretically, and independently of empirical considerations, although empirical evidence was used to calibrate and test them.

On the contrary, the type of model we are going to examine in this chapter is built empirically. More specifically, whereas the deductive theoretical models proceed from the general (model building) to the specific (model calibration), inductive statistical models result from calibrating standard mathematical models (such as the linear form) to given empirical situations, as represented by observational data. Deductive models can be considered to be *causal*, in the sense that they represent the "explanation," in terms of formulas, of the relationships between variables and parameters (e.g., the effect of birth and death rates on the growth of population). Inductive models are descriptive, in that they represent the identification of joint patterns of variations (not necessarily always with meaning, but sufficiently reliable to be operational) among the variables.

An important operational advantage of statistical regression models is that (provided that data are available) their development can always be attempted a priori, i.e., in the absence of insights into the nature of the relationship between the variables, as is required for the deductive models. This very convenient characteristic for the purposes of modeling should not be made to replace, or worse supersede, the need for an ex-post-facto rational validation of the model. In other words, although a deductive model is in principle preferable if it is possible to build it, an inductive statistical approach may result in a heuristic model that can then be used for operational purposes as well as for further investigation of the phenomenon it deals with.

Another important difference between the regression models and the theoretical models is that, as we shall see later, the regression models will be automatically calibrated. More precisely, the process of model building in this case is equivalent to the process of model calibration, since the regression models result from the direct fitting of ready-made "forms" to specific situations. Furthermore, in the special case of *linear regression models* (to which we shall confine this chapter), the form of the models allows the use of standardized measures of their fit. This, contrary to the criteria we have used in Sections 6.6 and 6.7, will allow for comparative model performance assessments. Finally, under certain conditions, linear regression models also provide for built-in measures of precision regarding the estimation of parameter values in the probabilistic sense that we have seen in Sections 6.3 to 6.5.

These features make linear regression models extremely useful from an operational point of view and compensate, in a sense, for their lack of explanatory power. Also, the fact that the regression models are nonsubstantive, i.e., that they are not restricted to application to a specific area of planning and analysis, such as population analysis or economic analysis, further enhances their practical appeal.

7.2   The Method of Least Squares for the Calibration of Linear Regression Models

Let us now present the simplest case of a statistical regression model, that of a linear model in two or more variables. This model postulates a priori the existence of a linear relationship between the *predicted* variable Y, and a set of *predicting* variables X_i of the form

$$Y = a_0 + a_1 X_1 + a_2 X_2 + \ldots + a_i X_i + \ldots + \ldots + a_n X_n \quad (7.1)$$

A linear model thus specifies that the (*dependent*) variable Y is a linear function of the (*independent*) variables X_i.

We have already seen a number of examples of relationships of this form between quantities intervening in some of the models in previous chapters. However, it is important to distinguish between the origins of such linear formulations in these cases. For instance, the linear model (2.1) of *population projection* was derived analytically from the statement of the mechanisms of growth. The regional employment multiplier models (3.51) to (3.53), which represent sets of linear relationships between the variables, were also rationally derived from the implications of specific assumptions about the effects of new jobs. The models were conceptual and were validated (or refuted) against empirical evidence, through the process of calibration.

On the other hand, the linear model intervened in a different fashion in conjunction with several substantive areas. For instance, the *travel demand generation model* (4.56) assumed that the level of travel generated by a given zone was a linear function of its characteristics. The *shift-and-share model* of economic regional forecasting postulated that the regional shifts in employment levels were linear functions of the population levels of the regions. In both these cases, the choice of a linear model is primarily motivated by the fact that this is the simplest form that a potential mathematical relationship can take. Therefore, although in some cases they may well empirically "work," and thus approximate a more elaborate and rationally valid description of the relationship between the variables, the use of linear models in this latter case will be primarily justified by a close calibration to the given data.

Let us therefore describe the procedure for the development of a linear regression model in a practical case beginning with the simplest linear model, a model in two variables (sometimes called the *univariate* linear model) of the form

$$Y = a_0 + a_1 X \qquad (7.2)$$

Let us assume that we have surveyed a sample of 10 areas ($i = 1$ to 10) and that the observed levels of mass transit trips per day generated in the zones Y_i, as well as the levels of total residential population of the zones X_i, were recorded as given in Table 7.1. Naturally, we could apply the general methods of model calibration of Sections 6.6 and 6.7 to this particular case. (See Exercise 7.1.) However, the fact that the model has a linear form, combined

TABLE 7.1

Zone, i	1	2	3	4	5	6	7	8	9	10	$\sum\limits_i$
Population, X_i (thousands)	40	60	80	20	40	60	80	40	20	60	500
Number of transit trips, Y_i (thousands)	6.0	7.5	9.6	4.0	5.4	6.8	8.7	6.4	4.8	8.0	67.2

with the use of the first criterion, S (the minimum sum of squared errors), results in very advantageous special features.

First, the use of the method of least sum of squared errors for the calibration of linear models affords another major advantage over the use of other criteria and/or other forms of models. Specifically, standard measures of the performance of the model can be derived *prior* to the development of the model, or as by-products of the calibration of the model. Consequently, the overall precision of a potential linear model can be assessed immediately on the basis of the observed values alone, and not, as we have done in Chapter 6, after the model has been calibrated and applied to compute the predicted values. This powerful advantage of linear models of the form (7.2) over other models is due to the fact that the parameters a_i can be expressed analytically in terms of the observed values of the variables, as we shall see later, and consequently, the predicted values Y_i, which are themselves [through (7.2)] simple expressions of the parameter values, can also be expressed as functions of the observed values. Therefore, the errors (differences between observed and predicted values), and thus the efficiency of the model as measured by the criteria R or R^2 can also be evaluated before the actual calibration of the model, using the observed values only.

To summarize, as was noted above, although R and R^2 or related measures such as ρ^2 can be used in connection with any type of predictive model, the fundamental advantage of the use of a linear model is that, if a model of the form (7.2) is to be fitted to a set of data $(\hat{X}_i, \hat{Y}_i)$, for instance, as given in Table 7.1, using the minimum-sum-of-squared-errors criterion, the resulting precision of the model can be evaluated on the basis of the values of only the $\hat{X}_i$'s and $\hat{Y}_i$'s. This very advantageous feature of linear models therefore allows us to determine the highest level of precision (minimum level of error) that can be hoped for. This can then be used as the basis for the decision of whether the development of the model is warranted. It can be shown in the case of linear models of the form (7.2) that R^2 can be computed as

$$R^2 = \frac{\left[\sum_{i=1}^{n} (\hat{X}_i - \bar{X})(\hat{Y}_i - \bar{Y})\right]^2}{\left[\sum_{i=1}^{n} (\hat{X}_i - \bar{X})^2\right]\left[\sum_{i=1}^{n} (\hat{Y}_i - \bar{Y})^2\right]} \tag{7.3}$$

Alternatively, it can be shown that the value of R, the square root of R^2 (which is called the *coefficient of linear correlation*), can be computed as

$$R = \frac{\frac{1}{n} \sum_i \hat{X}_i \hat{Y}_i - \left(\frac{1}{n} \sum_i \hat{X}_i\right)\left(\frac{1}{n} \sum_i \hat{Y}_i\right)}{\sqrt{\frac{1}{n} \sum_i (\hat{X}_i - \bar{X})^2} \sqrt{\frac{1}{n} \sum_i (\hat{Y}_i - \bar{Y}_i)^2}} \tag{7.4}$$

where the $\hat{Y}_i$'s and the $\hat{X}_i$'s are the n observed values ($i = 1, \ldots n$) for the variables Y and X, respectively, and $\bar{Y}$ and $\bar{X}$ the corresponding averages.

(Note that these formulas do not include the predicted values Y_i for Y.) Also, in spite of their forbidding appearance, these expressions are in fact rather simple, since using the expressions for the sample variance for the $\hat{Y}_i$'s and the $\hat{X}_i$'s, they can be simplified to

$$R^2 = \frac{\left[\sum_{i=1}^{n} (\hat{X}_i - \bar{X})(\hat{Y}_i - \bar{Y})\right]}{(ns_{\hat{x}}^2)(ns_{\hat{y}}^2)} \qquad (7.5)$$

and

$$R = \frac{(\overline{\hat{X}\hat{Y}}) - (\bar{X})(\bar{Y})}{s_{\hat{x}}s_{\hat{y}}} \qquad (7.6)$$

Furthermore, it can be shown that, in the case of linear models, the values of R^2 will be between 0 and 1, corresponding to worst and best (linear) fit, respectively. (See Exercise 7.23.) Correspondingly, the values of R will be between -1 and 0 (for negatively sloped models) or between 0 and $+1$ (for positively sloped models). The fact that the variations and R^2 for linear models are within the fixed interval from 0 to 1 makes R^2 a "universal" scale for measuring the effectiveness of the linear model. This is not true for any model, where the lower bound for R^2 could be any negative value (if s_e^2 is greater than $s_{\hat{y}}^2$), although the maximum value of R^2 is also 1 (when $s_e^2 = 0$).

As an example of the application of the foregoing formulas, let us determine the level of error of the best linear model in two variables of the form (7.2) which can be fitted to the data in Table 7.1. We need to compute the values of the various terms that appear in the expression(s) for R^2 (and R). The results are presented in Table 7.2. Therefore,

$$\bar{X} = \frac{1}{n}\sum_i \hat{X}_i = \frac{500}{10} = 50 \qquad \bar{Y} = \frac{1}{n}\sum_i \hat{Y}_i = 6.72$$

$$s_{\hat{x}}^2 = \frac{1}{n}\sum_i (\hat{X}_i - \bar{X})^2 = 420 \qquad s_{\hat{y}}^2 = \frac{1}{n}\sum_i (\hat{Y}_i - \bar{Y})^2 = 2.79$$

From formula (7.3), the value of R^2 is therefore

$$R^2 = \frac{(330)^2}{(4200)(27.9)} = 0.93$$

Alternatively, we might have used formula (7.4) or its compact version, (7.6). The only new term we need to compute is $\sum_i \hat{X}_i\hat{Y}_i$. This is easily found to be equal to 3690. Thus, the value of R would be

$$R = \frac{1}{10}\frac{(3690) - (50)(6.72)}{\sqrt{4200/10}\sqrt{27.9/10}} = 0.96$$

so that $R^2 = (0.96)^2 = 0.93$. (It is worth noting that, as expected, the value of R^2 is found between 0 and 1, and that the value of R is between -1 and $+1$.

TABLE 7.2

$i =$	1	2	3	4	5	6	7	8	9	10	$\sum_i$
$\hat{X}_i - \bar{X}$	-10	10	30	-30	-10	10	30	-10	-30	10	
$(\hat{X}_i - \bar{X}_i)^2$	100	100	900	900	100	100	900	100	900	100	4200
$(\hat{Y}_i - \bar{Y}_i)$	-0.72	0.78	2.88	-2.72	-1.32	0.08	1.98	-0.32	-1.92	1.28	
$(\hat{Y}_i - \bar{Y}_i)^2$	0.52	0.61	8.29	7.40	1.47	0.01	3.92	0.10	3.67	1.64	27.90
$(\hat{X}_i - \bar{X})$ $\cdot (\hat{Y}_i - \bar{Y})$	7.2	7.8	86.4	81.6	13.2	0.8	59.4	3.2	57.6	12.8	330

Having found otherwise would have meant that a computational error had occurred.)

In the same sense as in Chapter 6, this value for R^2 can now be interpreted to mean that 93% of the variations in the observed values of the zonal levels of transit trip making would be "reproduced" by the best linear model which can be fitted to the data in Table 7.1. In other words, a model of the form (7.2) would be 93% "effective." The value of ρ^2 is equal to

$$\rho^2 = 1 - R^2 = 1 - 0.93 = 0.07$$

This means that the *residual variance* s_e^2 (the average squared error) would only be equal to 7% of the variance $s_{\hat{Y}}^2$. Thus, the reproductive power of the model relative to the amount of information provided is fairly high. Another measure of the precision of the model to be developed would be the ratio of the standard error of estimate s_e (the square root of the residual variance s_e^2) to the standard deviation $s_{\hat{Y}}$ of the observed values. This indicator, sometimes called the *coefficient of determination*, measures the prediction error from the model as a percentage of the error in prediction when using the "worst" model, as seen in Chapter 6. This ratio is simply equal to the square root of ρ^2,

$$\boxed{\rho = \frac{s_e}{s_{\hat{Y}}} = \sqrt{1 - R^2}} \qquad (7.7)$$

in this case, $\sqrt{0.07} = 0.26$. This value can be interpreted to mean that the order of magnitude of the prediction error using the best possible linear model (7.2) is only about 26% of the error that would be made when the information represented by the model is not used, i.e., when all values for the zonal trip levels are predicted to be equal to the mean of the observed values, $\bar{Y} = 6.72$. Equivalently, the use of a linear model (7.2) for prediction purposes would result in a reduction of $100 - 26 = 74\%$ of the error in a prediction made in this worst case.

Let us now assume that, based on these results, we decide to go ahead with the calibration of the model. Here, again, the methods of Chapter 6 can be used. In particular, this calibration can be performed empirically, using an "eyeball" graphical procedure, by plotting the values of the observed levels of transit trip making versus the levels of population, and fitting a straight line to the resulting plot, as represented on Figure 7.1.

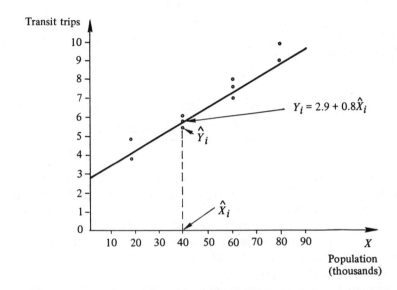

Figure 7.1   Plot of the linear regression.

Since the value of the parameter a_0 in (7.2) is represented by the Y-axis *intercept* and the value of a_1 by the *slope* of the straight line, we see that an approximate heuristic model would be

$$Y = 2.9 + 0.8X$$

However, the other very attractive advantage of the use of linear models, in conjunction with the minimum-sum-of-squares criterion for calibration, is that the values of the parameters can be determined analytically, i.e., "exactly," without the drawbacks of the trial-and-error approach used in Chapter 6 (such as guessing the original range of values of the parameters, in which direction to change their subsequent values, when to stop the search procedure, etc.). (See Exercise 7.1.)

The translation of the minimum sum of squared error condition, in the case of the univariate linear model (7.2), results in two simple equations in the two unknown parameters. Going directly to the solution of these two equations, in terms of the observed values $\hat{X}_i$ and $\hat{Y}_i$, the values of a_0 and

a_1 in (7.2) are, respectively, equal to

$$a_1 = \frac{\sum_{i=1}^{n} (\hat{Y}_i - \bar{Y})(\hat{X}_i - \bar{X})}{\sum_{i=1}^{n} (\hat{X}_i - \bar{X})^2} \tag{7.8}$$

$$a_0 = \bar{Y} - b\bar{X} \tag{7.9}$$

with the same notation as in formulas (7.3) and (7.4) for R and R^2. Alternatively (see Exercise 7.3), a_0 and a_1 can also be expressed as

$$a_1 = \frac{n(\sum_i \hat{X}_i \hat{Y}_i) - (\sum_i \hat{X}_i)(\sum_i \hat{Y}_i)}{n(\sum_i \hat{X}_i^2) - (\sum_i \hat{X}_i)^2} \tag{7.10}$$

$$a_0 = \frac{n(\sum_i \hat{X}_i)^2(\sum_i \hat{Y}_i) - (\sum_i \hat{X}_i)(\sum_i \hat{X}_i \hat{Y}_i)}{n(\sum_i \hat{X}_i^2) - (\sum_i \hat{X}_i)^2} \tag{7.11}$$

Let us illustrate the exact calibration procedure for the linear models in the case of the data in Table 7.1. It is worth noting that the terms that appear in the expressions of the parameters a_0 and a_1 have already all been computed above, for the determination of the value of R^2. Thus, another very useful feature of linear models is that their calibration requires only a minimal amount of additional computational work, after the prior determination of their precision has been performed.

In any case, using the results presented in Table 7.2, and using, for instance, formulas (7.8) and (7.9), we obtain

$$a_1 = \frac{\sum_i (\hat{X}_i - \bar{X})(\hat{Y}_i - \bar{Y})}{\sum_i (\hat{X}_i - \bar{X})^2} = \frac{330}{4200} = 0.0786$$

and

$$a_0 = \bar{Y} - a_1\bar{X} = 6.72 - 0.0786(50) = 2.79$$

Therefore, the best linear model of the number of transit trips Y_i per day in a given zone i, as a function of its population X_i, is

$$Y_i = 2.79 + 0.0786 X_i \tag{7.12}$$

The same expression for the model would have been obtained using the alternative formulas (7.10) and (7.11). (See Exercise 7.4.)

As stated above, another attractive property of the linear models is that the evaluation of their level of precision can, alternatively, be obtained simultaneously with the results of the calibration. Specifically, the value for R^2 (again when resulting from the minimization of the sum of squared errors) can be expressed in terms of the parameter a_1 of the model and of the observed data. That is, mathematical manipulation shows that when the parameters a_0 and a_1 have the values in formulas (7.8) and (7.9) or (7.10) and (7.11), the value of R can be expressed as

$$R = a_1 \frac{s_{\hat{X}}}{s_{\hat{Y}}} \tag{7.13}$$

Thus, formula (7.13) allow us to compute the value of the indicator R^2 from the observed values $\hat{Y}_i$ and $\hat{X}_i$ after the model is calibrated, without computing the predicted values Y_i.

For instance, let us evaluate the precision of model (7.12) developed in the illustrative example above. We have already computed the values of the respective samples variances $s_{\hat{X}}^2$ and $s_{\hat{Y}}^2$ for X and for Y in Table 7.2. Therefore, the value for R^2, using formula (7.13), is equal to

$$R = \frac{(0.0786)\sqrt{420}}{\sqrt{2.79}} = 0.96$$

and we retrieve the previously computed value.

A few comments are in order at this point. First, the evaluation of the precision of the model can, of course, be conducted using the methods outlined in Chapter 6, i.e., directly form the 10 predicted values for the levels of transit usage. The value of R^2, as given, for example, by formula (6.41), would be found to be the same. (See Exercise 7.5.)

Also, if the other criterion, the log-likelihood value, were used instead of the minimum sum of squares to determine the values of the parameters a_0 and a_1, the same values would also be found. (See Exercise 7.2.) (This is not necessarily the case for any model.) Finally, the log-likelihood approach can also be conducted analytically in the case of the linear model, although we shall not describe the procedure here.

In summary, this remarkable set of properties for calibration and precision estimation make the linear class of models especially useful for practical purposes.

7.3   The Statistical Reliability of the Linear Regression Model

The advantages of the linear model would alone explain, if not justify, its wide use in modeling. However, as we shall now see, it offers other distinct advantages over other types of models, specifically in connection with the estimation of its level of precision. In the same fashion as we have described the calibration and precision estimation of linear models in the (simplest) case of the *univariate model* (7.2) (i.e., in one independent variable), we shall remain with this particular model in this section, and generalize the results in Section 7.4.

The values that were obtained for the coefficients a_0 and a_1 of the model, as well as those for R^2 and R, were computed on the basis of the observed (sample) values $\hat{Y}_i$ and $\hat{X}_i$. Thus, since these values (as all sample values) are subject to fluctuations from sample to sample, we are faced with the same questions as in Section 6.3: What is the precision on the determination of the values of a_0, a_1, and R^2? In other words: What is the order of magnitude of potential fluctuations in these values in a given calibration? For example, whereas we obtained a value of 2.79 for a_0 and of 0.0786 for a_1, and of 0.96 for R on the basis of the data in Table 7.1, how would these values be changed if we used another set of 10 observations, i.e., if we measured the levels of transit travel in the same zones, but on different days? It is clear that this question is of the same nature as those we asked in Section 6.3. That is, the values for a_0, a_1, and R are *random variables*, and in order to assess the reliability of the model, we need to evaluate the reliability of their estimation. It is important to note in this respect that the concept of *reliability* of the model is fundamentally different from that of its *precision*. The former, as we shall see, relates to the "precision" with respect to true values (in the sense used in Chapter 6), whereas the latter is in relation to observed values.

The great advantage of linear models is that, provided that the data used in the calibration and the precision evaluation possess certain features, the probabilistic characteristics of the a_i's and of R can be ascertained. Consequently, the answers to the question posed above can be obtained in the same fashion as in Section 6.3. Let us illustrate this, using the same data. We must first assume that the values of the variable X (the population levels X_i) are *given* (fixed) and are not subject to error. On the contrary, if we were to measure again the levels of transit patronage within each area, we would obtain other values corresponding to random fluctuations. We do *not* need to know the probability distribution of these measurements within a given area. However, their variance should be (or is assumed to be) the same in all areas. Finally, we make the assumption that the linear model applies, i.e., that there is a linear relationship between the true value of the average daily transit usage and the population level. This set of requirements is graphically illustrated in Figure 7.2. If repeated measurements of the level of transit usage were made in a given area with a population level X_i, we would get varying values for Y_i, say Y_{ij}. Their distribution is represented above the line parallel to the Y axis, going through the point of coordinate X_i on the population level axis. These assumptions mean that:

1. The true means of the respective distributions of the Y_{ij}'s, i.e., μ_{Y_1}, μ_{Y_2}, ..., are arranged along the straight line

$$\mu_{Y_i} = a_0 + a_1 X_i \qquad (7.14)$$

This is the assumption of a linear model.

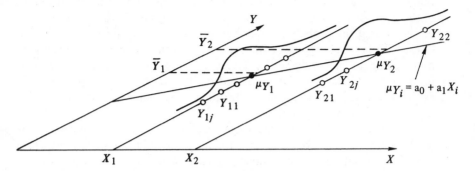

Figure 7.2 The statistical assumptions of the linear regression model.

2. The variances of the distributions of the Y_{ij}'s within a group of observations for Y_i (i.e., for a given i), are all equal.
3. We assume that the random variables Y_{ij} are independent of each other, in the sense of Section 1.4 and formula (1.10).
4. The X_i's are not random variables but deterministic values.

These kinds of assumptions are not as restrictive in practice as they may at first sound. For instance, in our case, it is not unreasonable to assume that (even if it is not strictly observed in the data) there is a linear (i.e., proportional) relationship between the average transit level in a given area and its population level. Nor is it unreasonable to assume that the variations in the transit usage (e.g., on a daily level, if the observations are conducted daily), as measured by the sample variances, equal. Also, it should be the case that the level of transit usage on a given day in a given area is independent of the level in another day in a different area. Finally (at least compared to the daily numbers of trips), the population levels can be considered to be deterministic.

Under these conditions, it can be shown that estimates for the standard deviations of the parameters a_0 and a_1 in model (7.2) can be computed, from the residual variance $s_e^2 = (1/n) \sum_i (Y_i - \hat{Y}_i)^2$, as

$$s_{a_0}^2 = \frac{s_e^2}{n-2} \tag{7.15}$$

$$s_{a_1}^2 = \frac{n}{n-2} \left[\frac{s_e^2}{\sum_i (\hat{X}_i - \bar{X})^2} \right] \tag{7.16}$$

Therefore, we can evaluate the precision, in the probabilistic sense of Section 6.3, of the estimated values of the parameters a_0 and a_1 using formula (6.3).

Under slightly more restrictive conditions, we can obtain a better evalua-tion of the reliability of the model. If it can be assumed that the distributions of the Y_{ij}'s for a given value of i are *normal probability distributions*, it can be shown that the probability distributions of a_0 and a_1 are both T distribu-tions, with $(n - 2)$ degrees of freedom, n being the sample size. This allows us to compute the probabilities associated with various levels of error as probabilities of the T variable, instead of the Tchebyscheff approximation, as described in Section 6.3, using formula (6.8), but where the T variable replaces the normal Z variable.

For instance, in the example above, each of the observed values for the levels of transit Y_i can be considered to be a binomial random variable which records the total number of residents in each of the large zonal populations that use the transit system. Therefore, it should be normally distributed, since, as we have seen in Section 6.3, a binomial variable with a large parameter n is approximately normal. Therefore, the parameters a_0 and a_1 of the model (7.12) both have a T distribution, with a number of degrees of freedom equal to $n - 2 = 10 - 2 = 8$. Let us compute the estimate of their repective vari-ances, through formulas (7.15) and (7.16). The quantities $s_{\hat{Y}}^2$ and $\sum (\hat{X}_i - \bar{\bar{X}})^2$ were computed in Table 7.2. Since from formula (7.7), $s_e^2 = (1 - R^2)s_{\hat{Y}}^2 = 0.195$, we get

$$s_{a_0}^2 = \frac{0.195}{8} = 0.0244 \quad \text{and} \quad s_{a_0} = 0.156$$

$$s_{a_1}^2 = \frac{10}{8}\left(\frac{0.195}{4200}\right) = 0.000058 \quad \text{and} \quad s_{a_1} = 0.00762$$

Therefore, at a level of confidence of, say, 95%, the value of the T variable with 8 degrees of freedom such that it leaves out a probability of 5% on both tails or 2.5% on either tail of the probability curve (i.e., $T_{0.475}$ in the nota-tion of Section 6.3) is equal to 2.306. Therefore, the maximum level of error for the parameter a_0 would be, from formula (6.8), where s_{a_0} plays the role of $\sigma\sqrt{n}$:

$$\delta_{a_0} = T_{p/2}s_{a_0} = 2.306(0.156) = 0.360$$

and, similarly,

$$\delta_{a_1} = T_{p/2}s_{a_1} = 2.306(0.00762) = 0.0176$$

Therefore, we know with 95% certainty that the true value of a_0 would be around the estimated value of 2.79 ± 0.360 (i.e., anywhere between 2.43 and 3.15).

In the same fashion, the value of a_1 could be anywhere between

$$0.0786 - 0.0176 = 0.061 \quad \text{and} \quad 0.0786 + 0.0176 = 0.0956$$

consequently, all linear models of the form (7.2), where a_0 and a_1 can be chosen respectively within the two ranges of values above, are equally valid representations of the variations of the transit usage as a function of the population levels, given our data. Of course, this relatively large degree of imprecision in the specification of the model is due to the very small sample size. When the sample size for the observed values $\hat{Y}_i$ and $\hat{X}_i$ is large, the T distributions become *standard normal distributions*, and the standard normal table replaces the T table in the procedure above. (See Exercise 7.6.)

The above determination of the level of error on the specification of the two parameters allows us to determine the corresponding level of error in the value of $Y_i = a_0 + a_1 X_i$. It is however, important to distinguish here between the estimation of the true value of the *mean* of Y_i and that of the true value of a *single* predicted value of Y_i. The true value of the mean of Y_i is, from the assumption represented by formula (7.14) and illustrated by Figure 7.2, equal to

$$\mu_{Y_i} = a_0 + a_1 X_i$$

Since X_i is assumed to be given, Y_i is then a random variable, the sum of the random variables a_0 and $a_1 X_i$, respectively. It can be shown that its variance is equal to

$$\sigma^2_{\mu_{Y_i}} = \sigma^2_{a_0} + (\hat{X}_i - \bar{X})^2 \sigma^2_{a_1}$$

for which an estimate is

$$s^2_{\mu_{Y_i}} = s^2_{a_0} + (\hat{X}_i - \bar{X})^2 s^2_{a_1} \tag{7.17}$$

or, by replacing $s^2_{a_0}$ and $s^2_{a_1}$ by their expressions in (7.15) and (7.16),

$$s^2_{\mu_{Y_i}} = s^2_e \left[\frac{1}{n-2} + \left(\frac{n}{n-2} \right) \frac{(\hat{X}_i - \bar{X})^2}{\sum_i (\hat{X}_i - \bar{X})^2} \right] \tag{7.18}$$

Under the same conditions as above, if the Y_{ij}'s for a fixed value X_i are normally distributed, their mean is also normally distributed. Therefore, the evaluation of the level of error on the true value μ_{Y_i} of the mean of the predicted values Y_i, using the estimate of its variance (7.18), can be obtained in the same fashion from a T table, again with $(n-2)$ degrees of freedom, or from the standard normal table when the sample size is large.

For instance, in the example above, the three observations for the transit level usage for an area with a population of $X_6 = 60$ were, respectively, 7.5, 6.8, and 8. Those were the Y_{6j}'s. Their observed average was thus equal to $(7.5 + 6.8 + 8.0)/3 = 7.43$. From formula (7.18), the variance of this observed value is equal to

$$s^2_{\mu_{Y_6}} = 0.195 \left[\frac{1}{10-2} + \left(\frac{10}{10-2} \right) \frac{(60-50)^2}{4200} \right] = 0.03018$$

and

$$s_{\mu_{Y_6}} = \sqrt{0.03018} = 0.174$$

Since μ_{Y_6} is distributed with a T distribution with $n-2 = 8$ degrees of freedom, repeating the procedure used above for a_0 and a_1, the level of maximum error on the observed value of μ_{Y_6} of 7.43 is, at a level of confidence of 95%:

$$\delta_{\mu_{Y_6}} = T_{0.475} s_{\mu_{Y_6}} = 2.306(0.174) = 0.401$$

Therefore, the average value of the level of transit corresponding to a population of $X = 60,000$ would be predicted to be between

$$7.43 - 0.40 = 7.03 \quad \text{and} \quad 7.43 + 0.40 = 7.83$$

However, it is critical to understand that this error-level estimation concerns the *average* of the predictions for Y_6 over a large number of calibrations of the model (7.2) on independent sets of 10 data points. To evaluate the level of precision corresponding to a *single* prediction of the value of the transit usage level when $X = 60$, i.e., a single calibration of the model, we need to add to the variance $s_{\mu_{Y_t}}^2$ in (7.18) the variance of a single value Y_{ij} around its mean. This variance, as was assumed above, is independent of the index i and can be estimated from the residual variance s_e^2, correcting as above for the number of degrees of freedom $(n - 2)$ of the T variable Y_{ij}. Therefore,

$$s_{Y_{ij}}^2 = \frac{n}{n-2} s_e^2 \tag{7.19}$$

Consequently, the variance of a single predicted value Y_t is equal to

$$s_{Y_t}^2 = s_{\mu_{Y_t}}^2 + s_{Y_{ij}}^2 \tag{7.20}$$

Replacing the terms on the right-hand side by their expressions from (7.18) and (7.19), we get

$$s_{Y_t}^2 = s_e^2 \left[\frac{n+1}{n-2} + \left(\frac{n}{n-2} \right) \frac{(\hat{X}_i - \bar{X})^2}{\sum_i (\hat{X}_i - \bar{X})^2} \right] \tag{7.21}$$

For instance, in the example above, since we have already evaluated the variance of the average of the predictions of the level of transit usage when $X = 60$ as being equal to 0.03024, the variance of a prediction of the level of transit using the specific (single) model (7.12) would be equal to that value, plus the variance of a single value Y_{ij}. As was evaluated immediately above, s_e^2 is equal to 0.07 (2.79) × 0.1953. Therefore, from (7.19),

$$s_{Y_{0j}}^2 = \left(\frac{10}{8} \right) 0.195 = 0.244$$

and from (7.20) or (7.21),

$$s_{Y_6}^2 = s_{\mu_{Y_6}}^2 + s_{Y_{0j}}^2 = 0.03024 + 0.244 = 0.274$$

and

$$s_{Y_6} = \sqrt{0.274} = 0.523$$

Therefore, at the same level of confidence of 95%, the level of maximum error on Y_6 will be

$$0.523\,(2.306) = 1.222$$

The predicted value of Y_6 from model (7.12) would be equal to

$$Y_6 = 2.79 + 0.0786X_6 = 2.79 + 0.0786(60) = 7.47$$

Therefore, the "true" predicted value could lie anywhere between

$$7.47 - 1.22 = 6.25 \quad \text{and} \quad 7.47 + 1.22 = 8.69$$

As we would expect, the level of imprecision on the prediction of Y_6 is greater than on that of μ_{Y_6}, for the same reason that the precision is better on the averages of a series of predictions than on single values, as we have seen in Section 6.3. Also, it can be seen from formulas (7.18) or (7.21) that the level of error is not uniform, but rather a parabolically increasing function of the deviation of the value $\hat{X}_i$ from the mean $\bar{X}$. In other words, since the mean for the $\hat{X}_i$'s was equal to 50, we can expect the error on the estimation of Y_7 (corresponding to $X_7 = 80$, which is farther away from $\bar{X} = 50$ than $X_6 = 60$) to be larger than that on the estimation of Y_6. (See Exercise 7.7.)

Finally, when the value of the $\hat{X}_i$'s cannot be considered to be deterministic, as we have assumed above, but rather a random quantity like the $\hat{Y}_i$'s, all the results above are still valid, provided that the prediction errors $(Y_i - \hat{Y}_i)$ can be considered probabilistically independent [in the sense of formula (1.10)] of the random variables $\hat{X}_i$. Practically, this would mean that the distributional properties of these errors are not dependent on the values of $\hat{X}_i$.

Thus, the properties of the linear model are such that they allow us to evaluate analytically not only the overall precision of the model, as in Chapter 6, but much more interestingly for operational purposes, the individual level of precision of single predicted values. This unique feature among forecasting models adds to the practical advantages of the linear regression model.

7.4 Multivariate Linear Regression Models

As we have often done for several models that have been considered in this text, let us now generalize those previous results to the case of the multivariate model (7.1):

$$Y = a_0 + a_1X_1 + a_2X_2 + \ldots + a_nX_n$$

In this case, although the concepts remain the same, the resulting formulas, as well as the computational procedures they entail, are substantially more cumbersome than in the simple univariate case discussed above. However, for that reason, multivariate linear regressions are almost always implemented using standard, widely accessible computer programs. The output of these programs is typically an estimated equation of the form

$$Y = 4.3 + 3.9X_1 - 0.005X_2 - 0.13X_3 - 0.012X_4 \quad (7.22/4.57)$$

which might express Y, the total rate of trip generation per household in a given area as a linear function of X_1, the average car ownership; X_2, the density of residential dwelling units per acre; X_3, the distance from the CBD; and X_4, the average family income in thousands of dollars.

Together with the calibration of the model represented by the values of the coefficients a_i of the X_i's, the program output will contain estimates of the values of the standard deviations s_{a_i} of these parameters, i.e., the equivalents of the s_{a_0} and s_{a_1} in the univariate case. Since the parameters are in the multivariate case, again distributed with T distributions with $(n - m - 1)$ degrees of freedom (m being the number of independent variables X_i), or a normal distribution when the sample size n is large), the values of the s_{a_i}'s can then be used to compute the resulting level of error on the estimation of the model's parameters. (See Exercise 7.8.) They can also be used, through a generalization of formula (7.17), to compute the variance of the mean of a given Y_i:

$$s_{\mu_{Y_i}} = s_{a_0}^2 + \sum_{k=1}^{n} s_{a_k}^2 (\hat{X}_{ki} - \bar{X}_k)^2 \quad (7.23)$$

where $\hat{X}_{ki}$ is the ith observed value for the kth variable X_k, and $\bar{X}_k$ the sample mean for X_k.

Finally, the standard deviation for a single predicted value of Y_i would be obtained by adding to the variance in (7.23) the value of the residual variance s_e^2, weighed for the number of degrees of freedom:

$$s_{Y_i}^2 = s_{\mu_{Y_i}}^2 + \frac{n}{n - m - 1} s_e^2 \quad (7.24)$$

The value of the residual variance s_e^2 is also usually a part of the output of the regression programs, as well as that of $s_{Y_i}^2$ in (7.24). Finally, the *coefficient of multiple correlation*, which, in the multivariate case is noted as $R_{Y;X_1X_2...X_m}$, is again computed as

$$R_{Y;X_1X_2...X_m}^2 = 1 - \frac{s_e^2}{s_{\hat{Y}}^2} \quad (7.25)$$

All this information will allow evaluation of the level of error on the prediction of the values Y_i for all values of the X_k's. (This is also, in most cases, performed as part of the linear regression programs.)

The multivariate case, however, introduces the question (also present in any model with several variables) of the relative contributions of the variables to the overall efficiency of the model. This is of some practical importance, since if it can be determined empirically that the presence of a given variable does not significantly affect the overall precision of a model, it may then be deleted from its specification, resulting in conceptual and methodological economy. This question, which in general cannot be answered except heuristically (i.e., following the trial and error approach of the previous chapter) may be answered analytically prior to the development of linear models of the form (7.1).

Let us illustrate this procedure in the case of a model in three variables. Assume that we would like to forecast the level of migration into a given area from the levels of total residential populations and the size of the work force. Such a model would establish a connection between the population projection models of Chapter 2 and the employment projection models of Chapter 3. To that effect, 10 geographical areas in a certain region have been surveyed, with the results described in Table 7.3, where X_1 is the residential population (in thousands), X_2 is the size of the work force (also in thousands) and Y is the number of people in-migrating to the area (in hundreds).

TABLE 7.3

Zone $i =$	1	2	3	4	5	6	7	8	9	10
$\hat{X}_{1i}$	21	27	32	38	43	53	61	71	76	78
$\hat{X}_{2i}$	6.3	5.2	7.7	5.4	4.1	5.3	10.2	9.6	12.3	22
$\hat{Y}_i$	4.8	4.0	5.4	5.8	5.6	8.0	8.7	7.5	9.6	6.8

Next, using the procedure described in Section 7.3, a univariate model of the level of migration Y as a function of the size of the population X is developed. This results in the formulation

$$Y = 3.047 + 0.0715X_1 \qquad (R^2 = 0.683, R = 0.826)$$

(See Exercise 7.9.) Since the resulting R^2 is somewhat low, a multivariate model is attempted, on the premise that the inclusion of more information about the zonal characteristics should result in a better prediction of the level of migration into the zone. Therefore, a model of the form

$$Y = a_0 + a_1X_1 + a_2X_2 \qquad (7.26)$$

is considered. However, the question arises as to whether the additional effort presented by the inclusion of the variable X_2 and a new calibration will be justified in terms of the gain in the resulting precision of the new model.

The major advantage of multivariate linear models mentioned earlier—that the multivariate coefficient R^2 can be determined before calibration—can now be utilized to answer that question. Moreover, it is possible to express its value as a function of the values of the respective coefficients R_k

corresponding to the univariate models between the dependent variable Y and the individual independent variables X_k. Although the formula in the general case is somewhat involved, in the two variable case ($k = 2$) we are considering, it can be written

$$R^2_{Y;X_1X_2} = \frac{R^2_{YX_1} + R^2_{YX_2} - 2R_{YX_1}R_{YX_2}R_{X_1X_2}}{1 - R^2_{X_1X_2}} \qquad (7.27)$$

with an obvious notation. Since all the R's in this formula can be computed from the observed data, e.g., using any of formulas (7.3) through (7.6), so does the value of the multiple coefficient $R^2_{Y;X_1X_2}$.

Formula (7.27) offers the added advantage of showing the respective contributions of the individual variables X_1 and X_2 (and in the general case the X_k's) to the overall efficiency of the model. First, it can be seen that the total efficiency in terms of R^2 values is not equal to the sum of the respective efficiencies of separate models between Y and X_1, on the one hand, and Y and X_2, on the other. This would be true only when the precision of a model between X_1 and X_2 as measured by $R_{X_1X_2}$ is equal to zero, in which case formula (7.27) simplifies to

$$R^2_{Y;X_1X_2} = R^2_{YX_1} + R^2_{YX_2} \qquad (7.28)$$

At the other extreme, if a perfect linear model between X_1 and X_2 can be calibrated, i.e., $R_{X_1X_2} = R^2_{X_1X_2} = 1$, then it can be shown that

$$R^2_{Y;X_1X_2} = R^2_{YX_1} = R_{YX_2} \qquad (7.29)$$

In that case, the linear model in the two variables is not better than either of the two univariate linear models in the single variables.

Going back to the illustrative example, we can now estimate what overall level of precision for a potential model of the form (7.26) we can expect, by first computing, respectively, $R^2_{YX_2}$ for a univariate model of the migration as a function of the work force, and $R^2_{X_1X_2}$ for a model of the population as a function of the work force. (See Exercises 7.9 and 7.10.) The value of R_{YX_1} has already been computed and is equal to 0.683. The other values are found to be equal to

$$R_{YX_2} = 0.399 \qquad R^2_{YX_2} = 0.159$$

$$R_{X_1X_2} = 0.731 \qquad R^2_{X_1X_2} = 0.534$$

Therefore, from formula (7.27) the value of the coefficient of multiple correlation $R_{Y;X_1X_2}$ is equal to

$$R^2_{Y;X_1X_2} = \frac{0.683 + 0.159 - 2(0.826)(0.399)(0.731)}{1 - 0.534} = 0.773$$

Thus, the inclusion of the work force in the set of predicting variables would result in a decrease of the residual variance from $1 - R^2 = (1 - 0.683) = 0.31.7$ or 31.7% to $(1 - 0.773) = 0.22.7$, or 22.7% of the variance

$s_\hat{Y}^2$ of the migration levels. Equivalently, the efficiency of the model would be increased from reproducing 68.3% of the variance of the migration levels to 77.3%. Since the variance $s_\hat{Y}^2$ is easily evaluated as being equal to 8.58, corresponding to a standard deviation $s_\hat{Y}$ of 2.93, the typical order of magnitude of the error on the reproduction of the migration levels (standard error of estimate), which was previously equal to

$$s_e = \sqrt{1 - R^2}\ s_\hat{Y} = \sqrt{1 - 0.683}\ (2.93) = 1.65$$

would now be equal to

$$s_e = \sqrt{1 - 0.773}\ (2.93) = 1.39$$

Based on this assessment, we might then decide to go ahead and calibrate model (7.26) on the basis of the data in Table 7.3. Although in the general multivariate case the expressions of the coefficients require the use of matrix notation, in the three-variable case, as here, the computation of their values is still relatively simple. (See Exercise 7.11.) The resulting model is then found to be

$$Y = 3.130 + 0.0417X_1 + 0.1595X_2 \tag{7.30}$$

We might also have asked a slightly more precise question which again, for the case of a nonlinear model could only be answered experimentally. Specifically, although the foregoing analysis measures the role of the variable X_2 in increasing the precision of the multivariate model over the univariate model, it does not compare the contributions of X_1 and X_2 when they are both included. That is, we examined only the role of X_1 and X_2 in isolation, as represented by R_{YX_1} and R_{YX_2}. We also examined the effects of X_1 and X_2 together, as represented by $R_{Y;X_1X_2}$. We did not examine the effect of either variable as a supplement to the other. This is the purpose of another type of coefficient R, the *coefficient of partial correlation*, which we shall now define.

The coefficient of partial correlation between the variable Y and the variable X_2 with respect to the variable X_1, which is represented as R_{YX_2/X_1}^2, measures the additional effect of the inclusion of X_2 in a model in X_1 and X_2 respective to the individual effect of X_1. This is evaluated as the percentage of the residual variance of a first model between Y and X_1, which can then be reproduced by a model in X_2 and X_1. (Note the difference in notation between $R_{YX_2/X}^2$ and $R_{Y;X_1X_2}^2$.) In accordance with its definition, the coefficient of partial correlation R_{YX_2/X_1} is therefore related to the coefficient of multiple correlation $R_{Y;X_1X_2}$ through the equality

$$R_{Y;X_1X_2}^2 = R_{YX_1}^2 + R_{YX_2/X_1}^2(1 - R_{YX_1}^2) \tag{7.31}$$

In physical terms, this means that the square of the coefficient of multiple correlation, which measures the percentage of the variance of Y explained from both X_1 and X_2, is equal to the percentage of the variance first explained by X_1 individually, plus the fraction of unexplained percentage $(1 - R_{YX_1}^2)$ that X_2 reproduces after the effect of X_1 has been already taken into account.

That fraction is, by definition, the coefficient of partial correlation of Y and X_2 with respect to X_1: hence formula (7.31).

This formula can be turned around and used to compute the value of the coefficient of partial correlation from the values of the coefficient of multiple correlation and of the univariate correlation of Y and the other variables as

$$R^2_{YX_2/X_1} = \frac{R^2_{Y;X_1X_2} - R^2_{YX_1}}{1 - R^2_{YX_1}} \qquad (7.32)$$

In the example above, since $R^2_{Y;X_1X_2}$ is equal to 0.773 and $R^2_{YX_1}$ is equal to 0.683, the value of $R^2_{YX_2/X_1}$ is therefore equal to

$$R^2_{YX_2/X_1} = \frac{0.773 - 0.683}{1 - 0.683} = 0.284$$

This indicates that after the contribution of the variable "population size" has been taken into account, the second variable, "size of the work force," reproduces, or accounts for, only 28.4% of the residual (unreproduced) variance of the level of migration. Therefore, in terms of additional effectiveness, the model in the two variables "work-force size" and "population size" is only 28% more effective than the model in the single variable "population size." Conversely, we can evaluate the effectiveness of the population size's contribution of the reproduction of the migration levels, coming after the contribution of the work-force size. This is measured by the corresponding coefficient of partial correlation R_{YX_1/X_2} between Y and X_1 with respect to X_2. Its value is given by a formula that is symmetrical to formula (7.31), which results from an interchange of the roles of X_1 and X_2:

$$R^2_{Y;X_1X_2} = R^2_{YX_2} + R^2_{YX_1/X_2}(1 - R^2_{YX_2}) \qquad (7.33)$$

which can be rewritten as

$$R^2_{YX_1/X_2} = \frac{R^2_{Y;X_1X_2} - R^2_{YX_2}}{1 - R^2_{YX_2}} \qquad (7.34)$$

In this case, this is equal to

$$R^2_{YX_1/X_2} = \frac{0.773 - 0.159}{1 - 0.159} = 0.730$$

Therefore, the comparative roles of the two variables in the overall efficiency of the model can be characterized as follows. When X_1 is used alone, it can account for $R^2_{YX_1} = 0.683$, or 68.3% of the total variations of Y. When X_2 is used alone, it can account for $R^2_{YX_2} = 0.59$, or 59%. When X_2 is used after X_1, it accounts for an additional $R^2_{YX_2/X_1} = 0.284$, or 28.4% of the variance unaccounted for by X_1, whereas when the order of incorporation of these two variables in a multivariate model is reversed, X_1 can account for an additional $R^2_{YX_1/X_2} = 0.730$, or 73% of the variance unaccounted for by X_2. Finally, both X_1 and X_2 can account for 0.733, or 77.3% of the original variance.

Alternatively, the computation of the values of the respective coefficients of partial correlation can be effected without the prior computation of the value of the coefficient of multiple correlation. They can be evaluated through the formulas

$$R_{YX_1/X_2} = \frac{R_{YX_1} - R_{YX_2}R_{X_1X_2}}{\sqrt{1 - R_{YX_2}^2}\sqrt{1 - R_{X_1X_2}^2}} \qquad (7.35)$$

$$R_{YX_2/X_1} = \frac{R_{YX_2} - R_{YX_1}R_{X_1X_2}}{\sqrt{1 - R_{YX_1}^2}\sqrt{1 - R_{X_1X_2}^2}} \qquad (7.36)$$

These formulas offer the advantage that the comparative contributions of the variables can therefore be assessed prior to the development of the multivariate model, if desired. (See Exercise 7.12.)

In any case, the coefficients of partial correlation in the case of more than two variables X_i, which can be computed through generalizations of formulas (7.35) and (7.36), can be used in connection with the optimization of the order of inclusion of potential predicting variables in a multivariate linear model. For instance, let us assume that we want to determine the most economical model in the least number of variables corresponding to a minimum value for the multiple R^2 of, say, 0.90. Instead of examining more or less at random which combination of variables achieves that value, we can first compute the values of the partial coefficients of correlations of the individual candidate variables X_m, with respect to the $(m - 1)$ other variables, i.e., their respective individual contributions after the others have been incorporated into the model. The variable with the least partial coefficient value would then be dropped (if, of course, the multiple R^2 for the m variables is in excess of our requirement). Next, we compute the $(m - 1)$ coefficients of partial correlation between the variables remaining under consideration, and reiterate the procedure until the value of the multiple R^2 decreases to its minimum acceptable value. This procedure, known as *stepwise regression*, has a number of variants and can also be used in connection with the identification of the least reliable variables X_k in terms of the estimation of the corresponding parameter a_k in (7.1). Indeed, although we shall not present it here, there is a connection between the value of the variance "explained" by a given predicting variable X_k and the reliability of its associated parameter a_k. Finally, it is also possible to assess the reliability of the measure of the overall precision of the model, i.e., the level of error on R^2 itself.

7.5 Pseudo-Linear Models

A number of other models which have been seen throughout this text are not linear in nature. However, after suitable transformations, they can be written as linear models, thus allowing us to avail ourselves of the operational advantages of the linear regression models which have been stressed in the preceding sections of this chapter. Such models are sometimes called *pseudo-linear* or *intrinsically linear*. Let us therefore examine these various models in terms of the type of functional form they represent.

The first example of a pseudo-linear model is the *exponential model* of the form

$$Y = \alpha_0(\alpha_1)^X \qquad (7.37)$$

This exponential form was first encountered in the population forecasting model of Chapter 2, under the formulation

$$P_n = P_0(1 + r)^n \qquad (7.38/2.4)$$

This exponential model can readily be transformed into a linear model (as, indeed, we have already done in Section 2.3) by taking the logarithms of both sides:

$$\log P_n = \log P_0 + n \log (1 + r) \qquad (7.39)$$

Therefore, if we consider the quantity $\log P_n$ to be the new variable, called Y, and if we call the constants $\log P_0$ and $\log (1 + r)$, a_0 and a_1, respectively, model (7.39) can be rewritten

$$Z = a_0 + a_1 r$$

where

$$Z = \log P \longleftrightarrow P = e^Z \qquad (7.40)$$

$$a_0 = \log P_0 \longleftrightarrow P_0 = e^{a_0} \qquad (7.41)$$

$$a_1 = \log (1 + r) \longleftrightarrow 1 + r = e^{a_1} \qquad (7.42)$$

if we use the natural (or Neperian) logarithms of base $e = 2.718\dots$. Model (7.39) is now the univariate model (7.2) in the dependent variable $\log (P_n)$ and the independent variable n. Thus, after transformation of the observed values of the dependent variable into their logarithms, the techniques of linear regression of Section 7.2 can be applied. When the value of the parameters a_0 and a_1 have been found, the values of the parameters P_0 and r in the original model (7.38) can be evaluated through formulas (7.41) and (7.42). Finally, the predicted values can be computed from the transformed model (7.39) or from the original model (7.38). (See Exercise 7.13.)

In general, a model of the form (7.37) can be transformed into a linear model using the same transformation of the variables:

$$\log Y = \log \alpha_0 + X \log \alpha_1$$

or

$$Z = a_0 + a_1 X$$

where

$$Z = \log Y \longleftrightarrow Y = e^Z \qquad (7.43)$$

$$a_0 = \log \alpha_0 \longleftrightarrow \alpha_0 = e^{a_0} \qquad (7.44)$$

$$a_1 = \log \alpha_1 \longleftrightarrow \alpha_1 = e^{a_1} \qquad (7.45)$$

Another example of an exponential model that can be transformed into a linear model is the *double-exponential* population projection model,

$$P = P_\infty a^{b^t} \tag{2.10}$$

which becomes, after taking the logs twice and some simple manipulations,

$$\log\left[\log\left(\frac{P_\infty}{P}\right)\right] = \log\left[\log\left(\frac{1}{a}\right)\right] + t \log b \tag{2.11}$$

(see Section 2.5), so that it is now a linear model,

$$Z = \alpha_0 + \alpha_1 t$$

where

$$Z = \log\log\left(\frac{P_\infty}{P}\right) \longleftrightarrow P = P_\infty e^{-e^Z} \tag{7.46}$$

$$\alpha_0 = \log\log\left(\frac{1}{a}\right) \longleftrightarrow \frac{1}{a} = e^{e^{\alpha_0}} \longleftrightarrow a = e^{-e^{\alpha_0}} \tag{7.47}$$

$$\alpha_1 = \log b \longleftrightarrow b = e^{\alpha_1} \tag{7.48}$$

(See Exercise 7.15.)

Another example is the *intervening opportunity model* of spatial interaction,

$$R_{ij} = K_j O_j e^{-\lambda N_{ij}} \tag{4.40}$$

which becomes

$$\log R_{ij} = \log K_j + \log O_j - \lambda N_{ij}$$

or

$$Z = \alpha_0 + \alpha_1 N_{ij}$$

where

$$Z = \log R_{ij} \longleftrightarrow R_{ij} = e^Z \tag{7.49}$$

$$\alpha_0 = \log K_j + \log O_j \longleftrightarrow K_j = e^{\alpha_0 - \log O_j} \tag{7.50}$$

$$\alpha_1 = -\lambda \longleftrightarrow \lambda = -\alpha_1 \tag{7.51}$$

(See Exercise 7.16.)

A final example is the *spatial impedance model*,

$$F(d_{ij}) = \alpha e^{-\beta d_{ij}} \tag{4.6}$$

which becomes

$$\log F(d_{ij}) = \log \alpha - \beta d_{ij}$$

or

$$Z = a_0 + a_1 d_{ij}$$

where

$$Z = \log F(d_{ij}) \tag{7.52}$$

$$a_0 = \log \alpha \longleftrightarrow \alpha = e^{a_0} \tag{7.53}$$

$$a_1 = -\beta \longleftrightarrow \beta = -a_1 \tag{7.54}$$

(See Exercise 7.17.)

An example of a *multivariate exponential model* that can be transformed into a multivariate linear model is the logit model of modal choice:

$$P_1^k = \frac{1}{1 + e^{G_2^k - G_1^k}} \qquad (4.61)$$

which when $(G_2^k - G_1^k)$ is a linear function, is equivalent to

$$\log\left(\frac{P_1^k}{1 - P_1^k}\right) = (\alpha_0^1 - \alpha_0^2) + \sum_{i=1}^{n}(\alpha_i^1 - \alpha_i^2)X_i \qquad (4.64)$$

(See Section 4.9.) This is a model of the form (7.1).

Another class of models that can be transformed into linear models is the class of *power function models* of the form

$$Y = \alpha X^\beta \qquad (7.55)$$

An example of such a model is the other form of the "interaction impedance function,"

$$F(d_{ij}) = \alpha d_{ij}^{-\gamma} \qquad (4.5)$$

By again taking the logarithms of both sides, we get

$$\log F(d_{ij}) = \log \alpha - \gamma \log d_{ij}$$
$$Z = a_0 + a_1 \log d_{ij}$$

with

$$Z = \log F(d_{ij}) \qquad (7.56)$$

$$a_0 = \log \alpha \longleftrightarrow \alpha = e^{a_0} \qquad (7.57)$$

$$a_1 = -\gamma \longleftrightarrow \gamma = -a_1 \qquad (7.58)$$

In its *multivariate* version, the power function model (sometimes called multiplicative model) has the form

$$Y = \alpha_0 X_1^{\alpha_1} X_2^{\alpha_2} \ldots X_m^{\alpha_m} \qquad (7.59)$$

An example of such a model is the *travel production* function of a given zone i:

$$O_i = \alpha_0 U_{i1}^{\alpha_1} U_{i2}^{\alpha_2} \ldots U_{ik}^{\alpha_k} \qquad (4.4)$$

which specifies the number of trips O_i originating in a zone as a function of its k characteristics U_{ik}. By again taking the logarithms of both sides of (7.59), we get

$$\log O_i = \log \alpha_0 + \alpha_1 \log U_{i1} + \alpha_2 \log U_{i2} + \ldots + \alpha_m \log U_{im} \quad (7.60)$$

This is a model of the form (7.1):

$$Z = a_0 + a_1 \log X_1 + a_2 \log X_2 + \ldots + a_m \log X_m$$

where

$$Z = \log O_i \longleftrightarrow O_i = e^Z \qquad (7.61)$$

and

$$\alpha_i = a_i \longleftrightarrow a_i = \alpha_i \qquad (7.62)$$

These transformations of the original formulations of these respective models thus allows for the analytical determination of the values of their parameters, using the techniques of linear statistical regression. The determination of the precision of the model is not affected by the definition of its variables, since the criteria used (R, R^2, ρ^2, etc.) are normalized; i.e., they do not depend on the unit of measurement of the variables (absolute values or logarithms). Also, determination of the interval of estimation of the predicted values can be performed first on the transformed values Z as we have done above, and then translating the resulting intervals in terms of the original scale of values. For instance, if the estimation interval for the value Z_{ij} in a transformed model (4.40) turned out to be between 7.131 and 7.185, at a certain level of confidence, this would mean that the corresponding estimation interval for the original variable R_{ij} would be between $e^{7.131} = 1250$ and $e^{7.185} = 1319$ at the same level of confidence.

7.6 Problems and Extensions of the Linear Model

In conclusion, let us briefly review some of the typical difficulties that may be encountered in the development of the linear statistical model. This may be a fitting conclusion (pun not intended) to a text that has stressed the advantages of analytical models and generally overlooked some of the more mundane difficulties of their implementation.

First, some or all of the basic assumptions required by the linear model may not be verified. For instance, the variances of the observed values within individual levels of the predicting variable(s) may not be equal. In other words, the $s_{Y_i}^2$ in equation (7.20) may not be equal for various i. This will distort the calibration and the precision of the linear model to the extent that the variance of the Y_i's will not be uniform, since it will be larger for values of i corresponding to larger values of $s_{Y_i}^2$. In turn, the values of the parameters a_i will be distorted. This is sometimes called the problem of *heteroscedasticity*. One way around this particular difficulty is to minimize the criterion

$$\sum_i \sum_j \frac{(Y_i - \hat{Y}_{ij})^2}{s_{Y_{ij}}^2}$$

instead of $\sum_i (Y_i - \hat{Y}_i)^2$. This will give less "weight" to (i.e., minimize) the effect of large errors on the Y_i's.

Another typical problem may be caused by the dependence of the error term $(Y_i - \hat{Y}_i)$ on the predicting value(s) $\hat{X}_{ki}$. This is again a problem of uniformity of the error term across the prediction range, which can be attenuated through using the difference between observed values corresponding to consecutive levels of the predicting variable(s) as the predicted variable.

Finally, another important special situation is when some of the predicting variables in a multivariate model are themselves related through linear relationships. This is called the problem of *multicolinearity*. Because it is then possible (to some degree) to predict the values of the predicting variables from one another, the information provided by the individual predicting variables overlaps. This, in turn, results in poor model efficiency, as well as a large indeterminacy in the attribution of the respective contributions of the predicting variables.

Although there are numerous other problematic situations of this type, they can be usually accommodated through special modifications of the basic procedure of linear regression. That is one of the main objects of the methods of *econometrics*, which is a very important area of modeling, and one for which this chapter can be considered an introduction.

EXERCISES

7.1 Using the data of Table 7.1 and the minimum-sum-of-squared-errors criterion as used in Section 6.6, calibrate the univariate linear model (7.2).

7.2 Using the same data as in Exercise 7.1 but this time using the log-likelihood criterion, verify that both criteria result in the same values for the parameters a_0 and a_1.

7.3 Starting from formulas (7.8) and (7.9), respectively, derive the alternative formulas (7.10) and (7.12) for the parameters a_0 and a_1. (*Hint:* Develop fully the products of factors and replace $\bar{Y}$ and $\bar{X}$ by their expressions in terms of the $\hat{X}_i$'s and $\hat{Y}_i$'s.)

7.4 Use the alternative formulas for a_0 and a_1, (7.10) and (7.11), to calibrate the model (7.2) on the data of Table 7.1.

7.5 Using the results of Exercise 7.1, compute the optimal value of the coefficient R^2 at calibration, using formula (6.41). Compare the result with the value obtained analytically in Section 7.2.

7.6 How would the precision of the estimation of parameters a_0 and a_1 be affected if the sample size had been 100 instead of 10? [Assume the same observed values for $s_{\hat{Y}}^2$ and $(\hat{X}_i - \bar{X})$.] What effect would that have, in turn, on the estimation of the value of the mean of Y_4 and on a single prediction of Y_4, respectively?

7.7 Complete the estimation of the level of error on the prediction of the mean of the Y_i's, and on the Y_i's for all values of i, which was started in Section 7.3. Draw a plot of the upper and lower bounds on the estimation intervals for both quantities, as a function of $\hat{X}_i$.

7.8 Assume that together with the specification of model (7.22/4.57), the following values for the standard deviations of the coefficients have been obtained (the number of degrees of freedom is 85):

$$s_{a_0} = 0.06 \quad s_{a_1} = 0.04 \quad s_{a_2} = 0.003 \quad s_{a_3} = 0.008 \quad s_{a_4} = 0.06$$

Determine the respective levels of precision on the estimation of the various parameters of the model.

7.9   Using the data in Table 7.3, develop a linear model expressing the level of migration Y as a function of the size of the residential population X_1. Compute the value of $R^2_{YX_1}$.

7.10   Symetrically, develop a model of Y as a function of the size of the work force X_2, as well as the resulting value for $R^2_{YX_2}$. Estimate a model of X_1 as a function of X_2 and the corresponding $R^2_{X_1X_2}$.

7.11   It can be shown that in the case of a linear model with two predicting variables,

$$Y = a_0 + a_1 X_1 + a_2 X_2 \qquad (7.63)$$

the value of the coefficients a_0, a_1, and a_2 can be computed from the observed values as the solution of the system of three equations in the three unknowns: a_0, a_1, and a_2:

$$a_0(n) \quad\;\; + a_1(\sum_i \hat{X}_{1i}) \quad\;\; + a_2(\sum_i \hat{X}_{2i}) \quad\;\; = \sum_i \hat{Y}_i$$

$$a_0(\sum \hat{X}_{1i}) + a_1(\sum \hat{X}^2_{1i}) \quad\;\; + a_2(\sum \hat{X}_{1i}\hat{X}_{2i}) = \sum \hat{X}_{1i}\hat{Y}_{i1} \qquad (7.64)$$

$$a_0(\sum \hat{X}_{2i}) + a_1(\sum \hat{X}_{1i}\hat{X}_{2i}) + a_2(\sum \hat{X}^2_{2i}) \quad\;\; = \sum \hat{X}_{2i}\hat{Y}_i$$

Using formulas (7.63) and (7.64) and the data in Table 7.3, calibrate a model of the form (7.26).

7.12   Using the alternative formulas (7.35) and (7.36) for the value of the coefficients of partial correlation, verify that they result in the same values as were found in the illustrative example.

7.13   Using the data for Exercise 2.4, apply the techniques of linear modeling regression after transforming the observed values according to formula (7.40). Determine through formulas (7.41) and (7.42) the value of the original coefficients α_0 and α_1 of the model. Compare the results with those of an "eyeball" procedure.

7.14   Use the results of Exercise 7.13 to answer the forecasting questions in the remainder of Exercise 2.4.

7.15   Using the data of Exercise 2.2, apply the formulas of linear regression modeling to the transformed values Z given by formula (7.46). Determine the values of the parameters of the double-exponential model from formulas (7.47) and (7.48).

7.16   Using the data of Table 4.15 and formulas (7.49) through (7.51), develop a linear model corresponding to the transformed intervening opportunities model (4.40). [Note that R_{ij} is equal to $(15{,}000 - \sum_{k=1}^i r_k)$ and N_{ij} is equal to N_i.] Use formulas (7.50) and the known value of $O_j = 15{,}000$ to determine the value of the scaling factor K_j. Use formula (7.51) to determine the value of the parameter λ. Compare the results with those obtained in the empirical approach of the illustrative example in Section 4.6.

7.17 Using the data in Figure 6.6 and transforming the values of $F(d_{ij})$ according to formula (7.52), apply a linear regression to the three observed values to determine the value of the parameter β in (4.6) through formula (7.54). Compare with the result obtained in the illustrative example following Figure 6.6.

7.18 The survey that produced the data in Table 7.1 used in the illustrative example of Section 7.2 also recorded the variations of the size of the respective areas, X_2 (in square miles), as follows:

i	1	2	3	4	5	6	7	8	9	10
X_{2i}	15	25	28	8	17	23	29	17	9	27

Using formulas (7.61) given in Exercise 7.11, develop a linear model of the variations of the number of mass transit trips per zone Y_i as a function of X_1 and X_2. Compare with the model between Y and X_1 obtained in the text in terms of R^2.

7.19 On the basis of the results of Exercise 7.18:
(a) Compute the value of the coefficients of partial correlation between (Y and X_1) and (Y and X_2), respectively.
(b) Elaborate on the implications for the potential contributions of these two variables to a multivariate model.
(c) Compute the overall precision of a model in the two variables, as measured by the coefficient of multiple correlation $R_{Y;X_1X_2}$.

7.20 Show that the average of the error in prediction using the linear model

$$Y = a_0 + a_1 X_1 + a_2 X_2 + \ldots + a_i X_i + \ldots + a_n X_n$$

which can be written as $(1/N) \sum (Y_i - \hat{Y}_i)$, is always zero. (*Hint:* Replace Y_i by its expression in terms of $X_{1i}, X_{2i}, \ldots, X_{ni}$.)

7.21 Given the accompanying data from a survey of the number of trips Y originating from 20 cities, and of the mean per capital income X_1 and median age X_2 observed in the cities, perform a linear regression of Y on X_1 and X_2. Specifically, find the value of:
(a) The coefficient of multiple correlation between the number of trips and both the mean income and the median age.
(b) The coefficient of partial correlation of the number of trips and the mean income with respect to the median age.
(c) The coefficient of partial correlation of the number of trips and the median age with respect to the mean income.
Compute each of these coefficients in two different ways, and interpret their meaning in physical terms in each case. Elaborate on the precision of the model, and on the respective contributions of the two predicting characteristics to the "explanation" of the variations of the number of trips originating in a zone.

$i =$	1	2	3	4	5	6	7	8	9	10
Y_i (thousands)	30	32	40	29	42	48	29	37	41	50
X_{1i} (thousands of dollars)	7.2	7.9	8.1	7.5	8.0	8.1	7.3	9.1	8.7	9.0
X_{2i} (years)	32	35	39	40	35	40	35	44	38	42

$i =$	11	12	13	14	15	16	17	18	19	20
Y_i	52	34	43	48	28	32	44	53	47	45
X_{1i}	8.3	7.6	7.2	8.3	5.9	6.9	6.8	7.9	8.4	8.8
X_{2i}	36	38	35	42	31	31	35	39	43	46

7.22   Using the data of Table 7.1 and the model (7.12), determine the value of $R^2_{YX_1}$ directly from the differences between the predicted and observed values. Compare with the value obtained analytically in the text.

7.23   Show that

$$(\hat{Y}_i - Y_i)^2 + (Y_i - \bar{\bar{Y}}_i)^2 = (\hat{Y}_i - \bar{\bar{Y}}_i)^2$$

when Y_i is the predicted value from a linear model. [*Hint:* Start from

$$(\hat{Y}_i - Y_i) + (Y_i - \bar{\bar{Y}}_i) = (\hat{Y}_i - \bar{\bar{Y}}_i)$$

Raise both sides to their square, and show that the double product is equal to zero.] Using this result, demonstrate that the value of $R^2_{Y;X_1X_2...X_m}$ is always between zero and 1 for linear models.

7.24   The accompanying table presents the results of a survey of the average number of trips per family per day in three areas, as a function of the average number of cars owned by a family.

	Region A			*Region* B			*Region* C		
	1	*2*	*3*	*4*	*5*	*6*	*7*	*8*	*9*
Average number of trips, $\hat{Y}_i$	1.24	1.31	1.04	1.56	0.53	0.49	0.86	1.60	1.15
Average number of cars, $\hat{X}_i$	0.75	0.78	0.76	0.84	0.68	0.65	0.71	0.82	0.75

(a)   Plot the variations of the average number of trips/family/day versus the average number of cars owned.

(b)   Compute the equation of the linear model that best approximates these variations. Confirm your results graphically.

(c)   Estimate the efficiency of this model. State your definition of efficiency (performance, fit, etc.). Elaborate on the meaning of your numerical answer(s).

7.25 Using the data for Exercise 7.24, investigate the effect of the geographical location on the average level of trip making. (Assume that the distribution of the levels of trip making is normal. State and substantiate other required assumptions.) Specify the level of confidence of your conclusion. Verbalize, and perhaps qualify, the result of the test. (*Hint:* Develop three models, for each of the regions, and evaluate the significance of the variations in the parameters in terms of the level of precision on their estimation.)

7.26 In a tenth area, the measurement for the average number of cars owned was 1.47.
   (a) At what level would you estimate the corresponding level of trip making?
   (b) What level of precision would you give to your prediction?

REFERENCES

ALLEN, E. *Introduction to Linear Regression and Correlation*. San Francisco: W. H. Freeman & Company, 1976.

GRAYBILL, F. *Theory and Application of the Linear Model*. North Scituate, Mass.: Duxbury Press, 1976.

ROGERS, A. *Matrix Methods in Urban and Regional Analysis*. San Francisco: Holden-Day, Inc., 1972.

SEARLE, S. *Linear Models*. New York: John Wiley & Sons, Inc., 1971.

WONNACOTT, R. J., AND T. H. WONNACOTT. *Econometrics*. New York: John Wiley & Sons, Inc., 1968.

Appendix A
Statistical Tables

TABLE A.1 A Thousand Random Digits

25	65	24	72	54	69	90	47	0	60	31	2	96	78	92	95
80	34	39	84	40	32	89	31	84	83	18	86	39	5	31	4
88	80	31	43	8	41	82	76	6	9	60	96	24	35	50	18
33	96	45	29	58	91	72	89	58	52	49	49	93	65	50	34
82	69	43	41	50	70	44	92	61	97	58	52	29	40	61	65
55	81	83	74	31	13	47	89	55	86	61	87	90	88	27	15
25	19	7	77	77	36	54	43	69	74	82	80	14	62	61	41
52	31	82	63	60	92	43	19	56	30	8	6	83	37	15	45
45	33	73	83	10	78	9	32	27	8	8	62	10	45	67	7
58	27	21	72	72	79	41	76	19	20	91	77	51	47	76	94
35	11	93	23	25	49	76	31	39	24	64	34	87	48	90	19
72	11	15	95	2	65	59	69	21	7	79	15	72	33	69	94
93	97	41	55	84	83	29	59	45	49	31	17	41	72	39	28
0	21	81	85	47	49	73	41	22	47	14	62	55	54	24	76
46	64	13	66	9	67	86	88	75	87	14	17	48	91	2	4
19	71	52	8	5	81	12	37	58	90	95	1	74	15	17	99
27	11	27	99	28	14	0	30	49	79	75	39	99	93	64	18
83	45	86	81	45	17	37	69	91	97	86	89	66	32	86	94
15	81	52	49	68	51	90	47	98	30	98	84	19	58	17	69
27	7	91	0	23	95	42	8	36	17	46	98	38	78	57	24
15	74	19	44	72	24	26	95	43	9	80	1	54	33	43	44
11	81	0	92	17	40	38	55	73	52	67	40	68	38	50	7
70	49	5	38	95	71	68	24	13	56	89	93	5	13	72	20
87	5	98	82	20	49	83	44	1	87	41	97	87	89	31	66
72	46	58	31	94	80	34	42	12	17	18	68	72	87	5	18
26	53	73	78	25	36	35	60	54	7	71	81	81	11	82	56
72	38	44	9	85	75	18	84	45	92	45	94	70	73	4	85
55	33	63	33	21	63	35	66	49	12	22	78	81	41	75	50
69	26	84	32	35	15	77	92	0	56	53	30	23	35	3	4
90	99	24	74	24	41	82	33	77	61	18	39	63	29	98	1
46	39	52	83	87	20	80	56	85	34	81	36	14	12	85	80
28	92	36	83												

TABLE A.2 Standard Normal Probability Distribution

The entry in the table represents the probability p_z that a standardized normal random variable Z takes a value between 0 and the value Z, when Z is positive, or by symmetry, between Z and 0 when Z is negative. The value of the cumulative distribution $\Phi(z)$ is the probability of a value between $-\infty$ and Z. Thus, it is equal to $0.5 + p_z$ when Z is positive, and $0.5 - p_z$ when Z is negative.

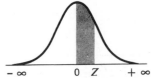

z	.00	.01	.02	.03	.04	.05	.06	.07	.08	.09
0.0	.0000	.0040	.0080	.0120	.0160	.0199	.0239	.0279	.0319	.0359
0.1	.0398	.0438	.0478	.0517	.0557	.0596	.0636	.0675	.0714	.0753
0.2	.0793	.0832	.0871	.0910	.0948	.0987	.1026	.1064	.1103	.1141
0.3	.1179	.1217	.1255	.1293	.1331	.1368	.1406	.1443	.1480	.1517
0.4	.1554	.1591	.1628	.1664	.1700	.1736	.1772	.1808	.1844	.1879
0.5	.1915	.1950	.1985	.2019	.2054	.2088	.2123	.2157	.2190	.2224
0.6	.2257	.2291	.2324	.2357	.2389	.2422	.2454	.2486	.2517	.2549
0.7	.2580	.2611	.2642	.2673	.2703	.2734	.2764	.2794	.2823	.2852
0.8	.2881	.2910	.2939	.2967	.2995	.3023	.3051	.3078	.3106	.3133
0.9	.3159	.3186	.3212	.3238	.3264	.3289	.3315	.3340	.3365	.3389
1.0	.3413	.3438	.3461	.3485	.3508	.3531	.3554	.3577	.3599	.3621
1.1	.3643	.3665	.3686	.3708	.3729	.3749	.3770	.3790	.3810	.3830
1.2	.3849	.3869	.3888	.3907	.3925	.3944	.3962	.3980	.3997	.4015
1.3	.4032	.4049	.4066	.4082	.4099	.4115	.4131	.4147	.4162	.4177
1.4	.4192	.4207	.4222	.4236	.4251	.4265	.4279	.4292	.4306	.4319
1.5	.4332	.4345	.4357	.4370	.4382	.4394	.4406	.4418	.4429	.4441
1.6	.4452	.4463	.4474	.4484	.4495	.4505	.4515	.4525	.4535	.4545
1.7	.4554	.4564	.4573	.4582	.4591	.4599	.4608	.4616	.4625	.4633
1.8	.4641	.4649	.4656	.4664	.4671	.4678	.4686	.4693	.4699	.4706
1.9	.4713	.4719	.4726	.4732	.4738	.4744	.4750	.4756	.4761	.4767
2.0	.4772	.4778	.4783	.4788	.4793	.4798	.4803	.4808	.4812	.4817
2.1	.4821	.4826	.4830	.4834	.4838	.4842	.4846	.4850	.4854	.4857
2.2	.4861	.4864	.4868	.4871	.4875	.4878	.4881	.4884	.4887	.4890
2.3	.4893	.4896	.4898	.4901	.4904	.4906	.4909	.4911	.4913	.4916
2.4	.4918	.4920	.4922	.4925	.4927	.4929	.4931	.4932	.4934	.4936
2.5	.4938	.4940	.4941	.4943	.4945	.4946	.4948	.4949	.4951	.4952
2.6	.4953	.4955	.4956	.4957	.4959	.4960	.4961	.4962	.4963	.4964
2.7	.4965	.4966	.4967	.4968	.4969	.4970	.4971	.4972	.4973	.4974
2.8	.4974	.4975	.4976	.4977	.4977	.4978	.4979	.4979	.4980	.4981
2.9	.4981	.4982	.4982	.4983	.4984	.4984	.4985	.4985	.4986	.4986
3.0	.4987	.4987	.4987	.4988	.4988	.4989	.4989.	.4989	.4990	.4990

Reproduced by permission from Paul Hoel, *Introduction to Mathematical Statistics*, 4th ed., John Wiley & Sons, Inc., New York, 1971.

TABLE A.3 T Probability Distribution

The entry in the table is the value of the T random variable such that it leaves out a right hand-tailed probability for higher values equal to the heading P of the column. The row index v represents the value of the number of degrees of freedom.

v \ P	.10	.05	.025	.01	.005
1	3.078	6.314	12.706	31.821	63.657
2	1.886	2.920	4.303	6.965	9.925
3	1.638	2.353	3.182	4.541	5.841
4	1.533	2.132	2.776	3.747	4.604
5	1.476	2.015	2.571	3.365	4.032
6	1.440	1.943	2.447	3.143	3.707
7	1.415	1.895	2.365	2.998	3.499
8	1.397	1.860	2.306	2.896	3.355
9	1.383	1.833	2.262	2.821	3.250
10	1.372	1.812	2.228	2.764	3.169
11	1.363	1.796	2.201	2.718	3.106
12	1.356	1.782	2.179	2.681	3.055
13	1.350	1.771	2.160	2.650	3.012
14	1.345	1.761	2.145	2.624	2.977
15	1.341	1.753	2.131	2.602	2.947
16	1.337	1.746	2.120	2.583	2.921
17	1.333	1.740	2.110	2.567	2.898
18	1.330	1.734	2.101	2.552	2.878
19	1.328	1.729	2.093	2.539	2.861
20	1.325	1.725	2.086	2.528	2.845
21	1.323	1.721	2.080	2.518	2.831
22	1.321	1.717	2.074	2.508	2.819
23	1.319	1.714	2.069	2.500	2.807
24	1.318	1.711	2.064	2.492	2.797
25	1.316	1.708	2.060	2.485	2.787
26	1.315	1.706	2.056	2.479	2.779
27	1.314	1.703	2.052	2.473	2.771
28	1.313	1.701	2.048	2.467	2.763
29	1.311	1.699	2.045	2.462	2.756
30	1.310	1.697	2.042	2.457	2.750
40	1.303	1.684	2.021	2.423	2.704
60	1.296	1.671	2.000	2.390	2.660
120	1.289	1.658	1.980	2.358	2.617
∞	1.282	1.645	1.960	2.326	2.576

Reproduced by permission from Paul Hoel, *Introduction to Mathematical Statistics*, 4th ed., John Wiley & Sons, Inc., New York, 1971.

TABLE A.4 Binomial Probability Distribution

he entry in the table represents the probability that a binomial random variable with parameters (number of observations) and π (probability of an individual observation showing a given haracteristic) takes the value x. [Probabilities for values of π between 0.6 and 1 are obtained by hanging π into $(1 - \pi)$ and x into $(n - x)$.]

n	x	$\pi =$ .05	.1	.2	.3	.4
2	0	.9025	.8100	.6400	.4900	.3600
	1	.0950	.1800	.3200	.4200	.4800
	2	.0025	.0100	.0400	.0900	.1600
3	0	.8574	.7290	.5120	.3430	.2160
	1	.1354	.2430	.3840	.4410	.4320
	2	.0071	.0270	.0960	.4890	.2880
	3	.0001	.0010	.0080	.0270	.0640
4	0	.8145	.6561	.4096	.2401	.1296
	1	.1715	.2916	.4096	.4116	.3456
	2	.0135	.0486	.1536	.2646	.3456
	3	.0005	.0036	.0256	.0756	.1536
	4		.0001	.0016	.0081	.0256
5	0	.7738	.5905	.3277	.1681	.0778
	1	.2036	.3280	.4096	.3602	.2592
	2	.0214	.0729	.2048	.3087	.3456
	3	.0011	.0081	.0512	.1323	.2304
	4		.0005	.0064	.0284	.0768
	5			.0003	.0024	.0102
6	0	.7351	.5314	.2621	.1176	.0467
	1	.2321	.3543	.3932	.3025	.1866
	2	.0305	.0984	.2458	.3241	.3110
	3	.0021	.0146	.0819	.1852	.2765
	4	.0001	.0012	.0154	.0595	.1382
	5		.0001	.0015	.0102	.0369
	6			.0001	.0007	.0041
7	0	.6983	.4783	.2097	.0824	.0280
	1	.2573	.3720	.3670	.2471	.1306
	2	.0406	.1240	.2753	.3176	.2613
	3	.0036	.0230	.1147	.2269	.2903
	4	.0002	.0026	.0287	.0972	.1935
	5		.0002	.0043	.0250	.0774
	6			.0004	.0036	.0172
	7			.0002	.0002	.0016

n	x	$\pi =$ .05	.2	.3	.2	.4
8	0	.6634	.4305	.1678	.0576	.0168
	1	.2793	.3826	.3355	.1977	.0896
	2	.0515	.1488	.2936	.2965	.2090
	3	.0054	.0331	.1468	.2541	.2787
	4	.0004	.0046	.0459	.1361	.2322
	5		.0004	.0092	.0467	.1239
	6			.0011	.0100	.0413
	7			.0001	.0012	.0079
	8				.0001	.0007
9	0	.6302	.3874	.1342	.0404	.0101
	1	.2985	.3874	.3020	.1556	.0605
	2	.0629	.1722	.3020	.2668	.1612
	3	.0077	.0446	.1762	.2668	.2508
	4	.0006	.0074	.0661	.1715	.2508
	5		.0008	.0165	.0735	.1672
	6		.0001	.0028	.0210	.0743
	7			.0003	.0039	.0212
	8				.0004	.0035
	9					.0003
10	0	.5987	.3487	.1074	.0282	.0060
	1	.3151	.3874	.2684	.1211	.0403
	2	.0746	.1937	.3020	.2335	.1209
	3	.0105	.0574	.2013	.2668	.2150
	4	.0010	.0112	.0881	.2001	.2508
	5	.0001	.0015	.0264	.1029	.2007
	6		.0001	.0055	.0368	.1115
	7			.0008	.0090	.0425
	8			.0001	.0014	.0106
	9				.0001	.0016
	10					.0001

n	x	$\pi =$ .5	n	x	$\pi =$ .5	n	x	$\pi =$ .5	n	x	$\pi =$ .5	n	x	$\pi =$ .5
2	0	.2500	11	0	.0005	16	0	.0000	20	1	.0000	24	2	.0000
	1	.5000		1	.0054		1	.0002		2	.0002		3	.0001
				2	.0269		2	.0018		3	.0011		4	.0006
3	0	.1250		3	.0806		3	.0085		4	.0046		5	.0025
	1	.3750		4	.1611		4	.0278		5	.0148		6	.0080
				5	.2256		5	.0667		6	.0370		7	.0206
4	0	.0625					6	.1222		7	.0739		8	.0438
	1	.2500					7	.1746		8	.1201		9	.0779
	2	.3750	12	0	.0002		8	.1964		9	.1602		10	.1169
				1	.0029					10	.1762		11	.1488
5	0	.0312		2	.0161	17	0	.0000					12	.1612
	1	.1562		3	.0537		1	.0001	21	1	.0000			
	2	.3125		4	.1208		2	.0010		2	.0001	25	2	.0000
				5	.1934		3	.0052		3	.0006		3	.0001
6	0	.0156		6	.2256		4	.0182		4	.0029		4	.0004
	1	.0938					5	.0472		5	.0097		5	.0016
	2	.2344	13	0	.0001		6	.0944		6	.0259		6	.0053
	3	.3125		1	.0016		7	.1484		7	.0554		7	.0143
				2	.0095		8	.1855		8	.0970		8	.0322
7	0	.0078		3	.0349					9	.1402		9	.0609
	1	.0547		4	.0873					10	.1682		10	.0974
	2	.1641		5	.1571	18	0	.0000					11	.1328
	3	.2734		6	.2095		1	.0001	22	1	.0000		12	.1550
							2	.0006		2	.0001			
			14	0	.0001		3	.0031		3	.0004			
8	0	.0039		1	.0009		4	.0117		4	.0017			
	1	.0312		2	.0056		5	.0327		5	.0063			
	2	.1094		3	.0222		6	.0708		6	.0178			
	3	.2188		4	.0611		7	.1214		7	.0407			
	4	.2734		5	.1222		8	.1669		8	.0762			
				6	.1833		9	.1855		9	.1186			
9	0	.0020		7	.2095					10	.1542			
	1	.0176				19	1	.0000		11	.1682			
	2	.0703	15	0	.0000		2	.0003						
	3	.1641		1	.0005		3	.0018						
	4	.2461		2	.0032		4	.0074	23	2	.0000			
				3	.0139		5	.0222		3	.0002			
10	0	.0010		4	.0417		6	.0518		4	.0011			
	1	.0098		5	.0916		7	.0961		5	.0040			
	2	.0439		6	.1527		8	.1442		6	.0120			
	3	.1172		7	.1964		9	.1762		7	.0292			
	4	.2051								8	.0584			
	5	.2461								9	.0974			
										10	.1364			
										11	.1612			

Appendix B
Solutions to Selected Exercises

1.1 (a) $\quad A + B = \begin{bmatrix} 22 & 47 & 52 & 34 \\ 37 & 97 & 31 & 51 \\ 37 & 27 & 22 & 81 \\ 52 & 72 & 28 & 76 \end{bmatrix}$

(b) $\quad A - B = \begin{bmatrix} 0 & -3 & 14 & -6 \\ -7 & 25 & 11 & -15 \\ 1 & -7 & 0 & -17 \\ -16 & 16 & 2 & -24 \end{bmatrix}$

(c) $\quad 3A + 4B = \begin{bmatrix} 77 & 166 & 175 & 122 \\ 133 & 327 & 103 & 186 \\ 129 & 98 & 77 & 292 \\ 190 & 244 & 97 & 27 \end{bmatrix}$

(d) $\quad AB = \begin{bmatrix} 1675 & 2020 & 974 & 3263 \\ 2497 & 3432 & 1360 & 4242 \\ 1715 & 1918 & 998 & 2849 \\ 2320 & 3017 & 1285 & 3847 \end{bmatrix}$

1.2   Matrix of cofactors:

$$\begin{bmatrix} 0.675 & 0 & 0 \\ 0.075 & 0.667 & 0 \\ 0.210 & 0.267 & 0.801 \end{bmatrix}$$

Determinant $= 0.60$.

$$B^{-1} = \begin{bmatrix} \dfrac{0.675}{0.600} & \dfrac{0.075}{0.600} & \dfrac{0.210}{0.600} \\ \dfrac{0}{0.600} & \dfrac{0.66}{0.600} & \dfrac{0.267}{0.600} \\ \dfrac{0}{0.600} & \dfrac{0}{0.600} & \dfrac{0.801}{0.600} \end{bmatrix} = \begin{bmatrix} 1.125 & 0.125 & 0.350 \\ 0 & 1.111 & 0.445 \\ 0 & 0 & 1.335 \end{bmatrix}$$

1.3   (a) $\sum\limits_{i=1} X_i = 16$

(b) $\sqrt{\sum\limits_i X_i} = 4$

(c) $\sum\limits_i \sqrt{X_i} = 7.614$

(d) $\sum\limits_i X_i^2 = 84$

(e) $(\sum\limits_i X_i)^2 = 256$

(f) $\sum\limits_i 2X_i = 32$

1.4   (a) $\sum\limits_i \sum\limits_j X_{ij} = 27$

(b) $\sum\limits_i \sum\limits_j \dfrac{1}{X_{ij}} = 4.283$

1.5 $X = \tfrac{8}{5} = 1.6$

1.7 $X \le 1$

1.10 (a) $\mu = 6.4$

(b) $\sigma^2 = 7.84$

(c) $\sigma = 2.8$

1.11 (c) $\bar{X} = 4$

(d) $s_X^2 = 10.50, s_X = 3.24$

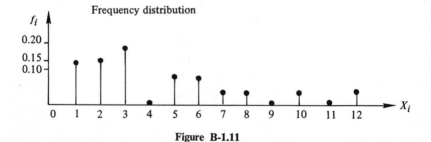

Figure B-1.11

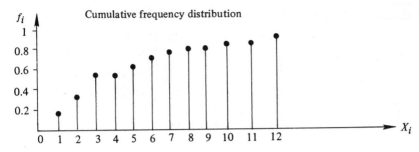

Figure B-1.11   (Cont.)

1.12 $\frac{1}{N} \sum_{i=1}^{N} (X_i - \bar{X}) = \frac{1}{N} \sum_{i} X_i - \sum_{i} \frac{\bar{X}}{N} = \bar{X} - N\frac{\bar{X}}{N} = 0$

2.1 (a) $t_0 = \frac{\log 1.3}{\log 1.05} = 5.38$ years

2.2 (a) $P_t = 250{,}000(0.48)^{0.93t}, P_{10} = 175{,}253$
   (b) $t_0 = 16.41$ years

2.3 (a) $P_t = 50 + 1.96t; P_{15} = 79.4$
   (b) $P_{19} = 87.2$

2.4 (a) Exponentially decreasing with (5-year) rate of 0.08, or 8%:
       $P_n = 500(0.92)^n;$
   (b) $P = 350$ for $n = 3.45$ or $t_0 = 1950 + 5(3.45) = 1967$

2.7 (a) Logistic model with parameters $P_0 = 11; a = 0.08; b = 0.002$
   (b) $P_t = 20$ for $t_0 = 12.11;$
   (c) $P_\infty = 40$

2.8 $\frac{P_{\text{met}}}{P_{\text{state}}} \simeq 0.35$

   $\frac{P_{\text{rest}}}{P_{\text{state}}} \simeq 0.65$

2.9 (a) $\left(\frac{P_\infty - P_5}{P_\infty - P_4}\right)\left(\frac{P_\infty - P_4}{P_\infty - P_3}\right)\left(\frac{P_\infty - P_3}{P_\infty - P_2}\right)\left(\frac{P_\infty - P_2}{P_\infty - P_1}\right) = v \cdot v \cdot v \cdot v = v^4$
   Thus,

$$\frac{P_\infty - P_5}{P_\infty - P_1} = v^4 = \frac{5000 - 2000}{5000 - 1000} = 0.75$$

$$4 \log v = \log 0.75 \text{ and } \log v = \frac{\log 0.75}{4} = -0.0719$$

$$v = e^{-0.0719} = 0.93, \text{ or } 93\%$$

   (b) $P_t = P_\infty - v^t(P_\infty - P_0)$. If $P_{10} = 0.9P_\infty$, then $0.9P_\infty = P_\infty - v^{10}P_\infty$, or
   $0.9 = 1 - v^{10}$; or $v^{10} = 0.1$; $v = \sqrt[10]{0.1} = 0.79$, or 79%.

2.10 (a) Leaving male births out, since we tie them to the females:

$$\mathbf{P}^M_{1970} = \begin{bmatrix} 0.012 & 0 & 0 \\ 0.994 & 0.008 & 0 \\ 0 & 0.990 & 0.992 \end{bmatrix} \begin{bmatrix} 8,000 \\ 10,000 \\ 9,000 \end{bmatrix} = \begin{bmatrix} 100 \\ 8,032 \\ 18,828 \end{bmatrix}$$

$$\mathbf{P}^F_{1970} = \begin{bmatrix} 0.011 & 0.018 & 0 \\ 0.995 & 0.017 & 0 \\ 0 & 0.987 & 0.989 \end{bmatrix} \begin{bmatrix} 7,500 \\ 6,000 \\ 9,000 \end{bmatrix} = \begin{bmatrix} 190 \\ 7,564 \\ 14,823 \end{bmatrix}$$

$$\text{Total male births} = [0.013 \quad 0.013 \quad 0] \begin{bmatrix} 7,500 \\ 6,000 \\ 9,000 \end{bmatrix} = 176$$

This is now added to the male population in the first age group:

$$\mathbf{P}^M_{1970} = \begin{bmatrix} 276 \\ 8,032 \\ 18,828 \end{bmatrix}$$

The population distributions for year 2000 are obtained by reiteration using these new distributions.

(b) The combined population distribution is obtained by adding $\mathbf{P}^M_{1970}$ and $\mathbf{P}^F_{1970}$.

2.12 The transition to the first (5-year) period can be registered as

$$\begin{bmatrix} p^1_1 \\ p^1_2 \\ p^1_3 \\ p^1_4 \\ p^1_5 \\ p^1_6 \\ p^1_7 \\ p^1_8 \\ p^1_9 \end{bmatrix} = \begin{bmatrix} 0 & 0 & 0 & 0.022 & 0.055 & 0.043 & 0.024 & 0.010 & 0.003 \\ 0.993 & 0 & 0 & 0 & 0 & 0 & 0 & 0 & 0 \\ 0 & 0.998 & 0 & 0 & 0 & 0 & 0 & 0 & 0 \\ 0 & 0 & 0.998 & 0 & 0 & 0 & 0 & 0 & 0 \\ 0 & 0 & 0 & 0.998 & 0 & 0 & 0 & 0 & 0 \\ 0 & 0 & 0 & 0 & 0.998 & 0 & 0 & 0 & 0 \\ 0 & 0 & 0 & 0 & 0 & 0.997 & 0 & 0 & 0 \\ 0 & 0 & 0 & 0 & 0 & 0 & 0.997 & 0 & 0 \\ 0 & 0 & 0 & 0 & 0 & 0 & 0 & 0.997 & 0.997 \end{bmatrix}$$

$$\times \begin{bmatrix} 59.85 \\ 53.06 \\ 41.84 \\ 32.03 \\ 34.40 \\ 36.23 \\ 39.03 \\ 37.27 \\ 31.09 \end{bmatrix} = \begin{bmatrix} 5.55 \\ 59.38 \\ 52.99 \\ 41.72 \\ 31.94 \\ 34.33 \\ 36.09 \\ 38.88 \\ 68.20 \end{bmatrix}$$

(Population levels are in hundreds)

Repeating, for the second time period:

$$\begin{bmatrix} p_1^2 \\ p_2^2 \\ p_3^2 \\ p_4^2 \\ p_5^2 \\ p_6^2 \\ p_7^2 \\ p_8^2 \\ p_9^2 \end{bmatrix} = \begin{bmatrix} 5.61 \\ 5.51 \\ 59.26 \\ 52.88 \\ 41.64 \\ 31.88 \\ 34.23 \\ 35.98 \\ 106.76 \end{bmatrix} ; \text{ etc.}$$

3.1   (a) $A = \begin{bmatrix} 0.11 & 0.1 & 0.2 \\ 0 & 0.1 & 0.3 \\ 0 & 0 & 0.25 \end{bmatrix}$; $(I - A)^{-1} = \begin{bmatrix} 1.12 & 0.12 & 0.35 \\ 0 & 1.11 & 0.45 \\ 0 & 0 & 1.33 \end{bmatrix}$

(b) $Y = (I - A)^{-1}X = \begin{bmatrix} 1.12 & 0.12 & 0.35 \\ 0 & 1.11 & 0.45 \\ 0 & 0 & 1.33 \end{bmatrix} \begin{bmatrix} 100 \\ 120 \\ 40 \end{bmatrix} = \begin{bmatrix} 140 \\ 151 \\ 53 \end{bmatrix}$

(c) $X = Y - AY = \begin{bmatrix} 150 \\ 200 \\ 150 \end{bmatrix} - \begin{bmatrix} 0.11 & 0.10 & 0.20 \\ 0 & 0.10 & 0.30 \\ 0 & 0 & 0.25 \end{bmatrix} \begin{bmatrix} 150 \\ 200 \\ 150 \end{bmatrix} = \begin{bmatrix} 83 \\ 135 \\ 112 \end{bmatrix}$

3.2   If $\Delta Y^{(1)} = A\Delta X$ and $\Delta Y^{(k)} = A\Delta Y^{(k-1)}$,

$$Y = X + \Delta Y^{(1)} + \Delta Y^{(2)} + \ldots + \Delta Y^{(k)}$$

$$= \begin{bmatrix} 100 \\ 120 \\ 40 \end{bmatrix} + \begin{bmatrix} 31 \\ 24 \\ 10 \end{bmatrix} + \begin{bmatrix} 8 \\ 5 \\ 3 \end{bmatrix} + \begin{bmatrix} 2 \\ 1 \\ 1 \end{bmatrix} = \begin{bmatrix} 141 \\ 150 \\ 54 \end{bmatrix}$$

3.3   The matrix equation $Y = AY + X$ can be written in the traditional form as

$$Y_1 = 100 + 0.11Y_1 + 0.10Y_2 + 0.20Y_3 \qquad (1)$$
$$Y_2 = 120 + \quad 0 \quad + 0.10Y_2 + 0.30Y_3 \qquad (2)$$
$$Y_3 = \ \ 40 + \quad 0 \quad + \quad 0 \quad + 0.25Y_3 \qquad (3)$$

From equation (3); $Y_3 - 0.25Y_3 = 40$ and $0.75Y_3 = 40$ or $Y_3 = 40/0.75$ = 53.3. Replacing $Y_3 = 53$ in equation (2), we get

$$Y_2 = 120 + 0.10Y_2 + 0.30(53.3)$$
$$= 120 + 0.10Y_2 + 16 = 136 + 0.10Y_2$$

and $Y_2 - 0.10Y_2 = 136 = 0.90Y_2$ or $Y_2 = 136/0.90 = 151.1$.

Finally, replacing both values of Y_2 and Y_3 in equation (1), we get $Y_1 = 100 + (0.11Y_1) + 0.10(151) + 0.20(53)$, or $Y_1 - 0.11Y_1 = 100 + 15.1 + 10.6$. Thus, $0.89Y_1 = 125.7$ and $Y_1 = 125.7/0.89 = 141.2$. Summarizing,

$$Y_1 = 141$$
$$Y_2 = 151$$
$$Y_3 = 53$$

3.6 (a) $\mathbf{A} = \begin{bmatrix} 0.25 & 0.50 \\ 0.50 & 0.25 \end{bmatrix}; \ (\mathbf{I} - \mathbf{A})^{-1} = \begin{bmatrix} 2.4 & 1.6 \\ 1.6 & 2.4 \end{bmatrix}$

   (b) $\begin{bmatrix} Y_A \\ Y_B \end{bmatrix} = \begin{bmatrix} 2.4 & 1.6 \\ 1.6 & 2.4 \end{bmatrix} \begin{bmatrix} 150 \\ 100 \end{bmatrix} \begin{bmatrix} 520 \\ 480 \end{bmatrix}$

   (c) $\begin{bmatrix} X_A \\ X_B \end{bmatrix} = \begin{bmatrix} 1 \\ 1 \end{bmatrix} - \begin{bmatrix} 0.25 & 0.50 \\ 0.50 & 0.25 \end{bmatrix} \begin{bmatrix} 1 \\ 1 \end{bmatrix} = \begin{bmatrix} 0.25 \\ 0.25 \end{bmatrix}$

   (d) $\begin{bmatrix} Y_A \\ Y_B \end{bmatrix} = \begin{bmatrix} 2.4 & 1.6 \\ 1.6 & 2.4 \end{bmatrix} \begin{bmatrix} 1 \\ 0 \end{bmatrix} = \begin{bmatrix} 2.4 \\ 1.6 \end{bmatrix}$

3.8 $\mathbf{P} = \mathbf{HE}^p + \mathbf{H(SH)E}^p + \mathbf{HSHSHE}^p + \ldots$

$\mathbf{P} = (\mathbf{HE}^p + \mathbf{(HS)HE}^p + \mathbf{(HS)^2 HE}^p + \ldots)$

$= (\mathbf{I} + \mathbf{HS} + \mathbf{(HS)^2} + \ldots + \mathbf{(HS)}^n + \ldots)\mathbf{HE}^p = (\mathbf{I} - \mathbf{HS})^{-1}\mathbf{HE}^p$

3.9 $\mathbf{E} = \mathbf{SHE}^p + \mathbf{SHSHE}^p + \mathbf{SHSHSHE}^p + \ldots$

$\mathbf{E} = \mathbf{S(I)HE}^p + \mathbf{S(HS)HE}^p + \mathbf{S(HS)^2 HE}^p + \ldots$

$= \mathbf{S(I} - \mathbf{HS})^{-1}\mathbf{HE}^p$

3.10

$$\mathbf{E} = \mathbf{E}^s + \mathbf{E}^p \tag{1}$$

$$\mathbf{P} = \mathbf{HE} \tag{2}$$

$$\mathbf{E}^s = \mathbf{SP} \tag{3}$$

We must now express $\mathbf{E}$, $\mathbf{P}$, and $\mathbf{E}^s$ as functions of the given $\mathbf{E}^p$. Replacing $\mathbf{E}$ in (2) by its expression in (1), we get

$$\mathbf{P} = \mathbf{H(E}^s + \mathbf{E}^p) = \mathbf{HE}^s + \mathbf{HE}^p$$

Replacing $\mathbf{E}^s$ by its expression in (3), we get

$$\mathbf{P} = \mathbf{HSP} + \mathbf{HE}^p \quad \text{and} \quad \mathbf{IP} - \mathbf{HSP} = \mathbf{HE}^p$$

or

$$(\mathbf{I} - \mathbf{HS})\mathbf{P} = \mathbf{HE}^p$$

and multiplying both sides by $(\mathbf{I} - \mathbf{HS})^{-1}$, we get

$$(\mathbf{I} - \mathbf{HS})^{-1}(\mathbf{I} - \mathbf{HS})\mathbf{P} = (\mathbf{I} - \mathbf{HS})^{-1}\mathbf{HE}^p = \mathbf{IP}$$

$$(\mathbf{I} - \mathbf{HS})^{-1}\mathbf{HE}^p = \mathbf{P} \tag{a}$$

Since $\mathbf{E}^s = \mathbf{SP}$, we immediately have

$$\mathbf{E}^s = \mathbf{S(I} - \mathbf{HS})^{-1}\mathbf{HE}^p \tag{b}$$

Finally, $\mathbf{P} = \mathbf{HE}$ or $\mathbf{E} = \mathbf{H}^{-1}\mathbf{P}$ and

$$\mathbf{E} = \mathbf{H}^{-1}(\mathbf{I} - \mathbf{HS})^{-1}\mathbf{HE}^p \tag{c}$$

3.15 $\mathbf{E} = \mathbf{E}^p + \mathbf{E}^s = \mathbf{E}^p + (\mathbf{SHE}^p + \mathbf{SHSHE}^p + \mathbf{SHSHSHE}^p + \ldots)$

$= \mathbf{H}^{-1}\mathbf{H}[\mathbf{E}^p + \mathbf{SHE}^p + \mathbf{SHSHE}^p + \mathbf{SHSHSHE}^p + \ldots]$

$= \mathbf{H}^{-1}[\mathbf{HE}^p + \mathbf{HSHE}^p + \mathbf{HSHSHE}^p + \mathbf{HSHSHSHE}^p + \ldots]$

$= \mathbf{H}^{-1}[\mathbf{I} + \mathbf{HS} + \mathbf{HSHS} + \mathbf{HSHSHS} + \ldots]\mathbf{HE}^p$

$$= H^{-1}[I + HS + (HS)^2 + (HS)^3 + \ldots]HE^p$$
$$= H^{-1}(I - HS)^{-1}HE^p$$

4.2 $\quad W_{ij} = O_j \left[\dfrac{D_i F(d_{ij})}{\sum\limits_i D_i F(d_{ij})} \right]$

4.4 (a) New values:

$A_{ij} = P_i^2 d_{ij}^{-2}$	$j = 1$	2	3
$i = 1$	$\frac{9}{4}$	$\frac{9}{64}$	$\frac{1}{4}$
2	$\frac{1}{16}$	$\frac{4}{9}$	$\frac{1}{4}$
3	$\frac{1}{9}$	$\frac{1}{4}$	$\frac{4}{9}$
Total	2.42	0.83	0.94

$a_{ij} = A_{ij}/\sum\limits_i A_{ij}$	$j = 1$	2	3
$i = 1$	0.93	0.17	0.27
2	0.03	0.53	0.27
3	0.04	0.30	0.47

$W_{ij} = E_j a_{ij}$	$j = 1$	2	3	Total: W_i
$i = 1$	$2(0.93) = 1.86$	$3(0.17) = 0.51$	$4(0.27) = 1.08$	3.45
2	$2(0.03) = 0.04$	$3(0.53) = 1.59$	$4(0.27) = 1.08$	2.71
3	$2(0.04) = 0.08$	$3(0.30) = 0.90$	$4(0.47) = 1.88$	2.86
				9.02

4.7 $P_2 \geq 0.30 \rightarrow P_1 \leq 0.70 \rightarrow \Phi_{(u)} \leq 0.70 \rightarrow U \leq 0.525 \rightarrow 0.525 \geq U = 0.8 + 0.11(T_2 - T_1) + 0.1(C_2 - C_1) + 0.01(40) + 0.05(30) \rightarrow 2.175 \leq 0.11(T_1 - T_2) + 0.1(C_1 - C_2)$; or, assuming that $T_1 \leq T_2$ and $C_1 \geq C_2$,

$$2.175 + 0.11(T_2 - T_1) \leq 0.1(C_1 - C_2)$$

4.8 (a) $P_2 = \frac{1}{3} \longrightarrow P_1 = \frac{2}{3} = \dfrac{1}{1 + e^{-[(0.7 + 0.3(1.5 - 1) + 0.2(t_2 - t_1)]}}$

$$1 + e^{-[0.85 + 0.2(t_2 - t_1)]} = \left(\frac{1}{\frac{2}{3}} \right) = 1.5$$

$$e^{-[0.85 + 0.2(t_2 - t_1)]} = 0.5$$

or, taking the logs

$$-[0.85 + 0.2(t_2 - t_1)] = \log(0.5) = -0.693$$

or

$$0.2(t_2 - t_1) = 0.693 - 0.850 = -0.157$$

and

$$t_2 - t_1 = -0.785; \text{ i.e., } t_2 = t_1 - 0.785 \text{ hour, or 47 minutes.}$$

4.9 (a)

A_{ij} $i=$	$j=$ 1	2	3
1	3/0.5 = 6	3/6 = 0.5	3/3 = 1
2	1.5/6 = 0.25	1.5/0.3 = 5	1.5/3 = 0.5
3	0.5/3 = 0.17	0.5/3 = 0.17	0.5/0.2 = 2.5
Total	6.42	5.67	4.0

a_{ij}

0.94	0.09	0.25
0.04	0.89	0.12
0.02	0.02	0.63

$$O_1 = (0.7)3 = 2.1$$
$$O_2 = (0.6)1.5 = 0.9$$
$$O_3 = (0.5)0.5 = 0.25$$

(b) Trip distribution (in millions):

$T_{ij} = O_j a_{ij}$ $i=$	$j=$ 1	2	3	Total
1	2.1(0.94) = 1.96	0.9(0.09) = 0.08	0.25(0.25) = 0.06	2.1
2	2.1(0.04) = 0.08	0.9(0.89) = 0.79	0.25(0.12) = 0.03	0.91
3	2.1(0.03) = 0.05	0.9(0.03) = 0.03	0.25(0.62) = 0.16	0.24

4.11 Shortest path: $A \longrightarrow B \longrightarrow C \longrightarrow G$; length = 4.

4.12

M_{ij}

	A	B	C
1	1.04	1.74	1.07
2	0.39	0.87	0.20
3	1.57	1.39	0.73

5.1 X_1 = number of jobs created in the first industrial sector (in hundreds)
X_2 = number of jobs created in the second industrial sector (in hundreds)

$$Max \ (X_1 + \quad X_2)$$

Such That amounts of funds available in the 4 years will be less than

$$1.3X_1 + 0.35X_2 \le 4.55 \ \text{(1st year)}$$
$$0.6X_1 + 0.7 \ X_2 \le 4.30 \ \text{(2nd year)}$$

$$0.65X_1 + 0.5X_2 \le 3.25 \text{ (3rd year)}$$
$$0.3X_1 + 0.4X_2 \le 2.40 \text{ (4th year)}$$
$$X_1 \ge 0; \quad X_2 \ge 0$$

Solution (see Figure B-5.1): $X_1^* = 1.1$, $X_2^* = 5.2$
Total number of jobs created: 630

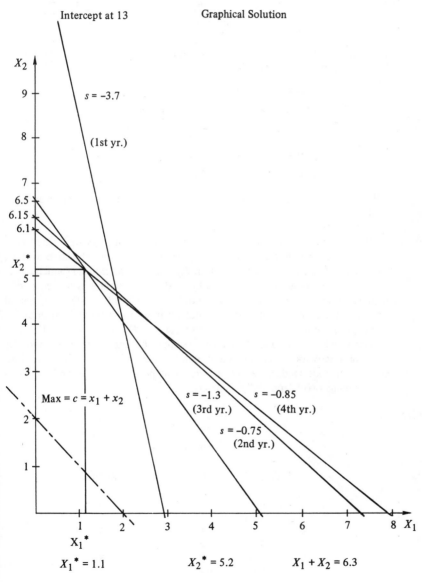

Figure B-5.1

5.9 We want the maximum of either what comes out of node 1, or what goes into node 7. We use F_{ij} for the flow on the link $i\text{—}j$. We want $Max\,(F_{12} + F_{13} + F_{14}) = Max\,(F_{57} + F_{67})$. However, all flows must be positive and less than the capacities. Therefore:

$$0 \leq F_{12} \leq 1 \qquad 0 \leq F_{24} \leq 4 \qquad 0 \leq F_{45} \leq 2$$

$$0 \leq F_{14} \leq 3 \qquad 0 \leq F_{34} \leq 6 \qquad 0 \leq F_{46} \leq 3$$

$$0 \leq F_{13} \leq 2 \qquad 0 \leq F_{57} \leq 5 \qquad 0 \leq F_{67} \leq 3$$

Finally, at each node, the sum of flows going in must be equal to the sum of flows going out. Therefore,

At node 2: $F_{12} = F_{24}$

At node 3: $F_{13} = F_{34}$

At node 4: $F_{24} + F_{14} + F_{34} = F_{45} + F_{46}$

At node 5: $F_{45} = F_{57}$

At node 6: $F_{46} = F_{67}$

All these equations are linear and we thus have a linear programming problem.

5.10 In the general case, a maximum flow problem can always be written as a linear programming problem in the variables F_{ij}. The objective will be $Max\,(F_{01})$. The constraints will be that $F_{ij} = F_{jk}$ for all nodes j (which represents the equality of the sum of the flows that are coming into each node j to the sum of the flows that are going out of it). Also, $F_{ij} - F'_{ij} = c_{ij}$ for all links $i\text{–}j$ (which represents the fact that all flows must be at least equal to some given minimum level c'_{ij}). Finally, $F_{ij} + F''_{ij} = c''_{ij}$, for all links $i\text{–}j$ (which represents the fact that all flows must be under the given capacity c''_{ij}). For a network with n nodes and m links, there will be $n + 2m$ equations, since each node leads to a "conservation of flow" equation, and an equal link leads to two "capacity" equations.

5.12 (a)

Plans (1 + 2)

$X_1 + X_2$	X_1	X_2	Return
0	0	0	0
1	0	1	3
2	1	1	5
3	2	1	7
4	3	1	8
5	4	1	9

Plans (1 + 2 + 3)

$(X_1 + X_2)$; X_3	X_1	X_2	X_3	Return
0	0	0	0	0
1	0	1	0	3
2	1	1	0	5
3	2	1	0	7
4	2	1	1	8
5	2	1	2	9

Plans (1 + 2 + 3 + 4)

Total	X_1	X_2	X_3	X_4	Return
0	0	0	0	0	0
1	0	1	0	0	3
2	0	1	0	1	5
3	2	1	0	0	7
4	0	1	0	3	9
5	1	1	0	3	11

5.13 $g_{1\ldots i}(x, y)$ is the optimal return for the combination $(x; y)$ for the first i locations, and P_i is the corresponding current allocation for x and y, in that order

$g_1(X; Y)$ — $Y \backslash X$

0	1	3	6
2	3	5	7
4	5	6	8
6	6	7	9

P_1 — $Y \backslash X$

0;0	0;1	0;2	0;3
1;0	1;1	1;2	1;3
2;0	2;1	2;2	2;3
3;0	3;1	3;2	3;3

$g_{12}(X; Y)$ — $Y \backslash X$

0	2	4	6
2	2	6	7
4	6	8	9
6	8	10	11

P_2 — $Y \backslash X$

0;0	0;1	0;2	0;0
0;0	0;1	0;2	0;3
0;0	0;1	2;0	2;0
0;0	0;1	0;2	0;3

$g_{123}(X; Y)$ — $Y \backslash X$

0	3	5	7
2	5	7	9
4	7	9	11
6	9	11	13

P_3 — $Y \backslash X$

0;0	0;1	0;1	0;3
0;0	0;1	0;1	0;3
0;0	0;1	2;1	0;3
2;0	0;1	0;1	0;3

5.14   Following is a flow diagram of the tasks:

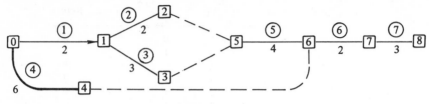

Figure B-5.14

where the activity numbers are circled and the dummy links are in dashed lines.

Node (point in time)	Earliest Start of Next Activity	Latest Start	Slack	Critical Point?
0	0	0	0	Yes
1	2	2	0	Yes
2	4	5	1	No
3	5	5	0	Yes
4	6	10	4	No
5	5	5	0	Yes
6	10	10	0	Yes
7	12	12	0	Yes
8	15	15	0	Yes

(a)   Minimum total completion time: 15 days.

(b)   Critical path: 0 to 1 to 3 to 5 to 6 to 7 to 8.

5.15   Expected completion time for activity i: $\bar{t}_i = (t_i^p + 4t_i^e + t_i^o)/6$.

Activity, $i =$	1	2	3	4	5	6	7
$\bar{t}_i$	2.33	2.66	3.17	6.17	4.5	1.83	3.83

The new activity flowchart is as follows:

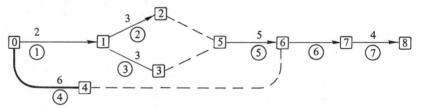

Figure B-5.15

The minimum completion time is now 15.66 days, with the same critical path: 0 to 1 to 3 to 5 to 6 to 7 to 8.

Standard deviations of the critical activities: $\sigma_i = (t_i^p - t_i^0)/6$.

Activity, $i =$	1	3	5	6	7
σ_i	0.66	0.50	0.83	0.16	1.16
σ_i^2	0.44	0.25	0.69	0.03	1.36

Variance of the minimum completion time $\sigma_{t*}^2 = \sum\limits_{i \text{ crit}} \sigma_i^2 = 2.63$.

Standard deviation: $\sigma_{t*} = \sqrt{2.63} = 1.62$.

(a) Thus, the probability that the completion time will be less than 15 days is the probability that the standard normal variable will be less than

$$\frac{15 - 15.66}{1.62} = -0.41$$

That probability is 0.34, or 34%.

(b) Similarly, the probability that the completion of the study is effected between 14 and 16 days is the probability that the standard normal variable takes a value between

$$\frac{14 - 15.66}{1.62} = -1.02 \quad \text{and} \quad \frac{16 - 15.66}{1.62} = 0.21$$

That probability is 0.26, or 26%.

6.1 (a) For a binomial random variable, $\sigma_X^2 = np(1 - p)$. Since $p = X/n$,

$$\sigma_p^2 = \sigma_X/n^2 = \frac{p(1 - p)}{n} = \frac{(0.2)(0.8)}{100} = 0.0016 \quad \text{and}$$

$$\sigma_p = \sqrt{0.0016} = 0.04$$

The error would then typically be of the order of 4%, or 4 percentage points.

(b) Large sample size gives $\bar{X}$ a normal distribution. $Z_{0.475} = 1.96$. Therefore,

$$0.23 - 1.96(0.04) \leq \mu_{\bar{X}} \leq 0.23 + 1.96(0.04)$$

or

$$0.15 \leq \mu_{\bar{X}} \leq 0.31 \qquad \text{i.e., } 0.15 \leq p \leq 0.31$$

(c) Correction factor for small population:

$$\sqrt{\frac{P - N}{P - 1}}$$

Then

$$s_{\bar{X}} = 0.04\sqrt{\frac{850 - 100}{850 - 1}} = 0.037$$

New estimation interval: $0.23 - 1.96(0.037) \leq \mu_p \leq 0.23 + 1.96(0.037)$; $0.16 \leq \mu_p \leq 0.30$.

6.2 $Z_{0.49} = 2.33$; $\sigma_{\bar{X}} = 1500/\sqrt{100} = 150$

$$7900 - 150(2.33) \leq \mu_{\bar{X}} \leq 7900 + 150(2.33) \quad \text{or} \quad 7550 \leq \mu_{\bar{X}} \leq 8250$$

Since last value 7500 is outside this interval, true value has changed.

6.3 $\delta = s Z_{0.475} = 0.25(1.96) = 0.49\%$

6.4 $s = \sqrt{s_1^2 + s_2^2} = \sqrt{(0.25)^2 + (0.25)^2} = 0.35$

      $\delta = 0.35(1.96) = 0.69\%$

6.5   Small samples. Assume that the variances are equal. From formula (6.10),

$$s_{\bar{X}} = \sqrt{\frac{(n_1 - 1)s_1^2 + (n_2 - 1)s_2^2}{n_1 + n_2 - 2}} \sqrt{\frac{1}{n_2} + \frac{1}{n_1}}$$

$$= \sqrt{\left[\frac{14(0.25)^2 + 24(0.25)^2}{15 + 25 - 2}\right]\left[\frac{1}{25} + \frac{1}{15}\right]} = 0.082$$

$$s_X = s_{\bar{X}}\sqrt{n} \approx s_{\bar{X}}\sqrt{\frac{n_1 + n_2}{2}} = 0.082\sqrt{20} = 0.367$$

The difference in rates is not distributed normally anymore, but with a T distribution with $(n_1 + n_2 - 2) = 18$ degrees of freedom, $T_{0.475} = 2.101$. Thus,

$$\delta = s_X T_{0.475} = 0.367(2.101) = 0.77\%$$

6.7 $p = 0.54;\ \sigma_p = \sqrt{\frac{(0.54)(0.46)}{200}} = 0.035$

At a level of confidence of 95%: $0.47 \leq \mu_p \leq 0.61$. Therefore, the assumption may not hold in the overall population.

6.14   Model 2 results in a sum of squared errors of 0.012 and is therefore better. Optimal values:

$$a = 0.08 \qquad b = 0.002$$

6.16   Model 2 results in a log-likelihood value of -709.17; model 3 in -680.26. Model 4 is therefore better.

7.9 $\sigma_{\hat{Y}}^2 = 2.93;$ $\sigma_{\hat{Y}} = 1.71$

      $\sigma_{\hat{X}_1}^2 = 391.8;$ $\sigma_{\hat{X}_1} = 19.80$

      $R_{YX_1}^2 = 0.683;$ $R_{YX_1} = 0.826$

      $a_0 = 3.047;$ $a_1 = 0.0715$

7.10 $\sigma_{\hat{X}_2}^2 = 25.54;$ $\sigma_{\hat{X}_2} = 5.05$

       $R_{YX_2}^2 = 0.159;$ $R_{YX_2} = 0.399$

       $a_0 = 5.43;$ $a_1 = 0.135$

       $R_{X_1X_2} = 0.731;$ $R_{X_1X_2}^2 = 0.534$

       $a_0 = 24.78;$ $a_1 = 2.86$

7.11 $10a_0 + 500a_1 + 88a_2 = 66.2$

      $500a_0 + 28918a_1 + 5136a_2 = 3590$

      $88a_0 + 5136a_1 + 1032a_2 = 618$

      Solution: $a_0 = 3.1298;\ a_1 = 0.0417;\ a_2 = 0.1595$.

      Model: $Y = 3.1298 + 0.0417X_1 + 0.1595X_2$.

7.13

$n =$	0	1	2	3	4	5
$\hat{Y}_n$	500	435	400	370	345	323
$Z = \log \hat{Y}_n$	6.214	6.075	5.991	5.913	5.844	5.778

$R_{Zn} = -0.989$; $R^2_{Zn} = 0.979$
$a_0 = 6.1799$; $a_1 = -0.0843$ or $Z_n = 6.18 - 0.0843n$
$\alpha_0 = 482.97$; $\alpha_1 = 0.919$ or $Y = 482.97(0.919)^n = 482.97(1 - 0.081)^n$
The population is exponentially decreasing at a rate of 8.1% per year.

Predicted Z_n	6.180	6.096	6.011	5.927	5.843	5.758
Predicted $Y_i = e^{Z_n}$	482.97	443.92	408.02	375.03	344.70	316.83

7.14 $Y_t = 482.97(0.919)^n = 350$
$(0.919)^n = 0.725$
$n(\log 0.919) = \log (0.725)$
$n = \dfrac{\log 0.725}{\log 0.919} = 3.81$ and $t = 1950 + 3.81(5) = 1969$

7.15

$t =$	0	5	∞
Y	120	150	250
$Z_t = \log\log \dfrac{250}{Y_t}$	-0.3093	-0.6717	∞

$R_{Zt} = -1.0$; $R^2_{Zt} = 1.0$ (always when a linear model is calibrated on only two values)
$a_0 = -0.3093$; $a_1 = -0.07248$ and $Z = -0.3093 - 0.0725t$
$a = 0.48$; $b = 0.93$ and $Y = 0.48^{0.93^t}$

7.16

$i =$	1	2	3	4
$R_i = 15,000 - \sum_{k=1}^{i} r_k$	12,300	3,800	275	0
$\hat{Y}_i = \log \hat{R}_i$	9.4174	8.2428	5.6167	∞
N_i	5,000	35,000	100,000	110,000

$R_{YN} = -0.99$; $R^2_{YN} = 0.98$
$a_0 = 9.6287$; $a_1 = 0.00004007$
$\log O_j = \log 15,000 = 9.6158$
$K_j = e^{9.6287-9.6158} \approx 1.013$
$\lambda = -a_1 \approx 4.01 \times 10^{-5}$
$R_i = O_j K_j (e^{-4.01 \times 10^{-5} N_i}) = 15,000(1.013)e^{-4.01 \times 10^{-5} N_i}$
$r_i = R_i - R_{i-1} = 15,195[e^{-4.01 \times 10^{-5} N_i} - e^{-4.01 \times 10^{-5} N_{i-1}}]$
with $R_0 = 15,000$.

$i =$	1	2	3	4
R_i	12,434	3,734	276	185
$r_i = R_i - R_{i-1}$	2,566	8,700	3,458	91

7.17

$X = d_{tj}$	1.5	4.5	8
$F(d_{tj})$	0.027	0.010	0.002
$Y = \log F$	-3.6119	-4.6052	-6.2146

$R_{YX} = -0.966;\ R_{YX}^2 = 0.992$
$a_0 = -2.934;\ a_1 = -0.402$
$\alpha = 0.0532;\ \beta = 0.402$
$F(d_{tj}) = 0.0532e^{-0.402d_{tj}}$

7.18 (a) From equations (7.59),

$$10a_0 + \quad 50a_1 + \quad 19.8a_2 = 67.2$$
$$50a_0 + \quad 292a_1 + 117.6a_2 = 369.0$$
$$19.8a_0 + 117.6a_1 + 44.56a_2 = 144.68$$

or in matrix notation,

$$\begin{bmatrix} 10 & 50 & 19.8 \\ 50 & 292 & 117.6 \\ 19.8 & 117.6 & 44.56 \end{bmatrix} \begin{bmatrix} a_0 \\ a_1 \\ a_2 \end{bmatrix} = \begin{bmatrix} 67.2 \\ 369.0 \\ 144.68 \end{bmatrix}$$

Solution: $a_0 = 3.036;\ a_1 = 0.325;\ a_2 = 1.040$
$Y = 3.036 + 0.325X_1 + 1.040X_2$

(b) $\sigma_{\hat{Y}} = 2.792;\ \sigma_{\hat{X}_1} = 20.494;\ \sigma_{\hat{X}_2} = 7.318$
$R_{YX_1} = 0.96;\ R_{YX_2} = 0.95;\ R_{X_1X_2} = 0.97$
The roles of X_1 and X_2 are nearly equal ($R_{YX_1} \simeq R_{YX_2}$) and are interchangeable. Therefore, from (7.29), we expect that $R_{Y;\,X_1X_2} \simeq R_{YX_1} \simeq R_{YX_2}$. From (7.28),

$$R_{Y;\,X_1X_2}^2 = \frac{(0.96)^2 + (0.95)^2 - 2(0.96)(0.95)(0.97)}{1 - (0.97)^2} = 0.93$$

Either of the models

$$Y = 2.79 + 0.0786X_1$$
$$Y = 2.423 + 0.217X_2$$

is about as efficient as the bivariate model shown above.

(c) $R_{Y;\,X_1X_2}^2 = 0.93;\ R_{Y;\,X_1X_2} = 0.96$

7.21 $\bar{Y} = 40.2;\ \bar{X}_1 = 7.85;\ \bar{X}_2 = 37.8$
$\sigma_{\hat{Y}} = 8.07;\ \sigma_{\hat{X}_1} = 0.79;\ \sigma_{\hat{X}_2} = 4.116$
$Y = -6.130 + 4.231X_1 + 0.347X_2$
$R_{YX_1} = 0.55;\ R_{YX_2} = 0.51;\ R_{X_1X_2} = 0.83$

(a) $R_{Y;X_1X_2} = 0.56$
(b) $R_{YX_1/X_2} = 0.27$
(c) $R_{YX_2/X_1} = 0.13$

7.22 Model: $Y = 2.79 + 0.0786X_1$.

	1	2	3	4	5	6	7	8	9	10	$\sum_i$
	6.00	7.50	9.60	4.00	5.40	6.80	8.70	6.40	4.80	8.00	$\bar{Y} = 6.72$
$+0.0786X_i$	5.93	7.55	9.08	4.36	5.93	7.50	9.08	5.93	4.36	7.50	
$-\hat{Y}_i)$	0.07	−0.05	0.52	−0.36	−0.53	−0.70	−0.38	0.47	0.44	0.50	
$\hat{Y}_i)^2$	0.05	0.02	0.27	0.13	0.28	0.49	0.14	0.22	0.19	0.25	2.04
$\bar{Y})$	−0.72	−0.22	2.88	−2.72	−1.32	0.08	1.98	−0.32	−1.92	1.28	
$\bar{Y})^2$	0.52	0.05	8.29	7.34	1.74	0.01	3.92	0.10	3.69	1.64	27.36

$$R^2 = 1 - \frac{s_e^2}{s_{\hat{Y}}^2} = 1 - \frac{0.204}{2.736} = 0.93; \ R = 0.96$$

Appendix C
List of Symbols

C.1 Parameters and Coefficients

Statistical Models.

$\bar{X}$	sample average for X
s_X	sample standard deviation for X
s_e	standard error of estimate
s_e^2	residual variance
μ_X	true value of the mean of X
σ_X^2	true value of the variance of X
R_{YX}	coefficient of linear correlation between Y and X
ρ	ratio of residual to original standard deviations
$R_{Y;\,X_1\,X_2\dots X_m}$	coefficient of multiple correlation between Y and the set of X_i's.
R_{YX_1/X_2}	coefficient of partial correlation between Y and X_1 with respect to X_2
p	level of probability of error
δ	absolute error

Population Projection Models.

a	constant unit time population increment
r	exponential rate of growth
v	modified exponential rate of growth

B   matrix of birth rates b_i
S   matrix of survivorship rates $s_{i,i-1}$
M   column vector of migration levels M_i
m   matrix of migration rates m_i
$\mathbf{M}^{kl}$ matrix of interregional migration rates $m_{i,i-1}^{kl}$
$\mathbf{D}^i$ matrix of regional birth rates b_k^i, regional survivorship rates
                   $s_{k,k-1}^i$, and external net migration rates m_k^i, for each region i

Economic Analysis Models.
c propensity to consume
α ratio of service jobs to basic jobs
β ratio of service jobs to total population
γ ratio of total population to total employment
A   matrix of production coefficients a_{ij} in input-output model *or* of
                   "work to home" coefficients a_{ij} in multi-regional employ-
                   ment and population multiplier model
Γ   matrix of regional γ_i's
Q   column vector of regional service jobs Q_i
B   matrix of regional β_i's
C   matrix of "home to shop" travel coefficients c_{ij}
G   matrix of employment migration coefficients g_{ij}
α^{kl} matrix of interregional structural coefficients α_{ij}^{kl}
$\mathbf{a}$ matrix of interregional production coefficients a_{ij}^{kl}
$\mathbf{b}$ row vector of value-added coefficients b_i^{kl}

Models of Land Use and Travel Demand.
k_i scaling factor for area i
l_i scaling factor for area j
d_{ij} friction factor (impedance) between areas i and j
O_j level of activity originating in area j
D_i level of activity terminating in area i
λ coefficient of proportionality between level of opportunity in
                   area and probability of choosing area
n_{ij} level of opportunity in area i for residents of area j
N_{ij} cumulative level of opportunities up to and including area i

Variables

General and Statistical Models.
X_i ith value of X (predicted or theoretical)
$\hat{X}_i$ ith value of X (observed or sampled)
Z standard normal random variable

T	T-distributed random variable
L	value of the log-likelihood function
S	value of the sum of squares

Population Projection Models.

P_n	population level at time n
$\mathbf{P}^n$	column vector of age groups' population levels at time n
$[P^i]^n$	column vector of regional age groups' population levels at time n
E_p	basic (production) employment level
E_s	service (nonbasic) employment level
E	total employment level
E_{ij}^n	employment in sector j of region i at time n
$\tilde{E}_{ij}^n$	expected employment in sector j of region i at time n
X_i	basic production of sector i
Z_i	nonbasic production of sector i
Y_i	total production of sector i
X_{ik}	production of sector (region) i acquired by sector (region) k
I_{ij}	external input into sector (region) j from sector (region) i
$\mathbf{X}$	column vector of regional basic productions
$\mathbf{Z}$	column vector of regional nonbasic productions
$\mathbf{Y}$	column vector of regional total productions
$\mathbf{X}_k$	column vector of external demands from sector (region) k
$\mathbf{E}^p$	column vector of regional basic (production) jobs
$\mathbf{E}^s$	column vector of service (nonbasic) jobs
$\mathbf{E}$	column vector of regional levels of total employment
$\mathbf{P}$	column vector of regional levels of residential population

Models of Land Use and Travel Demand.

I_{ij}	level of spatial interaction between areas i and j
r_{ij}	number of residents of area j choosing area i
R_{ij}	cumulative number of residents of area j choosing areas beyond area i
W_{ij}	number of employed residents of area j living in area i
G_i^k	utility of mode i for travelers in group k
P_i^k	probability of an individual traveler in group k choosing mode i.

Appendix D
Glossary

Algorithm. A systematic computational procedure, in most cases consisting of an organized sequence of steps, often repeated.

Analytical (solution, model, etc.). Mathematically formulated and precisely formalized.

Behavioral model. A model that translates and/or reflects assumptions about behavior, attitudes, preferences, etc.

Calibration of a model. The process of finding the specific values of the model's parameters that correspond to a given empirical situation.

Causal model. A model that reflects a cause—effect relationship.

Coefficient. A numerical (constant) value, usually the multiplier of a variable in a model.

Confidence level. The probability with which an inferred statistical statement or conclusion is made.

Constraint A physical requirement translated as part of a model, i.e., in equation form.

Continuous (variable, model, etc). Refers to a variable, or model, etc., that can take an infinity of values, states, etc.

Convergence. The mathematical property of tending to a specific, stable ultimate value or state.

Criterion. A quantititive yardstick, the value of which is used for comparative purposes.

Deductive. Proceeding from a general proposition to a specific conclusion.

333

Degrees of freedom. The number of independent pieces of information (e.g., data measurements) that intervene in the computation of the value of a statistical entity.

Dependent variable. The variable whose value is a function of the given variables (*see Independent variable*).

Descriptive model. A model that is not explicitly behavioral, causal, or otherwise explanatory.

Deterministic (model, variable, etc.). That which is certain, or non-fluctuating, in a probabilistic sense.

Differential (model, equation, etc.). A model, or equation, etc. that involves continuous variables and their instantaneous rates of change.

Disaggregated (data, model, etc.). A model or data whose level of specification is at the elementary, unit level, or some small unit.

Discrete variable. A variable that can take only a limited, finite number of values. Opposite of continuous.

Distribution. A particular arrangement of a set of values across several categories, e.g., of probabilities, numbers of jobs, etc.

Dummy (link, variable, etc.). A fictional link, or variable, etc., that does not have a physical correspondent but is helpful conceptually and/or computationally.

Dynamic Involving the element of time.

Empirical Based on actual experience, as opposed to theory.

Endogeneous (variable, parameter, etc.). A variable or parameter whose value is determined internally. Opposite of exogeneous.

Feasible solution. A solution that fulfills the requirements but that may not possess other desirable properties, e.g., optimality, etc.

Finite. Refers to a quantity that has a limited value. Opposite of infinite.

Fitting a model. Same as calibrating a model.

Forecast. Hypothetical future condition.

Heuristic (solution, method, etc.). One that may be useful, although not fully understood, rationalized, or formalized.

Hypothesis. A proposition subject to proving or disproving. Not to be confused with assumption or postulate.

Independent variable. A variable whose value determines the value of the output (dependent variable).

Indicator. A quantity whose numerical value is used to represent and/or summarize a given situation.

Inductive. Proceeding from a specific proposition to a general law.

Infinite. Refers to a value that is as large as it can be.

Infinitesimal. Refers to a value that is as small as it can be.

Inter-. Between or among groups.

Intra-. Within a group.

Iteration. Repetition.

Iterative. Consisting of the repetition of a basic routine.

Longitudinal. Addressing the same element at periodic points in time.

Macroscopic. Large scale. Opposite of microscopic.

Microscopic. Small scale.

Model. A mathematical representation consisting of variables and their interrelationships, together with the appropriate constraints.

Multivariate. Involving several variables. Opposite of univariate.

Normalized (value, variable, etc.). Having been rescaled to conform to certain requirements.

Normative model. Designed to indicate desirable (i.e., usually best) conditions.

Objective function. A mathematical expression translating certain goals, and whose value is to be optimized.

Observed value. An empirical measurement for the value of a variable.

Operational. That which is susceptible to practical implementation.

Operations research. The branch of mathematics devoted to the optimization of management, production, or general activity systems.

Optimal. Best, in some sense to be defined.

Optimize. To find the best value, condition, state, etc.

Order (of a variable, equation, etc.). The highest of the powers of the variable(s).

Order of magnitude. Scale, level of value of a quantity, e.g., hundreds, millions, fractions, etc.

Parameter. A quantity which intervenes in the specification of a general model and whose value adapts it to a specific empirical situation.

Predicted variable. Same as dependent variable.

Predicting variable. Same as independent variable.

Primary data. Original data that is obtained directly through field research.

Probabilistic. Having uncertain (individual) values, but possessing certain long term, stable characteristics, and therefore susceptible to prediction.

Projection. A prediction based on past trends.

Regression. A statistical technique of modeling the observed variations of a predicted variable as a function of some predicting variable(s).

Scaling factor. A quantity intervening in a model for the sole purpose of normalizing its variables or of balancing other quantities. Not synonymous with parameter.

Secondary data. Data that is obtained indirectly, i.e., not as the result of field surveys.

Sensitivity analysis. Designed to determine the effects of small changes in the values of the independent variables, or the parameters, constraints, etc., on the value of the dependent variable.

Sequential model. A model involving an ordered series of equations.

Significance level. Minimum probability under which the occurrence of the corresponding event is considered dismissible.

Simulation. The process of replicating, with the aid of computers and models, the workings of physical phenomena.

Simultaneous model. A model involving several equations that must be considered at the same time. Opposite of sequential model.

Standardized.   Same as normalized.

Static model.   A model that does not involve the element of time. Opposite of dynamic model.

Statistic.   An indicator whose value is derived from sampled measurements.

Statistical model.   A model representing a pattern found in empirical data.

Stochastic.   Same as probabilistic.

Structural.   Concerned with the relationships rather than the numerical values.

System.   A set of interdependent, interacting parts.

Theory.   A rational set of statements that purports to explain, or at least represent abstractly, certain phenomena.

Typology.   A classification that is based on logical principles and that stresses the relationships between classes

Univariate.   Depending only on a single variable.

Validation of a model.   The demonstration that the structure of a given model is applicable in a given situation. Not to be confused with model calibration.

Appendix E
Selected Bibliography

ALONSO, W. "Predicting Best with Imperfect Data." *Journal of the American Institute of Planners*, 34 (1968), 248–55.

ALONSO, W. *The Quality of Data and the Choice and Design of Predictive Models.* Highway Research Board Special Report 97. Washington, D.C.: 1968.

ANGEL, S., AND G. M. HYMAN. "Urban Spatial Interaction." *Environment and Planning*, 4 (1972), 99–118.

ARTLE, R. "External Trade, Industrial Structure, Employment Mix and the Distribution of Incomes: A Simple Model of Planning and Growth." *Swedish Journal of Economics* (1965).

BARBER, G. "Land Use Planned Design via Interactive Multiple Objective Programming." *Environment and Planning*, 8 (1976), 625–36.

BATTY, M. "Some Problems of Calibrating the Lowry Model." *Environment and Planning*, 2 (1970), 95–114.

BATTY, M. "Exploratory Calibration of a Retail Location Model Using Search by Golden Section." *Environment and Planning*, 3 (1971), 411–32.

BATTY, M. "Modelling Cities as Dynamic Systems." *Nature*, 231 (1971), 425–28.

BATTY, M. "Spatial Entropy." *Geographical Analysis*, 6 (1974), 1–32.

BAXTER, R., AND L. WILLIAMS. "An Automatically Calibrated Urban Model." *Environment and Planning*, 7 (1975), 3–20.

BELLMAN, R. *Dynamic Programming*. Princeton, N.J.: Princeton Univ. Press, 1957.

BEN AKIVA, M. *Passenger Transport Demand: Theory and Models*. Cambridge, Mass.: MIT Department of Civil Engineering, 1972.

BEN SHAHAR, H., et al. "Town Planning and Welfare Maximization." *Regional Studies*, 3 (1969).

BESHERS, J. "Demographic Applications of Computer Models," *Computer Methods in the Analysis of Large Scale Social Systems*. Cambridge, Mass.: MIT Press, 1968.

BONSALL, P., ed. *Urban Transportation Planning*. Montclair, N. J.: Allanheld and Osmun, 1977.

BOX, G. P. E. "Use and Abuse of Regression." *Technometrics*, 8(4) (1966), 625–29.

BOYCE, D., et al. *Metropolitan Plan Making*. Regional Science Research Institute. Philadelphia: 1970.

BRAND, D. "Theory and Method in Land Use and Travel Forecasting." *Highway Research Record*, 422 (1973), 10–20.

BROADBENT, T. A. "A Hierarchical Interaction-Allocation Model for a Two-Level Spatial System." *Regional Studies*, 5 (1971), 23–27.

BROMLEY, D. "An Alternative to Input/Output Models." *Land Economics* (May 1968), 125–33.

BROWN, H. "A Technique for Estimating the Population of Counties." *Journal of the American Statistical Association*, 50: 270 (1955).

CAMERON, B. *Input-Output Analysis and Resource Location*. London: Cambridge Univ. Press, 1968.

CARROTHERS, S. "An Historical Review of the Gravity and Potential Concepts of Human Interaction." *Journal of the American Institute of Planners*, 22 (1956), 94–102.

CATANESE, A. J., AND A. W. STEISS. *Systemic Planning: Theory and Application*. Lexington, Mass.: D. C. Heath, 1970.

CESARIO, F. J. "Parameter Estimation in Spatial Interaction Modelling." *Environment and Planning*, 5 (1973), 503–18.

CHAPIN, F. S., AND WEISS, S. F. "A Probablistic Model for Residential Growth." *Transportation Research*, 2 (1968), 375–90.

CHARLES RIVER ASSOCIATES. *A Disaggregated Behavioral Model of Urban Travel Demand*. Report to the U.S. Department of Transportation. Washington, D.C.: 1972.

CHOUCKROUN, J. M. "A General Framework for the Development of Gravity Type Distribution Models." *Regional Science and Urban Economics*, 5 (1975).

CORDEY HAYES, M. "Dynamic Frameworks for Spatial Models." *Socio-Economic Planning Sciences*, 6 (1972), 365–85.

CORDEY HAYES, M., AND A. G. WILSON. "Spatial Interaction." *Socio-Economic Planning Sciences*, 5 (1971), 73–95.

CRECINE, J. P. *TOMM (Time Oriented Metropolitan Model)*. CRP Technical Bulletin No. 6, Department of City Planning, Pittsburgh: 1964.

CRIPPS, E. L., AND D. H. FOOT. "The Empirical Development of an Elementary Residential Location Model for Use in Subregional Planning." *Environment and Planning*, 1 (1969), 81–90.

CZAMANSKI, S. *Methods of Regional Science*. Lexington, Mass.: D. C. Heath, 1975.

CZAMANSKI, S., AND E. MALIZIA. "Applicability and Limitations in the Use of National Input-Output Tables for Regional Studies." *Papers of the Regional Science Association*, 23 (1969).

DAVIS, H. C. T. "Regional Sectorial Multipliers with Reduced Data Requirements." *International Regional Science Review*, 1 (1977).

DELFT, A., AND P. NIJKAMP. "A Multiobjective Decision Model for Regional Development, Environmental Quality and Industrial Land Use." *Papers of the Regional Science Association*, 36 (1976), 35–57.

DOUGLASS, A. A., AND R. J. LEWIS. "Trip Generation Techniques: Household Least Square Regression and Analysis." *Traffic Engineering and Control*, 12(9) (1971).

EDENS, H. J. "Analysis of a Modified Gravity Demand Model." *Transportation Research*, 4 (1970), 51–62.

FARBEY, B. A., A. H. LAND, AND J. D. MURCHLAND. "The Cascade Algorithm for Finding All Shortest Distances in a Directed Graph." *Management Science*, 14 (1967), 19–28.

FORRESTER, J. W. *Urban Dynamics*. Cambridge, Mass.: MIT Press, 1969.

FOX, K., AND T. K. KUMAR. "The Functional Economic Area: Delineation and Implications for Economic Analysis and Policy." *Papers of the Regional Science Association*, 15 (1965).

FREUND, J. *Mathematical Statistics*. Englewood Cliffs, N. J.: Prentice-Hall, Inc., 1971.

GEORGE, S., AND C. E. PYERS. "The Application of Critical Programming to Large Scale Transportation Studies." *Highway Research News*, 12 (1966), 51–66.

GOLDNER, W. *Projective Land Use Model* (PLUM). BATSC Technical Report 219, Bay Area Transportation Study Commission. Berkeley, Calif.: 1968.

GOLDNER, W. "The Lowry Model Heritage." *Journal of the American Institute of Planners*, 37 (1971), 100–110.

GOLOB, T. F., AND M. J. BECKMANN. "A Utility Model for Travel Forecasting." *Transportation Science*, 5 (1971), 79–90.

GREENBERG, M. "A Test of Combination Models for Projecting the Population of Minor Civil Divisions." *Economic Geography*, 48 (1972).

GREENWOOD, M. J. "Urban Economic Growth and Migration: Their Interaction." *Environment and Planning*, 5 (1973).

GREENWOOD, M. J. "A Simultaneous-Equations Model of Urban Growth and Migration." *Journal of the American Statistical Association*, 70 (1975), 797–810.

HAGGETT, P., AND R. T. CORLEY. *Network Analysis in Geography*. London: Arnold, 1969.

HAMILTON, H., AND J. PERRY. "A Short Method for Projecting Population by Age from One Decenial Census to the Other." *Social Forces*, 41:22 (1962).

HAMMER, T. *The Estimation of Economic Base Multipliers*. Regional Science Research Institute. Philadelphia: 1968.

Handbook of Population Census Methods. United Nations Statistical Office. New York: 1958.

HARRIS, B. J. *Linear Programming and Projection of Land Uses*. Paper 20, Penn-Jersey Transportation Study. Philadelphia: 1962.

HARRIS, B. J. "The City of the Future: The Problem of Optimal Design." *Papers of the Regional Science Association*, 19 (1967).

HAYS, H. *Statistics for the Social Sciences*, 2 ed. New York: Holt, Rinehart & Winston, 1973.

HEWINGS, G. "Input-Output Aggregation Models for Regional Impact Analysis," *Growth and Change*, 3 (1972).

HILL, D. M. "A Growth Allocation Model for the Boston Region." *Journal of the American Institute of Planners*, 31 (1965), 111–20.

HILL, D. M., D. BRAND, AND W. B. HANSEN. "Prototype Development of Statistical Land Use Prediction Model for Greater Boston Region." *Highway Research Record*, 114 (1965), 51–70.

HILL, M. *Planning for Multiple Objectives*. Regional Science Research Institute. Philadelphia: 1973.

HOCHWALD, W. *Design of Regional Accounts*. Baltimore: Johns Hopkins Press, 1961.

HOOVER, E. M. *An Introduction to Regional Economics*. New York: Alfred Knopf, 1971.

HYMAN, G. M. "The Calibration of Trip Distribution Models." *Environment and Planning*, 1 (1969), 105–12.

ISARD, W. "A Simple Rationale for Gravity Type Behavior." *Papers of the Regional Science Association*, 35 (1975).

ISARD, W. *Introduction to Regional Science*. Englewood Cliffs, N.J.: Prentice-Hall, Inc., 1975.

JEWELL, W. S. "Methods for Traffic Assignment." *Transportation Research* (1967), 31–46.

KADANOFF, L. P. "From Simulation Model to Public Policy." *American Scientist*, 60 (1972), 74–79.

KAIN, J. F. "The Journey to Work as a Determinant of Residential Location." *Papers and Proceedings of the Regional Science Association*, 9 (1962), 137–60.

KARLQUIST, A., AND B. MARKSJO. "Statistical Urban Models." *Environment and Planning*, 3 (1971), 83–98.

KEYFITZ, N. *Introduction to the Mathematics of Population*. Reading, Mass.: Addison-Wesley, 1968

KILBRIDGE, M. D., R. P. O'BLOCK, AND P. V. TEPLITZ. "A Conceptual Framework for Urban Planning Models." *Management Science*, 15 (1969), B246–66.

KISH, L. *Survey Sampling*. New York: John Wiley, 1965.

KORCELLI, K. "Urban Spatial Interaction Models in a Planned Economy: A Review." *International Regional Science Review*, 2 (1976).

LAPATRA. *Systems Analysis for Urban Development*. Stroudsburg, Pa.: Dowden, Hutchinson and Ross, 1973.

LATHROP, G. T., AND J. R. HAMBURG. "An Opportunity-Accessibility Model for Allocating Regional Growth." *Journal of the American Institute of Planners*, 31 (1965), 95–103.

LATHROP, G. T., J. R. HAMBURG, AND G. F. YOUNG. "Opportunity-Accessibility Model for Allocating Regional Growth." *Highway Research Record*, 113 (1965), 54–66.

LAVE, C. "A Behavioral Approach to Modal Split Forecasting." *Transportation Research*, 3 (1969).

LEE, D. B. "Requiem for Large Scale Models." *Journal of the American Institute of Planners*, 39 (1973), 163–78.

LINDSAY, W. "Using Models for New Town Design." *Architectural Design*, 41 (1971), 286–88.

LOS, M. "Simultaneous Optimization of Land Use and Transportation." *Regional Science and Urban Economics*, 8 (1978), 21–42.

LOWRY, I. *Migration and Population Growth: Two Analytical Models*. San Francisco: Chandler, 1976.

LOWRY, I. "A Short Course in Model Design." *Journal of the American Institute of Planners*, 31 (1965).

MALONE, J. M., AND F. DiCESARE. "Calibration of Gravity Models." *Transportation Research*, 12 (1978), 181–84.

MASSER, I. "Possible Applications of the Lowry Model." *Planning Outlook*, 11 (1971), 46–59.

McCARTHY, G. M. "Multiple Regression Analysis of Household Trip Generation: A Critique." *Highway Research Record*, 297 (1969).

McGinnis. *Mathematical Foundations for Social Analysis.* Indianapolis: Bobbs-Merrill, 1965.

McLoughlin, J. B., and J. N. Webster. "Cybernetic and General-System Approaches to Urban and Regional Research." *Environment and Planning,* 2 (1970), 369–408.

Morrison, W. I., and P. Smith. "Nonsurvey Input–Output Techniques at the Small Area Level: An Evaluation." *Journal of Regional Science,* 14 (1974).

Muller, F. "An Operational Mathematical Programming Model for the Planning of Economic Activities in Relation to the Environment." *Socio-Economic Planning Sciences,* 7 (1973), 123–38.

Myernyk, W. *The Elements of Input-Output Analysis.* New York: Random House, 1965.

Niedercorn, J. H., and B. V. Berchdolt. "An Economic Derivation of the Gravity Law of Spatial Interaction." *Journal of Regional Science,* 9 (1969), 273–81.

Nijkamp, P., and P. Rietveld. Multiobjective Programming Models: New Ways in Regional Decision Making." *Regional Science and Urban Economics,* 6 (1976).

Oliver, R. M., and R. B. Potts. *Flows in Transportation Networks.* New York: Academic Press, 1972.

Paelinck, J. H. P. "Dynamic Urban Growth Models." *Papers of the Regional Science Association,* 24 (1970), 25–37.

Pittenger, D. B. "A Typology of Age-Specific Net Migration Rate Distributions." *Journal of the American Institute of Planners,* 40:3 (1974).

Preston. *Elementary Matrices for Economics.* Library of Modern Economics: 1975.

Projections of the Population of the U.S., 1975 *to* 2025. Current Population Reports, Series P-25, U.S. Bureau of the Census. Washington, D.C.: 1975.

Putnam, S. "Intraurban Employment Forecasting Models: A Review and a Suggested New Model Construct." *Journal of the American Institute of Planners,* 38 (1972).

Putman, S. H., and F. W. Ducca. "Calibrating Urban Residential Models: Procedures and Strategies." *Environment and Planning,* 10 (1978).

Quandt, R. E. *The Demand for Travel, Theory and Measurement.* Lexinton, Mass.: Lexington Books, 1970.

Rassam, P. "The *n*-Dimensional Logit Model and Applications." *Highway Research Record,* 369 (1972).

Reifler, R., and C. Tiebout. "Interregional Input–Output, an Empirical California–Washington Model." *Journal of Regional Science,* 10:2 (1970).

Reiner, T. "A Multiple Goals Framework for Regional Planning." *Papers of the Regional Science Association,* 26 (1971).

Rogers, A. "A Regression Analysis of Interregional Migration in California." *Review of Economics and Statistics,* 49 (1967).

Rogers, A. *Matrix Analysis of Interregional Population Growth and Movement.* Berkeley: Univ. of California Press, 1968.

Sakarovitch, M. "The k-Shortest Paths in a Graph." *Transportation Research,* 2 (1968), 1–11.

Santini, D. J. "An Econometric Model of Transportation Infrastructure as a Determinant in Intraurban Location." *Journal of Regional Science,* 18(1) (1978), 73–85.

Schaffer, W. A., and K. Chu. "Nonsurvey Techniques for Constructing Regional Interindustry Models." *Papers of the Regional Science Association,* 22 (1969), 83–101.

Schaffer, W. A. "Estimating Regional I/O Coefficients." *Review of Regional Studies,* 2 (1972).

Schmitt, R. C., and A. H. Crosetti. "Shortcut Methods of Forecasting City Population." *Journal of Marketing,* 17:417 (1953).

Schmitt, R. C. "A Method for Projecting the Population of Census Tracts." *Journal of the American Institute of Planners,* 20:2 (1954).

Scott, A. J. *Combinatorial Programming: Spatial Analysis and Planning.* London: Methuen, 1971.

Searle, S. R. *Linear Models.* New York: John Wiley, 1971

Seidman, D. *The Construction of an Urban Growth Model.* Delaware Valley Regional Planning Commission, 1. Philadelphia: 1969.

Senior, M. L. "A Review of Urban Economic, Ecological and Spatial Interaction Approaches to Urban Location Modeling." *Environment and Planning,* 5 (1973), 165–97.

Senior, M. L., and A. G. Wilson. "Exploration and Syntheses of Linear Programming and Spatial Interaction Models of Residential Location." *Geographical Analysis,* 6 (1974), 209–38.

Siegel, J. "Development and Accuracy of Projections of Populations and Households in the U.S." *Demography,* 9 (1972).

Siegel, J. "Forecasting the Population of Small Areas." *Land Economics,* 19:1 (1953).

Steger, W. A., and T. Laksmanan. *Plan Evaluation Methodologies: Some Aspects of Decision Requirements and Analytic Response.* Urban Development Models, Highway Research Board. Washington, D.C.: 1968.

Steines, D., and W. Fisher. "An Econometric Model of Residential Location." *Journal of Regional Science,* 14 (1974), 65–80.

Stillwell, F. J. B., and B. D. Boatwright. "A Method of Estimating Interregional Trade Flows." *Regional and Urban Economics,* 1 (May 1971), 77–87.

Stockwell, E. G. "Use of Socio-Economic Status as a Demographic Variable." *Public Health Reports,* 81:961 (1966).

Stopher, P. *Survey Sampling and Multivariate Analysis in Transportation Planning.* Lexington, Mass.: Lexington Books, 1976.

Swanson, C. V., and R. J. Waldmann. "A Simulation Model of Economic Growth Dynamics." *Journal of the American Institute of Planners*, 36 (1970), 314–22.

Thomlinson, R. "A Model for Migration Analysis." *Journal of the American Statistical Association* (1971).

Tiebout, C. *The Community Economic Base Study.* Committee for Economic Development. New York: 1962.

Tufte, E. R. *Data Analysis for Politics and Policy.* Englewood Cliffs, N.J.: Prentice-Hall, Inc., 1974.

Vickerman, R. W. "Accessibility, Attraction and Potential: A Review of Some Concepts and Their Use in Determining Mobility." *Environment and Planning*, 6 (1974), 675–91.

Wagon, D. J., and A. F. Hawkens. "The Calibration of the Distribution Model for the SELNEC Study." *Transportation Research*, 4 (1970), 103–12.

Warwick, D., and C. Lininger. *The Sample Survey.* New York: McGraw-Hill, 1975.

Watson, P. *The Value of Time: Behavioral Models of Modal Choice.* Lexington, Mass.: Lexington Books, 1974.

Watson, P. "Choice of an Estimation Procedure for Models of Binary Choice: Some Statistical and Empirical Evidence." *Regional and Urban Economics*, 4(2) (1974), 187–200.

Weiss, S. J., and E. C. Gooding. "Estimation of Differential Employment Multipliers in a Small Regional Economy." *Land Economics*, 44 (1968), 235–44.

Wilde, D. J. *Optimum Seeking Methods.* Englewood Cliffs, N.J.: Prentice-Hall, Inc., 1964.

Williams, E. J. "A Note on Regression Methods in Calibration." *Technometrics*, 11(1) (1969), 1891–92.

Williamson, "Simple I/O Models for Area Economic Analysis." *Journal of Land Economics*, 46 (1970).

Willis, K. G. *Problems in Migration Analysis.* Lexington, Mass.: D.C. Heath, 1974.

Wilson, A. G. "Models in Urban Planning: A Synoptic Review." *Urban Studies*, 5 (1968).

Wilson, A. G. *Entropy in Urban and Regional Modelling.* London: Pion Press, 1970.

Wilson, A. G. *Generalising the Lowry Model.* CES-WP-56, Centre for Environmental Studies. London: 1970.

Wilson, A. G. "A Family of Spatial, Interaction Models and Associated Developments." *Environment and Planning*, 3 (1971).

WILSON, A. G., ET AL. "Calibrating and Testing the SELNEC Transport Model." *Regional Studies*, 3 (1969),337–50.

WILSON, A. G., AND P. REES. *Spatial Population Analysis*. New York: Academic Press, 1977.

WOOTON, H. J., AND G. W. PICK. "A Model for Trips Generated by Households." *Journal of Transport Economics and Policy*, 1 (1967), 137–58.

YAN, C. S. *Introduction to Input-Output Economics*. New York: Holt, Rinehart & Winston, 1969.

Index